De Havilland Enterprises

A History

Graham M Simons

Pen & Sword
AVIATION

First Published in Great Britain in 2017 by
Pen & Sword Aviation
an imprint of
Pen & Sword Books Ltd
47 Church Street, Barnsley, South Yorkshire S70 2AS

Copyright © Graham M Simons
ISBN 9781473861381

A CIP catalogue record for this book is
available from the British Library.

Typeset in 10/9 Palatino
by GMS Enterprises

Printed and bound in England by
CPI Group (US) Ltd, Croydon, CR0 4YY

Pen & Sword Books Ltd incorporates the Imprints of Pen & Sword
Aviation, Pen & Sword Family History, Pen & Sword Maritime, Pen & Sword
Military, Pen & Sword Discovery, Wharncliffe Local History, Wharncliffe
True Crime, Wharncliffe Transport, Pen & Sword Select, Pen & Sword
Military Classics, Leo Cooper, The Praetorian Press, Remember When,
Seaforth Publishing and Frontline Publishing.

For a complete list of Pen & Sword titles please contact
PEN & SWORD BOOKS LIMITED

47 Church Street, Barnsley, South Yorkshire, S70 2AS, England
E-mail: enquiries@pen-and-sword.co.uk
Website: www.pen-and-sword.co.uk

Contents

* Totals built should to be considered very much an estimate only, for the records that date back over one hundred years are not totally verifiable to any high degree of accuracy.

Dedication

Since the early 1970s I have being tramping the airshow circuit, both here in the UK and further afield, regularly seeing the same old faces - that used to be young faces - that have, in many cases, become firm friends. Three such gentlemen are Ian Oliver, John Stride and Barry Dowsett. These three have been involved in all things 'De Havilland' for many years.

I have been actively supporting the Shuttleworth Collection at Old Warden in Bedfordshire - usually with a trade stand - for the past thirty years or so, and often we were 'next door' to other De Havilland groups, supported by John Stride and his father Cyril. They worked with the British Aerospace Mosquito RR299, the De Havilland Moth Club and the De Havilland Aircraft Heritage Centre known by many under its former name of the Mosquito Aircraft Museum.

Cyril and John worked tirelessly, doing all they could to preserve the name and in many cases a number of De Havilland products, and even after Cyril passed away, John continued with this. The thought was always in the back of my mind that although they never sought it, they both never received the recognition they deserved. John himself latterly worked on Comet G-ACSS, before passing away not long after research for this book started, but not before he was able to provide me with a large selection of photographs that could be used.

So I would like to dedicate this book to all the many volunteers that strive to support the vintage and veteran aircraft preservation movement, and to John Stride in particular - you are all an inspiration!

A bit of fun at Old Warden, 2003. Left to right: Ian Oliver, John Stride and Barry Dowsett aboard a very strange looking Bleariot!

Introduction

'*Ahhh!... De Havilland!*' For many years that phrase was a logo, a slogan, a concept.

Look back, and there was a time when every small biplane was 'a Moth', an entire air force trained on a 'Tiger' and a new Elizabethan age dawned with the introduction of the world's first jet airliner.

De Havillands were without doubt the most prolific of all British aircraft manufacturers owing their success to the vision, energy and genius of a small but highly dedicated team led by the founder and first designer, Captain Geoffrey de Havilland Kt, OM, CBE, AFC, RDI, Hon FRAeS, Hon FIAS who was knighted for his services to British aviation in 1944.

The story of how he and Francis Trounson Hearle CBE, FRAeS, MIProdE, Charles Clement Walker CBE, AMICE, Hon FRAeS, Wilfred Ernest Nixon, Francis Edward Noel St. Barbe, Arthur Ernest Hagg FRAeS and Alan

Samuel Butler guided the company's fortunes from 5 October 1920, the day it moved into Stag Lane, is an epic of true British resourcefulness and could fill several volumes ten times the size of this book.

It begins at Seven Barrows in Hampshire, moves to Hendon in North London amongst the military aeroplanes of the First World War, spends fifteen years at Stag Lane to investigate civil and military prototypes between the wars, to witness the birth and growth of the Moth family and the famous wooden utility transports, and moves finally to Hatfield, Chester and elsewhere to record thirty years' progress towards the jet transport descendants of the incredible Mosquito - the famous 'wooden wonder' of the Second World War.

The core - and indeed the main body - of this book is a numeric listing of all aircraft designs that carried a De Havilland type

Darryl Cott's delightful air-to-air of one of the most beautiful of the De Havilland products, DH.88 Comet G-ACSS, not long after its restoration to fly - the aircraft is in the care of the Shuttleworth Collection, Old Warden. *[DH via BAe Hatfield]*

Sir Geoffrey de Havilland, the founder of the Enterprise, with His Royal Highness Prince Philip, the Duke of Edinburgh. The occasion was the handing over of the first Heron for the Queen's Flight at Hatfield on 18 May 1955. *[DH via BAe Hatfield]*

number - this also includes the 'design projects' that never reached the hardware stage, and also reference to the duplicated contemporary Handley Page project numbers that by mutual agreement between the two companies were not used by De Havilland.

The story touches on the De Havilland Technical School's T.K. series and the products of the De Havilland companies in Australia and Canada are listed as they were all generically De Havilland types - the Cierva C.24 cabin autogiro is included for the same reason.

Many of the aircraft featured in this book deserve books written about them in their own right - indeed, I have done just that with

'*Mosquito, the original Multi-Role Combat Aircraft*' and '*Comet! The world's First Jet Airliner*' for Pen & Sword Aviation and a number of other monographs.

This book brings together in one place the concise details of every aircraft and every design conceived by the company to the point where it was absorbed into the Hawker Siddeley Group conglomorate.

Graham M Simons
Peterborough
6 September 2016

The Men...

Without a shadow of a doubt the De Havilland Aircraft Company was the most prolific of all the British aircraft manufacturers.

It was founded by Capt Geoffrey de Havilland on 25 September 1920 with the aid of some finance from George Holt Thomas, his former employer at Airco and the man who founded Brooklands aerodrome. De Havilland became director and chief designer. Other key people from Airco who joined as directors included Arthur E Turner, Charles Clement Walker as chief engineer, long-term friend and brother-in-law Frank Trounson Hearle as the general and works manager, Wilfrid Ernest Nixon as company secretary, and Francis Edward Noel St Barbe as sales manager. Chairman was Alan Samuel Butler. Geoffrey de Havilland had as his chief designer an old colleague from the days of The Aircraft Manufacturing Company at Hendon – the remarkable Arthur Ernest Hagg, who was responsible for so many successful 'DH' designs, in particular the Moth series culminating in the four-engined Albatross.

The company's first premises comprised a large field at the end of a country road in Edgware, to the north of London, that was the access road to Burnt Oak Farm, its access road being called Stag Lane. The field had been previously used for flying by the London & Provincial Aviation Company's flying school. On 5 October the new business moved into its two wooden sheds. The company's test and experimental pilot was Hubert Stanford Broad. The company made a conscious decision to build predominantly civil (including commercial) aircraft. Its creation of the first of the Moth series sealed the company's future and the aircraft and its maker gained world-wide status and reputation.

The extension of the London Underground railway system to Edgware marked the end of Stag Lane as an aerodrome for the area was quickly developed for housing. The business was converted into a public company on 18 December 1928 and the company set up The London Aeroplane Club flying Moths from Stag Lane. In 1930, De Havilland acquired land for a new airfield at Hatfield and the first part to be developed was accommodation for the Club. Besides Leopard Moth, Puss Moth, Hawk Moth and Fox Moth machines, some of which were used commercially (in particular the Fox Moth), the company produced a consistently good series of airliners that began with derivatives of the DH.4 and DH.9 and went on through the DH.66 to the Dragon, Dragon Rapide and Express airliners of the mid to late 1930s. Its last pre-war commercial products were the Albatross and, under the new chief designer that replaced Hagg, Ronald E Bishop, the Flamingo. De Havilland also built its own engines to the designs of Frank Bernard Halford [*b.* Nottingham, March 7th, 1894; *d.* April 16th, 1955], among these being the Gipsy series of four and six-cylinder engines. It also manufactured propellers. Geoffrey de Havilland, knighted for his services to the aircraft industry during the 1939-45 war, died in retirement on 26 May 1965 having lost both his sons in flying accidents.

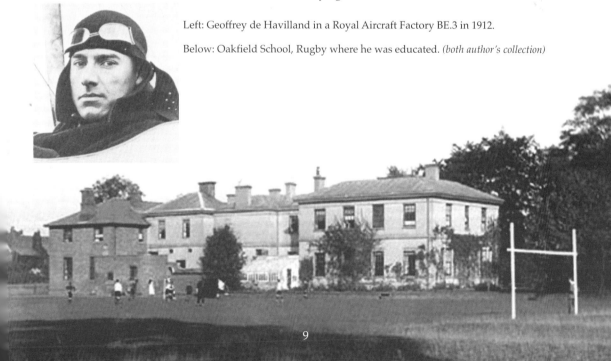

Left: Geoffrey de Havilland in a Royal Aircraft Factory BE.3 in 1912.

Below: Oakfield School, Rugby where he was educated. (*both author's collection*)

The early years

Geoffrey de Havilland and his brothers Ivon and Hereward were the sons of the Rev. Charles de Havilland of Crux Eaton, near Highclere, Hampshire. They were exceptionally mechanically minded, and Geoffrey was educated first at Oakfield in Rugby and then at St. Edward's School, Oxford, before moving to the Crystal Palace Engineering School in 1900 for a three year mechanical engineering course. He was neasrly 18 years old.

His elder brother Ivon had been apprenticed to the Brush Electrical Company at Loughborough in Leicestershire, then worked at the Daimler Motor Company at Coventry before becoming the Chief Designer for the Isis Motor Company at Willesden. Sadly, he was to pass away in his early twenties

In 1903, while at the Crystal Palace Engineering School, Geoffrey built one of Britain's earliest motor cycles with an engine from published drawings on which to commute to and from Crux Eaton.

From 1903 he worked as a student engineer with Willand & Robinson, a company manufacturing steam turbines and steam engines. Here he started work on internal combustion engines for motor vehicles, which also included building a second motorcyle for himself, this time with an engine of his own design.

In 1905 he joined the design office of the Wolseley Tool & Motor Car company, but left a year later for a more interesting job with the Motor Omnibus Construction Company, first in Moorgate and later at Walthamstow.

In 1906, while living in Walthamstow Geoffrey met Frank T. Hearle, a Cornish marine engineer working as a mechanic for the Vanguard Omnibus Company and destined to be his brother-in-law and life-long business associate.

Frank Hearle had served his apprenticeship with Cox's, the marine engineers of Falmouth, but had moved to London on 8 January 1908. It was not long before he had been intoduced to Geoffrey de Havilland and they used to meet to talk about aviation.

The free flight attempts of the early pioneers had held both men's attention since boyhood and inevitably. in 1908, with a £500 loan from grandfather. he forsook the motor bus to design a 45 hp flat four water-cooled engine to power an aeroplane of his own construction. It had a power/weight ratio only half that of the Wright brothers' engine and was built for £250 by the Iris Motor Company in their works at Scrubbs Lane, Willesden.

De Havilland then rented a workshop off Bothwell Street in Fulham, and with the assistance of F. T. Hearle built a wire-braced biplane with front elevator and bicycle wheel undercarriage; Geoffrey's young wife made the cotton covering on a hand sewing machine and the engine, mounted at right angles to the fuselage, drove two aluminium propellers through bevel gearing. In 1909 the finished aircraft was taken to Seven Barrows, just north of Lambourne on the North Hampshire Downs near Crux Eaton, and erected it in a shed recently vacated by J. T. C. Moore Brabazon but it was December before conditions were suitable for risking flight in such a flimsy structure. When the day came, de Havilland took off downhill and became briefly airborne before the port wings failed and the aircraft was wrecked, fortunately without serious injury to the pilot.

In his second biplane, inadequate spars of locally purchased whitewood gave way to straight grained spruce and ash, and the engine was mounted normally to drive a single pusher propeller. A successful quarter mile flight, made at Seven Barrows on 10 September 1910, was followed quickly by figure eights, a first passenger flight for Hearle and, in October, for his wife and eight month old son Geoffrey who, some thirty years later, was to be his Chief Test Pilot.

At the end of 1910 the aircraft was taken by road to Farnborough and following a successful one hour

The first De Havilland design to take shape is seen in the Fulham Palace Road workshop, along with its designer. (*DH via BAe Hatfield*)

acceptance test, flown by the designer on 14 January 1911. It was purchased by the War Office for £400 and used by de Havilland on 7 February to qualify for Royal Aero Club Certificate number 53.

He and Hearle were taken on by His Majesty's Balloon Factory (later the Army Aircraft Factory) as designer/pilot and mechanic respectively but the aircraft, now known as the FE.1, crashed on 15 August while being flown by the Assistant Superintendent, Lt. J T. Ridge. A redesigned version, the FE.2, with nacelle and 50 hp Gnôme rotary, flew for the first time three days later. In this aeroplane, which was not a rebuild of the FE.1 as has been widely supposed, de Havilland qualified for R.Ae.C. Special Certificate No. 4 for a 100 mile flight to Shrewton, near Larkhill, and back on 6 December 1911.

Early Days

When Farman, Wright and Curtiss first set out on the uncertain path towards fulfilment, Cody's contraption looked little different and probably flew with a comparable confidence. However, while Cody's fatal 1913 flight was in a machine little altered in technology from his 1909 machine, Geoffrey de Havilland's Farnborough-built B.E.2 biplane of 1912 looked remarkably advanced for its time and would not have looked all that out of place twenty years later. At the time Cody was clattering uncertainly into the air and reaching heights of several hundreds of feet, Geoffrey de Havilland and a passenger (Major Frederick Hugh Sykes) had already secured the British altitude record not just for a solo flight, but one with a passenger. They reached 10,560 feet.

Two pages from the Lloyd's Aviation record that show Geoffrey de Havilland flying career up to October 1921

LLOYD'S AVIATION RECORD.
PILOTS.

Confidential Information for the Use of Subscribers only.

G. De Havilland.

Date of Issue............10 OCT 1921

Name...... Geoffrey De Havilland, ...	Age.	Date of Birth.	Nationality.
Address....Stag Lane Aerodrome., EDGWARE., Middsx.		27th July 1882.	British.

Description of Certificates and Licences with dates.

'A' Licence No. 659 valid 16/9/21 to 15/3/22.
Royal Aero Club Certificate No. 53.

Types of Aircraft Licensed to fly.

V A R I O U S.

General Experience and Hours flown per type.	Source of Information and Date.
Is among the foremost of the world's aircraft designers. First flew in 1910, and has been constantly flying since, and has flown all his own designs of machines. Was test pilot at the Royal Aircraft Establishment, Farnborough, for three years.	Pilot. 21/9/21.

ACCIDENTS. 1911:- Forced landing due to engine failure. Ran into ditch; propeller and chassis broken.
    1913:- On Single-Seater Scout, S.E.1 at R.A.E., Farnborough. Machine spun into ground owing to too small a rudder. Machine wrecked. Pilot sustained broken jaw and general shock.
    1918:- While taking off in a D.H.9 at Hendon, failed to see a soldier standing in middle of aerodrome, and collided with him. Chassis and propeller fractured.

When last Medically Examined.	Date.						
Date of last Flight and Type of Aircraft.	Date.	20/9/21. D. H. Monoplane.					

The Stag Lane site in 1923. *[DH via BAe Hatfield]*

But the young de Havilland had already matched Cody's level of thinking with his early de Havilland Biplane No.1 of 1909, and the new machine, the Biplane No.2, flew for a quarter of a mile on 10 September 1909. After a one-hour acceptance flight on 14 January 1911, it was purchased by the War Office, re-named the F.E.1 (Farman Experimental) and flown extensively on a variety of tests until 15 August, when the engine broke and the aircraft was damaged beyond repair in the subsequent and premature return to earth. This machine had fore and aft planes, a pusher engine, and large ailerons.

The rights for de Havilland aircraft had rested with Holt Thomas's company, Airco, but in the post-war recession, Airco was sold to the Birmingham Small Arms Co Ltd (BSA). When, in April 1920, BSA decided to close down the aircraft business, Holt Thomas and de Havilland left. By now, 52-year-old George Holt Thomas was in failing health and saw little prospect of remaining in successful business himself. However, he had faith in his young designer and offered to put up the cash for Geoffrey de Havilland to start up his own business, the only condition being that Arthur Turner, Airco's former financial director, should be chairman of the board.

On 25 September 1920 came the announcement of the formation of a new private concern. It was called the De Havilland Aircraft Company Ltd and began its days with £50,000 capital in £1 shares. First directors were Geoffrey de Havilland, Arthur E Turner and Charles Clement Walker as Chief Engineer. A dynasty which was to have far-reaching effects on the British light aeroplane had been born.

A number of key men from Airco also joined the new company. Francis T Hearle as general Manager, Wilfred E Nixon as Company Secretary and Francis E N St.Barbe as Sales Manager. Arthur E Hagg also joined as Assistant Designer.

They rented a large field at the end of a country road in Edgware known as Stag Lane, recently vacated by the London and Provincial Aviation Company's flying school, and on October 5 moved into its two wooden sheds.

The founders of the company, as they appeared in 1937. Left to right: Francis T Hearle, Wilfred E Nixon, Geoffrey de Havilland, Charles C Walker, Francis E N St Barbe. *(DH via BAe Hatfield)*

Post first flight conference - Hubert Broad, down from the first flight of the DH.88 Comet Racer gives his first impressions to the men most concerned. On the left, with his back to the camera is Geoffrey de Havilland, also with his back to the camera are Arthur Hagg, the designer. On the right is Charles Walker and Major Frank Halford, responsible for the special DH Gipsy Six racing engines. *(DH via BAe Hatfield)*

An immediate decision was taken to build mainly civil aeroplanes - a bold step at a time when the market scarcely existed-and two half finished DH.18s were brought over from Hendon.

Hopes for lucrative military contracts during these lean years were quickly dispelled by the rigidity of Air Ministry specifications, which left designers little room for initiative and led to a crop of unimpressive aeroplanes. The rejection of the DH.27, DH.42 and DH.56 military prototypes led the company into the private venture field with the DH.65 Hound and DH.77 low-wing interceptor fighter of 1929. Both were faster than contemporary fighters but continued Air Ministry indifference eventually ended De Havillands military aircraft aspirations for a decade.

Onward and upward

1921 was memorable for the arrival of premium apprentice 18 year old Ronald E. Bishop. He was to join the company's design office in 1923, and became the Chief Designer in 1936, taking over Arthur Hagg.

Another of the 1921 'intake' was Alan S. Butler, wealthy owner of a private Bristol Tourer G-EAWB, who placed an order for a special three seat tourer to his own requirements. Butler backed this with an investment which allowed the site to be acquired outright from Warren and Smiles, directors of London and Provincial, who were demanding that De Havilland's either purchase the freehold or move out, and he was later made Chairman of the Company.

In 1921 the Company decided to embark on commercial flying to provide practical experience for their future designs and set up its own private hire service. This also met growing demands by Aerofilms Ltd., specialists in the air-to-ground photography of factories, public buildings and the like; by newspapers and film companies who wanted reporters, photographic plates or exposed ciné film rushed back from sporting events, disasters or State functions. The service was also used by jockeys or by wealthy people in a hurry.

Chief pilot and manager was Alan J. Cobham who had been flying for the aerial photography department of Airco. He ferried all his old photographic Siddeley Puma engined DH.9s over from Hendon to Stag Lane and these formed the nucleus of the new De Havilland Aeroplane Hire Service. His staff included Hubert S. Broad, Walter L. Hope, F. J. Ortweiler, Charles D. Barnard and R. E. Keyes.

The aircraft were in almost daily demand for flights from Stag Lane to Britain's major cities and business thrived until in 1925 Alan Cobham departed for the Cape on the first of his long distance air route survey flights. This marked the end of all Hire Service operations. Walter Hope left to form his own Stag Lane-based Air Taxis Ltd.; Charles Barnard took up an appointment as personal pilot to the Duchess of Bedford; and Hubert Broad became chief test pilot to the De Havilland Aircraft Co. Ltd.

It was not long after the Armistice which ended the Great War that four flying schools were established at which RAF Reservists could put in their annual flying hours, and the first was opened by De Havillands on 1 April 1923 with two DH.6s and four Avro 548s as primary trainers. These were supplemented by seven of the D.H. Aeroplane Hire Service DH.9 variants for advanced flying and, when the Hire Service closed, its aircraft went over entirely to schoolwork.

The first Chief Instructor at Stag Lane was named Edelston. He was followed by E. Burnaby Wilson and then by Flt. Lt. A. S. 'Jimmy' White, AFC who held the post until 1928 when he was succeeded by Flt. Lt. Robert W. Reeve, DFC, MM who had come from Beardmores in 1925. The instructional staff included John V. Holman, C. E. F. Riley, P. P. Grey, Charles D. Barnard and Clement A. Pike, who ran the School after Reeve left to become Chief Flying Instructor of De Havillands' second school at White Waltham in 1935.

To meet ever increasing Moth orders, additional workshops and flight sheds arose at Stag Lane and specially built Moth lock-up 'garages' were available when they qualified.

The success of the Moth family brought in much international business and the company was quick to realise the Empire's need for aviation. They quickly set up sites in Canada, Australia, New Zealand, South Africa and the USA. Thus was laid the foundations of the De Havilland Sales and Service organisation.

By 1926 all primary training was done on Moths, the veteran DH.9s were modernised and re-engined with Armstrong Siddeley Jaguar radials as DH.9Js by the School's engineers, several of whom were later to hold high office in the Industry. The Chief Engineer, H. M. Woodhams (holder of Ground Engineer's Licence No. 2), later became Managing Director of Armstrong Whitworth Aircraft Ltd., while his assistants, R. E Hardingham and James Norman joined the Air Registration Board as Secretary - and later Chief Executive - and Chief Surveyor, respectively when it was formed in 1937.

S. T. Weedon, one of the fitters who constructed the first hand-built Gipsy engine, became Chief Engineer of the School in 1935.

Additional duties undertaken by the School instructors included flight testing the wing flaps intended for the DH.50 and DH.51 in DH.9C G-EBAW; development tests on wing flaps fitted to Bristol Fighter J6721; distribution of newspapers during the 1926 general strike; development flying on behalf of Rolls-Royce Ltd. of the prototype F engine installed in their own DH.9A, J8110, from its first flight at Stag Lane on 11 November 1927 until Broad delivered it to Brooklands on 27 May 1929; production test flying of new Moths; and the supply of relays of pilots for the 600 hour Gipsy engine endurance test in 1929.

The syllabus now included advanced navigation, instrument flying, aerobatics, gunnery and photography. When the Expansion Scheme began in 1935 the School became 1 Elementary and Reserve Flying Training School and provided training for pilot entrants to the RAF. The second School, opened by Robert Reeve at White Waltham in November 1935 with Tiger Moths became 13 E&RFTS and trained 600 pilots before the aerodrome was handed over to Air Transport Auxiliary on 11 January 1941. De Havilland's also operated 90 RAF DH.82s at 17 EFTS North Luffenham during 1941/2.

With the outbreak of war a number of Hawker Harts that had been used were returned to the RAF, leaving the Hatfield School with seventeen Tiger Moths which rapidly increased to fifty-four. Flying staff were given service rank and in 1941, when there were forty-two instructors, 180 pupils and ninety Tiger Moths on strength, the School flew the amazing total of 43,693 hours. To achieve this, a relief airfield was opened at Holwell Hyde, later known as Panshanger, four miles north east of Hatfield. On 7 September 1942, the whole School moved there to clear Hatfield for all-out Mosquito production.

With the coming of peace, the School returned to Reserve flying and gradually ran down until only a handful of RAF Tiger Moths remained, closing on 31 March 1953.

Guaranteeing engine supply
Participation in the 1923 Lympne Light Aeroplane Trials and the 1924 Air Ministry Trials for two seaters

Above: The DH Gipsy I - the valve gear was later enclosed in the Gipsy II.

Below: The Gipsy III was the first inverted engine in the De Havilland stable.

Below: The Gipsy Major I, with wider cylinder bores was possibly the greatest of all pre-war aircraft engines, with 14,625 built.

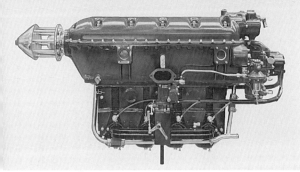

Above: The Gipsy Minor.

Below: The DH Gipsy Six, later called the Gipsy Queen.

Below: largest of the pre-war engines was the 405-425 horsepower 60 degree inverted vee-twelve, termed the Gipsy 12, and later the Gipsy King.

with engines under 1,100 cc., convinced Geoffrey de Havilland that machines of less than fifty horsepower were of little practical value. As no engine of this power existed, he approached Major Frank B. Halford of the Aircraft Disposal Co. Ltd., Croydon, who designed the 60 horsepower four cylinder Cirrus, a brilliant improvisation which used low cost cylinders and other components from the lirm's vast stock of war surplus Renault engines.

The rugged reliability of this engine, coupled with the simple lines and plywood construction of De Havilland's two seat Moth set a fashion in light aeroplane configuration which was often imitated but remained unsurpassed for over twenty years. It made the flying club movement possible, penetrated to all parts of the world in the hands of record breaking pilots and dramatically changed the company fortunes.

De Havilland's were determined to be independent of an outside firm which might not be able to maintain the supply and so decided to make its own engines. Frank Halford joined them to design a new 100 h.p. unit. Tuned to give 135 horsepower, it first flew in 1927 in the DH.71 monoplane in which Hubert Broad raised the Class speed record to nearly 187 m.p.h. Sales of the new Gipsy engine, as it was called, soon became big business and deliveries began on 28 June 1928 from a newly-built engine works in the south east corner of the aerodrome. Then, in 1929, the Gipsy was turned upside down and fitted into the new Puss Moth which, at the Olympia Aero Show, London, first introduced private pilots to cabin comfort.

Halford remained independant until the De Havilland Engine Co was formed under his leadership on 1 February 1944. The company pioneered the jet era with the Gobin, which first ran in April, 1942, only 248 days after the first drawings were issued to the shops. The engine was initially flight tested in March, 1943, in a modified Gloster Meteor prototype. The first Lockheed Shooting Star to fly did so powered by a Goblin and during 1944 this aircraft and the Goblin-powered Vampire became the first aircraft ever to exceed 500 m.p.h. The Goblin received the first ever official 150-hr. military type test certificate.

The Ghost turbojet, which first fiew in an Avro Lancastrian, was developed both as a civil and a military engine. It powered the Comet 1 and 1A in which aircraft it became the first turbojet to enter service with commercial aviation. The engine also received the first 150 hr. civil type approval certificate to be issued. Nearly 2,000 Ghosts were built in the United Kingdom and under licence abroad as the powerplant for Venom and Saab J-29 fighters. In its variants the engine has maximum ratings of 4,850-5,300 pounds of thrust.

De Havilland's big Gyron turbojet, the first De Havilland axial flow engine, ran initially during January, 1953 and following development over the next five years achieved a thrust of more than 29,000 pounds with reheat, equivalent to almost twice its original performance.

The Gyron axial turbojet of 24,000 pounds thrust was flight tested in de-rated form in 1955 in a modified

Finishing touches are put to the London Flying Club clubhouse and light aircraft showroom at the new Hatfield Aerodrome. *[DH via BAe Hatfield]*

Short Sperrin bomber. The engine, the first turbojet to be specifically designed for propulsion at high Mach numbers, was originally specified for a number of projected supersonic fighter and bomber aircraft.

The Gyron Junior, a scale variant of the Gyron first ran in August 1955, in its DGJ.1 form and in October 1957 in its DGJ.10 configuration. Flight testing commenced in May, 1957, in an English Electric Canberra. It was the first British turbojet to be developed specifically for propulsion at speeds in excess of Mach 2.5, and the DGJ.10 powered the Bristol Type 188 research aircraft. The Gyron Junior's application in the 188 provided official recognition of the advanced ideas formulated in the early 1950s by Major Halford on supersonic propulsion.

When Frank Halford died in April 1955, he left behind a well-knit team of engineers and technical services worthy of his name.

The company also entered the burgeoning helicopter market with the Gnome engine, derived from the General Electric T58, entered production in June, 1959, and three months later flew as the powerplant of a modified Westland Whirlwind helicopter. The engine was subsequently ordered by the Ministry of Aviation for powering all Whirlwind aircraft of the Royal Air Force. Other helicopters with which the Gnome was associated included the Westland Wasp in which aircraft the engine first flew in May, 1960, and the Italian Agusta 101G and Agusta-Bell 204 for which aircraft the Gnome was selected as the power unit.

De Havilland's did not stop at just jet engines - their rocket experience which was initiated in 1946, progressed from the early Sprite assisted take-off rocket (ATO) for the Comet, through the Super Sprite ATO unit for the Vickers Valiant to the Spectre family of turbo-pump rockets. Flight testing of the Spectre in its fully variable thrust version started in December, 1956, in a specially modified English Electric Canberra, and in May, 1957, the engine flew in the Saunders-Roe SR.53, the first research interceptor employing mixed turbojet and rocket powerplants. In October, 1959, the Double Spectre which combined a variable thrust Spectre with a fixed thrust Spectre flew for the first time during flight trials with test vehicles of the Avro Blue Steel stand-off bomb.

Outgrowing Stag Lane.

Although still in rural country, with Burnt Oak Station and 'The Bald Faced Stag' (the firm's 'local') as the only sizeable buildings in sight, Stag Lane was already doomed as an aerodrome because the extension of the Underground railway to Edgware changed the area into a London dormitory suburb and it was soon engulfed in a sea of houses.

Consequently, in 1930, a new airfield site was acquired at Hatfield, and during the next twelve months the De Havilland School of Flying and the London Aeroplane Club moved out. By the end of 1932 the entire airframe factory had departed, but not before the immortal Tiger Moth trainer, the Fox Moth light transport and the twin engined Dragon had been launched. The aerodrome was closed officially by NOTAM No. 4 in January 1934 but the Engine Division remained. After the landing ground had been sold to the building contractors, the grass area gradually shrank until only a narrow strip remained from which the last machine, Hornet Moth G-ACTA piloted by Capt. Geoffrey de Havilland took off for Hatfield on 28 July 1934.

From Hatfield's new factory there emerged a growing stream of Tiger Moth and Moth Minor trainers; Leopard and Hornet Moth tourers; Dragon, DH.86 and Rapide light transports; the Comet racers; the Albatross and Flamingo airliners; and finally 1,440 Airspeed Oxford twin engined trainers before the works was turned over to de Havillands' main contribution to the 1939-1945 war - the Mosquito.

The wartime total of 6,710 of these high performance, multi-role combat aircraft built by De Havilland's at Hatfield and in their new No. 2 Factory at Leavesden; by sub-contractors; and by the Canadian and Australian companies, a figure which rose to 7,781 by the time production ceased in 1950.

The De Havilland Repair Organisation repaired 2,962 Mosquitoes, Hurricanes, Spitfires and miscellaneous De Havilland types at Hatfield and Witney, Oxon.; and in 4½ years its Merlin Repair Dept. overhauled 9,022 of these engines.

When the DH.88 Comet racers drew attention to the advantages of variable pitch airscrews, de Havillands acquired a licence to manufacture the American-designed Hamilton propeller and equipped a factory at Stag Lane which began deliveries in July 1935. Over

Above: The initial layout of the London Flying Club facility at Hatfield. In the distance can be seen Harpsfield Hall and Sinclair's Farm. At the time of this picture, there were only five hangars and the swimming pool and squash courts were not yet built. The road in the foreground is the Barnet bypass, for many years designated the A1.

Below: By the mid-1930s the London Aero Club had established a major sporting facility on the aerodrome at Hatfield. The main clubhouse in the centre of the picture was later to become the aerodrome restaurant. The squash court is in the foreground right, with the swimming pool across the road.The line of hangars (now increased to eight), beyond which can be seen a number of lock-up garages, later became a manufacturing facility for plastics, sheet metal and wood detail. *[both DH via BAe Hatfield]*

Proudly flying the Union Flag, the Headquarters building at Hatfield gleams in the summer sun. *[DH via BAe Hatfield]*

102,000 were made during the war years, 23,210 of them at Stag Lane, where the Engine Division - reconstituted as The De Havilland Engine Co. Ltd. in 1944 - built 10,212 Gipsy Major and Gipsy Queen engines over the same period. Over 8,000 Tiger Moths were built at home and abroad, nearly half by Morris Motors Ltd., Cowley, Oxfordshire; and 200 Rapides and Dominie navigation trainers were built at Hatfield. In 1943 production of these was transferred to Brush Coachworks Ltd., at Loughborough where another 275 were produced; while the associated Airspeed Company, taken over in 1940, built 4,462 Oxfords as well as 695 Horsa gliders.

The Mosquito was followed by a family of Vampire cannon-firing interceptors powered by Frank B. Halford's Goblin turbojet engine, the Vampire prototype being flown on 20 September 1943, only sixteen months after the go-ahead was given. It exceeded 500 mph in the spring of 1944 and was the first UK or USA aircraft to do so. The classically beautiful Merlin engined Hornet single seat fighter development of the Mosquito, first flown on 28 July 1944, was too late to join combat.

Post War Pinnacle!

The company knew that the war was coming to a close and so prepared for peace. They flew their all-metal Rapide replacement, the Dove, on the company's 25th anniversary, 25 September 1945, only six weeks after the end of hostilities.

The Witney Repair Unit sold nearly 100 refurbished Rapides by February 1946 and production of the Vampire and its variants continued at the Preston works of the English Electric Co. Ltd. until greatly

Chief Test Pilot Group Captain John Cunningham CBE, DSO and two Bars, DFC and Bar, DI. *[DH via BAe Hatfield]*

Right: John Cunningham and the rest of the flight crew receive congratulations after the first flight of the Comet.

Left: Head of the design team, Ron Bishop alongside the team's creation.

Below: Roll-out of the DH.106 from the Experimental Shop, with the Class B marks G-5-1 on its polished skin.
(all DH via BAe Hatfield)

expanded by the acquisition of the former Shadow Factory at Hawarden, Chester, in 1948.

During the next eleven years more than 3,500 aircraft were built there, including nearly 500 Doves and some 140 of its four engined development, the Heron.

The Vampire was followed by the Venom with Halford's bigger Ghost Engine. The Ghost powered the DH.108 tailless research monoplanes and the early Comet airliner with which the British Overseas Airways Corporation made the world's first revenue earning jet flight in May 1952.

The tragedies which overtook both these types shed light worldwide on the little known phenomena of compressibility and fatigue problems and paved the way for highly reliable Comets of later marks, the second generation Trident short-haul transports and the DH.125 executive jets.

It was in 1935 that De Havilland introduced the manufacture of variable-pitch propellers into Great Britain. The merit of propellers of this type had been convincingly demonstrated during the previous year by the DH.88 Comet with variable-pitch aluminium propellers made by the French company Ratier. The success of the Comet Racer gave further impetus to the growing feeling within the company that this type of propeller was essential to the future of

aviation, and a manufacturing licence was purchased from Hamilton Standard of America.

The easily-repaired aluminium-alloy blades enabled the De Havilland factories in London and at Lostock to renovate and send back into the fray a total of 40,708 propellers like these, damaged during the war. Between 1939 and 1945, de Havilland factories in Great Britain produced a total of 146,000 propellers for a wide range of aircraft types, representing the major share used throughout the war by the Royal Navy and the RAF.

De Havilland Propellers Ltd., formed as a separate company in 1946 with a new factory at Hatfield, produced propellers for most postwar transports and later designed and manufactured Firestreak and Red Top air to air missiles.

In February, 1949, studies began on a new method of construction for large propellers, using hollow-steel in place of aluminium as the blade material. In the light of the knowledge then available, it was thought that aluminium would be too heavy in the larger diameters called for by such aircraft as the Britannia and the Beverley, which were then under design.

Hamilton Standard and De Havilland, working together, mastered the difficult techniques of

In the light of their successful development of Firestreak, de Havilland Propellers were appointed the overall design authority for the Blue Streak missile, leaders of a team whose other major members were de Havilland Aircraft, Rolls-Royce and Sperry. Blue Streak, which was designed to carry a thermo-nuclear
warhead over a range of several thousand miles to a ground target with extreme accuracy, was one of the most challenging problems ever faced by the British aircraft industry.

The last aeroplane type sold under the familiar De Havilland label before the De Havilland Enterprise, by then employing some 37,000 people, was absorbed into the Hawker Siddeley Group in 1960 was a small number of early marks of DH.125.

As the company house magazine *De Havilland Gazette* said in October 1959: ' *Blue Streak, the British Long-range Ballistic Missile, is seen here in one of the test towers which have been constructed at Hatfield by De Havilland Propellers Limited, the overall design authority for work on this project. At Spadeadam, in Cumberland. a vast new rocket test establishment is being built to facilitate complete system testing of the missile, and at Woomera, in Australia, tremendous efforts are being made in expanding and developing the missile-firing range to accommodate the flight trials of a vehicle which will cross the whole of the Australian Continent in a matter of a few minutes.'* (DH via BAe Hatfield)

One of the De Havilland Propellers production hung on a Vickers Vanguard airliner. *[DH via BAe Hatfield]*

manufacturing hollow-steel blades, and many hundreds of propellers of this type were put into service. Propeller technology then advanced again, and it was once more possible to use aluminium as the blade material in the largest of sizes before progressing to composites.

In 1959 the decision was taken that the Propeller Company should diversify its interests further by using its wide knowledge of many engineering skills to produce equipment for markets outside the aircraft industry, and a System Engineering Group was set up to develop automatic control equipment for the process industries. In the same year a licence agreement was concluded which entitled the Company to manufacture the Pottermeter, a precision turbine-type flowmeter employing a novel principle of operation whereby the rotor 'floats' in the stream of fluid being metered with the minimum of friction. This leads to extreme accuracy and long life, and thus the de Havilland Pottermeter aroused keen interest throughout many industries.

In addition to propellers and missiles, the Propeller Company manufactured a wide range of aircraft equipment, including alternators - compact power supply units used in many British guided missiles-airborne radar scanners, electric fuel control systems for turbine aero-engines, and cold-air-units and complete air-conditioning systems for a number of civil and military aircraft.

The Machines...

De Havilland No.1

Captain Geoffrey de Havilland's first aircraft - the De Havilland Biplane No. 1 - was a single seat biplane of cotton covered, white wood construction with a fixed tailplane, front elevator, large rudder above the tailplane, uncompensated ailerons, and no fixed fin. It was braced with piano wire and mounted on an undercarriage of cycle tubing with four cycle wheels.

The pilot sat in a wicker chair with a lever on the left controlling the elevator, one on the right for the rudder, and a footbar controlling the ailerons.

The four cylinder, horizontally opposed, water-cooled engine, designed by Geoffrey de Havilland and made by the Iris Motor Company at Willesden, developed 45 hp at 1,500 rpm. It weighed 224 lbs and was mounted at right angles to the direction of flight so as to drive two pusher propellers with adjustable aluminium blades through steel shafting and bevel gears.

No working drawings were made, so the aircraft was completed from sketches early in 1909 in a rented workshop off Bothwell Street, Fulham, London, with the assistance of Frank T. Hearle and Mrs Louise de Havilland, who sewed on the cotton covering. In May 1909 it was taken on a lorry to

Geoffrey de Havilland's first biplane, supposedly seen in the fields at Seven Barrows in 1909.
This picture is something of a mystery - many claim it is a photograph of the actual aircraft, but in 50th Anniversary of the company edition of *DH Gazette,* the company stated that the photo was that of a model. *(DH via BAe Hatfield)*

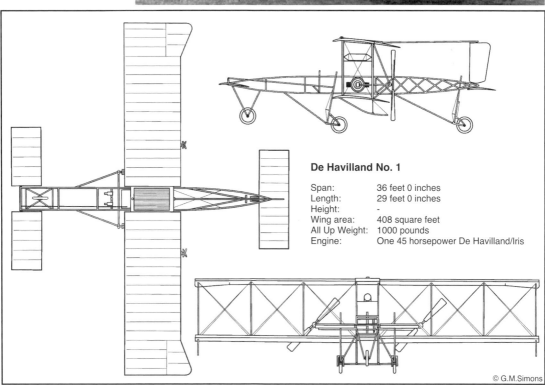

De Havilland No. 1

Span:	36 feet 0 inches
Length:	29 feet 0 inches
Height:	-
Wing area:	408 square feet
All Up Weight:	1000 pounds
Engine:	One 45 horsepower De Havilland/Iris

© G.M.Simons

The wrecked remains of Geoffrey de Havilland's original 45 hp Iris-built engine lying in the wreckage of his first biplane. *(DH via BAe Hatfield)*

The remains of the aircraft following its crash. *(DH via BAe Hatfield)*

Seven Barrows, near Newbury, but over six months elapsed before undercarriage, propeller drive, engine and control adjustments were finished so that fast taxying could be attempted whenever the wind was calm.

The machine flew just once - in December 1909 after a downhill take-off into wind. Without pilot training and deprived of instinctive control by his complex system of levers, de Havilland overcorrected when he felt himself airborne and pulled the nose up so steeply that the wing spars failed and the aircraft broke up when it crashed from a height of fifteen feet. Geoffrey was uninjured and the engine was salvaged.

De Havilland No.2

After the failure of his first aircraft design Geoffrey de Havilland began construction of his second aircraft, re-using the engine that he had designed for the earlier machine. Like the Bristol Boxkite and several other contemporary British designs, this closely followed the general lines of the Farman III, being a two-bay pusher biplane, with the pilot and passenger seated on the lower wing directly in front of the engine. Lateral control was effected by a pair of ailerons mounted on the upper wing. The so-called De Havilland Biplane No.2 was of spruce and ash construction with interconnected tail and front elevators, balanced ailerons and simplified undercarriage, built in the same Fulham workshop. The engine, salvaged from Biplane No. l, drove a single pusher propeller and a first successful flight of one mile was made by de Havilland at Seven Barrows on 10 September 1910. Records suggest that the engine was both rebuilt and 'tweaked' for now it was producing fifty horsepower.

After de Havilland was appointed assistant designer and test pilot at Army Balloon Factory (later the Royal Aircraft Factory) the machine went by road to Farnborough during December 1910 where, after a one hour acceptance flight on 14 January 1911, it was purchased by the War Office for £400 and restyled as the F.E.1 (Farman Experimental).

It was repeatedly modified and de Havilland flew it on 31 March with a larger tailplane and rear elevator; and again on 11 April with wing and aileron extensions, sixty-five square feet in area, which were removed and refitted several times.

Trials over the measured course on Laffan's Plain on 15 May gave the maximum speed as 38 mph, but

The De Havilland Biplane Number 2 at Farnborough. *(author's collection)*

Geoffrey de Havilland's second biplane. This photograph is thought to have been taken at Seven Barrows. *(author's collection)*

Once at Farnborough Biplane Number 2 was soon re-designated as the F.E.1. *(author's collection)*

with the extensions fitted aileron drag made the aircraft unstable in yaw, partially cured on 26 May by installing new rudders above and below the tailplane. It flew again on 3 July with the front elevator removed, but this pushed the C of G too far back, corrected next day by moving the upper mainplane rearwards.

Geoffrey de Havilland carried many passengers in this aircraft, completing eighty miles of circuit flying with seventeen officers and men of the London Balloon Company on 28 July and three days later reached an altitude of 1,000 feet. On 2 August he flew to Laffan's Plain with Lt. Ridge, who then taxied the machine and flew a few yards. During his next lesson on 5 August the aircraft nosed over, but when Lt. Ridge took it out again on 15 August after repairs, a broken bolt loosened two cylinders. The engine was beyond repair and the aircraft did not fly again in this form.

Span:	33 feet 6 inches.
Length:	29 feet 0 inches.
Wing area:	356 square feet.
All-up-Weight:	1000 pounds
Max speed:	38 mph.
Endurance:	1 hour 20 minutes.

Royal Aircraft Factory F.E.2

According to some records, the crashed F.E.1 was 'rebuilt' in August 1911 as the F.E.2. However, this was a 'rebuild' in name only, as it was a completely new design, incorporating few if any actual components of the original. The reason for this was that at this stage Farnborough was still not authorised to build aircraft from scratch, so it seems to be a good way of dealing with the paperwork! The Iris engine, seriously damaged in the F.E.1 crash, was replaced by a fifty horsepower Gnôme rotary engine, a two-seater canvas-covered nacelle was fitted, and the fore-elevator was replaced with one incorporated into a sesquiplane tail in the conventional manner.

On its first outing at Farnborough on 16 August 1911 it taxied only fifty yards before a piston broke up and the pieces were ejected through an exhaust port but, at 6.30 a.m. on 18 August Geoffrey de Havilland successfully flew it the short distance to Laffan's Plain and made four landings. Tail heaviness made gliding difficult but with over fifty pounds of lead in the nose it flew well, although this was reduced when a monoplane tail unit was fitted.

On 6 December 1911 de Havilland flew the F.E.2 to

The F.E.2 in its original form, with an 'open' pilot's nacelle. *(author's collection)*

The F.E.2 on its central float at Fleet Pond, Farnborough in 1912. Note the small wingtip float. *(author's collection)*

Left and below: The F.E.2 in 1912 with a 70 hp Gnôme and Maxim machine gun in the nose. By now the pilot's nacelle has been covered with canvas.

Bottom: The F.E.2 in 1913 after major modifications and the fitment of a 70 hp V-8 engine. *(all author's collection)*

Shrewton, near Larkhill and return having covered 100 miles in two and three-quarter hours flying time. Following a 'height test' to 1,900 feet before the official observer, Capt. Burke, on 23 December, Geoffrey de Havilland qualified for the Royal Aero Club's Special Aviator's Certificate.

The aircraft flew persistently right wing low but, after rigging adjustments, this was corrected. The aircraft was then taken over to Fleet Pond where the wheels were removed and the remaining structure was bolted to a single shallow-draught float, and tail and wing tip floats fitted. First flights from the water, totalling forty-five minutes were made by de Havilland on 12 April 1912 but, with the drag of the float, the engine was not powerful enough and so it went back to

Farnborough where it was replaced by a 70 hp Gnôme. It first flew with this engine on 26 April and was flown to the Pond next day for the float to be refitted. With extra power, water take-offs with pilot and passenger were reasonable and the aircraft then went on to enjoy a comparatively long career on both wheels and floats.

It was employed in 1912 for trials with a Maxim machine gun mounted in the nose and in 1913 was extensively reworked with 70 hp Renault V-8 engine, streamlined nacelle, new outer wing panels which

increased the span to 42 feet, the tailplane raised to the top longerons, and a smaller rudder. In this form it resembled the larger and later F.E. types which were built in quantity.

The new nacelle was deeper and more spacious, the mainplanes 'identical to those of the BE.2A'. Effectively, although the factory now routinely constructed original aircraft, it was another case of a new design reusing the designation of an older one. During a trip to the South Coast piloted by Royal

Aircraft Factory test pilot Ronald Kemp on 23 February 1914, it spiralled into the ground from 500 feet. at West Wittering, seven miles from Chichester, Sussex, due it was said, to the absence of fixed fin area to offset the increased keel surface of the new nacelle. Passenger E. T. Haynes, a civilian scientist at the Factory, was killed and the aircraft destroyed.

Span:	33 feet 0 inches, increased to 42 feet.
Length:	28 feet 0 inches
Wing area:	340 square feet.
All-up-Weight:	1200 pounds
Max speed	47.5 mph.

Royal Aircraft Factory S.E.1

The first aircraft type designed under Geoffrey de Havilland's direction after his appointment to the Royal Aircraft Factory was a canard pusher biplane which, due to the peculiarities of aircraft nomencature at the time, had to be described as the rebuild of a crashed Army Blériot monoplane. In reality, nothing but the Blériot's 60 hp E.N.V. engine was used in its construction. Two bay biplane wings were mounted at the rear end of a long, narrow nacelle, with twin rudders on outriggers behind and a front wing, or elevator, in the extreme nose. It received RAF

The S.E.1 canard biplane with centrally mounted engine driving a pusher propeller through an extension shaft. *(author's collection)*

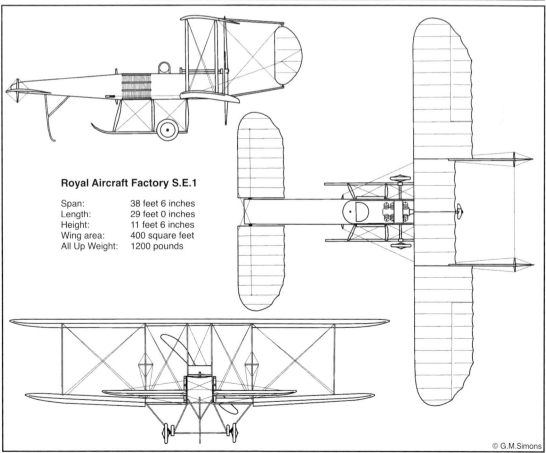

Royal Aircraft Factory S.E.1

Span:	38 feet 6 inches
Length:	29 feet 0 inches
Height:	11 feet 6 inches
Wing area:	400 square feet
All Up Weight:	1200 pounds

© G.M.Simons

designation S.E. l, signifying Santos Experimental at first but it came to mean Scouting Experimental.

Roll-out took place at 5 a.m. on 7 June 1911 but the wheels were too far aft of the centre of gravity, causing the front skids to dig into the ground when taxying and it was next day, after adjustments, before a first straight flight of about a mile was possible. Longer flights followed on 10 June, and a flight to Laffan`s Plain on 28 June showed that the hinge line of the front wing was too far ahead of the centre of pressure and progressive reductions in area were necessary before the S.E.1 became stable in pitch. Turns were difficult and although side area was reduced by stripping fabric from the sides of the nacelle, improvement was only achieved when the all-moving front wing was replaced by a fixed aerofoil with trailing edge elevator.

Geoffrey de Havilland, its only pilot up to that time, flew it for the last time on 16 August 1911, when he made two return trips to Laffan's Plain with a misfiring engine. This was rectified, but two days later, on 18 August, Lt. T. J. Ridge, Assistant Superintendent of the Royal Aircraft Factory but a pilot of only limited experience, stalled it off a gliding turn over Farnborough, spun it and was killed.

Royal Aircraft Factory B.E.1

The B.E.1, just as the S.E 1 before it, was disguised as repairs to an existing aeroplane. It masqueraded as a Voisin biplane presented to the War Ofiice by the Duke of Westminster but only its 60 hp Wolseley water-cooled engine lived on in the new aircraft.

Construction of Geoffrey de Havilland and F. M. Green's two seat tractor biplane, was orthodox to modern eyes with slightly greater span to the upper wing but with no fixed fin and lateral control by wing warping. It was pushed out for first engine runs at Farnborough on 4 December 1911 and first flew in the hands of de Havilland on 27 December. The first passenger was Frank T. Hearle on 3 January 1912 but the rest of the month was spent in solving rigging problems. It eventually flew well, once at night, and carried a large number of passengers, but before long the cumbersome Wolseley engine installation, with its drag-producing radiator between the front centre section struts, was scrapped in favour of an air-cooled 60 hp Renault. This engine was completely uncowled but was later faired to give protection to the occupants.

The B.E.1, forerunner of the mass produced B.E.2s used during the First World War, had a comparatively long career and was equipped with early radio apparatus by Capt. H. P. T. Lefroy, Royal Engineers. With Geoffrey de Havilland as pilot he then used it for pioneer wireless controlled artillery shoots on Salisbury Plain. On 11 March 1912 it was handed over to Capt. Charles James Burke, Commanding Officer of the Air Battalion, accepted as airworthy next day, and later taken on charge by 2 Squadron, Royal Flying Corps with serial number 201. In the hands of Capt. Burke and other pilots it took part in a number of experimental flights at Farnborough during 1913 and 1914 and eventually crashed there in January 1915.

Right: The B.E 1 with 60 hp Wolseley and radiator between the centre-section struts.

Below: The B.E 1 now fitted with an uncowled 60 hp Renault engine. *(both author's collection)*

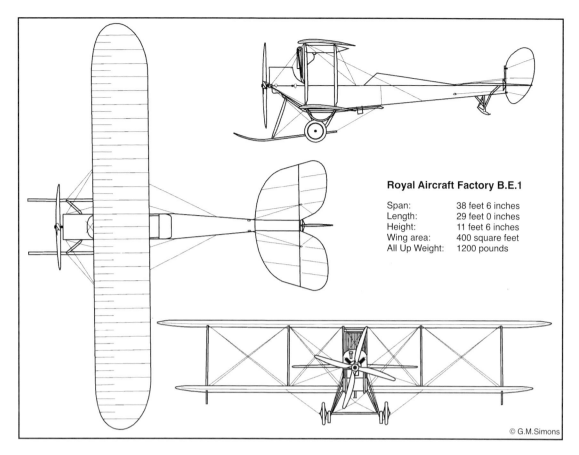

Royal Aircraft Factory B.E.1

Span:	38 feet 6 inches
Length:	29 feet 0 inches
Height:	11 feet 6 inches
Wing area:	400 square feet
All Up Weight:	1200 pounds

© G.M.Simons

Royal Aircraft Factory B.S.1

The last aircraft designed by Geoffrey de Havilland before he left Farnborough to join the Aircraft Manufacturing Co. Ltd. was the B.S.1 single seat biplane flown early in 1913. Powered by a 14 cylinder, two row Gnôme rotary, it was the first aeroplane in the world specifically designed as a fast single seat scout and as Blériot was said to have originated the tractor biplane, was known as the Blériot Scout, or B.S. 1.

Its wooden, circular section monocoque fuselage was years ahead of its time and merged smoothly into the lines of the closely cowled engine to give the B.S.1 a streamlined shape. Lateral control was by warping the single bay wings and the tail unit featured a diminutive rudder, without fixed fin, mounted above a one-piece tailplane and elevator.

For its time the B.S.1 was fast, and in March 1913 its designer, now Lt. de Havilland, Special Reserve, was timed over the speed course at 91.4 mph. Unfortunately the rudder was too small for the keel

The B.S.1 with Geoffrey de Havilland seated at the controls.. This picture was taken after the rudder modification was completed and designation changed to B.S.2, *(author's collection)*

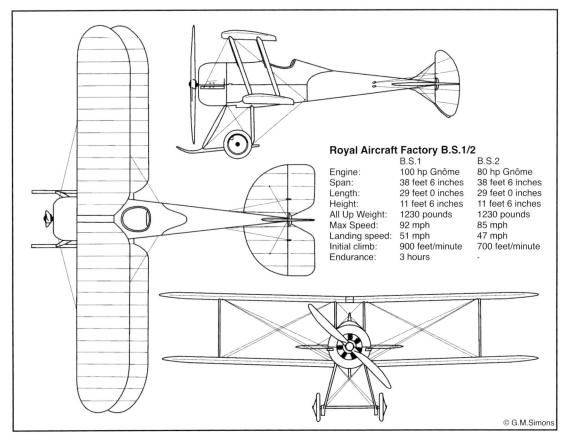

Royal Aircraft Factory B.S.1/2

	B.S.1	B.S.2
Engine:	100 hp Gnôme	80 hp Gnôme
Span:	38 feet 6 inches	38 feet 6 inches
Length:	29 feet 0 inches	29 feet 0 inches
Height:	11 feet 6 inches	11 feet 6 inches
All Up Weight:	1230 pounds	1230 pounds
Max Speed:	92 mph	85 mph
Landing speed:	51 mph	47 mph
Initial climb:	900 feet/minute	700 feet/minute
Endurance:	3 hours	-

© G.M.Simons

surface of the deep front fuselage and directional control was poor. Later, on the day of the speed trials, it went out of control in a turn and de Havilland was injured as it struck the ground in a fiat spin.

During extensive repairs the aircraft was re-engined with an 80 hp Gnôme and fitted with a divided elevator to accommodate a tall, high aspect ratio rudder with small fixed fins above and below the fuselage. It was then redesignated B.S.2, later changed

to S.E.2, but within a few months the rudder was enlarged still more and the machine reappeared with a fabric covered strut-and-longeron rear fuselage.

It was taken over by 5 Squadron RFC in January 1914 and also served with 3 Squadron at Netheravon. It was sent to Moyenneville, France in October 1914 and flew offensive patrols until March 1915. Armament was two rifles mounted on the sides of the fuselage to fire outside the arc of the propeller.

DH.1

Captain Geoffrey de Havilland's first design after joining the Aircraft Manufacturing Co. Ltd (AirCo) in June 1914, and the first to be given the famous 'DH' type number, was a two seat reconnaissance machine, armed with a forward firing machine gun.

It was a twin boom, two bay, wire braced biplane of fabric covered wooden construction, the mainplanes having two spars, wire braced internally. A pusher layout gave the observer/gunner the best possible arc of fire from the front cockpit. The design included three unusual features; coil springs in the undercarriage to absorb landing shocks, a form of oleo leg to damp out the rebound, and the provision of air brakes. These were rotatable aerofoils protruding three feet on each side of the nacelle just behind the front centre section struts. Non-availability of supplies

of the 120 hp watercooled Beardmore engine resulted in the 70 hp aircooled Renault being fitted instead.

The prototype, designated the Airco DH.I, was completed and flown at Hendon in January 1915. Contemporary reports record that the designer '...demonstrated his confidence in it by taking off without any preliminary straight hops and at once commencing to circle'. He also piloted it during tests which not only showed it to be inherently stable and capable of being flown 'hands off' but also that the air brakes were ineffective, so they were removed.

A small number of DH.ls were built but these had rubber cord shock absorbers in the undercarriage, forward facing exhaust pipes and the front cockpit coaming lowered to the top longerons to improve the pilot's view and to permit free rotation of the single Lewis gun on its pillar mounting. Five reached Royal Flying Corps (RFC) training units during 1915.

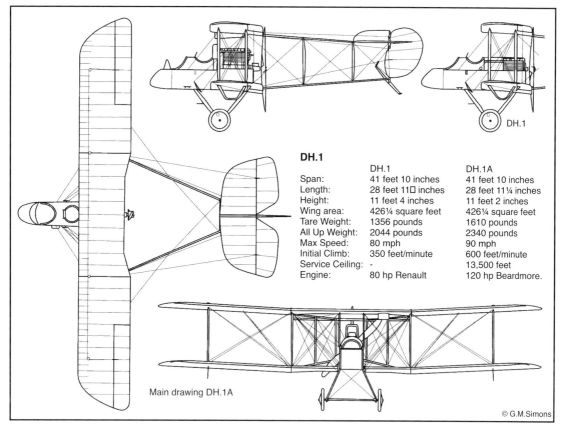

DH.1

	DH.1	DH.1A
Span:	41 feet 10 inches	41 feet 10 inches
Length:	28 feet 11☐ inches	28 feet 11¼ inches
Height:	11 feet 4 inches	11 feet 2 inches
Wing area:	426¼ square feet	426¼ square feet
Tare Weight:	1356 pounds	1610 pounds
All Up Weight:	2044 pounds	2340 pounds
Max Speed:	80 mph	90 mph
Initial Climb:	350 feet/minute	600 feet/minute
Service Ceiling:	-	13,500 feet
Engine:	80 hp Renault	120 hp Beardmore.

Main drawing DH.1A

© G.M.Simons

Production was delayed until the 120 hp Beardmore was available in quantity and manufacture was finally undertaken by Savages Ltd. at King's Lynn, leaving Airco free to develop newer types. Savages, founded in 1851 by Frederick Savage, normally built fairground and traction engines, steam wagons, ploughing engines and fairground locomotives designed to run on a circular track. They also made engines for steam yachts.

With the Beardmore engine it carried the designation DH.IA and was identified by the upright engine, a large radiator behind the pilot's head and the gravity fuel tank mounted under the port upper wing root. The prototype DH.1A, serialled 4606, was converted from an Airco-built DH.1. Seventy-three DH.ls and DH.lAs were delivered to the RFC, but they saw little war service and in 1916 six were shipped to the Middle East Brigade for operational use by 14 Squadron. Home Defence squadrons received twenty-four and a further forty-three went to training units such as 35 Reserve Squadron at Northolt and 199 Training Squadron. The type remained operational until early in 1917, after which it was relegated to second line duties and were withdrawn from use at the end of 1918.

Production amounted to the prototype and 100 production machines with RFC serial blocks 4600-4649 and A1611-A1660 used.

Left: Captain Geoffrey de Havilland sits on board the prototype DH.1 - seen here fitted with auxilliary aerofoils behind and below the cockpit - at Hendon in January 1915. *(DH via BAe Hatfield)*

Right: the prototype DH.1A, serialled 4606, with the 120 horsepower Beardmore engine. *(DH via BAe Hatfield)*

DH.2

The DH.2 single seat pusher fighter resembled a scaled down DH.I, its main components being similar but smaller versions of those of the earlier type. It came about because the British military mind was slow to see the importance of interrupter gear in order to allow the use of a machine gun firing forward through the propeller of a tractor aeroplane. Therefore the DH.2 appeared as an unstaggered two bay biplane of orthodox fabric covered wooden construction, powered by a 100 hp Gnôme Monosoupape rotary aircooled engine, using tubular steel instead of wooden tail booms and employing a steerable tail skid.

The prototype was first flown by Geoffrey de Havilland on 1 June 1915, and proved to be initially tail heavy but next day, with thirty pounds of ballast in the nose, he reached 3,500 feet in five minutes, a remarkable rate of climb for the time. On 3 June the machine went back into the works for the nacelle to be moved four inches forward and to have a gun and a larger rudder fitted, after which large scale production for the RFC was conducted by the Airco

factory at Hendon and four hundred DH.2s were delivered.

The machine carried a single Lewis gun on a flexible mounting in front of the pilot, necessitating a slightly reshaped nacelle, and a few aircraft were fitted with the 110 hp Le Rhône rotary in place of the Gnôme. RFC pilots quickly learned the technique of aiming the whole machine at their targets using the Lewis gun as a fixed weapon. Sensitivity of control, a limited speed range, and the inexperience of pilots, resulted in a number of early accidents through spinning, while others were caused by structural damage following the disintegration of the rotary engines in flight. However, despite this, there was an appreciation of its immensely strong structure and delightful handling qualities, so

Above: The prototype DH.2, fitted with the 100 horsepower Monosoupape rotary engine.

Left: A production DH.2, serialled 5943. The aircraft is fitted with a gravity fuel tank and two-bladed propeller. *(both DH via BAe Hatfield)*

A DH.2 seen 'somewhere in France.
author's collection)

that it became a fully acrobatic fighting machine.

The first operational DH.2 squadron was 24, commanded by Major Lanoe G. Hawker, who led his twelve machines from Hounslow to St. Omer, France on 7 February 1916. Within three months 29 and 32 Squadron had also been re-equipped and sent to France and the three squadrons took part in the Battle of the Somme and fought continuously against the Germans until the early part of 1917. 266 DH.2s served with the British Expeditionary Force with 5, 11, 16 and 18 Squadrons.

The DH.2 took part in many events. On 1 July 1916 Major Lionel Wilmot Brabazon Rees, Commanding Officer of 32 Squadron, won the Victoria Cross for a single-handed attack on a formation of ten German two seaters, destroying two. Later that year, on 28 October, a DH.2 of 24

Squadron inadvertently caused of the death of German fighter pilot Oswald Boelcke. He had set out for his sixth sortie of the day with his two best pilots, Manfred von Richthofen and Erwin Böhme, and three others. The patrol eventually led them into a dogfight with a number of DH.2 fighters In the ensuing dogfight, Boelcke and Böhme, unaware of each other's presence, closed in on the same aircraft, flown by Captain Arthur Knight. Boelcke swerved to avoid a collision with the interceding aircraft. Böhme's landing gear brushed Boelcke's upper wing. As the fabric peeled off the upper wing of his aircraft, Boelcke struggled for control. He and his aircraft fell out of sight into a cloud. When it emerged, the top wing of the Fokker DR.1 Triplane was gone. However, Boelcke made a relatively soft crash-landing but was nevertheless killed.

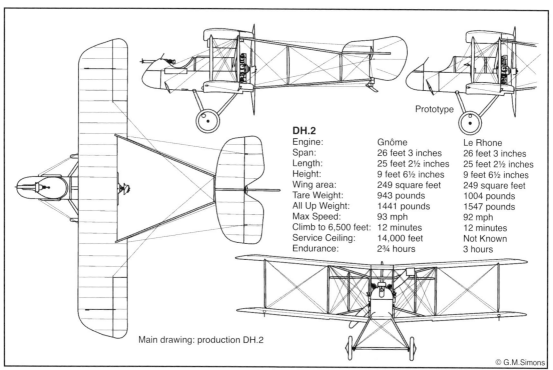

Prototype

DH.2

	Gnôme	Le Rhone
Engine:		
Span:	26 feet 3 inches	26 feet 3 inches
Length:	25 feet 2½ inches	25 feet 2½ inches
Height:	9 feet 6½ inches	9 feet 6½ inches
Wing area:	249 square feet	249 square feet
Tare Weight:	943 pounds	1004 pounds
All Up Weight:	1441 pounds	1547 pounds
Max Speed:	93 mph	92 mph
Climb to 6,500 feet:	12 minutes	12 minutes
Service Ceiling:	14,000 feet	Not Known
Endurance:	2¾ hours	3 hours

Main drawing: production DH.2

© G.M.Simons

A few weeks afterwards, on 23 November, another well-known German pilot, Manfred von Richtofen, shot down Major Lanoe G. Hawker in his DH.2 after one of the longest single combats of the war. In 774 combats, the DH.2s of 24 Squadron was recorded as having destroyed 44 enemy aircraft.

Two aircraft were issued to Home Defence squadrons and on 17 June 1917 a machine from the Orfordness Experimental Station flown by Captain R H M S Saundby, (later Air Marshal Sir Robert Henry Magnus Spencer Saundby KCB, KBE, MC, DFC, AFC) took part in an attack on Zeppelin L48.

When ousted from the Western Front by the DH.5 and other tractor fighters, thirty-two DH.2s were despatched to the Near East where they saw service in Palestine with 17 and 111 Squadrons and in Macedonia with 47 Squadron and the RFC/RNAS Composite Fighting Squadron. At home, one hundred DH.2s were issued to training units including 10 Reserve Squadron at Joyce Green, but by the autumn of 1918 all DH.2s had been struck from RAF charge.

Production: 4732 (prototype) RFC blocks 5916-6015, 7842-7941, 8725. A2533-A2632, A4764-A4813, A4988-A5087. Not all were delivered.

DH.3

The DH.3, Captain Geoffrey de Havilland's third design, appeared in 1916, and was a large two-bay biplane capable of bombing German industrial centres. The design seemed to owe something to the Royal Aircraft Factory's FE.4, in the early design of which Captain de Havilland had collaborated. The DH.3 was equipped with two 120 hp Beardmore water-cooled engines in nacelles between the mainplanes. The long, slender, wire braced Warren girder fuselage was built of spruce, covered with plywood at the forward end and carried low to the ground on a wide track, short legged undercarriage. A pair of bumper wheels was provided under the nose to prevent any possibility of tipping onto its nose. As might be expected on such a large design, it was necessary to ensure good handling qualities by using an elevator with generous horn balances.

The four bladed, nine foot diameter pusher airscrews were carried clear of the mainplane trailing edges by short extension shafts and the DH.3 was also the first aircraft to feature the curving rudder that was to become the characteristic 'signature' of almost every future De Havilland design. The crew of three consisted of the pilot in an open cockpit just ahead of the mainplanes, and front and rear gunners whose cockpits were each equipped with two Lewis guns on pillar mountings. The DH.3 had a sprightly performance and when engaged on long range duties could carry a military load of 680 pounds and fuel for eight hours.

Only the prototype was built and as far as is known, it carried no serial number. A second version, carrying the serial 7744 was powered by two 160 hp Beardmore engines and so modified as to warrant the designation DH.3A. These included the cutting back of mainplane trailing edges

In order to obviate the use of engine extension shafts, while to lighten the controls still further, the rudder was given increased balance area. An order was placed for fifty production DH.3As but when the first, A5088, was still under construction, the War Office cancelled the contract in the belief that strategic bombing of Germany was unnecessary and

The prototype DH.3 being assembled at Hendon with 120 horsepower Beardmore engines. *(DH.BAe Hatfield)*

Left: a side view of the same aircraft. Without any crew on board, the aircraft tended to tail-sit. *(DH.BAe Hatfield)*

A rear view of the prototype DH.3 at Hendon apparently fitted with two-bladed propellers. *(DH.BAe Hatfield)*

The mainplanes of the DH.3 were designed to fold in order to save hangar space. *(DH via BAe Hatfield)*

that the twin engined bomber was impracticable. Both prototypes were flown by pilots of the Upavon evaluation unit but were then relegated to storage behind the Hendon hangars. Legend has it that the prototype DH.3s were burning on the factory scrap heap on 7 July 1917 while London was being bombed by their German counterpart, the Gotha.

This and later bombardments encouraged a rapid change of official attitude which resulted in the DH.3 being redesigned and built in quantity as the DH.10.

Production: Prototype unmarked, DH.3A serial 7744. 7745, A5088 to A5137 unfinished.

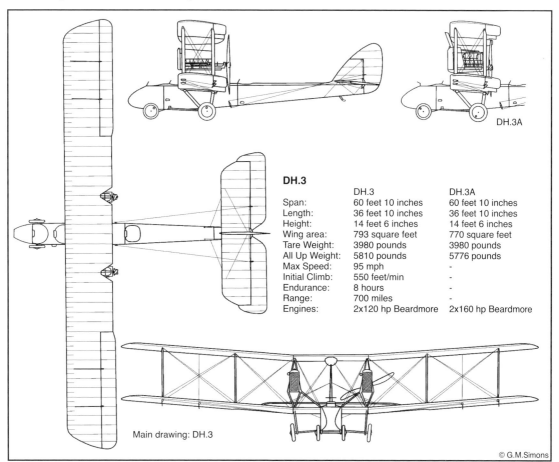

DH.3A

DH.3

	DH.3	DH.3A
Span:	60 feet 10 inches	60 feet 10 inches
Length:	36 feet 10 inches	36 feet 10 inches
Height:	14 feet 6 inches	14 feet 6 inches
Wing area:	793 square feet	770 square feet
Tare Weight:	3980 pounds	3980 pounds
All Up Weight:	5810 pounds	5776 pounds
Max Speed:	95 mph	-
Initial Climb:	550 feet/min	-
Endurance:	8 hours	-
Range:	700 miles	-
Engines:	2x120 hp Beardmore	2x160 hp Beardmore

Main drawing: DH.3

© G.M.Simons

DH.4

The prototype DH.4 bomber, serialled 3696, first flew at Hendon in August 1916. Its fabric covered, wire braced, spruce and ash structure was typical of the day but the front fuselage, housing the cockpits and main fuel tanks, was additionally strengthened with a plywood covering. Mainplanes and tailplane followed the then standard two spar layout but the spars were lightened by spindling between the ribs and the tailplane was fitted with variable incidence gear. Rubber cord suspension was used in the undercarriage and the fin and rudder conformed to the De Havilland family shape first used on the DH.3. Armament consisted of one synchronised forward firing Vickers gun mounted on top of the fuselage, single or twin Lewis guns on a Scarff ring for the observer, and two 230 lb. and four 112 lb. bombs were carried in racks under the fuselage and wings respectively.

The prototype was fitted with a 230 hp Beardmore-Halford-Pullinger (BHP) six cylinder watercooled engine and was unique in having rear centre section struts which raked sharply forward. Production DH.4s had the rear struts shortened and made parallel to the front and were powered by a variety of engines, including the 200 hp RAF 3A, 230 hp Siddeley Puma, 250 hp Rolls-Royce III and 260 hp Fiat. Pilots were warned of the risk to the propeller when taking off with the tail too high. When more powerful engines were installed, it was necessary to fit a taller undercarriage and this eventually became standard on all DH.4s. The incidence was also increased to shorten the landing run. All these engines were cooled by frontal radiators except the Fiat, first installed in A7532, the radiator being fitted between the front undercarriage legs, permitting the use of close fitting cowlings as in the of the later DH.9. In addition to the modified undercarriage late production DH.4s had the rear Scarff ring raised to improve the field of fire and the rear decking was made flat. Orders were placed with Airco and four sub-contractors for 1,700 DH.4s, of which 1,449 were delivered.

The first DH.4s in France, delivered by air to 55 Squadron on 6 March 1917, were first used operationally at Valenciennes on 6 April. Towards the end of the war it bombed munitions factories at Frankfurt, Mannheim and Stuttgart but French and Belgian based DH.4s were also used for high level photographic reconnaissance flights, fighter sweeps and anti-Zeppelin and submarine patrols.

More squadrons were equipped with the type to increase the bombing capacity of the RFC, two squadrons re-equipping in May, and a total of six squadrons by the end of the year. As well as the RFC, the RNAS used the DH.4, both over France and over

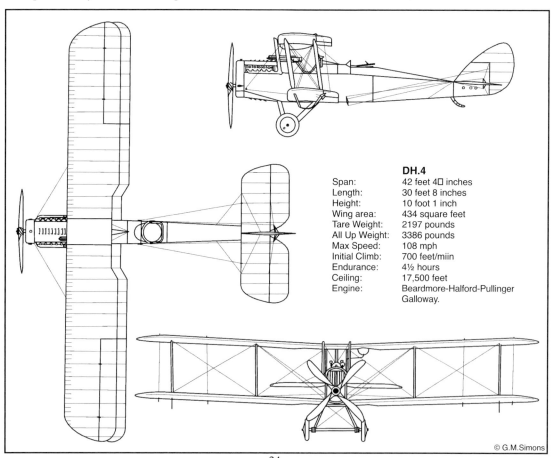

DH.4

Span:	42 feet 4☐ inches
Length:	30 feet 8 inches
Height:	10 foot 1 inch
Wing area:	434 square feet
Tare Weight:	2197 pounds
All Up Weight:	3386 pounds
Max Speed:	108 mph
Initial Climb:	700 feet/miin
Endurance:	4½ hours
Ceiling:	17,500 feet
Engine:	Beardmore-Halford-Pullinger Galloway.

© G.M.Simons

Left: The prototype DH.4, identifiable by the raked-forward rear centre-section struts. The aircraft is seen at Hendon in Augusat 1918.

Below: A2129 was an early production example with a short-length undercarriage, a Scarff ring fitted to the upper longerons and a 250hp R-R engine. *(DH.BAe Hatfield)*

Italy and the Aegean front. The DH.4 was also used for coastal patrols by the Royal Naval Air Service (RNAS). One, crewed by Major Egbert Cadbury and Captain (later Air Vice-Marshal) Robert Leckie as gunner, shot down Zeppelin L70 on 5 August 1918. Four RNAS DH.4s were credited with sinking the German U-boat UB 12 on 19 August 1918.

Most naval DH.4s were among 150 built under sub-contract by the Westland Aircraft Works. They were Eagle powered and fitted with twin, instead of single front guns and a raised Scarff ring mounting for the rear gunner, but increases in weight and parasitic drag reduced their performance.

Pilots who flew the DH.4 were unanimous in praise of its handling qualities, speed range and performance which made it almost immune from interception. No previous aircraft had so wide a speed range (45-143 mph on the Eagle VIII version) and pilots' notes emphasised its slow speed docility, recommending that the approach be made at 60 and the touch down at 50 mph. Operating at heights above 15,000 feet the machine could easily outfly contemporary single seat fighters but if caught was an easy victim because the cockpits were so far apart that the speaking tubes were useless as a means of coordinating defence and the aircraft went down in flames when bullets punctured the sixty gallon fuel tank between the seats. Later in 1917 fire hazards were reduced when the pressurised fuel system was replaced by two wind driven pumps on top of the fuselage behind the pilot.

The first DH.4 to be built by Westlands at Yeovil was flight tested by Bentfield Charles Hucks (later of 'Hucks Starter' fame) in April 1917 and delivered in France next morning. Coastal patrols were undertaken by RNAS Squadrons and at least one DH.4 was experimentally fitted with twin floats for this task. 202 Squadron also took a complete set of oblique and

DH.4 A7710 *'Elizabeth Campbell of Inverell Station'* a BHP Galloway powered machine. The was a so-called 'presentation aircraft' named after Miss Campbell of Inverell Station, Melbourne, Australia, who gave £2,700 to supposedly pay for it and to have it so inscribed. (*DH.BAe Hatfield*)

vertical photographs of Zeebrugge in preparation for a raid on the harbour on 22-23 April 1918 during which the lock-gates on the Mole were bombed with by Wing Commander Peregrine Forbes Morant Fellowes flying DH.4 A8065.

At the time of its entry into the war, the United States Army Air Service lacked any aircraft suitable for front line combat. It therefore procured various aircraft from the British and French, one being the DH.4. As the DH-4 - note the use of the an American-style hyphenated model number - it was manufactured mostly by Dayton-Wright and Fisher Body for service with the United States from 1918, the first American built DH-4 being delivered to France in May 1918, with combat operations commencing in August 1918. The powerplant was a Liberty L-12 of 400 hp and it was fitted with two .30 inch Marlin machine guns in the nose and two .30 inch Lewis guns in the rear and could carry 322 lb of bombs. it could also be equipped with various radios like the SCR-68 for artillery spotting missions. The heavier engine reduced performance compared with the Rolls-Royce powered version, but as the 'Liberty Plane' it became the US Army Air Service standard general purpose two-seater, and on the whole was popular with its crews.

The Home Defence DH.4s were operated far over the North Sea and efforts were made at the Marine Aircraft Experimental Establishment (MAEE), Isle of Grain, to equip them with flotation gear or as an alternative, hydrovanes and wing tip floats for use after the undercarriage was jettisoned. These devices

were developed and test flown by Harry Busteed using DH.4s A7457 and D1769. The latter aircraft was also used for trailing mine experiments and hydrovanes were also fitted to an American built DI I-4 at McCook Field, Dayton, Ohio. Two DH.4s, were fitted with one-and-a-half pounder Coventry Ordnance Works (COW) quick firing anti-Zeppelin guns. In 1917-18 the type was used overseas in small numbers, while in 1919-21 many went as Imperial Gifts to assist the formation of air forces in Canada and South Africa. Airco-built DH.4s A7893 and A7929, taken to New Zealand in 1919 by Col. A. V. Bettington were stationed at Sockburn and A7893, piloted by Capt. T. Wilkes and L. M. Isitt was the first aircraft to fly over Mount Cook.

As an engine test bed the DH.4 made a major contribution to Allied technical superiority and among the several experimental installations were those of the 300 hp Renault 12Fe in A2148, the 400 hp Sunbeam Matabele in A8083, the 353 hp Rolls-Royce G and the Ricardo-Halford inverted supercharged engine. One of the new American 400 hp Liberty 12 engines was fitted into a British built DH.4 delivered at McCook Field in August 1917. It first flew with the Liberty on 29 October of that year and heralded the mass production of the DH.4 in America. By the Armistice 3,227 had been built, 1,885 of which were shipped to France, and by the end of 1918 the total of American built DH-4s had risen to 4,587, or more than three times the British production of 1,449. Eventually, the three American contractors delivered 4,846 examples of the

A wonderfully detailed view of this unidentified DH.4, showing photographic plates being handed to the gunner of a DH4 aircraft, Serny airfield, France sometime in February 1917. *(author's collection)*

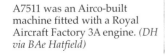

A7511 was an Airco-built machine fitted with a Royal Aircraft Factory 3A engine. *(DH via BAe Hatfield)*

DH-4, but after the war they were disposed of in considerable numbers to the Nicaraguan and other Latin American army air services.

In the USA, the Boeing Airplane Corporation, Dayton-Wright Airplane Company, the Fisher Body Corporation, and the Standard Aircraft Corp produced the DH-4 with the Liberty L-12 engine for the American air services. 9,500 DH-4s were ordered from American manufacturers, of which 1,885 reached France during the war.

The Americans built a single Dayton-Wright DH-4A which was fitted in July 1918 with an improved fuel system by the Engineering Division of the Army's Department of Aircraft Production. This aircraft should not be confused with the British cabin conversion designated the DH.4A. In October 1918, more extensive modifications by the Engineering Division produced the DH-4B in which the pilot's cockpit was moved back next to that of the gunner.

After the war, a number of firms, most significantly Boeing, were contracted by the US Army to remanufacture surplus DH-4s to DH-4B standard. Known by Boeing as the Model 16, deliveries of 111 aircraft from this manufacturer took place between March and July 1920, with 50 of them returned for further refurbishments three years later.

American conversions fell into two main categories - specialised versions for military purposes and experimental conversions of the early DH-4B, mainly as engine testbeds or trial installations aircraft. Military models included the DH-4B-2 trainer, known as the

Blue Bird, the DH-4B-5 two passenger 'Honeymoon' cabin transport devised by the Engineering Division of the Bureau of Aeronautics, and ambulance versions for one or two stretchers. Two of the last named, U.S. Marine serials A5811 and A5883, were used in 1922 in the island of Haiti, starting point of the longest flight in US history up to that time, made in 1924 by two US Army DH-4Bs which successfully covered the 10,953 miles to San Francisco and back.

The total of such conversions made in 1918-24 reached 1,540 when the two final rebuilds were made by the De Havilland Aircraft Co. Ltd. to the order of Maj. Davidson for the use of Naval and Military Attaches of the US Embassy in London. These aircraft were test flown by Hubert Broad in August 1926 and based at Kenley and Stag Lane in full US military markings until replaced by a DH.60 Moth in 1927.

Steel tube fuselages were built by the Boeing and Atlantic companies in 1920-25 to extend the useful lives of these veterans under the designations DH-4M, DH-4M-1 and DH-4M-2, 186 of which were by Boeing and

A DH.4 fitted with twin floats used for coastal patrols. (DH.BAe Hatfield)

An American-built DH-4B fitted with Grain floatation gear seen at McCook Field, Dayton Ohio. *(USAF Museum)*

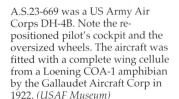

A.S.23-669 was a US Army Air Corps DH-4B. Note the re-positioned pilot's cockpit and the oversized wheels. The aircraft was fitted with a complete wing cellule from a Loening COA-1 amphibian by the Gallaudet Aircraft Corp in 1922. *(USAF Museum)*

at least 135 by Atlantic.

DH-4 variants remained in military service with the U.S. Army, Navy and Marines until 1929, one DH-4B-3 being re-engined with a Packard 2A-1500 by the US Navy at Quantico in 1926. They were built for the Corps Observation role, three by the Boeing company and one by Atlantic. The Boeings were ungainly sesquiplanes using steel DH-4M-1 fuselages and thick section wings of new design. The first, designated XCO-7, became the XCO-7A when fitted with a wide track undercarriage but crashed and was replaced by the XCO-7B, a similar machine powered by a 420 hp Liberty V-1410 experimental inverted engine. These prototypes scarcely resembled the DH-4B at all but the origins of the remaining Corps Observation conversion, XCO-8, could hardly be mistaken, being a reproduction of an undesignated conversion made in 1922 by the Gallaudet Aircraft Corporation which fitted a standard Liberty powered DH-4B with the mainplanes and N type interplane struts from a Loening COA-1 amphibian. The true XCO-8 was an exactly similar conversion made two years later by the Atlantic company.

Steel tube fuselages were built by the Boeing and Atlantic companies in 1920-25 to extend the useful lives of the DH.4s under the designations DH-4M, DH-4M-1 and DH-4M-2, 186 of which were by Boeing and at

least 135 by Atlantic. Considerable interest was aroused when two re-worked and specially modified DH-4s took off from Rockwell Field, San Diego, California on 27 June 1923 to conduct one of the first flight refuelling experiments. Lts. Lowell Smith and Paul Richter remained airborne for six and a half hours, during which time they were refuelled twice by hose from the DH-4 flown by Lts. Hine and Seifert. After minor adjustments they kept aloft for thirty-seven and a quarter hours on 27-28 August and landed only when fog prevented further contact with the tanker. On 13 December 1923 a DH-4 with supercharged Liberty, piloted by Lt H. Harris and carrying a passenger, climbed to an altitude of 27,000 feet over McCook Field, increased later to 30,500 feet, reached in 69 minutes in a special DH-4B fitted with a Roots type supercharger behind the engine. In 1927 a DH-4M-2 with Model II Roots blower, reached 26,500 feet in fifty-one minutes.

Under a contract signed in February 1923, Boeing undertook to equip three DH-4s with steel fuselages using the Boeing developed arc-welding process. These were known as XDH-4M-1s - the 'M' standing for modernised. This, plus the 'X' and the '-1' was used to differentiate from those built by Anthony Fokker in his new American factory, the Atlantic Aircraft Corp, which had been founded in May 1924.

The upward firing one-and-a-half pounder COW quick-firing anti-Zepplin gun fitted to fire through the upper centre-section of this DH.4. *(DH.BAe Hatfield)*

The interior of the Boeing factory in Seattle on 21 July 1921, showing the large-scale production of steel-tube fuselages for use on the rebuilt DH-4 aircraft. *(author's collection)*

Manufacturers and serial blocks.

The Aircraft Manufacturing Co. Ltd., Hendon, London, N.W.9. Serials A2125-A2174, A7401-A8089, B1482, C4501-C4540, D8351-D8430, D9231-D9280, F1551-F1552, F7595-F7598.

F. W. Berwick and Co. Ltd., Park Royal, London, N.W.l0. Serials B2051-B2150.

Glendower Aircraft Co. Ltd., 54 Sussex Place, South Kensington, London, S.W.7. Serials F2633-F2732, H5290.

Palladium Autocars Ltd., Felsham Road, Putney, London, S.W.15. Serials F5699-F5798.

The Vulcan Motor and Engineering Co. (1906) Ltd., Southport, Lancs. Serials B5451-B5550.

Waring and Gillow Ltd., Cambridge Road, Hammersmith, London, W.6. Serials H5894-H5939.

Westland Aircraft Works, Yeovil, Somerset. Serials B3954-B3990, B9476-B9500, D1751-D1775, N5960-N6009, N6380-N6429.

A number were re-built after the war from salvaged components.. These included: B7747, B7812, B7910, B7933, B7941, B7950, B7969, B7987, B799l, B9994, F5809, F5827, F5828, F5833, F5837, F5846, F6001, F6096, F6104, F6114, F6115, F6139, F6167, F6168, F6187, F6222, F6234, F6253, H7118, H7123, H7147, H7148.

A number of companies overseas made DH.4s, sometimes applying their own type numbers.

SABCA, Haren Airport, Brussels, Belgium (15 built in 1926 for Belgian Air Force)

Atlantic Aircraft Corporation, Teterboro, New Jersey, USA.

Boeing Airplane Company, Seattle, Washington, USA built a number issuing their own type numbers.

Model	C/N	Qty	Type	Client
16	88-198	111	DH-4B	US Army
	412-461	50	DH-4B	US Army
	462-511	50	DH-4M	US Army
	515-517	3	XDH-4M-1	US Army
	519-615	97	DH-4M-1	US Army
42	616	1	XCO-7	US Army
	617	1	XCO-7A	US Army
	618	1	XCO-7B	US Army
16	619-648	30	DH-4M-1	US Marines
	653-658	6	DH-4M	Cuba

The Dayton-Wright Airplane Co., Dayton, Ohio, USA. (3,106 built)

The Fisher Body Corporation, U.S.A. (1,600 built)

Standard Aircraft Corporation, Elizabeth, New Jersey, USA. (140 built)

DH.4 (Civil)

Hundreds of DH.4s - the majority brand new from the Airco and Waring and Gillow factories, were acquired by Handley Page Ltd. in 1919-20 and reconditioned by the Aircraft Disposal Co. Ltd. (AirDisCo) at Croydon

A DH-4C fitted with a 300 hp Packard 1a-116 engine. *(USAF Museum)*

Boeing-built DH-4Ms delivered to the US Marines were given the naval designation of O2B-1. The Navy colouring of silver overall with yellow top to upper wing and tail surfaces. *(author's collection)*

to become the postwar equipment of the air forces of Spain, Belgium, Greece, Japan and other small nations. With few exceptions these were powered by the 375 hp Rolls-Royce Eagle VIII engine and those for Spain and Belgium were flown out in the autumn of 1921 under temporary civil marks. In Spain the DH.4 formed the main equipment of the Air Force training establishment at Cuatros Vientos and was used extensively in the Moroccan War.

Two Eagle powered machines were also used in a purely civil capacity on the Continental services of Aircraft Transport and Travel Ltd. late in 1919 and two others were shipped to Australia by Clement John De Garis, an Australian entrepreneur and aviator. Once there he fitted both machines with cockpits for two passengers behind the pilot. One of them, the former F2691, now registerd G-AUCM, was erected and test flown at Glenroy on 27 November 1920 and piloted by Francis Stewart Briggs. De Garis's first major interstate flight was in the DH.4 from Melbourne to Perth, the first time Australia had been crossed by air from east to west, a distance of 2,169 miles. The aircraft landed at Belmont Park Racecourse on 2 December 1920, after 19 hours 10 minutes. One stretch of 1,105 miles was flown in eight and three quarter hours. De Garis, Briggs and their mechanic, Sergeant Stoward, were given a mayoral reception on their arrival in Perth. On

14 December they flew from Perth to Sydney, a distance of 2,462 miles in a time of twenty-one and a half hours.

Another notable flight was from Mildura to Sydney (five and a half hours) and on to Brisbane (four hours fifty minutes), in January 1921. Then, on 16 January, they set off on a one-day flight from Brisbane to Melbourne, leaving at 6:15 am local time and reaching their destination at 7:20 pm, a flying time of ten and a half hours. Stopovers were made in Grafton, Sydney and Cootamundra.

In August 1924 it carried mail on the Adelaide-Sydney service of Australian Aerial Services Ltd. with the name *'Scrub Bird'* and was still flying miners and supplies between Port Moresby and Lae, New Guinea for Bulolo Goldfields Ltd. in 1927.

de Garis sold the other DH.4, F2682/G-AUBZ to Raymond. J. P. Parer who flew it to victory in the first Australian Aerial Derby on 28 December 1920 at 142 m.p.h. It was then used for joyriding and other pioneering work until delivered to QANTAS at Longreach by rail on 12 August 1922. In the last two months of the year it covered over 5,000 air miles, mainly on the Charleville-Cloncurry mail service but was extensively damaged when it struck telephone wires while landing at Gilford Park station, south west of Longreach, on 6 June 1923. During repairs the two

A US Navy DH-4Amb-1 conversion, complete with turtle-back for the carriage of a stretcher patient. *(author's collection)*

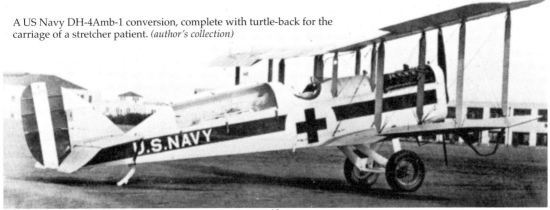

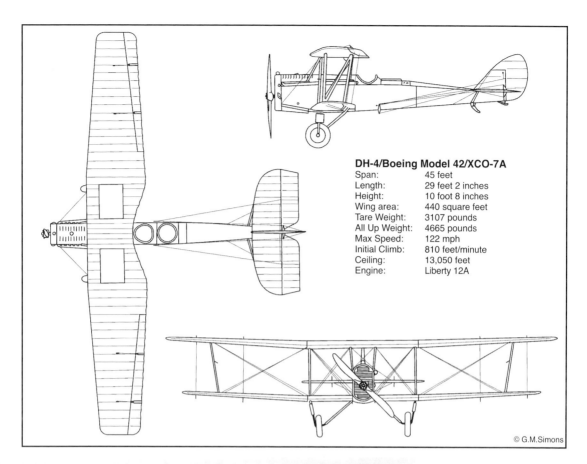

DH-4/Boeing Model 42/XCO-7A

Span:	45 feet
Length:	29 feet 2 inches
Height:	10 foot 8 inches
Wing area:	440 square feet
Tare Weight:	3107 pounds
All Up Weight:	4665 pounds
Max Speed:	122 mph
Initial Climb:	810 feet/minute
Ceiling:	13,050 feet
Engine:	Liberty 12A

© G.M.Simons

The XCO-7A was a standard Boeing-built DH-4M fuselage fitted with tapered wings, a wider tailplane and a new landing gear to Boeing design. *(USAF Museum)*

The XCO-7B was identical to the XCO-7A apart from the inverted Liberty engine. The new components did little to improve the original DH-4 performance figures. *(USAF Museum)*

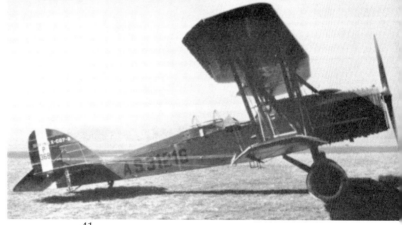

Variations of Engines and Design.

The different engines fitted in the DH.4 created a who range of slightly different aircraft specifications and data. These can be best considered by looking at the following British machines:

Engine:	Siddeley Puma	R-R Eagle Mk III/IV	R-R Eagle VII	R.A.F. 3A
H.P:	230	250	275	200
Span:	42 feet 4⅝ inches	42 feet 4⅝ inches	42 feet 4⅝ inches	42 feet 4⅝ inches
Length:	30 feet 8 inches	30 feet 8 inches	30 feet 8 inches	29 feet 8 inches
Height:	10 feet 1 inch	10 feet 5 inches	11 feet 0 inches	10 feet 5 inches
Wing area:	434 square feet	434 square feet	434 square feet	434 square feet
Tare Weight:	2230 pounds	2303 pounds	2387 pounds	2304 pounds
All Up Weight:	3344 pounds	3313 pounds	3472 pounds	3340 pounds
Max Speed:	106 mph	119 mph	143 mph	122 mph
Initial Climb:	1000 feet/min	1000 feet/min	1350 feet/min	-
Endurance:	4½ hours	3½ hours	3.75 hours	-
Ceiling:	17,400 feet	16,000 feet	22,000 feet	15,500 feet

Engine:	Fiat	Liberty 12
H.P.	260	400
Span:	42 feet 4⅝ inches	42 feet 6 inches
Length:	29 feet 8 inches	29 feet 8 inches
Height:	10 feet 5 inches	10 feet 5 inches
Wing area:	434 square feet	434 square feet
Tare Weight	2306 pounds	2306 pounds
All Up Weight:	3360 pounds	3360 pounds
Max Speed:	114 mph	114 mph
Initial Climb:	1000 feet/min	1000 feet/min
Endurance:	4½ hours	4½ hours
Ceiling:	17,500 feet	17,500 feet

The Americans built many DH-4s using different engines and designations:

Designation:	DH-4	DH-4B	DH-4M-1	DH-4M-2
Engine	Liberty 12	Liberty 12A	Liberty 12A	Liberty 12A
H.P.	400	435	435	435
Span:	42 feet 5 inches	42 feet 5½ inches	42 feet 5½ inches	42 feet 5½ inches
Length:	29 feet 11 inches	29 feet 11 inches	29 feet 11 inches	29 feet 11 inches
Height:	9 feet 8 inches	-	-	-
Wing area:	440 square feet	-	-	-
Tare Weight	2939 pounds	-	-	-
All Up Weight:	4595 pounds	4600 pounds	4595 pounds	4595 pounds
Max Speed:	118 mph	124 mph	118 mph	118 mph
Initial Climb:	760 feet/min	-	-	-
Ceiling:	12,800 feet	-	-	-

Designation:	XCO-7	XCO7A	XCO-7B	XCO-8
Engine:	Liberty 12A	Liberty 12A	Liberty V-1410	Liberty 12A
H.P.	435	435	420	435
Span:	45 feet	45 feet	45 feet	45 feet
Length:	30 feet 4 inches	30 feet 4 inches	30 feet 11 inches	30 feet
Height:	-	-	-	-
Wing area:	-	-	-	-
Tare Weight:	-	-	-	-
All-Up-Weight:	4798 pounds	4800 pounds	4652 pounds	4680 pounds
Max Speed:	130 mph	122 mph	-	130 mph
Initial Climb	-	-	-	-
Ceiling:	-	-	-	-

open passenger cockpits were roofed over to make an open-sided cabin and it first flew in this form in May 1924. It opened the extension service between Cloncurry and Camooweal on 7 February 1925 piloted by Capt. L. J. Brain but, when ousted by the new DH.50s at the end of 1927, was sold to Matthews Aviation Ltd. at Essendon Aerodrome, Melbourne where the fuselage was modified for joyriding with no less than four separate passenger cockpits behind the pilot. At this stage it was named 'Cock Bird' on the fin but in 1930 it returned to taxi work with a full DH.4A-style cabin with sliding windows as 'Spirit of Melbourne'. It was last in service with Pioneer Air Services, who acquired it in September 1934.

Left: the three-seat DH.4 G-AUBZ of Queensland and Northern Territory Aerial Services Ltd (QANTAS) at Longreach in March 1923.. (*DH.BAe Hatfield*)

Below: the same aircraft in 1929 modified for joyriding at Essendon with five open cockpits and a pair of ex-QANTAS FK.8 fuel tanks above the centre-section. (*QANTAS*)

In Canada, all twelve Imperial Gift DH.4s were equipped with air to ground wireless telegraphy sets for use on forestry patrol work by the Air Board Civil Operations Branch and in 1921 one of these aircraft made the first recorded geological reconnaissance flights. From August 1920 their pilots spotted hundreds of forest fires and helped save millions of dollars worth of timber, operating mainly from an airstrip at High River, Alberta, where the DH.4's performance could combat the turbulent skies near the Rockies. Special skis were designed for winter flying and as late as 1924 these veterans continued to give photographic coverage of the district but by that time showed such deterioration that they were permanently grounded at the end of the season. The one exception, G-CYDM, still airworthy in 1927, was reworked to DH.4B standard with underslung radiator and observation panels in the lower wing roots.

The DH.4's greatest contribution to the embryo air transport industry was made in Europe by four machines supplied by Handley Page Ltd. to the Belgian concern Syndicat National pour l'Etude des Transports Aeriens (SNETA). In company with a number of DH.9s, they ran spasmodically on the Brussels-London, Brussels-Paris and Brussels-Amsterdam services in 1920-21, and although their normal London terminal was Croydon, many flights terminated at Cricklewood for convenience of servicing. After the departure to Brussels of DH.4 O-BABI on 15 January 1921, Cricklewood was used no more and the DH.4's commercial life ended soon afterwards in two major crashes and the destruction of most of the SNETA fleet in a disastrous hangar fire at Brussels on 27 September 1921.

Apart from two machines employed by Aircraft Transport and Travel Ltd. as temporary replacements for crashed DH.4As, the standard DH.4 saw little civilian service in England. On June 21, 1919 however, Marcus D. Manton came third at an average speed of 117-39 m.p.h. in the Aerial Derby at Hendon in K-142, a new aircraft with Rolls-Royce Eagle VIII, specially

The DH.4R racer K141 photographed after the 1919 Aerial Derby. (*author's collection*)

'209' the DH-4B mail aircraft for the US Postal Service fitted with the Aeromarine wings and underslung mail compartment. *(USAF Museum)*

A DH-4B mailplane fitted with the Witteman-Lewis unstaggered wing and strengthened centre-section. *(USAF Museum)*

demilitarised by the Aircraft Manufacturing Co. Ltd. It competed against a 'one-off racing version registered K-141 and designated DH.4R to signify Racer. This was built in ten days by a team led by Frank T. Hearle, who fitted a 450 hp Napier Lion with chin radiator, clipped the lower mainplane at the first bay and braced the overhanging portion of the upper wing by slanting struts. Without stagger and with the rear cockpit faired over, it was scarcely recognisable as a DH.4 derivative but Airco test pilot Capt. Gerald Gathergood flew it twice round London in 1 hour 2 minutes and set up a British closed circuit record of 129.3 mph.

The one other British civil example was G-EAMU acquired by the shipping firm of S. Instone and Co. Ltd., primarily for the fast carriage of ship's papers but also accommodating two passengers in the open rear cockpit. With Capt. F. L. Barnard as pilot and appropriately named *'City of Cardiff'* it emulated the Aerial Derby machines by making its first flight on the morning of 13 October 1919, a return flight to the Welsh capital in the afternoon and its maiden trip to Paris next day. During 1920 several trips were made to Paris, Brussels, Nice, and on one occasion, to Prague.

In the USA DH-4s with Liberty 12 engines were placed in regular service with the US Postal Service on 12 August 1918 and from June 1919 onwards a considerable number of DH-4Bs and DH-4Ms were converted for the carriage of 400 pounds of mail in a watertight compartment that had once been the front cockpit. The aircraft was flown from the rear as a single seater. In addition, thirty machines were reconstructed by the Lowe, Willard and Fowler Engineering Company to have increased span, two 200 hp Hall-Scott L-6 watercooled engines outboard and a large mail compartment in the nose. One normal DH-4B, marked '299', was given a special fuselage having a cargo hold for 800 pounds of mail between the undercarriage legs. New wings of modified section were built by the Aeromarine Company and in 1922 No. 299 carried a record load of 1,032 lb. from New York to Washington at its economical cruising speed of 68 m.p.h. Other important and unusual DH-4 mailplanes included one fitted with Wittemann-Lewis unstaggered wings and strengthened centre section as well as several rebuilt by G. I. Bellanca with new, single bay, sesquiplane wings braced by his patent inclined

One of a number of US Postal Service DH-4Ms rebuilt by Bellanca with single bay sesqui-plane wings braced by Bellanca lift-struts and fitted with ailerons on the upper wing only. *(USAF Museum)*

Possibly the ultimate DH.4 conversion, one of the Lowe, Willard and Fowler DH-4B postal aircraft with two 200 hp Hall-Scott L-6 engines Other machines had 150 hp Hispano-Suizas. *(USAF Museum)*

lift struts. Pioneer mail pilots flew the DH-4s night and day in any weather between New York, Washington, Cleveland, Chicago and Omaha, finally linking the East and West coasts when the final section to San Francisco was opened in August 1920. DH-4s spanned the continental USA until 1927, by which time many had been equipped with large belly tanks giving incredible range, and enormous cone shaped floodlights for night landings in rough pasture at small townships en route.

DH.4A

Immediately following the cessation of hostilities there was an urgent demand for the ability to carry people across the channel to meet the demands of the armistice. Formed in March 1919 under the command of Major J. Ronald McCrindle 2 (Communication) Squadron, 86th Wing, RAF operated between Kenley and Buc, near Paris with DH.4s. During the sittings of the Peace Conference a daily courier and mail service was operated in each direction and many Cabinet Ministers availed themselves of this new means of transport, including Bonar Law, Winston Churchill, Lord Milner, Major General Sykes and William Morris 'Billy' Hughes, Prime Minister of Australia.

At the special request of Bonar Law, a number of Eagle VIII powered DH.4s were modified to accommodate a Minister and his secretary face to face in a glazed cabin so that work and conversation might be continued in comfort during the flight. The cabin top was a lightweight structure fully-glazed with Triplex windows along both sides and having a hinged starboard side and roof so that entry was both simple and discreet. A steeply curved hump decking over the cabin faired in to the tail. Normal DH.4 fuel tanks were retained behind the pilot and the

two familiar wind driven fuel pumps were mounted above them, but to compensate for the weight of the extra passenger so far back, the aircraft was re-rigged with the upper mainplane twelve inches aft of its usual position to allow for the rearwards shift in the centre of gravity. Thus, unlike the DH.4, the cabin model was unstaggered and therefore a major variant to which the designation DH.4A was allotted.

Under the command of Wing Commander W. Harold Primrose, the Communication Squadron made history on 28 June 1919 not only by flying four DH.4As in line astern over the Palace of Versailles during the signing of the Peace Treaty but also by carrying Bonar Law from Buc to Kenley with the Prime Minister's letter to the King advising him that the Treaty had been signed. When the squadron disbanded in September 1919 the DH.4As were sold to Handley Page Ltd. among hundreds of other war surplus machines.

In July 1919 four new DH.4s on Airco's Hendon production line were also converted into DH.4As for the operating subsidiary Aircraft Transport and Travel Ltd. and flew initially with enlarged military serial numbers. Piloted by Capt. Eardley Hayden 'Bill' Lawford, one, G-EAJC, is now famous as the machine which carried G. M. Stevenson-Reece of the *Evening Standard* and a consignment of grouse, newspapers, leather and Devonshire cream from Hounslow to Le

DH.4 F5764 was built by Palladium Autocars of Putney, and converted to DH.4A standard and used by 2 Communications Squadron for the carriage of British negotiators for the Armistice talks. It was later registered G-EAWH. *(author's collection)*

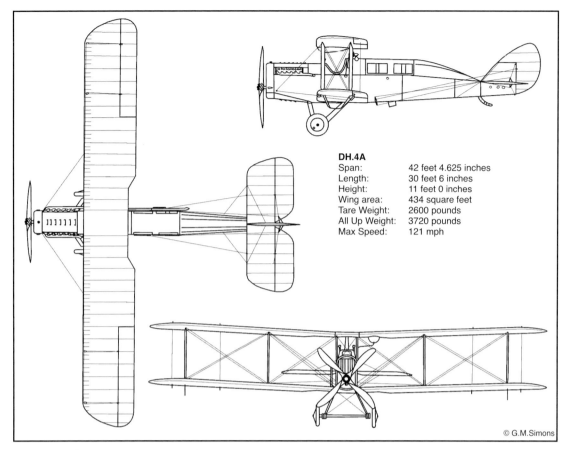

DH.4A

Span:	42 feet 4.625 inches
Length:	30 feet 6 inches
Height:	11 feet 0 inches
Wing area:	434 square feet
Tare Weight:	2600 pounds
All Up Weight:	3720 pounds
Max Speed:	121 mph

© G.M.Simons

Bourget in 2 hours 30 minutes on 25 August.

Later that same month another DH.4A, G-EAHG, was demonstrated by Captain Howard John Saint at the First Air Traffic Exhibition (ELTA) at Amsterdam and in the following October at Interlaken, Switzerland by Major Stewart-Wortley. On 10 November its sister craft 'HF carried the first civilian air mail to France at a fee of 2/6 per ounce. Unfortunately both 'HF and 'HG were lost in serious crashes while trying to maintain their schedules without wireless during the appalling winter of 1919, and were replaced by open cockpit DH.4s G-EANK and 'NL. All the A.T. & T. aircraft were based at Hendon, positioning flights being made to Hounslow to pick up passengers and clear Customs until the new terminal aerodrome opened at Plough Lane, Croydon on 1 April 1920. The DH.4s then operated both to Le Bourget in France and Schiphol in the Netherlands, but with fares at 20 guineas a head, could not compete with subsidised foreign air lines and were scrapped when A.T. & T. Ltd. went into liquidation on 15 December 1920.

It was a popular and robust machine especially for joy-riding and, with its Eagle engine, easy to maintain. The direct-drive Eagle was a slow-runner, full power emerging at just 1,355 rpm. This meant that it produced a good low-pitched throaty roar as it crossed the skies.

A number of nil hour DH.4s had been obtained by Handley Page Ltd. direct from Waring and Gillow Ltd., and one of these was converted to DH.4A standard as G-EAVL for use on the Cricklewood-Le Bourget and Schiphol services of Handley Page Transport Ltd. On 4 December 1920 piloted by Lt. Vaughan Fowler, it created a record by flying to Paris in half a gale with two passengers in an hour and 48 minutes. Two other DH.4As, O-BARI and O-BATO, were also produced for the company's Belgian customer SNETA, which used them on the Brussels-Croydon route in 1920-21. They were joined in April 1921 by one of the Communications Squadron DH.4As, F5764, acquired by Handley Page Ltd. among the surplus stock and reconditioned for civil use as G-EAWH.

Another of the original military DH.4As was shipped to Buenos Aires by Maj. S. G. Kingsley of the River Plate Aviation Co. Ltd., who in August 1920 made a pioneer business trip of 1,250 miles from Buenos Aires to Porto Alegre on charter to an Argentine bank. In the following year this DH.4A was joined by a DH.6 and a DH.16 which together covered a total of 40,000 miles in the Argentine, Brazil and Uruguay.

Another DH.4A also existed, in the shape of the Instone DH.4 G-EAMU, fully converted to DH.4A standard at Hamble by A. V. Roe and Co. Ltd. in February 1921. Renamed 'City of York' it flew the Croydon-Paris route in the livery of Instone Air Line

Another view of DH.4A F5764, showing the unstaggered wings and the fixed ladder allowing access to the passenger cabin. (*author's collection*)

The port side view of G-EAMU with the top open. Named *City of York*, this Instone Air Line DH.4A was formerly H5939 and went on to join Imperial Airways. It was the unlikely winner of the first King's Cup Air Race, averaging 123 mph on the Croydon-Renfrew leg. (*author's collection*)

Ltd., and made numerous charter flights. After reconditioning at Northolt by the Central Aircraft Company, 'MU made history on 8-9 September 1922 by flying from Croydon to Renfrew and back, piloted by Capt. F. L. Barnard, at an average speed of 123 mph to win the first of the King's Cup Air Races.

DH.5

Continued use of the DH.2 and other pusher scouts by the Royal Flying Corps in 1916 was mainly due to the lack of a suitable interrupter gear to enable the guns to fire forward through the propeller arc. However, George Constantinesco perfected such a mechanism and Capt. Geoffrey de Havilland was at last able to produce the DH.5, which combined the enhanced performance of the tractor biplane with the pusher's ability to fire forward. He also sought to retain the pusher pilot's magnificent all round view by rigging the DH.5 with twenty-seven inches of backward stagger to bring the pilot's cockpit in front of the leading edge of the upper mainplane. The fuselage of the prototype, A5172, was a wire braced, wooden box girder, strengthened with plywood at the forward end. It had rounded top

decking and flat sides carrying short fairings behind the familiar circular cowling of the 110 hp Le Rhone rotary. The main fuel tank was behind the pilot's seat with the oil tank on top of it, but there was also an auxiliary gravity tank fitted on top of the starboard mainplane. Mainplanes were of the usual two spar type, with spindled spars and a horn balanced rudder was of typical de Havilland outline. Flight trials showed the rudder to be ineffective during take off and a slightly larger one of similar shape was then fitted. Armament consisted of a single Vickers gun on top of the front fuselage, conveniently placed where the pilot could clear any stoppages.

550 DH.5s were built, 200 by the Aircraft Manufacturing Co. Ltd. and the remainder by three

The flat-sided prototype DH.5 with a small horn-balanced rudder. (*author's collection*)

main sub-contractors, but only 483 went into service with the RFC. A single aircraft, B7775, was built by 1 (Southern) Aeroplane Repair Depot. Production aircraft differed from the prototype by virtue of their unbalanced rudders, and their fuselages were faired to a circular section behind the engine and tapered to an octagonal section towards the tail. One was experimentally fitted with a 110 hp Clerget rotary and another, A9186, was fitted with a Vickers gun firing forwards and upwards at a 45 degree angle. Service trials were conducted in France at the end of 1916 and 24 and 32 Squadrons, which had taken the first DH.2s to France two years earlier, were issued with the first production versions in May 1917. Several other squadrons were also re-equipped.

The DH.5 was immensely strong, fully acrobatic aircraft to fly but a number of training accidents led to a widespread and unfounded belief that its unorthodox layout imparted a high stalling speed and made recovery from a spin difficult. In squadron service, flown by experienced pilots, it

proved quite docile but at heights above 10,000 ft. was easily outflown by contemporary fighters such as the Sopwith Pup. German combat reports claimed the shooting down of several DH.5s including some by Manfred von Richtofen on 23 November 1917 and the rest by other pilots a week later. The DH.5 was then relegated to ground attack duties and in the Battle of Ypres in August 1917, enemy trenches and machine gun posts received close attention from DH.5s of 41 Squadron. In November 1917 those of 64 and 68 Squadrons carried out low level formation attacks during the Battle of Cambrai, each aircraft carrying four 25 pound Cooper bombs. As in the case of the DH.4, many aircraft were provided by public subscription and received individual names.

A Darracq-built DH.5, A9403, was tested at Farnborough in September 1917 with plywood

A9456 was a Darraq-produced production DH.5. *(author's collection)*

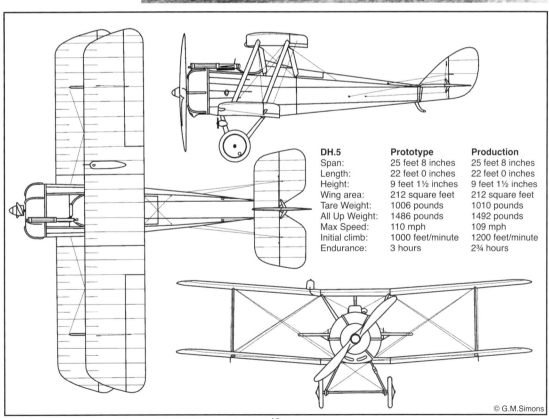

DH.5	Prototype	Production
Span:	25 feet 8 inches	25 feet 8 inches
Length:	22 feet 0 inches	22 feet 0 inches
Height:	9 feet 1½ inches	9 feet 1½ inches
Wing area:	212 square feet	212 square feet
Tare Weight:	1006 pounds	1010 pounds
All Up Weight:	1486 pounds	1492 pounds
Max Speed:	110 mph	109 mph
Initial climb:	1000 feet/minute	1200 feet/minute
Endurance:	3 hours	2¾ hours

© G.M.Simons

covered fuselage and Lott detachable petrol tank but the project was brought to an end by poor engine performance.

Manufacturers and serial blocks.
The Aircraft Manufacturing Co. Ltd., Hendon, London, N.W.9. Serials A5172, A9163-A9362.

The Darraq Motor Engineering Co. Ltd, Townmead Road, Fulham, London SW 6. Serials A9363-A9562.

British Caudron Co. Ltd, Broadway, Cricklewood, London N.W.2. Serials B331-B380

March, Johns and Cribb, Leeds. Serials B4901-B5000.

DH.6

The DH.6 was a primary trainer conceived in 1916 to meet the needs of the Royal Flying Corps, at that time expanding in readiness for the decisive battles of 1917-18. As the requirement was urgent, beauty of line and fine performance were sacrificed for ease and speed of manufacture and cheapness and simplicity of repair. All major assemblies were straight sided, upper and lower mainplanes were interchangeable and the wing tips were square cut. The airframe was of fabric covered, wire braced, wooden construction but the front fuselage was plywood covered for additional strength, the tail surfaces were of steel tubing with wooden ribs and the rubber-sprung axle of the undercarriage lay between two protecting steel spreader bars. Both occupants sat in a communal cockpit.

Power was provided by a 90 hp R.A.F. 1A eight cylinder Vee aircooled engine, bolted straight to the top longerons without any cowlings other than a scoop on the top to direct cooling air to the back cylinders, while vertical stacks led the exhaust fumes away over the top wing. On 90 horsepower the performance was not exactly sparkling but the DH.6 was viceless and would remain airborne at an air speed of 30 mph. It was a remarkable aeroplane, which the designer deliberately made unstable so that it would be an efficient elementary trainer.

The prototype DH.6s, A5175 and A5176, were fitted with the typical De Havilland

rudder and boasted an arched plywood decking to the rear fuselage, but production machines, built by Airco and seven sub-contractors, had flat sided decking and rectilinear rudders. At least 2,282 DH.6s were built, some 600 less than those actually ordered, and most saw widespread service with Training Squadrons during 1917 in the United Kingdom, the Near East and at Point Cook in Australia. It also became the communications aircraft of many Home Defence Squadrons, so that production soon outstripped that of the R.A.F. 1A engine, making it necessary to equip some production batches with the 80 hp Renault and the 90 hp Curtiss OX-5. The Curtiss OX-5 powered DH.6 was selected as an alternative in the event of difficulty being experienced with the Canadian JN-4 programme. Although this contingency did not arise, the single DH.6 completed in July 1917 by Canadian Aeroplanes Ltd. and successfully flown, was the first British designed aircraft built in Canada.

At the end of 1917 the Avro 504K became the RFC's standard trainer and over 300 DH.6s were transferred to the Royal Naval Air Service for anti-submarine

Above: The prototype DH.6 was powered by the RAF (Royal Aircraft Factory) 1A 90 hp upright Vee engine with over top-wing exhaust pipes. It used the DH-style of fin and rudder, although production machines adopted a sharp-pointed angular rudder

Left: Joy-riding operator Midland Aviation Services Ltd ran this DH.6. G-EARR (B3067), in Nottinghamshire during the summer of 1921. (*both author's collection*)

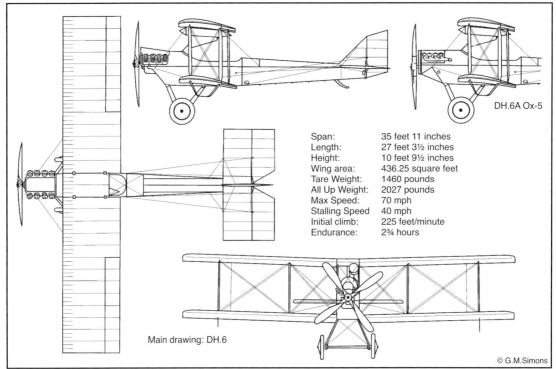

Span:	35 feet 11 inches
Length:	27 feet 3½ inches
Height:	10 feet 9½ inches
Wing area:	436.25 square feet
Tare Weight:	1460 pounds
All Up Weight:	2027 pounds
Max Speed:	70 mph
Stalling Speed	40 mph
Initial climb:	225 feet/minute
Endurance:	2¾ hours

DH.6A Ox-5

Main drawing: DH.6

duties around British coasts, and for operation by US Navy personnel on similar patrols off the North East coast of Ireland. Usually they were flown solo and carried up to 100 lb. of bombs under the wings but their only noteworthy attack was the unsuccessful bombing of U boat U.C.49 on 30 May 1918.

F3386 was modified by Airco and tested at the RAE Farnborough in July 1918 with ten inches of back stagger and a less cambered wing section, obtained by reducing mainplane chord from 6 feet 3 inches to 6 feet. Elevator chord was also reduced from 2 feet 6 inches to 1 foot 6 inches. In an otherwise identical set of modifications made to B2963 by the RAE, elevator chord shrank to 17 inches. Another experiment involved the re-rigging of B2840 with 13½ inches of back stagger. Ultimately the Airco modification was standardised and the aircraft was referred to as the DH.6A. Forced landings at sea were frequent and one R.A.F. engined machine was tested with flotation gear, but even without this the DH.6 had been known to remain afloat for ten hours.

At the end of 1918 the RAF had 1,050 DH.6s on charge, and in the following year most were declared obsolete and sold. Surplus aircraft auctioned at Hendon on 2 June 1919 realised prices that ranged from £60 to £100 depending to condition. A number were overhauled for pleasure flying in the UK during the ensuing fourteen years and others were privately owned. In Australia the Point Cook machines were also declared redundant and six of them, together with one built from spares, did valuable pioneer work.

In the USA Chamberlain Aircraft Inc. of New Jersey offered remodelled DH.6s with forward stagger, individual cockpits and an improved fuel system. At

least one is said to have been fitted with a 150 hp Benz engine, and as late as 1929 others were re-engined with 110 hp Clerget rotaries for 'barnstorming' purposes.

As a result of a sales tour made in 1919-20 by Maj. Hereward de Havilland in a Lion engined DH.9, a number of DH.6s were sold in Spain. One of these, M-AAAB, registered to Hispano-Britannica S.A. of Madrid in February 1920, is believed to have acted as 'prototype' for sixty built under licence at Guadalajara from 1921 onwards. These were used at the Air Force training establishment at Cuatros Vientos and also at Alcala de Henares. At least one belonged to a Royal Flight. Hispano-built DH.6s had centre section fuel tanks of aerofoil section, wings of reduced camber and the 140 hp Hispano-Suiza engine. A few were later sold for civil use, one being flown by the Aero Club of Barcelona in 1932 and three by Aero Popular S.A. of Madrid in 1933.

The civil DH.6, numbered K-100, was noteworthy as the first aeroplane in the UK to fly in civil markings. It also differed from other DH.6s in combining wings of reduced camber with normal unstaggered rigging, vertical tail surfaces of DH outline as fitted to the prototypes, separate cockpits and a curved cowling round the lower half of the engine.

To begin with the majority of civilian conversions were as two-seaters but eventually the Director of Research at the Air Ministry approved their conversion to three-seaters. This second fare-paying passenger brought the all-up weight to 2,380 lb and suddenly the aircraft became more profitable to operators and for a short time they were able to earn their keep with a rich return. The major operator was the Giro Aviation Co. Ltd., whose seven Renault and R.A.F. 1A engined

DH.6 with A2098 fitted with a R.A.F. 1A engine and floatation bags at the Isle of Grain on 14 June 1918. (*author's collection*)

machines made thousands of pleasure flights from Southport Sands in the period 1921-33. In the South the Martin Aviation Company's three DH.6s acquired from the Brompton Motor Co. Ltd. were fitted with 80 hp Renault engines and did similar business on the Isle of Wight during the 1921 and 1922 seasons.

This turned out to be a short-term pot of gold for the tiny hand-to-mouth existences of the new-era barnstormers. The slump of the 1920s put out of business many of the operators that had sprung up to make easy money from joy-riding. Numbers of aircraft were therefore abandoned and forgotten while others changed hands at unbelievably low prices. A considerable number belonged to small firms engaged on itinerant joyriding in the Midlands, Lancashire, the North Wales beaches and the Isle of Man. C. V. Maddocks and Charles Kingsford Smith, later to become the most famous of all Australian long distance pilots, acquired four DH.6s from RAF Henlow with the intention of shipping them to Australia. After the scheme fell through they formed one of the typical 'mushroom firms' of the period and gave pleasure flights near London, taking as much as £40 in an afternoon!

One was modified at Sherburn-in-Elmet in 1920 by the Blackburn Aeroplane and Motor Co. Ltd. and fitted with the Alula parasol wing designed by A. A. Holle of the Commercial Aeroplane Wing Syndicate Ltd. Powered by a 200 hp Bentley B.R.2 rotary, it was registered G-EAWG and first flown by Capt. Clinch on 2 January 1921. The wing was modified in April with dihedral instead of anhedral and also braced to a rigid structure below the wing. After flight tests by F. T. Courtney it was dismantled and despatched to St. Cyr for completion of the tests.

The success of the DH.6 on the domestic front was thus short-lived, being cut short by circumstances outside its control. While it looked nothing like the Moth of 1925, it demonstrated many of the characteristics that would distinguish that famous light aeroplane in the decade to come.

Fifty two appeared on the British register and possibly half as many again were converted for export.

Manufacturers and serial blocks.

The Aircraft Manufacturing Co. Ltd., Hendon, London, N.W.9. Serials A5175-A5176; B9563-B3100; B9031-B9130; D8581-D8780; F3346-F3445.

The Grahame-White Aviation Co. Ltd, Hendon, London, N.W.9. Serials A9563-A9762; C1951-C2150; C7601-C7900; D951-D1000.

Kingsbury Aviation Co.

Above: An Airco-built DH6A, B2840 with back-stagger, reduced rudder and elevator chord.(*John Stride collection*)

Right: One of the Spanish-built DH.6s with a rounded rudder, 140 hp Hispano-Suize water-cooled engine and Lamblin radiators between the undercarriage legs. (*author's collection*)

DH 6 variants			
Designation:	DH6 - 3 seater	DH6 - 2 seater	DH6 - 3 seater
Engine	R.A.F. 1A	Curtiss OX-5	Renault
H.P.	90	90	80
Span:	35 feet 11 inches	35 feet 11 inches	35 feet 11 inches
Length:	27 feet 3½ inches	27 feet 3½ inches	27 feet 3½ inches
Height:	10 feet 9½ inches	10 feet 9½ inches	10 feet 9½ inches
Wing area:	436.5 square feet	436.5 square feet	436.5 square feet
Tare Weight	1670 pounds	1539 pounds	1360 pounds
All Up Weight:	2380 pounds	1926 pounds	1900 pounds
Max Speed:	-	75 mph	-
Stalling speed:	45 mph	40 mph	40 mph
Endurance:	2¾ hours	2¾ hours	3½ hours.

G-EAWG, the DH.6 fitted with the Alula high lift wing and a 200 hp Bentley rotary by the Blackburn Aeroplane and Motor Co. in 1920. (*author's .collection*)

Ltd, Kingsbury, Middlesex. Serials C5126-C5275.

Harland and Wolff Ltd, Belfast. Serials C5451-C5750.

Morgan and Co., Leighton Buzzard, Bedfordshire. Serials C6501-C6700.

Savages Ltd, Stroud, Gloucs. Serials C6801-C6900.

Ransomes, Sims and Jefferies, Ipswich, Suffolk. Serials C7201-C7600.

The Gloucestershire Aircraft Co Ltd, Cheltenham. Serials C9336-C9485.

DH.7

This was a partially completed design for a single-seat tractor fighter powered by a Rolls-Royce Falcon engine. The design was abandoned due to the non-availability of engines.

DH.8

This was a projected pusher aircraft mounting a heavy calibre Coventry Ordnance Works 1.5 pounder gun. The design was not completed because engines were not available and also through development problems with the gun and mounting.

DH.9

Like the DH.4, the DH.9 had a number of variants and it is easy to become confused in attempting to understand the different models of this design. While the DH.9, 9C and 9J were variants, they bore a close relationship one to another. The DH.9A, however, was a very different machine and is subject to a seperate entry.

By the middle of 1917 it was clear there was a need for a bomber capable of carrying heavier loads over greater distances than the DH.4. Structurally similar to its predecessor, the DH.9 used identical mainplanes and tail surfaces but the pilot no longer sat between the engine and fuel tanks, but next to the gunner. The nose was better streamlined and the engine installation resembled the Fiat engined DH.4, but with a radiator retracting into the underside of the front fuselage as a means of temperature control. The prototype was DH.4 A7559, converted by the Aircraft Manufacturing Co. Ltd. and fitted with a 230 hp Galloway-built B.H.P. 'Adriatic' engine. Flight trials commenced at Hendon in July 1917 and contracts already awarded to sub-contractors were amended so that DH.9s rolled from the production lines instead of DH.4s.

Production machines were fitted initially with the Siddeley-built B.H.P. engine but the majority had the Siddeley Puma, a lightweight version of the B.H.P. modified for mass production by the Siddeley-Deasy Car Company. Teething troubles meant that the 300 hp Puma was derated to 230 hp, with the result that the

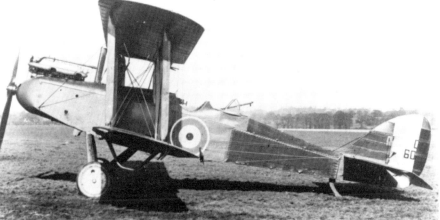

Left: DH.9 D6051.

Below: De Havilland Aircraft set up its 'Aeroplane Hire Service' at Stag Lane in 1919 with a number of aircraft modified for passenger-carrying. Closest to the camera is G-EAAC (formerly K-109), a DH.9B with a flat rear deck. Second in the line, G-EBAC, is a DH.9C with a faired deck. *(both author's collection)*

DH.9 was underpowered, with inferior performance to the aircraft it was replacing! With a full military load of 70 gallons of fuel, 4.5 gallons of oil, 6.5 gallons of water, one pilot's forward firing Vickers gun operated by Constantinesco interrupter gear, an observer's Lewis gun, two 230 lb. or four 112 lb. bombs, it was unable to climb above 13,000 feet.

Deliveries started with a batch of five at the end of 1917 and the type was in service with squadrons in France by April 1918. Engine troubles put an additional burden on crews, and 99 and 104 Squadrons alone suffered 123 engine failures out of 848 sorties flown before the Armistice. So the DH.4 was retained in service and the DH.9 supplemented rather than superseded it. In less hotly contested areas, the DH.9 enjoyed greater success, notably in September 1918 against the Turks in Palestine. Long range reconnaissance flights of over 300 miles were made against the Bulgars from bases in Macedonia, and ranges of over 400 miles were achieved by DH.9s locally modified in the Aegean Islands to carry overload fuel tanks for the bombing of Constantinople.

In the UK DH.9s joined DH.4s on coastal defence and anti-Zeppelin work, and at the end of the war replaced some of DH.6s on antisubmarine patrols. Thereafter the DH.9 was relegated to non-combatant roles and on 17 December 1918 99 Squadron, operating with DH.4s of 55 and 57 Squadrons, started the first cross-Channel air mail service. Twenty five bags of mail for the Army of Occupation on the Rhine were flown to Valenciennes in bad weather, en route to Cologne. By July 1919 no DH.9s remained on RAF charge, the last examples in service being the ambulance versions operating with 'Z Force' in Somaliland which carried one stretcher case in a coffin-like enclosure on top of the rear fuselage and had the upper trailing edge cut-out filled in.

Although the DH.9 failed in its intended role and faded from the RAF after suffering replacement by the DH.9A, its career was not over. Many modifications were made and, after the experimental installation of 250 hp Fiat A-12, a batch of one hundred was ordered from Short Brothers. As the engine resembled the Puma externally the main distinguishing feature was the exhaust manifold, fitted to the starboard side on Fiats and to the port side on Pumas, but in addition the radiator was fixed and equipped with vertical shutters because of the greater length of the Fiat installation. Some were later converted to Pumas for deck landing trials on HMS *Eagle* in 1921, and were fitted with DH.4 type front radiators instead of the underslung type, to minimise damage if forced to ditch.

In February 1918 one of the prototype Napier Lion engines was experimentally fitted at Farnborough to DH.9 C6078 and first flown on 16 March. The same machine was later fitted with a developed Lion engine and flown to Martlesham on 20 October, where on 2 January 1919 Capt. Andrew Lang flew it to 30,500 feet and established a new world altitude record. Throughout 1919 the RAE experimented with an RHA supercharger fitted to E630 and with alternative radiator positions on D2825.

The success of the Liberty engined DH.4 prompted the American Expeditionary Force to install the improved 435 hp Liberty 12A engine in the DH.9.

After the war surplus DH.9s took on a new lease of life in the service of other nations. Eighteen were supplied to Belgium, twelve to Poland, forty-eight

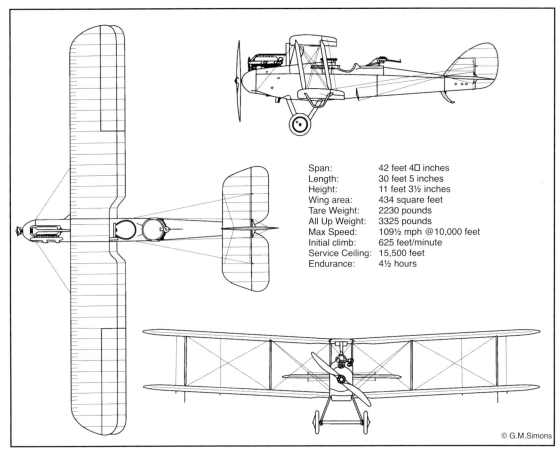

Span:	42 feet 4□ inches
Length:	30 feet 5 inches
Height:	11 feet 3½ inches
Wing area:	434 square feet
Tare Weight:	2230 pounds
All Up Weight:	3325 pounds
Max Speed:	109½ mph @10,000 feet
Initial climb:	625 feet/minute
Service Ceiling:	15,500 feet
Endurance:	4½ hours

© G.M.Simons

to South Africa as part of the Imperial Gift, nine to New Zealand, twenty-eight to Australia and others to Canada, India, Afghanistan, Greece, the Irish Free State, Holland and Latvia. One of the twenty Puma engined DH.9s supplied to Chile was flown by the Director of Civil Aviation, Capt. Aracena, 1,850 miles from Santiago to Rio de Janeiro in the autumn of 1922 and in the same year DH.9s of the Estonian Air Squadron, made the long flight from Tallinn to Riga.

The South African Air Force (SAAF) machines served for many years, and at least one, 159, was fitted with a 200 hp Wolseley Viper and unofficially named the DH. Mantis. Six saw service during the Boudeizvartz rebellion in 1922. Others were used in 1925 on an experimental air mail service between Cape Town and Durban, 450 pounds of mail being carried on each trip. The next year comparative trials took place at Roberts Heights between DH.9s fitted with the A.D.C. Nimbus, Armstrong Siddeley Jaguar and Bristol Jupiter engines. Final choice fell on the Jupiter and a number of SAAF DH.9s, rebuilt as the DH.9J M'pala I general purpose type with Jupiter VI or as the M'pala II for communications with Jupiter VIII and divided axle wide track oleo undercarriage, survived until 1937. The designation DH.9J was also used for the Jaguar engined conversions made at Stag ane.

A Puma DH.9 made a contribution to aerodynamic research when, in 1920, Frederick Handley Page equipped a standard aircraft, H9140, with his newly invented leading edge slots. These were full span, auxiliary aerofoils permanently fixed along both mainplanes to give maximum lift, thereby increasing the wing area by 34 square feet. Later a taller undercarriage was fitted and in September 1920 comparative trials took place at Farnborough against a standard DH.9, D5755. These showed a reduction in stalling speed from 51 to 44.5 m.p.h. and at a demonstration at Cricklewood on 21 October 1921 Maj. E. L. Foot took advantage of the ground angle created by the tall undercarriage and took off in a three point attitude and went straight into a incredible angle of climb. This aircraft carried the designation HP. 17 and its performance led to an order for the HP. 19 Hanley, similarly equipped.

Following Maj. Hereward de Havilland's tour of Spain in a Lion engined DH.9 in 1919, a number of surplus DH.9 airframes were sold to the Spanish Government. These were erected by the Hispano-Suiza company and fitted with 300 hp Hispano-Suiza 8Fb engines. From 1925 Hispano built the type under licence and a total production run in excess of 500 is often quoted. They were used in the African squadrons for reconnaissance and also at the Advanced Training School at Guadalajara. At the outbreak of the Civil War 25 were still in service

Right: D5748, a DH.9 fitted with a 250 hp FIAT A-12 engine, complete with exhaust on the starboard side.

Below: C6078, a DH.9 used as an airborne testbed for the Napier Lion engine with heated carburettor. *(both author's collection)*

Croydon by the Aircraft Disposal Co. Ltd. continued until 1924, but so great was their original stock that large numbers of unsold machines remained dismantled and neglected until burned in 1931.

Manufacturers and Serial Blocks
The Aircraft Manufacturing Co, Hendon, London N.W.9. Serials: C6051-C6350;   D2876-D3275; E5435-E5436;   E8857-E9056; H4216-H4315; H9113-H9412.

in Spain, of which 21 went over to the communists, and at least one, 34-18, was still active in 1940.

DH.9s equipping the Netherlands Army Air Service were unique, not only because they included ten built at Stag Lane in 1922 from unused components, but because these and others assembled in Holland by the Army Aircraft Factory were rejuvenated as late as 1934 with Wright Whirlwind radial engines. Dutch aircraft with Puma engines were mainly employed in the Netherlands East Indies, and had DH.50-type nose radiators. Both Puma and Whirlwind versions were fitted with enlarged horn balanced ailerons and elevators, and some, equipped as ambulances, closely resembled those used in Somaliland in 1919.

Demand for surplus DH.9s reconditioned at

The Alliance Aeroplane Co, Cambridge Road, Hammersmith, London W.6. Serials: H5541-H5890.

F. W. Berwick & Co., Park Royal, London N.W.10. Serials: C2151-C2230; D7301-D7400.

Cubitt Ltd, Croydon, Surrey. Serials: D451-D950.

Mann, Egerton & Co. Ltd, Aylesham Road, Norwich, Norfolk. Serials: D1651-D1750.

National Aircraft Factory No.1, Waddon, Surrey. Serials: F1-F300.

National Aircraft Factory No.2, Heaton Chapel, Stockport, Lancs. Serials: D1001-D1500.

Short Brothers, Rochester, Kent. Serials: D2776-D2875.

The Vulcan Engineering & Motor Co, Crossens, Southport, Lancs. Serials: B9331-B9430.

The former DH.9 H9140, now the Handley Page 17 slotted biplane, as seen at Cricklewood during the demonstrations held there on 21 October 1921. As part of these demonstrations it was flown against the unmodified DH9 G-EAUN seen in the background. *(author's collection)*

Right: A refurbished DH.9 has its rigging checked before dispatch from the Aircraft Disposal Company at Croydon.

Below: D1651, the first DH.9 built by Mann, Egerton & Co of Norwich. *(both author's collection)*

Thick mist was encountered and an hour later the machine was wrecked on Portsdown Hill, north of Portsmouth.

Some of the Amsterdam services were flown under contract to KLM, which at that time had no aircraft of its own, but when A.T. & T. closed down, four of its DH.9s were taken over by KLM to fly in competition with ten machines flown over the same route by Handley Page Transport Ltd. At least five DH.9s also operated between Croydon or Cricklewood and Brussels in 1920-21, often flying in groups of two or three on the services of the Belgian air line SNETA. Another of the former A.T. & T. DH.9s, G-EAQP, went to Newfoundland in 1922 to join the Aerial Survey Company, founded by F. Sydney Cotton for seal and fishery spotting and for taxi work during the gold rush at Stag Bay, Labrador.

Waring & Gillow Ltd, Cambridge Road, Hammersmith, London W.6. Serials: D5551-D5850; F1101-F1300.

G & W Weir Ltd, Cathcart, Glasgow. Serials: C1151-C1450; D9800-D9899; H7913-H8112.

Westland Aircraft Works, Yeovil, Somerset. Serials: B7581-B7680; D7201-D7300; F1767-F1866.

Whitehead Aircraft Co. Ltd, Townsend Road, Richmond, Surrey. Serials: E601-E700.

Aircraft were also built by SABCA, Haren Airport Brussels, Belgium and by Hispano-Suiza S.A, Guadalajara, Spain.

Civil DH.9s, DH.9B and DH.9C

Demilitarised DH.9s were used extensively by air transport concerns immediately after the First World War and to exploit the full load carrying capacity, modifications were designed by the Aircraft Manufacturing Co. Ltd., the de Havilland Aircraft Co. Ltd. and later by the Aircraft Disposal Co. Ltd.

Pioneer air services between London, Paris and Amsterdam operated by Aircraft Transport and Travel Ltd. (A.T. & T) in 1919-20 employed sixteen DH.9s, eight of which were erected by the fledgling De Havilland Aircraft Co. Ltd. at Stag Lane Aerodrome and the remainder surplus Government stock stripped of military equipment. Some were fitted with the B.H.P. engine and others with the Siddeley Puma. One of them, C6054, was the first aircraft to make a flight for other than military or experimental purposes in this country, and for this it was allotted, but did not carry, the first permanent British registration marking G-EAAA. Its commercial life was confined to the early hours of the morning of 1 May 1919 because bad weather delayed its departure from Hendon from midnight until it took off piloted by Capt. Howard J. Saint at 4.30 a.m. with newspapers for Bournemouth.

The earliest civil conversions just entailed the removal of military equipment, but by the end of 1919 nearly all DH.9s flying on Continental services were equipped to carry a second passenger in front of the pilot and designated DH.9B. In 1921 the de Havilland company further increased the load carrying capacity by a rearward extension of the back cockpit to accommodate light freight or a third passenger. The designation DH.9C was coined to cover this version and at least twelve were erected at Stag Lane in 1922-23, the first two leaving for Croydon on 23 September 1921 piloted by Alan. J. Cobham, F. J. Ortweiler and C. D. Barnard on delivery to the Cia Espanola del Trafico Aero for a subsidised air mail service started in January 1922 between Seville and Larache in Spanish Morocco. Three British pilots, F. W. Hatchett, Sidney St. Barbe and Charles F. Wolley Dod were employed, and the 9Cs gave quite extraordinary service for nearly seven years. Hatchett remained with the company and in 1929 was still flying over the original route in 9C M-AAGA which he had personally maintained through the years and considerably modified to suit changing conditions. All the pilot's controls and instrumentation were redesigned and moved into the rear cockpit and the front fuselage was widened to accommodate two passengers and mail and covered with a low cabin roof of local manufacture.

DH9C G-EBIG, in the scarlet and white colours of Northern Air Lines (Manchester) Ltd, then operating from Alexandra Park in Manchester. It is 22 April 1929 and a delegation from Manchester is on its way to London to collect the temporary licence for Wythenshawe Aerodrome. Flying to Croydon is Town Clerk F E Warbeck Howell (left), Alderman R A W Carter (with hat). The pilot, Edward Arnold Jones is being briefed by company chief pilot Archibald Norman Kingwill. The amount of room between the passengers hat and the roof is significant! *(author's collection)*

To improve passenger comfort, the de Havilland Aircraft Co. Ltd. modified the rear cockpit into a cabin for two passengers face to face. A light wood and fabric roof hinged about the port upper longeron for ease of entry and although at first the windows remained unglazed, hinged wind deflectors were fitted at the front end to make conversation possible. At this stage it was felt advisable to compensate for the aft movement of the centre of gravity and the wings were given eight inches of sweep back measured at the outer interplane strut. It was still known as the DH.9C, the first completed being the drab khaki G-EAFT in which Alan Cobham made several long distance charter flights to North Africa and the Near East. Its short life ended in the sea when fog overtook it while landing at Venice Lido in October 1922. For the carriage of light freight or for the convenience of cameramen, the cabin top was often removed and many of the Hire Service DH.9Cs flew permanently in this condition. Some 150,000 miles were flown in 1922-23, in the course of which the earliest recorded crop spraying sortie was made in Kent in June 1922. When pensioned off in 1924, DH.9C G-EAYU was sold with several military DH.9s to the Hedjaz Government but the ground crew fused some bombs incorrectly and 'YU and its Russian pilot were blown to pieces before reaching the rebel tribesmen.

Eight Stage Lane based DH.9Cs formed the fleet of the De Havilland Aeroplane Hire Service in 1922. They flew to all parts of Europe and the UK at a charge of £8 per hour, mostly on hire to film and newspaper companies wishing to cover distant events in time for their next editions. G-EBGU was fitted with an illuminated sign advertising the *Star* newspaper which Hubert Broad flew over London at night on 12 February 1924.

Two DH.9Cs, G-AUED and 'EF, supplied to QANTAS for the Charleville-Cloncurry route, opened on 3 November 1922, became the first successful cabin aircraft to operate scheduled services in Australia. They were joined by G-AUEU, converted by H. C. Miller, and by G-AUFM 'Ion' - wholly built at Longreach with a fuselage of QANTAS design which had DH.9C dimensions but DH.50 layout, with the pilot in an open cockpit behind a covered compartment for three passengers. It had the Puma from crashed DH.9C G-AUEF, DH.50 mainplanes, and also extended axles for dual wheel operation from boggy aerodromes. It first flew on 5 February 1927 but after a landing accident at Camooweal on 13 January 1928 was flown to Longreach and dismantled. The wings, engine and propeller were used in the construction of DH.50 G-AUJS in 1929.

DH.9C M-AAGA of Cia. Española del Trafico Aero following the widening of the fuselage and the installation of a glazed passenger cabin. by F. W. Hatchett. *(author's collection)*

Left: DH.9C G-EAYT, which Alan Cobham flew on many long-distance charters for the DH Hire Service during 1922.

Below: O-BELG fitted with a cabin top and underwing luggage containers by SNETA. *(both author's collection)*

A much more elaborate cabin conversion was made in Brussels by the Belgian concern SNETA, which equipped two of their DH.9s with the cabin tops and Triplex sliding windows removed from their defunct DH.4As. Additional luggage space was provided under the fuselage and also in special containers under the lower mainplane just outboard of the undercarriage. These aircraft were acquired by F/Os Nevill Vintcent and J. S. Newall in 1927 and flown to Stag Lane for modernisation, which included the fitting of nose radiators and centre section fuel tanks of the type then in production for DH.50s, an undercarriage incorporating the new D.H. system of rubber-in-compression, and Dunlop car tyres to reduce puncture risk. Leaving Stag Lane on 9 January 1928 they made a flight to India, arriving at Karachi on 26 April to start a tour of the sub-continent during which 5,000 passengers were given flights and the foundations of Indian air transport were laid.

The Aircraft Disposal Co. Ltd. at Croydon was responsible for the civil conversion of a considerable number of DH.9s, working independently of the manufacturers. One of the most famous was F1287/G-EAQM, in which Raymond J. P. Parer left Hounslow on 8 January 1920 with John C. McIntosh as co-pilot and succeeded in reaching Darwin in an extremely patched up condition on 2 August to complete the first flight ever made by a single engined aircraft between England and Australia. The

first flight from England to Cape Town, begun by a Vickers Vimy, was completed by Pierre van Ryneveld and Quintin Brand in DH.9 H5648 named *Voortrekker*. Discarded Imperial Gift DH.9s served in the Dominions for many years on scheduled services such as those run by the South African Air Force and QANTAS in Australia. New Zealand, having no Air Force, lent three each of its nine DH.9s free of charge to the N.Z. Flying School, Auckland (F1252, H5546, H5641); the Canterbury Aviation Co., Christchurch; and the N.Z. Aero Transport Co., Timaru. On 4 April 1922 Canterbury's DH.9 D3136/G-NZAH completed the first flight ever made between Gisborne and Auckland and the New Zealand Aero Transport DH.9 D31391G-NZAM later became the first aircraft to make the direct flight from Invercargill to Auckland.

The Disposals Company favoured neither the double rear cockpit nor the cabin top and their conversions were fitted mainly with four individual cockpits one behind the other. Entry to the rearmost

G-AUFM 'Ion' was built by QANTAS at Longreach in 1926/27 using DH.50 mainplanes. The pilot sat in an open cockpit behind the enclosed passenger cabin. *(author's collection)*

QANTAS at Longreach; G-AUEU by H. C. Miller at Albert Park Aerodrome, Adelaide, S.A.; H4890/G-EBDG by the Manchester Aviation Co. Ltd. at Alexandra Park and H5886J G-EBIG by Berkshire Aviation Tours Ltd. at Monkmoor Aerodrome, Shrewsbury. Both the latter served with Northern Air Lines on the abortive Stranraer-Belfast service in 1925 and afterwards as joyriding machines at Barton until 1930.

pair was simplified by hinging the decking along the port side, a device incorporated in most of the aircraft overhauled at Croydon during more than ten years. Over 60 four seat DH.9s of this type were supplied to Rumania by May 1922 and four to the Danish firm Det Danske Luftfartselskab A/S, whose first service with land aircraft was opened on 15 September 1920 when DH.9 T-DOGH flew from Copenhagen to Hamburg.

In 1924 a pair of two seat Puma Nines were shipped to the British and Egyptian Tea Co. Ltd., one of which was test flown at Rochester with Short wooden main and tail floats. Floats of this type were fitted to DH.9s used by the Air Survey Co. Ltd. during the Irrawaddy, Sarawak and Indian surveys in 1924-25, and for a number supplied to Bolivia. The first of these, AM-1, was erected and test flown by J. R. 'Joe' King at Riberalta on the Rio Beni in 1925.

After 1924 the A.D.C. company no longer fitted a cockpit ahead of the pilot and later conversions such as G-EBJW and 'JX, supplied to Northern Air Lines for a short lived Stranraer to Belfast service, were three seaters fitted with the 300 h.p. A.D.C. Nimbus, Major Frank Halford's re-design of the 230 h.p. Siddeley Puma. So, after ten years and two modifications, the designed power of the original B.H.P. engine was at last achieved. The Nimbus was also fitted to two special DH.9s G-EBPE and 'PF erected at Stag Lane in 1926 for an aerial survey of Northern Rhodesia by the Aircraft Operating Co. Ltd. They were equipped as two seaters with a camera position under the tail and twin metal floats 21 feet 9 inches long of the type built by Short Bros. for Sir Alan Cobham's DH.50J.

Conversions to full swept wing DH.9C standard by outside firms was confined to G-AUFM by

On 1 April 1923 the De Havilland company was awarded a contract for training RAF Reservists using Hire Service DH.9Cs. By the end of 1924 these had been replaced by seven Puma engined DH.9s equipped as two seat advanced trainers using six newly erected machines and the company's oldest aircraft, G-EAAC, specially preserved as a practical investigation into the longevity of aeroplanes under normal flying conditions. Two similar machines were also erected for the Beardmore School at Renfrew and another, G-EBHV, supplied to the Armstrong Whitworth Reserve School at Whitley.

In common with most open cockpit types the DH.9 occasionally appeared as a single seat racer as in the 1922 King's Cup Race when G-EAAC, G-EBEN and 'EP came third, fourth and tenth respectively. In the following year De Havilland Hire Service machine G-EBEZ was fitted temporarily with a 450 h.p. Napier Lion with which it came second at 144.7 m.p.h. piloted by Alan Cobham, and in 1927 W. G. R. Hinchliffe reached fourth place at 123.6 m.p.h. in a special single seater G-EBKO with A.D.C. Nimbus engine. The most spectacular result was achieved by the standard two seater VH-UHT in which H. C. Miller won the £1,000 first prize in the handicap section of the 2,200 mile Western Australia Centenary Air Race from Sydney to Perth in September 1929.

In 1934, when the type was nearly at the end of its career, Aerial Sites Ltd. of Hanworth employed G-AACP for banner towing and Sir Alan Cobham used 'CR for early flight refuelling experiments at Ford, Sussex. For this purpose the hinged decking to the rear cockpits was entirely removed to provide maximum working space.

DH.9A

Towards the end of 1917 demand for Rolls-Royce Eagle VIII engines vastly exceeded supply, so orders were placed in the USA for the 400 h.p. Liberty 12. These were earmarked for a new day bomber based on the DH.9, but by now the Aircraft Manufacturing Co. Ltd. were building the DH.10, so the extensive re-design of the earlier type was entrusted to the Westland Aircraft Works at Yeovil, Somerset.

Assisted by Mr. John Johnson on loan from Airco, the Westland design team, already experienced in building the DH. 4 and DH.9, took advantage of the extra power of the Liberty and combined the best of both designs to create an outstanding strategic bomber. The fuselage was strengthened to take the heavier engine by replacing the plywood partitions of the DH.9 with wire cross bracing, while improved climb and ceiling was guaranteed by fitting increased span and chord mainplanes.

The new machine was designated DH.9A, the prototype being a modified Westland built DH.9, B7664, fitted with a Rolls-Royce Eagle VIII to enable flight trials to proceed while awaiting delivery of the Liberties. Representatives of the Packard Motor Company, manufacturers of the Liberty, came to England to supervise its installation in production DH.9As, the first of which was C6122 and by December 1918 885 had been built by Westland and

other contractors. Armament was one forward firing Vickers gun on the port side of the front fuselage, single or double Lewis guns on a Scarff ring on the rear cockpit and up to 660 pounds of bombs carried on racks under the fuselage and lower mainplanes.

Many DH.9As were flight tested at Yeovil by Harry Hawker. The first squadron - 110 - arrived in France on 31 August 1918, flying aircraft presented by the Nizam of Hyderabad dropped some 10½ tons of bombs in daylight raids on Coblenz, Frankfurt, Mannheim and other German industrial centres.

As with the DH.9, two Airco-built DH.9As were sent to America, where it was planned to build 4,000. The Armistice terminated this project but four prototypes were built in August 1918, two by the Engineering Division of the Army's Bureau of Aircraft Production and two by Dayton-Wright, both designated USD-9. In October 1918 Dayton-Wright delivered four examples of a modified version known as the USD-9A which had the pilot's Browning gun on the starboard side and was fitted with a more rounded rudder. In the following month five more USD-9As were produced by the Engineering Division, which in February 1919 converted one of them to USD-9B with 435 h.p. Liberty 12A and wings of increased area. Another of these, serial A.S.40118, was a single seater fitted with a pilot's compartment of riveted steel plates and is believed to be the first machine ever to fly with a pressurised cockpit. The conversion was made at McCook Field, Dayton, Ohio in 1920 by the

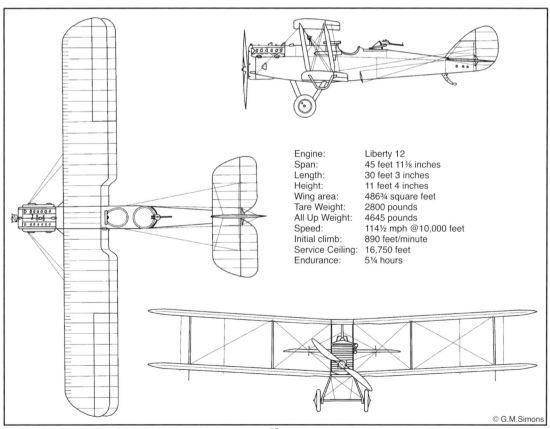

Engine:	Liberty 12
Span:	45 feet 11⅜ inches
Length:	30 feet 3 inches
Height:	11 feet 4 inches
Wing area:	486¾ square feet
Tare Weight:	2800 pounds
All Up Weight:	4645 pounds
Speed:	114½ mph @10,000 feet
Initial climb:	890 feet/minute
Service Ceiling:	16,750 feet
Endurance:	5¼ hours

© G.M.Simons

DH9A J.7067 in flight. *(author's collection)*

Engineering Division and was first flown by 'Art' Smith, a civilian test pilot, on 8 June 1921. Pressurisation was by a propeller driven pump on the port lower mainplane and the instrument panel was positioned on the trailing edge on the top centre section. The career of the USD-9A ended in 1922 when two examples appeared as the Ordnance IL-1 infantry liaison type at an all-up weight of 5,686 Ib. It was of grotesque appearance having triple instead of double interplane and undercarriage struts.

After the war the DH.9A continued in production in the UK and several hundred were built for Regular and Auxiliary day bomber squadrons at home, and for Flying Training Schools and squadrons stationed in the Near and Middle Easts. From June 21, 1921, DH.9As of 30 and 47 Squadrons were used on the Cairo-Baghdad mail service. Long term contracts were placed with Westland and de Havilland under Specification 45/22 for reconditioning DH.9As, and the type remained standard equipment, until struck off charge in 1931. It formed the initial equipment of the newly

formed Auxiliary Squadrons and under the nickname 'Ninak' became familiar to the populace for its inspiring displays at Hendon Pageants.

In Iraq and on the North West Frontier the tropicalised DH.9A became a general purpose aircraft equipped with an additional radiator under the nose and an overload fuel tank under the starboard upper mainplane. It was used mainly on policing duties and when working over difficult terrain, far from regular lines of communication, often carried spare wheels, goatskins of water, or tents and bedding on the sides of the fuselage or between the undercarriage struts.

Some DH.9As were converted for target towing or as dual trainers. Australia and Canada received the type in 1920 as part of the Imperial Gift, but most of

Above: J7307, with extra radiator, Handley Page slots, spare wheel and other assorted equipment, seen over Iraq in 1927.

Left: C6350, the second prototype, was a DH9 rebuild from the Aircraft Manufacturing Co. Ltd. *(both author's collection)*

61

The Aircraft Disposal Company's demonstrator machine G-EBCG - formerly F2868 - was powered by a 375 hp Rolls-Royce Eagle VIII. The cockpit access ladder is clearly seen. Registered in April 1922, it was cancelled in July 1924. (author's *collection*)

Left: One DH.9R single-seat racer was built. It had short span lower wings and powered by a 450 hp Napier Lion. G-EAHT (K-172) was registered on 23 July 1919 and flown by Capt Gerald Gathergood, winning a 137 mile closed circuit race in Amsterdam at average speed of 145 mph. It was scrapped in 1922. *(author's collection)*

the twenty-nine sent to Australia remained crated until commissioned by the Royal Australian Air Force under the type serial A1 in 1925. After modification by the Whitehead Aviation Company, all eleven Canadian DH.9As were handed over to the Air Board Civil Operations Branch for forestry patrol and survey work alongside the DH.4s.

In 1922 six were at Camp Borden and the remainder were on photographic survey work on wheels or skis at Rockcliffe, but most were destroyed in a hangar fire at Camp Borden on 16 October 1923. Development of the 450 hp Napier Lion, first flown in 1918 in a DH.9, led to a prototype, E775, and ten production installations, E746, E748-50, E752-57, being made in new Whitehead-built DH.9A airframes by the RAE at Farnborough. Although of broad arrow configuration, the Lion fitted snugly into close fitting cowlings and

was cooled by an underslung retractable radiator designed and constructed at the RAE, which also made the airscrew. After prototype trials with E775 in April 1919, the first production aircraft, E748, was completed with large mail boxes under the lower mainplane and first flown on 18 July. The boxes were fitted to several others but were subsequently removed and the rear cockpits enlarged for the internal stowage of mail bags. E775 was also tested in September 1919 with a Lion II giving 465 h.p. and during the following month six more aircraft were stripped of military equipment and delivered to AT&T at Hendon for use on the air mail service to the Army of Occupation on the Rhine. All six aircraft returned to the RAF between April and June 1920 and in the following year one of them, E752, made deck landing trials on HMS *Eagle* even though not fitted with arrester hooks. E746 made full load trials at

DH 9A variants			
Engine	R-R Eagle VIII	Napier Lion	Bristol Jupiter VI
H.P.	375	450	465
Span:	45 feet 11⅜ inches	45 feet 11⅜ inches	45 feet 11⅜ inches
Length:	30 feet 3 inches	30 feet 3 inches	30 feet 3 inches
Height:	11 feet 4 inches	11 feet 4 inches	11 feet 4 inches
Wing area:	491 square feet	491 square feet	491 square feet
Tare Weight	2705 pounds	2998 pounds	2740 pounds
All Up Weight:	4223 pounds	4814 pounds	4324 pounds
Speed @ 10,000 feet:	118 mph	123 mph	130 mph
Initial Climb:	850 feet/ minute	1100 feet/ minute	900 feet/ minute
Ceiling:	16,000 feet	19,000 feet	19,900 feet
Endurance:	3½ hours	-	-

Left: The Canadian Air Board DH9A G-CYAJ used by Flt Lt C. W. Cudemore on the first tran-Canada Air Mail service on 11 October 1920.

Below: The single-seat USD-9A fitted with a rudimentary pressure cabin under the P80 project number and serialled A.S.40118. *(both author's collection)*

Farnborough with the Lion II in 1920 and E748, with Lion II and 14 ft. 6 in. wide-track undercarriage, was delivered to Gosport on 10 August 1921. Another Lion II DH.9A, E775, fitted with experimental folding wings, first flew at Farnborough on 22 January 1924 and was delivered to Gosport for carrier trials on 29 March. The DH.9R sesquiplane racer erected from DH.9A components by the Aircraft Manufacturing Co. Ltd. was also Lion powered. Test pilot Gerald Gathergood made a fast trip from Hendon to Amsterdam in this machine in 2 hours 10 minutes to attend the ELTA Exhibition in July 1919 and while there won the 137 mile closed circuit race at an average speed of 145 m.p.h. During September comparative trials were made against the DH.4R, which proved to be marginally faster.

So vast were the stocks of DH.9A major assemblies and so limited the Air Ministry's financial resources that three contracts were awarded to the Westland Aircraft Works for aircraft using the maximum number of DH.9A components. The first, signed in 1920, was for thirty-six Westland Walrus fleet spotters, with Lion engines and unstaggered wings. In 1924 a small batch of somewhat similar Lion powered general purpose DH.9As was ordered and the third contract, awarded in 1926, was for the quantity production of the Westland Wapiti with Bristol Jupiter engine. The final DH.9A derivative, J7028, known as the DH.9AJ Stag, although designed for the Lion engine was also completed with a Bristol Jupiter and first flown at Stag Lane by Hubert Broad for 40 minutes on 15 June 1926.

In the experimental sphere, Westland built DH.9A numbered Fl632 was denuded of its mainplanes by Handley Page Ltd. in 1921 and fitted with a thick section cantilever monoplane wing bolted to a small cabane on top of the fuselage. Designated H.P.20, it completed the practical tests begun with a modified DH.9, H9140, on a full span, controllable slots, achieving a landing speed as low as 43 m.p.h. at a wing loading of 11 Ib./sq. ft. Another experimental aircraft was Liberty engined E870, which with Westland-built J6957 (Lion II), was used by the RAE for tests on steel airscrews in May 1924. E865 took part in similar tests on Fairey-Reed duralumin propellers in April 1925 and E8444 was used for immersion tests at Felixstowe.

In 1933 DH.9A H3588 was used at Farnborough for flight testing the aircooled Liberty 12 engine and in the same year E9895 was fitted at Brooklands with an experimental Vickers long stroke oleo undercarriage.

Due to its long RAF service the DH.9A figured less prominently on the secondhand market than did the DH.9. A few brand new aircraft were taken over from F. W. Berwick and Co.

E9895, a DH9A fitted with the experimental Vickers long-stroke undercarriage at Brooklands in 1933. *(author's collection)*

G-EAOG was one of the Lion-engined DH.9A mailplanes used by AT&T on the Cologne service during 1919-20. Surprisingly, it was returned to the RAF as E752 and made pioneer deck-landing trials aboard HMS *Eagle*. *(author's collection)*

J7787 was the first completely new DH9A built by De Havillands. It is seen here, ready for delivery at Stag Lane on 12 January 1926. *(author's collection)*

Ltd. by the Aircraft Disposal Co. Ltd., six of which were civilianised at Croydon for racing or overseas demonstration. The first, G-EAXC, converted in 1922, made fastest time in the race for the Coupe Lamblin over the course Le Bourget-Brussels-Croydon-Le Bourget piloted by Rex Stocken. A second conversion, G-EBCG, appeared in 1922 fitted with a 350 h.p. Rolls-Royce Eagle VIII for participation in the Croydon Whitsun Races. For the first King's Cup Race, which started at Croydon on 8 September 1922 the nose radiator was replaced with small side radiators. This Eagle conversion was made originally to the military demonstrator G-EBAN, which, fitted with Lamblin radiators between the undercarriage legs, left for Madrid in February 1922 to take part in Spanish Government trials which led to an order for a batch of similar machines for the Spanish Air Force.

Manufacturers and Serial Blocks.

The Aircraft Manufacturing Co. Ltd, Hendon, London, N.W.9. Serials: E8407-E8806; H1-H200; H4216-H4315; J5192-J5491; J7700.

F W Berwick & Co. Ltd, Park Royal, London N.W.10. Serials: F2733-F2882.

De Havilland Aircraft Co. Stag Lane, London.

Serials: J7787-J7798; J7877-J8482.

Gloster Aircraft Co. Cheltenham, Gloucs. Serials: J7249-J7258.

Handley Page Ltd, Cricklewood Aerodrome, London N.W.2. Serials: J6963-J6968.

H G Hawker Engineering Co. Ltd, Kingston Upon Thames and Brooklands Aerodrome, Surrey. Serials: J7835-J7854; J7867-J7876.

Mann, Egerton & Co.Ltd. Norwich, Norfolk. Serials: E9657-E9756; J551-J600.

George Parnell & Co. Ltd, Yate Aerodrome, Glocs. Serials: J8483-J8494.

Short Brothers Ltd, Rochester, Kent. Serials: J7823-J7834; J7884-7876.

The Vulcan Motor & Engineering Co. Ltd, Southport, Lancs. Serials: E9857-E9956; H3546-H3795.

Westland Aircraft Works, Yeovil, Somerset. Serials: F951-F1100;F1603-F1652; H3396-H3545; J401-J450; J6957-J6962; J7799-J7819; J7855-J7866; J8560-J8482.

Whitehead Aircraft Co. Ltd, TRichmond, Surrey. Serials: E701-E1100

The Dayton-Wright Airplane Co. Dayton, Ohio.

The Engineering Division of the US Army Air Service, McCook Field, Ohio.

DH.9J

The De Havilland School of Flying began training RAF reservists at Stag Lane on 1 April 1923 using Avro 548s and the DH.9s from their Hire Service. They were replaced in 1926 by Cirrus Moths, the DH.9s were modernised for advanced instruction and known as the DH.9J. This work entailed a shortened and strengthened front fuselage to carry the heavier 385

h.p. Armstrong Siddeley Jaguar III fourteen cylinder, two row, radial engine, behind which metal inspection doors gave access to the ancillary equipment. The old rigid V strut undercarriage, sprung with rubber bungees, was replaced with De Havilland rubber-in-compression units. Aileron circuits were also modified to incorporate the patent D.H. differential gear and Handley Page slots were fitted. The fuel system was changed to include a gravity tank in the centre section.

The pupil normally occupied the front cockpit, with

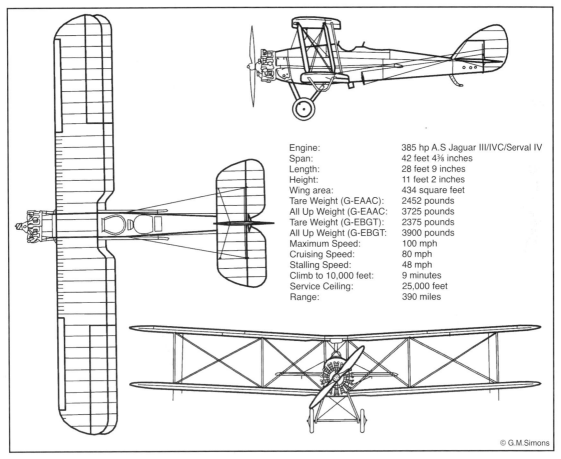

Engine:	385 hp A.S Jaguar III/IVC/Serval IV
Span:	42 feet 4⅜ inches
Length:	28 feet 9 inches
Height:	11 feet 2 inches
Wing area:	434 square feet
Tare Weight (G-EAAC):	2452 pounds
All Up Weight (G-EAAC:	3725 pounds
Tare Weight (G-EBGT):	2375 pounds
All Up Weight (G-EBGT:	3900 pounds
Maximum Speed:	100 mph
Cruising Speed:	80 mph
Stalling Speed:	48 mph
Climb to 10,000 feet:	9 minutes
Service Ceiling:	25,000 feet
Range:	390 miles

© G.M.Simons

the instructor in the rear, making it necessary to carry an equivalent weight of ballast when flying solo. It was found that the average pupil with only 10 hours on Cirrus Moths needed but 20 minutes dual before going solo in the larger and heavier DH.9J.

As the powerful Jaguar engine imparted a somewhat lively performance to the traditionally sedate DH. 9, it was necessary to fit a throttle stop to prevent the use of full power.

The Armstrong Whitworth Reserve School at Whitley also re-equipped with DH.9Js, two being erected at Stag Lane in 1926 and a further three in 1929, one of which G-AARS, was used as a testbed for the Armstrong Siddeley Serval IV nine

cylinder radial engine. Two other replacement aircraft were built at Stag Lane for the De Havilland School of Flying Ltd., one in 1927 and the other in 1929. In common with those built for Armstrong Whitworth, they had plywood covered fuselages.

The last DH.9J was not completed until the autumn of 1931, not long before the type went out of service. This machine, G-ABPG, built as an exercise by senior students of the Aeronautical Technical School, was fitted with an Armstrong Siddeley Jaguar IVC and employed on training duties by the Flying School.

DH.9J G-EBGT of the De Havilland School of Flying, with the Armstrong Siddeley Jaguar III engine and rubber-in-compression undercarriage. (*author's collection*)

65

DH.10 Amiens

The German bombing of London, the Home Counties and along the East Coast using twin-engined aircraft in 1917 pressured the Air Board into retaliatory action and to renew its interest in the DH.3. The Aircraft Manufacturing Co. Ltd. recieved a contract for prototypes of a larger version designated the DH.10.

The machine was structurally similar to its predecessor, the airframe being of spruce and ash construction, with fabric covered mainplanes. The fuselage consisted of a plywood covered, box-like front, to which was bolted the usual Warren girder tail section. Rudder and elevator trailing edges were of steel tubing to reduce the risk of accidental damage on the ground. Steel tubing was also used for the wide track divided undercarriage and for engine nacelle struts, the latter being faired to streamline shape with fabric doped over wooden formers. Two 230 h.p. B.H.P. watercooled engines were mounted as pushers and to give adequate airscrew clearance cut-outs were made in the trailing edges of upper and lower mainplanes as on the DH.3A. The crew of three was made up of front and rear gunners and pilot, but full dual control was fitted in the rear gunner's cockpit, the rudder bar being covered by hinged floorboards when not in use.

The prototype DH.10 first flew on 4 March 1918 but its performance was 6% down on estimate and it could carry only a small military load. To solve this, the second and third prototypes were fitted with more powerful engines arranged to drive tractor instead of pusher propellers, the second, C8659, flying for the first time on 20 April 1918 with 360 h.p. Rolls-Royce Eagle VIIIs. The first prototype was consequently the only DH.10 to have the cut out trailing edges. Engines of even greater power - 400 h.p. Liberty 12s - were fitted to the third prototype, C8660, which was the true pre-production version without nose wheels. It was built with 2½ instead of 4 degrees of mainplane sweepback, elongated nacelles, Scarff rings for front and rear gunners and horn balanced ailerons. Fuel was carried in the front fuselage in two 98 gallon tanks, either side of a bay carrying 900 pounds of bombs. Additional bomb loads were carried on external racks under the lower mainplane.

The Air Board gave the DH.10 the type name 'Amiens', so that the first two prototypes were Amiens Mks. I and II while the third and all production aircraft were Amiens Mk. III. Orders for 1,295 DH.10s were placed with the parent company and six sub-contractors but only eight were on RAF charge at the end of hostilities. Thus the DH.10 arrived too late to see war service, and the type was destined to use for technical refinement flying and mail carrying.

Performance improvements came from mounting the engines directly on the lower mainplane to eliminate the parasitic drag of the original strutted

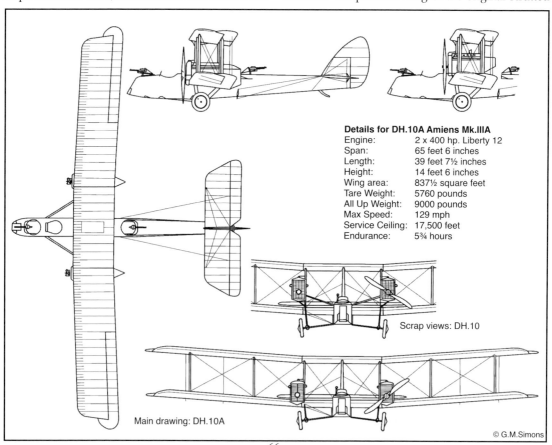

Details for DH.10A Amiens Mk.IIIA

Engine:	2 x 400 hp. Liberty 12
Span:	65 feet 6 inches
Length:	39 feet 7½ inches
Height:	14 feet 6 inches
Wing area:	837½ square feet
Tare Weight:	5760 pounds
All Up Weight:	9000 pounds
Max Speed:	129 mph
Service Ceiling:	17,500 feet
Endurance:	5¾ hours

Scrap views: DH.10

Main drawing: DH.10A

© G.M.Simons

Left: The first prototype DH.10 showing the pusher engines and trailing edge cut-outs for the propellers.

Below: DH.10C E5557 which was later to fly mails for AT&T. Note the difference in engine positions. *(both author's collection)*

arrangement. This gave rise to the Mann, Egerton-built DH.10A Amiens Mk. IIIA with Liberty engines. These were given a degree of upthrust and the aircraft was also equipped with heavy duty wheels. When Liberty deliveries stopped at the end of 1918 an up-rated Rolls-Royce Eagle VIII of 375 h.p. became standard on the final version, the DH.10C Amiens Mk. IIIC.

The first major experimental modification was the fitment of a 1½ pounder Coventry Ordnance Works quick firing gun in DH.10 E5458 and DH.10C E5550 for trials at Orfordness. Each had an enlarged bow cockpit and the old familiar nose wheels but trials were discontinued when air firing tests resulted in the crash of E5458.

The third investigation was devoted to improving asymmetrical flying in the event of engine failure and production DH.10 E6042 was modified by Airco and tested at Farnborough in 1921 with twin fins and rudders. A rectangular central fin was next added for comparison and in 1922 the assembly was replaced by an experimental tail unit with a horn balanced single rudder of greatly increased area. In 1923 the aircraft

was flown with twin rectangular rudders and between 29 April 1924 and 22 May 1926, fifteen or twenty test flights were made with the standard DH.10 rudder equipped with a small servo rudder on outriggers.

The DH.10 was used by 120 Squadron for the air mail service to the British Army of Occupation on the Rhine, daily flights being made between Hawkinge and Cologne. A DH.10 piloted by Capt. Barratt which left Hawkinge at 10.15 p.m. on 14 May 1919 and arrived at Cologne 3¼ hours later was the first aircraft to carry mails at night. Most of the DH.10s in India were sold as scrap at Ambala in February 1922 but a few were retained to police the North West Frontier with 97 Squadron and from 21 June 1921 to carry the desert air mail between Cairo and Karachi until superseded by Vickers Vimys in 1923. For this purpose they were fitted with an extra cockpit behind the pilot. One of the last recorded appearances of a DH.10 was at the 7 Group Display, Andover on 23 June 1923, when Flying Officer J. S. Chick performed a dog fight with two S.E.5As.

The designation DH.10B was supposedly reserved for a civil mail carrying version but only two aircraft were used for this purpose in England. Both

The second prototype, the DH.10 Amiens Mk.II with 360 hp Rolls-Royce Eagle VIII engines. *(author's collection)*

DH 10 variants			
	Mk.I	Mk.II	Mk.III
Engine	2 x 230 hp B.H.P	2 x 360 hp R-R Eagle VIII	2 x 400 hp. Liberty
Span:	62 feet 9 inches	62 feet 9 inches	65 feet 6 inches
Length:	38 feet 10 inches	38 feet 10 inches	39 feet 7½ inches
Height:	14 feet 6 inches	14 feet 6 inches	14 feet 6 inches
Wing area:	789¾ square feet	834¾ square feet	837½ square feet
Tare Weight	5004 pounds	-	5585 pounds
All Up Weight:	6950 pounds	8500 pounds	9000 pounds
Max Speed:	109 mph	117½ mph	-
Service Ceiling:	15,000 feet	-	16,500 feet
Endurance:	3½ hours	-	5¾ hours

Two views of G-EAJO as used by AT&T as a mailplane in 1919. The aircraft had long undercarriage radius rods which, coupled with the shoulder-mounted lower wings, gave the aircraft a somewhat spindly appearance.

In the picture below, the machine is being prepared for the ELTA Exibition in Amsterdam in August 1919. *(both author's collection)*

were operated by Aircraft Transport and Travel Ltd. but neither was actually known as a DH.10B because the first was the DH.10C prototype E5557 and the other a demilitarised DH.10, E5488, civil registered as G-EAJO. The latter was granted a full civil C. of A. before demonstration at the ELTA Exhibition at Amsterdam in August 1919 by Capt. Gerald Gathergood and on 30 September joined E5557 on regular mail flights between Hendon, Newcastle and Renfrew in an attempt to break the railway strike. A scheme was also considered for a conversion to carry pilot and four passengers, two side by side in the nose and two in the rear, the starboard passengers facing aft and the port forward.

At least one DH.10 supplemented the DH-4s on United States air mail routes. Powered by two Liberty VI engines and numbered 111, it had completed 31 hours 27 minutes flying on the New York - Cleveland-Omaha route by June 1920, average flying time for the initial stage of 200 miles being 3 hours.

Manufacturers and Serial Blocks.
The Aircraft Manufacturing Co. Ltd, Hendon, London, N.W.9. Serials: C8658-C8660, E5437-E5636, F1867-F1882, H2746-H2945.

The Alliance Aeroplane Co. Lt, Cambridge Road, London W.14. Serials: F7147-F7346.

The Birmingham Carriage Co., Birmingham. Serials: E6037-E6136.

The Daimler Co., Coventry. Serials: E9057-E9206.

Mann, Egerton and Co. Ltd, Norwich. Serials: F8421-F8495.

The National Aircraft Factory No.2, Heaton Chapel, Stockport. Serials: F351-F550.

The Siddeley-Deasy Motor Car Co. Ltd, Parkside, Coventry. Serials: E7837-E7986.

DH.11 Oxford

The DH.11 was intended as long distance day bomber to replace the DH.10, and retained the twin engined, three bay layout of the earlier type. They were structurally identical having fabric covered, wooden airframes incorporating steel tubing for highly stressed members such as engine mountings, undercarriage and the empennage trailing edges. Both types also had horn balanced ailerons and the characteristic de Havilland rudder, but there the similarity ended. Four degrees of dihedral on the upper mainplane compared with two degrees on the lower, gave the wings of the DH.11 a diverging appearance and the fuselage filled the whole mainplane gap, making it possible to put the rear gunner on a raised floor in the mid upper position with a commanding field of fire in all upward directions.

The main 170 gallon fuel tanks were slung from the top longerons of the centre fuselage, with a walk way beneath, giving the rear gunner access to the cockpit, in which the pilot sat on the starboard side, and thence to the front gunner. Entry was via a trap door between the spars of the lower wing opening on to the catwalk. Armament was a pair Scarff-ring-mounted Lewis guns fore and aft and 1,000 lb. of bombs carried internally. Two 320 h.p. A.B.C. Dragonfly radial engines were housed in nacelles fixed directly to the lower mainplane with a narrow track, cross-axle unit resembling that of a scaled up DH.9A.

Designs began early in 1918 when a contract was placed for three aircraft and by August the fuselage of the prototype, H5891, was well advanced in the Hendon factory. In September all work ceased because the Dragonfly engines were beset by problems and in November Siddeley Puma in-line, high compression engines were considered and the necessary engine

The prototype and only DH.11 Oxford. *(author's collection)*

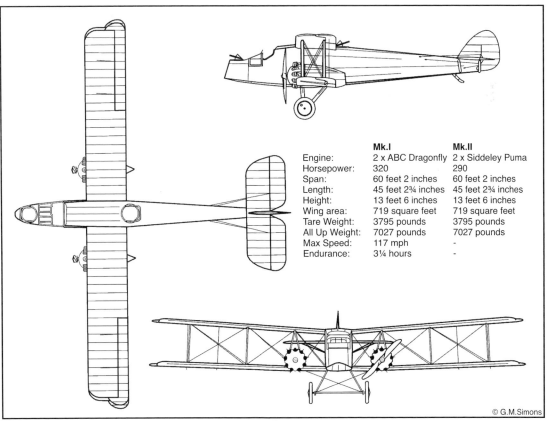

	Mk.I	Mk.II
Engine:	2 x ABC Dragonfly	2 x Siddeley Puma
Horsepower:	320	290
Span:	60 feet 2 inches	60 feet 2 inches
Length:	45 feet 2¾ inches	45 feet 2¾ inches
Height:	13 feet 6 inches	13 feet 6 inches
Wing area:	719 square feet	719 square feet
Tare Weight:	3795 pounds	3795 pounds
All Up Weight:	7027 pounds	7027 pounds
Max Speed:	117 mph	-
Endurance:	3¼ hours	-

© G.M.Simons

bearer modifications were put in hand.

By March 1919 the machine was ready and the mainplanes were being covered yet despite recurring magneto trouble it was decided to fit the Dragonflies after all. After the first few flights H5891 went back into the works for the engines to be repositioned but was short lived. Its last flight came when a connecting rod broke in one of the engines, which seized up just as the aircraft became airborne, but the pilot, F. T. Courtney, made a masterly forced landing without damage.

The projected Mk.II, H5893, fitted with Siddeley Puma high-compression engines, was not built.

DH.12

This was a modified version of the DH.11 Oxford that only reached the design stage before being cancelled.

It was to have a pair of 320 hp ABC Dragonfly engines and the mid-upper gunner was to be moved to a new position between the spars of the upper mainplane to give him a better field of fire.

DH.13

Type Number not used.

DH.14 Okapi

The DH.14 was a large single engined, two seat biplane of conventional appearance designed in 1918 as a replacement for the DH.4, DH.9 and DH.9A.

Although too late for the war, the DH.14 contract was not cancelled but construction was considerably delayed and in accordance with the system of aircraft nomenclature laid down in Technical Department Instruction No. 538, it was given the type name Okapi. Since 1917 the Rolls-Royce company had been developing a 12 cylinder vee-type watercooled engine similar to, but larger than, the Eagle. Fitted with four instead of two valves per cylinder, it gave 525 h.p. and was named the Condor. The DH.14 was one of the first aircraft fitted with this engine, which was cooled by a large nose radiator with controllable shutters.

Similar externally to a DH.9A and structurally orthodox, the design included a number of detail differences. Fuel tanks of 178 gallons capacity were housed in the fuselage aft of a fireproof engine bulkhead using gravity feed, the depth of the fuselage made it possible to blank off the upper portion of the main tank as a gravity tank and to rely on wind driven pumps only in cruising flight. The pilot's synchronised Vickers gun was located in a deep groove in the top decking, heavy gauge steel tubing was used for the engine mounting, strengthening blocks of aluminium were inserted in the lower longerons at undercarriage attachment points and the bomb load was stowed internally. Six 112 Ib. bombs were carried inside the lower wing between the spars and two in the fuselage

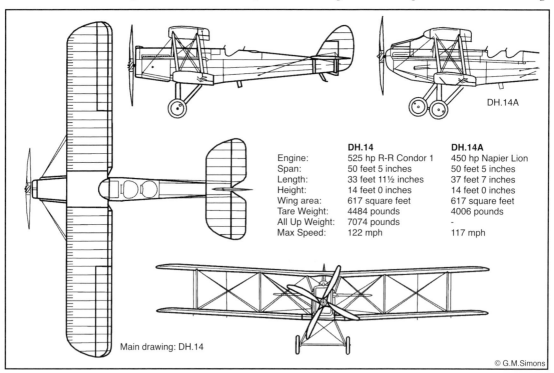

DH.14A

	DH.14	DH.14A
Engine:	525 hp R-R Condor 1	450 hp Napier Lion
Span:	50 feet 5 inches	50 feet 5 inches
Length:	33 feet 11½ inches	37 feet 7 inches
Height:	14 feet 0 inches	14 feet 0 inches
Wing area:	617 square feet	617 square feet
Tare Weight:	4484 pounds	4006 pounds
All Up Weight:	7074 pounds	-
Max Speed:	122 mph	117 mph

Main drawing: DH.14

© G.M.Simons

J1938, fitted with the 525 hp Rolls-Royce Condor I. *(author's collection)*

Cape Town. Registered G-EAPY and crewed by Cotton and Napier engineer W. A. Townsend, it left Hendon on 4 February 1920, and immediately forced landed at nearby Cricklewood with oil trouble eventually reaching Rome on 21 February. Despite two additional wheels fitted forward of the main undercarriage, it turned over while landing on a beach 18 miles north east of Messina, Italy, on 23 February after failing to find the aerodrome. G-EAPY was shipped back from Naples, rebuilt by Airco with three cockpits and sold to Cotton for the Aerial Derby of 24 July 1920.

under the pilot's seat. Bombs were released manually by the gunner, whose cockpit was fitted with twin Lewis guns on a Scarff mounting. Risk of shooting away his own tailplane bracing was eliminated by suppressing the top wires in favour of four faired tubular struts underneath, the rear pair of which were hinged to the bottom of the tail trimming tube and controlled tailplane incidence. This somewhat vulnerable gear, first fitted to the DH.11, was protected by an additional curved member aft of the main tail skid. The undercarriage consisted of the by now standard wooden Vee struts sprung by rubber cord wound round the axle.

Three airframes were laid down but postwar economies sounded the death knell. The first two aircraft, J1938 and J1939, were well advanced by July 1919 but the third airframe was finished first - completed by Airco as the private venture DH.14A for the *Daily Mail* transatlantic flight competition with a Napier Lion and fuel capacity increased to 586 gallons. When the arrival in Ireland of Alcock and Brown ended the project, the DH.14A languished at the Hendon works until first flown in the autumn of 1919 as Frederick Sidney Cotton's entry for the Australian Government England-Australia flight competition.

Ross and Keith Smith reached Darwin in their Vickers Vimy, G-EAOU, before Cotton was ready but Maj. Gen. Sefton Brancker, a director of Airco, then loaned him the aircraft for a flight to

On the first leg of the race a petrol leak started a fire and the aircraft was badly damaged when it struck telephone cables in a forced landing near Hertford.

When Airco closed down, the unfinished military DH.14s were completed at Stag Lane by the De Havilland Aircraft Co. Ltd. J1938, flown in September 1920, went to Farnborough where, on 22 December Squadron Leader Roderic Hill flew it on Condor engine trials. Except for brief visits to Martlesham on 3 and 17 March it spent the remainder of 1921 at Farnborough, making occasional test flights which culminated in an endurance test on 8 September and rate of climb trials on 24 November. It crashed at Burnham Beeches, Bucks, on 10 February 1922 while returning from Chingford, Flying Officer Robinson and observer Mitchell losing their lives.

After Cotton's aircraft was repaired at Stag Lane it emerged as J1940 and records show that test pilot Henry 'Jerry' Shaw, with W. K. Mackenzie as observer, made unsticking trials there on 13 March 1921 at all-up weights between 6,400 Ib. and 6,820 Ib., the shortest take-off in a 12 knot wind being a mere 215 yards.

The Napier Lion engined long-tange DH.14A G-EAPY in its original form, with a single-axle undercarriage. *(author's collection)*

Left: F. Sidney Cotton and W A Townsend at the start of their London- Cape Town flight in G-EAPY, showing the four-wheeled undercarriage.

Below: The same machine at Hendon following its rebuild by Airco and the installation of a third cockpit.
(both author's collection)

The second military machine, J1939, was delivered to Martlesham on 14 April 1921 but the DH. 14 remained on the Secret List and was not seen in public until one, probably J1939, was flown from Martlesham to Croydon by A. H. Orlebar for the Imperial Air Conference display of 3 to 6 February 1922.

DH.15 Gazelle

Built purely for experimental purposes, the DH. 15 was allotted the type name Gazelle, a name which, like those of its predecessors, was little used. The aircraft was basically a DH.9A, modified as a flying test bed for the 500 h.p. B.H.P. Atlantic vee-twelve water-cooled engine, built by the Galloway Engineering Co. Ltd., consisting of two 230 horsepower B.H.P. engines with a common crankcase. Its installation in the DH. 15 called for a large frontal radiator similar to that used with the Liberty 12 engine, long exhaust pipes and

vertical instead of raked front centre section struts as on the DH.14. Standard DH.9A armament, a synchronised forward-firing Vickers gun on the port side and a Lewis gun on a Scarff ring on the rear cockpit, was retained. Two DH.15s were ordered, but only one - J1937, the second machine - was completed.

In 1919-20, the aircraft, piloted by Gerald Gathergood completed extensive flight testing of the Atlantic engine.

J1937, the sole DH.15 Gazelle completed.
(author's collection)

Manufacturers and Serial Blocks.
The Aircraft Manufacturing Co. Ltd, Hendon, London, N.W.9. Serials: J1936, J1937.

Engine:	500 hp B. H. P. Galloway Atlantic	Wing Area:	486¾ square feet
Span:	45 feet 11⅜ inches	Tare Weight:	2312 pounds
Length:	29 feet 11 inches	All-Up Weight:	4773 pounds
		Max Speed:	139 mph
		Initial Climb:	1500 feet per minute
		Ceiling:	20,000 feet

DH.16

The war had barely ended when the Aircraft Manufacturing Co. Ltd. started to consider the best type of aircraft for the era of civil flying that stretched into the future. Experience gained in converting the rear cockpit of the military DH.4 into a cabin for two passengers and successful operation of the resultant DH.4A by RAF, influenced their decision to build a larger machine in the same configuration. The DH.16, Airco's first purely civilian type, was built from DH.9A components with the rear fuselage widened to seat four passengers in facing pairs in a glazed cabin. Although powered by the same 320 h.p. Rolls-Royce Eagle VIII engine as its predecessor, it was faster and carried four instead of two fare paying passengers, making it a more economical and commercially attractive aircraft.

The prototype first flew at Hendon in March 1919

The prototype DH.16 flew unmarked at Hendon during March 1919. (*author's collection*)

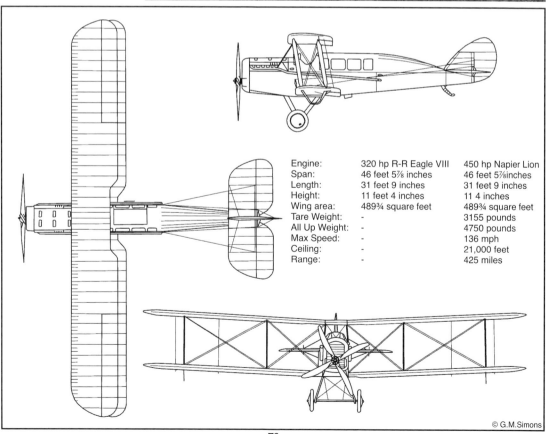

Engine:	320 hp R-R Eagle VIII	450 hp Napier Lion
Span:	46 feet 5⅞ inches	46 feet 5⅞inches
Length:	31 feet 9 inches	31 feet 9 inches
Height:	11 feet 4 inches	11 4 inches
Wing area:	489¾ square feet	489¾ square feet
Tare Weight:	-	3155 pounds
All Up Weight:	-	4750 pounds
Max Speed:	-	136 mph
Ceiling:	-	21,000 feet
Range:	-	425 miles

© G.M.Simons

Left: AT&Ts G-EALM was registered in August 1919, and is seen here at Hounslow for a publicity picture. Passenger entry was the same as for the DH.4A a fixed ladder and hinged roof!

Below: K-130 - later registered G-EACT - sets off on another 'Joy Loan' flght around the country. (both author's collection)

in contemporary khaki drab with red, white and blue rudder. In May it entered service with AT&T Ltd. bearing the temporary civil marking K-130. With 'Joy Loan' advertisements painted under the wings, it toured the provinces. In July 1919 the DH.16 flew to Amsterdam, where it was immaculately polished and put on display without mainplanes on the Airco stand at ELTA, the First Air Traffic Exhibition. Bearing the nationality mark G on the rudder, the same aircraft flew on the 12.30 p.m. service to Paris piloted by Major Cyril Patterson on 25 August, the inaugural day of the London-Paris air route.

Before production ceased in June 1920, nine had been built, one fitted experimentally with air brakes and flaps. One was sold to the Sociedad Rio Platense de Aviacion (River Plate Aviation Co. Ltd.) at Buenos Aires for a successful cross river ferry to Montevideo but the remainder were used on the continental services of AT&T Ltd. The final three were fitted with the heavier and more powerful Napier Lion engine, setting up new standards in reliability. During one week in the summer of 1920 the Lion powered DH.16 G-EAQS made seven return trips between Croydon and Paris within six days, making fastest time of the week in each direction.

In those days KLM, the Royal Dutch Air Line, had no aircraft of its own, so that the honour of making the first KLM scheduled service between Croydon and Amsterdam fell to Capt. H. 'Jerry' Shaw and the Eagle powered DH.16 G-EALU 'Arras'. This flight took place

in extremely bad weather on 17 May 1920 and carried two British journalists, a bundle of English newspapers and a congratulatory letter from the Lord Mayor of London to the Burgomaster of Amsterdam, in a flight time of 135 minutes. K.L.M. schedules were thereafter all flown by Aircraft Transport and Travel Ltd., but when the firm closed down in December 1920, its aircraft, including seven surviving DH.16s were stored in a Bessoneau hangar at Croydon, where all but two were broken up in 1922.

Survivors G-EALM and 'PT, were taken over by the De Havilland Aeroplane Hire Service in 1922 and after overhaul at Stag Lane went to Lympne for use on early morning newspaper flights to Ostend, four casual passengers per trip being brought back at £3 a head. The DH.16s were later based at Stag Lane, ready to go anywhere at £11 per hour.

On 5 December 1922 both DH.16s took part in an air freight experiment by flying consignments of a special Ulster edition of The Times from Sealand to Aldergrove on the day of issue, but after G-EALM crashed near Stag Lane during a test flight on10 January1923 with the loss of the pilot, R. E. Keyes, G-EAPT was dismantled and the type became extinct.

DH.17

This was a design for a large biplane carrying two crew and sixteen passengers. The machine was fitted with semi-retractable undercarriage and was powered by

two 600 hp Rolls-Royce Condor engines. Much design work was completed, and brochures produced but no orders were received due to the post-war slump. Span was 82 feet, length 46 feet 10½ inches, Wing area 1,650 square feet.

DH.18

The DH.18 was the first Airco machine designed and built from the outset as a commercial airliner. Its operating cost of 2s. 8d. per ton-mile was a remarkable reduction over those of its converted military predecessors. It was a two bay biplane of wooden construction carrying eight passengers in an enclosed cabin amidships, with the pilot in an open cockpit behind. Power was provided by a 450 h.p. Napier Lion mounted high in the nose above a radiator compartment into which cooling air was admitted by the pilot by means of controllable shutters. The rear fuselage was of standard de Havilland construction of a wire braced, wooden box girder but the cabin was a plywood covered wooden structure with a watertight door in case of forced landing at sea. Two passengers

sat with their backs to the engine bulkhead, two in the rear of the cabin and four in single seats amidships, those on the port side facing aft. Front and rear escape hatches were fitted in the cabin roof and a baggage compartment was provided under the pilot's cockpit. With seats removed, 256 cubic feet of cabin space was available for the carriage of 2,200 pounds of freight at a slight overload which somewhat reduced the performance and raised the landing speed.

To ensure uninterrupted utilisation, the Lion was arranged as a complete unit, with its attendant water and oil tanks and the entire mounting being quickly detached for replacement by another. Fuel tanks of 104 gallons capacity were housed under the centre section in the curved decking of the cabin roof, giving a minimum range of 400 miles, petrol being pumped initially to a streamlined gravity tank on top. An unusually tall undercarriage was fitted so that with the

After its C of A trials, the prototype DH.18, G-EARI was fitted with a three bladed propeller. Like many aircraft of the time, the fuel system determined that there was a need for a header tank above the upper. wing.
(author's collection)

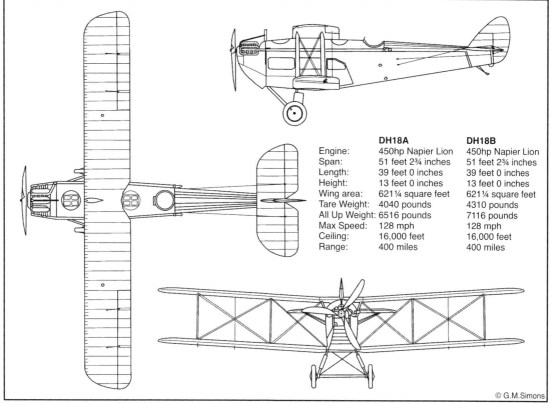

	DH18A	DH18B
Engine:	450hp Napier Lion	450hp Napier Lion
Span:	51 feet 2¾ inches	51 feet 2¾ inches
Length:	39 feet 0 inches	39 feet 0 inches
Height:	13 feet 0 inches	13 feet 0 inches
Wing area:	621¼ square feet	621¼ square feet
Tare Weight:	4040 pounds	4310 pounds
All Up Weight:	6516 pounds	7116 pounds
Max Speed:	128 mph	128 mph
Ceiling:	16,000 feet	16,000 feet
Range:	400 miles	400 miles

© G.M.Simons

Right: from the passengers' viewpoint the cabin of the DH.18 was interesting, if cramped. By placing seats facing alternate ways, the best legroom and shoulder space was achieved. By all accounts, the huge windows tended to rattle at speed.

Below: DH.18B G-EAWX, one of two built for the Instone Air Line and the last-built of the marque. The main difference is that instead of a fabric-covered fuselage with stringers, this version was plywood covered and thus had flat sides.

strengthened with plywood, they were handed over to Instone Air Line, together with the fourth aircraft, G-EAWO, built to Air Council order. By the end of September 1921, 'RO had flown more miles on the Paris, Brussels and Cologne routes than any other aeroplane and it was considered expedient to

tail on the ground, the mainplanes were at an angle of attack of seventeen degrees, allowing the aircraft to make really short landings. In a five five mph wind the landing run was just 163 yards. The traditional bungee shock absorbers were replaced with a rubber cord system in a streamlined casing through which ran an oleo damping leg.

G-EARI, the prototype DH.18, was built at Hendon in early 1920 and was flight tested by Francis T. Courtney before going to Martlesham Heath in March for trials. The two-bladed propeller was abandoned in favour of a three-blader and 'RI commenced service on the Croydon-Paris route of AT&T Ltd. on 8 April. It was wrecked in the August when Cyril Holmes forced landed with engine trouble in some back gardens at Wallington, Surrey. Two others, designated DH.18A, begun by Airco at Hendon, were the first aircraft completed by the embrionic De Havilland Aircraft Co. Ltd. at Stag Lane and embodied modifications resulting from flight experience with the prototype, including improved engine mountings, undercarriages and control cable fairleads.

When subsidised air services were authorised in March 1921, the Air Council was empowered to acquire up-to-date aircraft for lease to approved firms. The two DH.18As, G-EARO and 'UF were therefore purchased and after the top centre sections had been

withdraw it from service when the C. of A. expired two months later. This, and the loss of 'UF in a crash, so reduced the Instone fleet that two replacement aircraft were supplied by the Air Council. Total DH.18 production totalled six machines, the last two of which had plywood covering to the rear as well as to the front fuselage, additional emergency exits, improved cabin fittings and inertia engine starting under the designation DH.18B. The first DH.18B, G-EAWW, made its maiden trip from Croydon to Paris on 18 December 1921 piloted by F. T. Courtney and the other, 'WX, fitted with a Leitner-Watts three bladed metal propeller, went to Martlesham for type testing in January 1922 before delivery to Instone at Croydon a month later.

Pending delivery of its new DH.34s, Daimler Hire Ltd. commenced a Croydon-Paris service on 2 April 1922 using DH.18A 'WO transferred from Instone. Five days later it was in air collision in bad visibility with a Farman Goliath over Northern France, losing a wing and the tail unit to crash and burn with the loss of pilot R. E. Duke and a cabin boy. In the same month 'WX was loaned to Handley Page Ltd. to alleviate its fleet shortage, after which the two remaining aircraft of the type, 'RO and 'WW, were used almost exclusively on the Brussels route. When declared obsolete in 1923, 'RO had flown 90,000 miles without mishap and together

The restricted view of the pilot from his cockpit (just visible between the inboard interplane struts) was commented on by the Martlesham Heath test pilots.

with 'WW returned to the manufacturers for partial reconditioning for test purposes.

G-EAWW was used by the Technical Dept. of the Air Ministry for a flotation test to determine the length of time an aircraft with that type of cabin would remain afloat after a forced landing at sea. With all loose equipment and cowlings removed and with the cabin sealed, it took off from Martlesham on 2 May 1924 piloted by Squadron Leader C. A. Rea who put the DH.18B gently into the water off Felixstowe, where it floated for twenty-five minutes until a salvage crew recovered the engine.

On 16 April 1924 'RO was flown from Stag Lane to the RAE at Farnborough and was used on fuel consumption tests from 16 July until 5 December, and for experiments in cabin silencing from 3 February 1925 until 4 January 1926. In July 1926 it was testing a drift sight for aerial photography; on 7 July 1927 it was flown to Biggin Hill. Its return flight to Farnborough on 10 November is believed to have been its last.

Manufacturers

The Aircraft Manufacturing Co. Ltd, Hendon, London, N.W.9.

De Havilland Aircraft Co. Ltd., Stag Lane Aerodrome, Edgware.

DH.19

A two-seat cabin biplane powered by one 275 hp Rolls-Royce Falcon III, but the design was not completed.

DH.20

This was the designation of a layour prepared by the Aircraft Manufacturing Co. Ltd by Geoffrey de Havilland for a single seat sporting biplane with folding wings. It was to be powered by an 170 hp A.B.C. Wasp seven cylinder engine, which was never developed beyond the experimental stage. Span 33 feet, length 26 feet, Wing area 330 square feet.

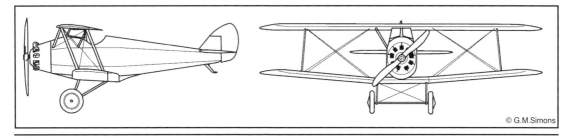

© G.M.Simons

DH.21

A design study by the Aircraft Manufacturing Co Ltd for a heavy civil transport aircraft with two engines geared to drive one propeller.

DH.22

A design study that included a layout for a pusher biplane with a normal rear fuselage in place of outriggers, the engine being mounted on the upper mainplane.

DH.23

A design for a four seat biplane flying boat powered by a single 450 hp Napier Lion engine mounted under the top centre-section and driving a tractor propeller.

An application was made to the Air Ministry for the civil registration G-AERN, including the issuing of certificate number 464 on 9 March 1920 under the constructors number E.58. Eventually, it was not built.

DH.24

A design study for a larger, developed version of the DH.18 cabin transport machine, powered by a 450 hp Napier Lion engine.

DH.25

A design study for a large transport biplane carrying ten passengers and two crew. Power was to be supplied by three 400 hp Liberty 12 water-colled engines houses in the fuselage, two side by side and a third aft, all geared to one propeller.

Span 86 feet, Length 63 feet Fuel 810 gallons, Oil 30 gallons, all-up-weight 15,440 pounds.

DH.26

A design study for a monoplane capable of carrying a commerical load of 1000 pounds with a thick section, internally braced cantilever wing. Powered by a 230 horsepower Siddeley Puma, the design showed so much potential that the Air Council ordered two examples of a larger version, the DH.29 powered by a 450 hp Napier Lion engine, so the DH.26 was not proceeded with.

DH.27 Derby

The DH.27 Derby was the De Havilland Company's first military machine and was a single engined long range, heavy day bomber built to Air Ministry Specification 2/20. It had been originally designed by Airco around the 525 horsepower Rolls-Royce Condor IA engine, and was first test flown by Hubert Broad at Stag Lane on 13 October 1922 with a 650 horsepower Condor III driving a four bladed wooden propeller.

It was a large two bay fabric covered biplane of, wire braced wooden construction that incorporated certain features which had been developed on De Havilland commercial aeroplanes, including the plywood covering to the long, slim fuselage, a variable incidence tailplane and the oleo damped rubber shock legs.

The wide track undercarriage was divided to make possible the carriage of a single heavy bomb centrally

J-6894, the first DH.27 Derby at Stag Lane in 1922. The central cabane housed the main fuel tanks, taking the place of the usual centre-section struts. *(DH via BAe Hatfield).*

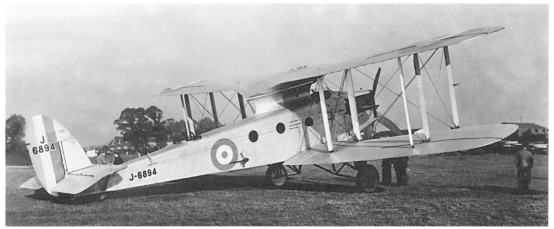

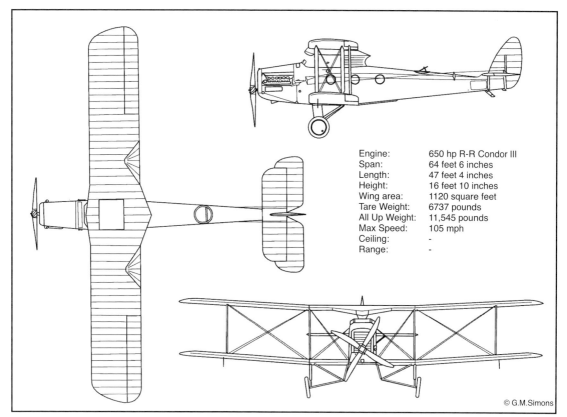

Engine:	650 hp R-R Condor III
Span:	64 feet 6 inches
Length:	47 feet 4 inches
Height:	16 feet 10 inches
Wing area:	1120 square feet
Tare Weight:	6737 pounds
All Up Weight:	11,545 pounds
Max Speed:	105 mph
Ceiling:	-
Range:	-

© G.M.Simons

under the fuselage and the wings were made to fold. In place of centre section struts, the upper mainplane was directly attached to a large streamlined cabane which housed 212 gallon fuel tanks, and three circular portholes were provided in the cabin for the benefit of the navigator/bomb aimer. The other members of the crew consisted of the pilot, whose cockpit was ahead of the wings, and a rear gunner with Scarff ring-mounted Lewis gun on top of the fuselage aft of the cabin. Two prototypes were used for competitive trials with the Avro Aldershot to determine the most suitable design for re-equipping 99 Squadron, Bircham Newton but the contract was awarded to the Aldershot. The Derby prototypes were then relegated to test duties at Martlesham Heath and at the naval experimental station in the Isle of Grain, from which J6894 made what was probably its last flight when it was flown to Farnborough on 1 February 1924.

DH.28

A design study for a troop carrier biplane to Air Ministry D of R Type 12 which did niot proceed beyond the design stage. It would have been powered by a 1000 horsepower Napier Cub. The two crewmembers sat in an open cockpit ahead of the main cabin that was 23 feet long. The fuselage had lines similar to the later DH.34. The span was 87 feet and length 65 feet.

DH.29 Doncaster

A pair of DH.29 long range aircraft were built at the Stag Lane works for the Research Department of the Air Ministry during the winter of 1920, construction not being completed until the summer of 1921. They were the first British transport monoplanes to be fitted with thick section, high lift, cantilever wings and their design was developed from the smaller DH.26 high wing project. The two crew sat in an open cockpit forward of a thirteen foot three inch glazed cabin of 345 cubic foot capacity. Well proven features were retained, including the oleo damped rubber shock absorbers, controlled cooling and fuselage construction. The main structure consisted of spruce longerons and cross struts strengthened with a plywood covering to keep the cabin free of internal bracing, but to provide a suitable anchorage for the extra wide track undercarriage - the floor was made wider than the roof.

The tapered, cantilever wing was of wooden construction, weighed 1,050 Ib. and was internally braced, fabric covered and fitted with differential ailerons designed by Arthur E. Hagg. Fuel was carried in leading edge tanks of 115 gallons capacity and fed to the carburettors by gravity.

Left: J6849 at Martlesham Heath in its original form with a frontal radiator and low-set cockpit.

Below: the same aircraft in its revised form with a raised cockpit and internal radiator compartment. *(both author's collection)*

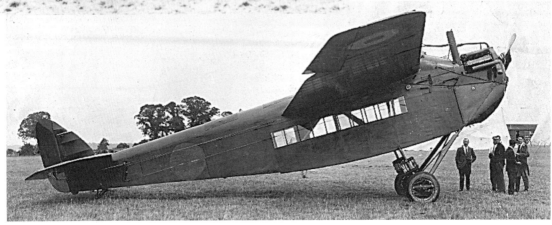

The prototype was first flown at Stag Lane on 15 July 1921 by Capt. Geoffrey de Havilland, but with the engine thrust line coinciding with the centre line of the fuselage, the cockpit received the full force of the slipstream, and the pilot was subjected to excessive buffeting. Emergency hatches and clear doped panels in the roof were stove in and performance was reduced by the disturbed airflow over the centre part of the wing. The ineffectiveness of the rudder was apparent when the machine did a large diameter ground loop to port as the speed fell below 30 mph on landing.

The first passenger was flight test observer W. K.

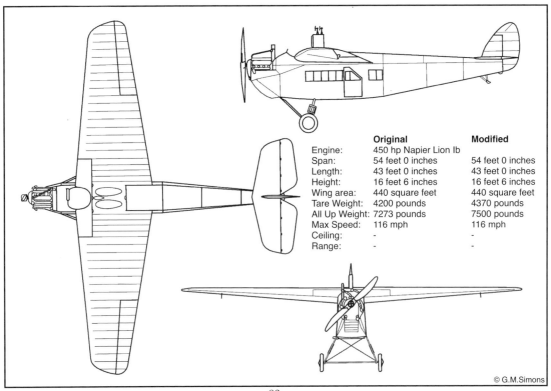

	Original	Modified
Engine:	450 hp Napier Lion Ib	
Span:	54 feet 0 inches	54 feet 0 inches
Length:	43 feet 0 inches	43 feet 0 inches
Height:	16 feet 6 inches	16 feet 6 inches
Wing area:	440 square feet	440 square feet
Tare Weight:	4200 pounds	4370 pounds
All Up Weight:	7273 pounds	7500 pounds
Max Speed:	116 mph	116 mph
Ceiling:	-	-
Range:	-	-

© G.M.Simons

Above: The unattractive lines of the Doncaster with its plank-like wing is evident in this view.

Right: one of the few air-to-air pictures of the DH.29 in flight. *(author's collection)*

Mackenzie, who flew in the left hand seat when Captain de Havilland made further test flights on 7, 11 and 12 July. In an attempt to improve directional control, a new nose was built to raise the power plant by 20 inches, but as the original fuel tanks no longer gave a sufficient head of petrol, a low pressure fuel system was installed which necessitated the addition of a streamlined header tank on top of the centre section, surmounted by two wind driven pumps. The original unbalanced elevator was replaced with a horn balanced unit.

The cabin was subsequently modified to have three small portholes in place of the original sliding windows, and was equipped for photographic and wireless experiments. A gunner's cockpit fitted with a Scarff ring was built on top of the fuselage aft of the wings and thereafter the aircraft was known officially as the Doncaster. It was flown from Martlesham to the RAE Farnborough on 17 April 1924 and in the following month was used for a series of 'Control of Doncaster' tests. The second DH.29 was completed in August 1921 as a commercial aircraft seating ten passengers. Wicker chairs were arranged with a gangway down the middle and a communicating door in the front bulkhead gave access to the pilot's cockpit.

Daimler Hire Ltd. showed considerable interest in the DH.29, but although its differential ailerons imparted exceptional lateral control other control problems came to light and the rudder was ineffective when taxying. The need for new flying stock was so urgent that the company was forced to order the DH.34 biplane instead and so the civil DH.29 G-EAYO saw no commercial service. Its only recorded public appearance was before delegates to the Imperial Air

The DH.29 in its final form with main cabin portholes and an rear gunners position. *(DH via BAe Hatfield)*

G-EAYO at the Imperial Air Conference demonstration at Croydon on 3 February 1922. *(DH via BAe Hatfield).*

Conference at Croydon on 3 to 6 February 1922, where it was exhibited statically in the Aircraft Disposal Company's hangar and flown on the final day. In the following November it joined the first prototype at Martlesham, where both aircraft took part in a very considerable programme of test flying and made valuable contribution to a fuller understanding of the behaviour of thick section cantilever wings. G-EATO returned to Stag Lane where Hubert Broad made the first of several test nights on 18 July 1923, climbing to 10,000ft. with Hessell Tiltman as observer on 20 and 24 July. They ferried it back to Martlesham on September 13 and next day made a full load test at the all-up weight of 7,500 pounds.

DH.30

A design study for a high wing reconnaissance aircraft to Air Ministry Specification D. of R. Type 3. This machine was derived from the DH.29 but the pilot's cockpit was situated midships as in the DH.18 and the thick section, cantiliver wing - which housed the 120 gallon fuel tank, was raised abaove the fuselage on short centre-section struts. An observer sat ahead of the bomb stowage and a tail gunner's position with Scarff ring and Vickers gun protected the rear.

There is some evidence to suggest that a fighter reconnaissance version was allocated the name 'Denbigh'to Specification D. of R Type 3A. and was referred to as such in Air Ministry records. Span 48 feet 6 inches, Length 41 feet.

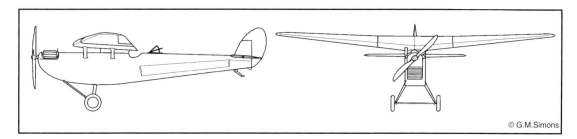

© G.M.Simons

DH.31

This was another design study for a reconnaissance biplane to Air Ministry Specification D. of R. Type 3 powered by a 450 hp Napier Lion (or similar) engine, with the pilot and gunner seated high up over a large cabin featuring four circular windows in each side, similar to the Avro Bison.

Stowage for three 112 pound bombs was provided in the centre of the cabin with a walkway on each side, giving the rear gunner access to the radio and camera positions forward.

Span 42 feet, Length 36 feet 9 inches.

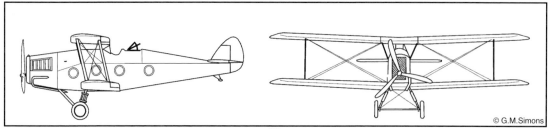

© G.M.Simons

DH.32

The technical and commercial success of the DH. 18 led to designs for an even better aeroplane of the same type to meet Air Ministry Specification 18/21. The first, although little more than a layout, was allotted the De Havilland type number DH.24, but the second, the DH.32, was a design study. It retained the best features of the DH.18, including the plywood covered fuselage, oleo damped and independently sprung undercarriage, controlled engine cooling and detachable power plant, but in the light of experience with the DH.29, refinements such as ball bearing controls and differential ailerons were added.

To reduce operating costs below those of the earlier machines, and to take full economic advantage of the aerodynamically refined DH.32 airframe, the 450 h.p. Napier Lion was changed for a special commercial version of the Rolls-Royce Eagle rated at 360 h.p.

Airline service inevitably revealed a number of shortcomings in the DH. 18 and as a result, all eight seats in the DH.32 faced forward, four on each side of a central gangway. The cabin door was on the starboard instead of the port side and the main baggage compartment was situated in the rear fuselage. Provision was also made for an elementary

form of air conditioning which, in conjunction with large DH.29-style sliding windows, was intended to reduce the possibility of air sickness. To this end petrol fumes were banished from the cabin and fire risks reduced by attaching the fuel tanks to the underside of the upper mainplanes.

In bad weather and without wireless, pilot-navigation had proved difiicult and even hazardous, with the result that the DH.32 was designed for operation by a crew of two which included a navigator. As on the DH.29, they were afforded a magnificent view in all directions by moving the open cockpit to a position forward of and on a level with, the upper mainplanes.

In September 1921 it was announced that construction of the first DH.32 was about to begin at Stag Lane and considerable interest was shown by DH.18 operators Instone Air Line Ltd. and Daimler Hire Ltd., then in urgent need of new equipment. As their existing fleets were Lion powered, this well tried engine was stipulated for the new machines.

The promising DH.32 design was shelved in favour of a Lion powered version of higher aspect ratio, carrying nine passengers at a higher cruising speed. This was the world famous DH.34.

Span 50 feet, length 39 feet, height 14 feet, wing area 618 square feet. Speed 98 mph, Duration 4 hours.

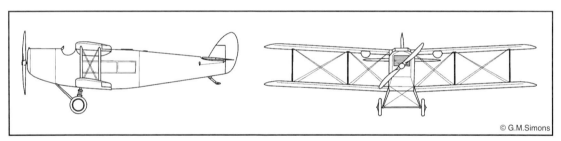

© G.M.Simons

DH.33

This was a layout for a small, single seat ship's fighter to Air Ministry Specification D. of R. Type 6. It was a small, heavily staggered biplane with a

radial engine and a high-camber hydrovane mounted forward of the undercarriage for alighting on water. The rear fueselage was detachable just aft of the cockpit for ease of stowage aboard ship. Span 29 feet, Length 23 feet.

DH.34

It took a few years after the outbreak of peace for the fledgling airline industry to understand the operating economics of air transport – and therefore have a clear idea of improvements that should be incorporated in a replacement type. It was evident that commercial aviation could only pay its way if the DH.18s were replaced by faster aircraft carrying more payload per horsepower. De Havilland's attempted to satisfy these requirements and had built the ten passenger DH.29 monoplane and completed designs for the eight passenger DH.32 biplane. After consultations between Daimler Hire Ltd., Instone Air Line Ltd., the Air

Council and the manufacturers, orders were placed for an improved version of the DH.32 modified to include the best features of the DH.29.

The fuselage was a wooden structure, plywood covered for strength and almost identical in appearance to that of the DH.29, but differing by having vertical sides and an internal diagonal strut in each bay to give triangulated strength. The Napier Lion was installed as a detachable power unit with internal radiator and controlled cooling, but without ladders the engine was inaccessible from the ground for maintenance or starting and one of the stipulations made at the design conference was for built-in service platforms. These took the form of hinged doors in the nose which could be let down for the engineer to stand

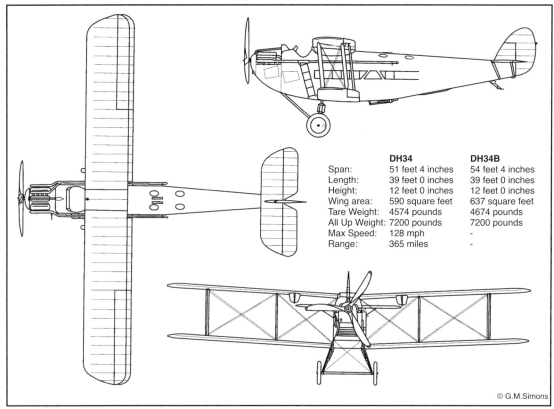

	DH34	DH34B
Span:	51 feet 4 inches	54 feet 4 inches
Length:	39 feet 0 inches	39 feet 0 inches
Height:	12 feet 0 inches	12 feet 0 inches
Wing area:	590 square feet	637 square feet
Tare Weight:	4574 pounds	4674 pounds
All Up Weight:	7200 pounds	7200 pounds
Max Speed:	128 mph	-
Range:	365 miles	-

© G.M.Simons

on when working on the engine or cranking it into life. Inertia starting was adopted as standard and brought to an end all propeller swinging on commercial aeroplanes. Wooden three bladed propellers were fitted as standard but a two bladed Leitner-Watts adjustable metal airscrew was fitted experimentally.

The two-bay mainplanes were of wooden construction and the ailerons were operated by differential gear first flown on the DH.29 and fitted as standard to all later de Havilland types. As in the DH.32, fire risk was reduced by fixing the 82 gallon fuel tanks to the underside of the upper mainplanes. Noise level was reduced by placing the pilot's cockpit between the cabin and the engine, from which warmth was obtained by means of a muff round an exhaust pipe. An almost triangular-shaped cabin door fitted in the starboard side to facilitate the loading of spare Lion engines, but the narrow fuselage made it necessary to cut a circular hole (normally fabric covered) in the port side to give sufficient room for aligning the engine fore and aft.

Two DH.34s were ordered by Daimler Hire Ltd., the first of which, G-EBBQ, made its first flight at Stag Lane on 26 March 1922 in the firm's all red colour scheme, piloted by Alan J. Cobham. It was the prototype of an initial batch of ten aircraft, seven of which were for the Air Council to Specification 17/21. After delivery to the owners at Croydon on 31 March, the inaugural flight to Paris was made by Captain Walter G. R. Hinchliffe on 2 April. Several of the Air Council's machines were leased to Instone Air Line Ltd., the first of which, the blue and silver G-EBBR 'City of Glasgow', went into service on the same day as the prototype, reaching Paris with full load in 2 hours 40 minutes piloted by Captain Frank L. Barnard. G-EBBQ forced landed at Berck in the Pas de Calais area

The prototype DH.34 G-EBBQ in Instone Air Line colours at Stag Lane, prior to delivery. *(DH via BAe Hatfield)*

84

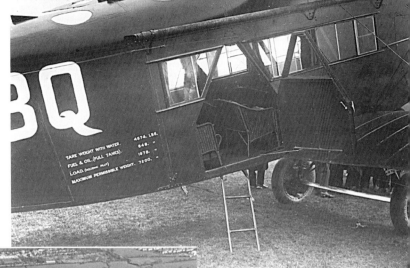

Right: Entry to the cabin of the DH.34 was by the starboard side through a door wide enough to admit a spare engine if required. Passenger seating was somewhat basic - while the foldaway ladder was essential.

Below: the maiden flight of the DH.34, flown by Alan Cobham. *(DH via BAe Hatfield)*

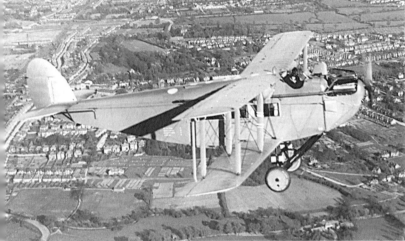

the small amount of traffic, the Director of Civil Aviation decided later that year to prevent undesirable competition by means of a route allocation system. The route to Brussels and Cologne was to be flown only by Instone Air Line Ltd., to Paris by Handley Page Ltd. and a new route to Berlin by Daimler Hire Ltd. This was opened on 15 September 11922 by G-EBBS piloted by Walter Hinchliffe and carrying Major Woods Humphery and Col. F. Searle, directors of the firm, but after the eighth trip, disagreement with the German Government forced a termination at Amsterdam until the service was resumed by 'BQ on 25 June 1923.

of France a fortnight later and turned over, leaving the second Daimler DH.34, G-EBBS, to maintain the service during its reconstruction at Stag Lane. The second Instone machine, G-EBBT *'City of New York'*, and the third Daimler, G-EBBU, were delivered during April and May 1922 but the latter also went back to Stag Lane to be rebuilt after another aircraft had landed on top of it at Croydon on 23 May.

G-EBBS was forced to carry on alone. Its first trip to Paris had been made on 13 April 1922 and on 1 May flown by Capt. E. D. C. Hearne, 'BS became the first aircraft to make two return trips between Croydon and Le Bourget in one day. On 2 June it increased this to five single trips in the day and by the end of 1922 G-EBBS established utilisation figures which, if impressive now, were hardly believable then. Scheduled services were flown on 122 days out of a possible 165, five days were spent on Air Ministry tests and double return journeys to Paris in one day were made on no less than forty-five occasions. By 5 December 100,393 miles had been flown in nearly 8,000 hours without incident or overhaul, to provide a foretaste of the enormous mileages that DH.34s were to fly during the next four years.

'City of New York', piloted by Captain Frank Barnard, inaugurated a new Croydon-Brussels service for Instone Air Line Ltd. on 2 May 1922 but in view of

Increases in traffic made necessary the delivery of one additional Air Council DH.34, G-EBBW *'City of Chicago'* to Instone on 13 August 1922, and another, G-EBBY, to Daimler. This left the Air Council with one spare DH.34, G-EBBX, which later went into service with Daimlers to replace G-EBBU, written off in an accident at Berck on 3 November 1922. The seventh production aircraft, built to the order of the Russian airline Dobrolet and first flown in June 1922, was crated and despatched by sea. Two additional aircraft, G-EBCX and 'CY, ordered by the Air Council at the end of 1922, brought DH.34 production to an end.

Daimler Hire Ltd. were in the unique position of owning two DH.34s outright and therefore able to operate services other than those earning subsidy. The Croydon-Amsterdam route was extended inland to Manchester and this daily service was inaugurated by the elderly G-EBBS on 23 October 1922.

Flights were also made to Castle Bromwich in connection with the British Industries Fair in March-April 1923 but on 14 September 'BS stalled while attempting a forced landing at Ivinghoe Beacon, Bucks, and was destroyed, with the loss of Capts. G. E. Pratt and L. G. Robinson and three passengers. This incident revived the controversy of the relatively high stalling

An unidentifiable DH.34 crosses the coast. The design racked up some remarkable milages and ultilization figures. *(DH via BAe Hatfield)*

speed of the DH.34 and the opportunity was seized of equipping Daimler's G-EBBX, at that time being rebuilt at Stag Lane after a forced landing in the sea off Ostend, with mainplanes of greater area. The increase was obtained by adding eighteen inches to the wing tip overhang so that the interplane struts remained in the same position relative to the centre line of the aircraft. At the same time an extra six inches of chord was added. When fitted with the new mainplanes the aircraft became the DH.34B, DH.34A being, it is believed, a preliminary design study. A reduction of 7 m.p.h. in the landing speed was obtained without any material effect on cruising performance and the aircraft was flown to Croydon for inspection by the owners on 23 February 1924. Trials for C. of A. were at once put in hand and maximum load tests were conducted during the second test flight on 1 March at an all-up weight of 7,200 pounds with 150 pounds of ballast in each of the nine seats and more in the rear locker.

When Imperial Airways Ltd. was formed on 1 April 1924 it inherited seven DH.34s from former operators and kept them in regular service on routes to Brussels and Amsterdam until 1926. One of the seven, G-EBBR, survived a forced landing by Capt. Wolley Dod in which it knocked down a 30 ft. tree at the foot of Whyteleafe Hill, near Kenley on 11 February 1924 to complete 127,000 miles in Instone service. Two months after becoming an Imperial Airways machine it was destroyed by fire when it struck a War Memorial on take off from Ostend piloted by Capt. A. L. Robinson on 27 May. Despite its modification, 'BX crashed and burned soon after leaving Croydon on 24 December 1924. Captain David A. Stewart and seven

passengers being killed in an attempted forced landing in circumstances very similar to those in which 'BS was lost. At the subsiquent enquiry, it was concluded that the aircraft was airworthy at the time of departure, there was no blockage in the petrol pipe, such damage being as a result of the firefighting operations subsequent to the crash. the aircraft was found to have crashed due to an unknown mechanical defect and subsequent stall whilst an emergency landing was being attempted. The pilot was cleared of any blame.

Another aircraft, G-EBBT, was then sent to Stag Lane for conversion to DH.34B and made its first flight in this condition piloted by Hubert Broad on 12 June 1925. Imperial Airways aircraft were not permitted to take part in races but DH.34 G-EBBYwas hired by a party of enthusiasts and left Croydon on July 3, 1925 piloted by Captain F. Minchin to follow the King's Cup machines. Later in the day it was damaged through running into a ditch while making a precautionary landing in bad weather at Carville near Newcastle. Again the opportunity was taken to make a DH.34B conversion and it first flew in modified form on 7 September. Unlike 'BX and 'BT, this aircraft was tested with an extra pair of interplane struts braced by wires at each wing tip. An order was also placed with de Havillands for a set of mainplanes fitted with Handley Page slots but before these could be delivered, Imperial Airways decided to re-equip with multi-engined aircraft and the remaining DH.34s, withdrawn from service at the end of the financial year on 31 March 1926, were dismantled at Croydon.

DH.35

This was a layout for a Corps Reconnaissance biplane to Air Ministry Specification D. of R Type 3A. The

aircraft was to have been a two-seater, resembling the Armstrong Whitworth Atlas and powered by an Armstrong Siddeley Jaguar aircooled radial engine. Span 46 feet, lenth 27 feet 6 inches.

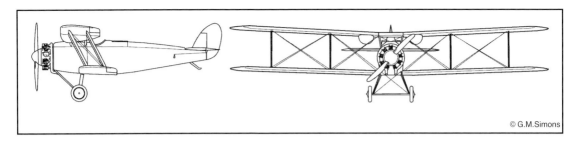

© G.M.Simons

DH.36

A layout for a coastal defence torpedo bomber to Air Ministry Specification D. of R. Type 9. It was similar in appearance to the DH.27 Derby but with centre section struts instead of the cabane. There was a crew of three - a pilot who sat forward of the wings, a gunner in the top rear fuselage and a bomb aimer in the lower centre fuselage, all three connected by a walkway. Span 86 feet, length 61 feet.

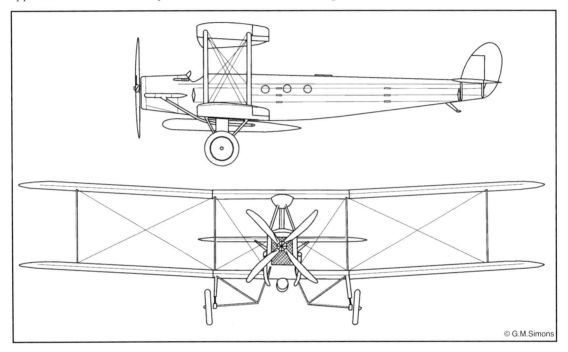

© G.M.Simons

DH.37

In November 1920 Alan S. Butler bought a Bristol Type 29 Tourer open two seater and became the first British private owner to tour at home and on the Continent. He also competed in the Aerial Derby at Hendon on 16 July 1921 and came second, but soon commissioned De Havillands to build a fast sporting and touring aeroplane. Economy of operation, space for two passengers in addition to the pilot, generous tankage and a simple structure needing a minimum of maintenance, were specified and the result was the DH.37, built in the early part of 1922 at a cost of some £3,000. So successfully did it meet the design requirements, that its owner put much needed capital into the company and became its chairman.

Powered by the 275 h.p. Rolls-Royce Falcon III, the new machine carried the two passengers in tandem in the front cockpit. Dual control was fitted and a removable, sliding deck enabled the DH.37 to be flown as a three, two or single seater. The strong fuselage construction used in previous designs of transport aircraft was used for the DH.37 and was also the first civil type to be rigged as a single bay biplane with differential ailerons on the lower mainplanes.

Eighty gallons of fuel were carried, half in a centre section tank mounted on splayed out 'N' struts and the remainder in a tank forward of the front cockpit. The Falcon was cooled by a nose radiator and drove a four bladed wooden propeller, and the undercarriage was of the independently sprung, oleo damped type.

Elevator control was via a cross shaft behind the pilot, running in external ball races and fitted with double ended cranks from which outside cables ran aft. These cranks, emerging from their acorn shaped ball race fairings, became a well known characteristic

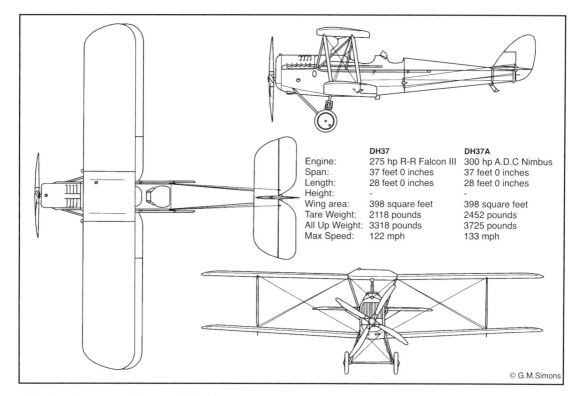

	DH37	DH37A
Engine:	275 hp R-R Falcon III	300 hp A.D.C Nimbus
Span:	37 feet 0 inches	37 feet 0 inches
Length:	28 feet 0 inches	28 feet 0 inches
Height:	-	-
Wing area:	398 square feet	398 square feet
Tare Weight:	2118 pounds	2452 pounds
All Up Weight:	3318 pounds	3725 pounds
Max Speed:	122 mph	133 mph

© G.M.Simons

of de Havilland aircraft during the biplane era.

Two DH.37s were laid down, the first of which, test flown in June 1922, became Mr. Butler's personal aircraft 'Sylvia', named after his sister, and the second, completed in 1924, was shipped to Australia.

Painted red with gold wings, 'Sylvia' made its debut as a single seater for the Aerial Derby at Croydon on 7 August 1922, but magneto trouble caused a late start and eventual retirement. In the first King's Cup Race which started at Croydon on 8 September 1922 Butler came 5th over the round-Britain course to Renfrew and back in a flying time of 7 hours 50 minutes. In the following month the British Government asked the De Havilland Hire Service to take Maj. Gen. Sir Warren H. Anderson to Constantinople. The DH.37 was chosen because of its relatively high cruising speed, and piloted by Alan J. Cobham left Croydon on 8 October, reaching its destination the same day. Three years later, on 6 June 1925, Cobham completed

a similar one day trip to Morocco.

Accompanied by his engineer, K. C. Brown, Alan Butler left Croydon on 17 April 1924 on the most extensive tour undertaken up to that time by a private owner. In four weeks 'Sylvia' visited the Riviera, Milan, Belgrade, Sofia, Bucharest, Vienna, Prague, Warsaw, Brussels and Paris. Between 11 and 13 May Broad flew it to Berlin and back in a flying time of 12 hours 45 minutes to bring back urgent press photos. On 30 May Butler left for the International Aero Exhibition in Prague, covering the 600 miles nonstop in 5½ hours. On 12 August 1924, again piloted by Butler, the DH.37 started from Martlesham and completed the 950 mile King's Cup course to Lee-on-Solent at an average speed of 112-65 m.p.h. and came in third.

In the following year, piloted by Maj. H. Hemming

DH.37 G-EBDO in its original form with the Rolls-Royce Falcon III engine. *(DH via BAe Hatfield)*

Left: G-EBDO, still named 'Sylvia' in single-seat racing trim.

Below: G-AUAA just after it was re-erected in Australia by Geelong Air Services. (both DH via BAe Hatfield)

and carrying two passengers, it was again third, completing two circuits of an 804 mile Croydon-Renfrew course on 3-4 July 1925 in a flying time of 16 hours 42 minutes.

To improve performance Butler had the Falcon engine replaced by the more powerful, and lighter, A.D.C. Nimbus for the King's Cup Race at Hendon on 9 July 1926. Hubert Broad and he first flew it with this engine as the single seat DH.37A, renamed 'Lois', on 6 July. He force landed near Cheltenham with a fractured induction pipe but flew it in several races at the Bournemouth Summer Aviation Meeting on 21-22 August 1926 and won the Boscombe High Speed Handicap event.

On 15 May 1927 it carried the owner into second place in the Morris Open Handicap Race at Hamble but on 4 June its career came to an end through striking the racecourse number board while competing as a two seater in the High Power Handicap at Ensbury Park during the Bournemouth Whitsun Meeting, Major H. Hemming receiving slight, and the passenger fatal, injuries.

The second DH.37 was shipped to Australia in 1924 for use by the Director of Civil Aviation and received that Dominion's first civil aircraft marking G-AUAA. Flown by Captain F. W. Follett, it competed 'hors concours' in the New South Wales Aerial Derby at Richmond Aerodrome, Sydney on 8 December 1924 and was adjudged the unofficial winner.

Two years later G-AUAA was acquired by the Guinea Gold Co. Ltd. and shipped to Rabaul, New Guinea, where an extra tank was fitted, enabling E. A. Mustar to ferry it to Lae on 31 March 1927. This 450 mile trip, mainly over the open sea, was completed in 5 hours 19 minutes. On 18 April Mustar groped his way through the mountains to make the first-ever landing on what was to become the goldfield's infamous sloping airfield at Wau. The DH.37 flew mining supplies up from Lae in 20 to 30 minutes compared with the 7 to 10 day trek by local porters.

DH.38

This design was a military biplane offered in either general duties or bombing versions, powered by one 450 h.p. Napier Lion engine with buried radiator.

In the bomber version the bomb sight was fitted in the floor of the pilot's cockpit and had a range from 45 degrees forward to vertically downwards. The gunner's position, sited close behind the pilot, was equipped with a Scarff ring. Small bombs were carried under the pilot's seat, with the larger ones in racks under the lower mainplane. Designs and performance calculations were prepared for the Greek Government for a long range heavy bomber, a short range bomber with increased bomb load and a long range photographic reconnaissance machine. No order was placed and the DH.38 was not built.

DH.39

An alternative version of the DH.38 fitted with one 360 h.p. Rolls-Royce Eagle VIII engine. A layout was prepared for the Greek Government but there were no detail designs and no order was placed. Span 51 feet 3 inches. Length 35 feet 6 inches.

DH.40

This was a projected two-seat forest patrol version of the DH.39 for civil operation by the Canadian Air Board. The engine was a 360 h.p. Rolls-Royce Eagle VIII. Span 51 feet 3 inches. Length 35 feet 6 inches.

DH.41

This was a two seat reconnaissance version of the DH.38 to Air Ministry Specification D. of R. Type 3.

Power was to come from a 450 hp Napier Lion, but the project did not proceed beyond the design phase. Span 51 feet 3 inches, length 36 feet 6 inches.

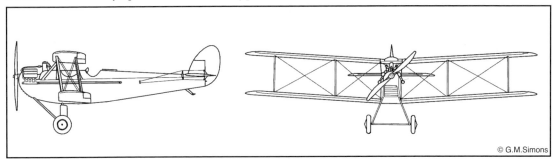

© G.M.Simons

DH.42 Dormouse / Dingo

This was a high performance two seat reconnaissance fighter designed to Air Ministry Specification D. of R. Type 22/22. The single prototype was built on standard De Havilland lines, with fuselage of spruce longerons and cross pieces covered with plywood, oleo damped undercarriage and a variable incidence tailplane. The upper and lower mainplanes were of unequal span and the narrow chord of the lower gave

the front interplane struts a considerable forward slope. For maximum view the pilot's cockpit, entered by a door on the starboard side, was placed high up to afford a commanding view in all upward directions through a large oval cutout in the top centre section. A generous V shaped trailing edge gap gave the gunner an equally good view forward and upward from his Scarff ring behind the pilot.

Powered by a 360 hp Armstrong Siddeley Jaguar II, Dormouse J7005 was first flown at Stag Lane on 25 July 1923 and made its public debut in the New Types

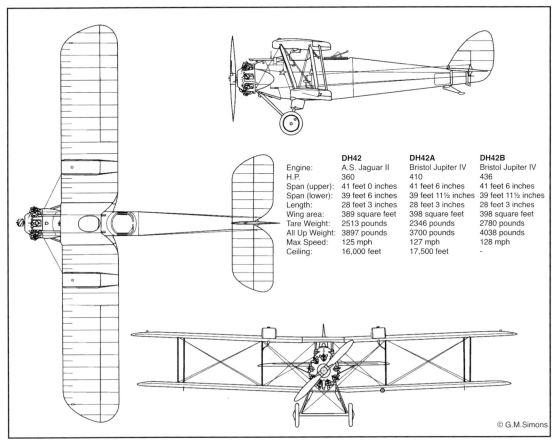

	DH42	DH42A	DH42B
Engine:	A.S. Jaguar II	Bristol Jupiter IV	Bristol Jupiter IV
H.P.	360	410	436
Span (upper):	41 feet 0 inches	41 feet 6 inches	41 feet 6 inches
Span (lower):	39 feet 6 inches	39 feet 11½ inches	39 feet 11½ inches
Length:	28 feet 3 inches	28 feet 3 inches	28 feet 3 inches
Wing area:	389 square feet	398 square feet	398 square feet
Tare Weight:	2513 pounds	2346 pounds	2780 pounds
All Up Weight:	3897 pounds	3700 pounds	4038 pounds
Max Speed:	125 mph	127 mph	128 mph
Ceiling:	16,000 feet	17,500 feet	-

© G.M.Simons

Above: DH.42 Dormouse J7005 in the New Types Park at RAF Hendon on 28 June during their 1924 Air Display.

Left: DH42A Dingo J7006 fitted with the Bristol Jupiter engine of 410 horsepower. *(both DH via BAe Hatfield)*

Park at the Hendon Display on 28 June 1924 alongside the Vickers Type 94 Venture I and Bristol Type 52 Bullfinch built to the same specification.

An Army Co-operation version to Specification D. of R. Type 8/24 - the DH.42A Dingo I - flew for the first time on 12 March 1924. As a result of fitting the large diameter 410 hp Bristol Jupiter III, the front fuselage differed considerably from that of the Dormouse. The two forward firing guns were no longer housed in neat tunnels but were fitted externally to fire over the engine. Front centre section struts which raked inwards at the top on the Dormouse were splayed out on the Dingo and the large oval cutout over the pilot's seat was reduced to a smaller circular opening. The gunner's trailing edge gap was cut right back to the rear spar and increased to fuselage width. The reduction of the pilot's aperture on the Dormouse to that on the Dingo was one of a number of modifications made in January 1925 before it was put through a new series of tests with a 420 h.p. Armstrong Siddeley Jaguar IV driving various propellers and at a variety of all-up weights.

The DH.42A Dingo I, J7006, was followed by a third prototype, J7007, termed as the DH.42B Dingo II, first flown by Hubert Broad on 29 September 1926. The Mk.II was similar to Mk.I and also intended for Army Co-operation duties but was steel instead of wooden construction. Although the original drawings called for an Armstrong Siddeley Jaguar, the actual engine fitted was a 436 hp Bristol Jupiter IV installed with full exhaust manifold and long exhaust pipes. Gravity fuel feed was used on all three machines, 60 gallons of fuel carried in two large aerofoil section tanks on top of the upper mainplane. Those of the Dingo II were larger and held 81 gallons and this aircraft was also equipped with an device under the rear fuselage for picking up messages.

Dormouse J7005 was delivered by air from Stag Lane to the RAE Farnborough on 27 March 1925 for use by the Wireless and Photographic Flight and was used for various W/T and magneto screening tests before being written off charge at the end of the year.

DH.43

This was a layout for a large, freight carrying biplane powered by a 400 hp Liberty 12 engine. The pilot sat in an open cockpit in front of the wings with a small cabin below and behind him for the loader/ground engineer The fuselage had a fifteen foot long cargo hold, with a large freight door on the port side. A pair of fuel tanks feeding the engine by gravity were located on the top wings and the aircraft was to be fitted with a variable incidence tailplane as was by now the standard De Havilland practice. There was no detail design completed and the aircraft was not built.

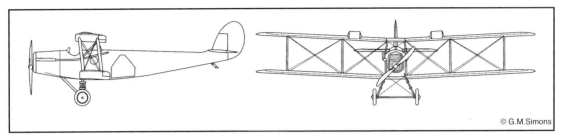

© G.M.Simons

DH.44

This was a preliminary design study made in 1923 for a civil transport airliner powered by a Siddeley Puma engine. It was not proceeded with.

DH.45

This was to be a twin engined torpedo-carrying coastal defence aircraft powered by a pair of 450 hp Napier Lion engines. It was intended to have a crew of three, pilot, front gunner/bomb aimer and rear gunner. No detail work was completed. Span 86 feet, Length 60 feet.

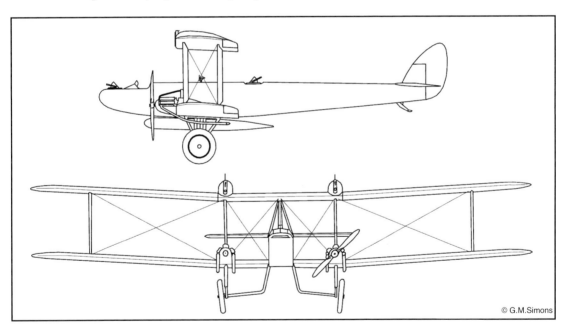

© G.M.Simons

DH.46

This was a layout for a single-seat sporting biplane, supposedly similar to the later DH.53 Hummingbird. Span 37 feet 6 inches. Length 24 feet 2 inches.

DH.47

This was a single seat glider design that was in many respects the forerunner to the DH.52. It was not proceeded with. Span 38 feet, length 27 feet 1 inch. Wheel track 2 feet 6 inches.

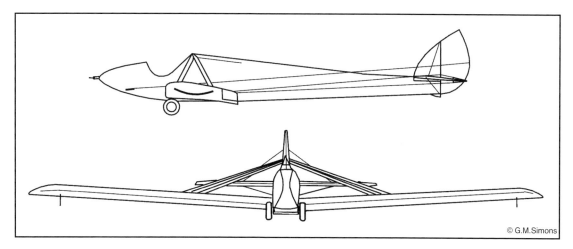

© G.M.Simons

DH.48

The DH.48 was a layout for a single seat survey and forestry patrol aircraft for the Royal Canadian Air Force, powered by a 200 h.p. Wolseley Viper engine. The fuselage was designed for the carriage of specialist equipment and was divided into compartments of the correct size and shape for the storage of furs, snow shoes, survival equipment, cameras, radio apparatus and luggage. No detail design was completed and the aircraft was not built. Span 37 feet. Length 25 feet 6 inches.

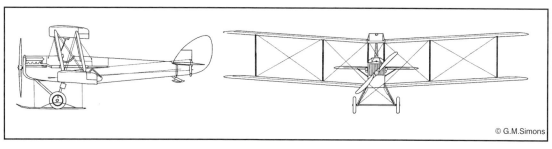

© G.M.Simons

DH.49

The DH.49 was to have been an updated version of the DH.9A with a plywood covered fuselage, oleo damped undercarriage, differential ailerons, ball bearing controls and cantilever tail unit.

Attention was paid to low speed controllability and the 370 h.p. Rolls-Royce Eagle IX watercooled engine, driving a four bladed airscrew, was specified as standard. Provision was also made for the alternative installation of the 400 h.p. Liberty 12 or the 450 h.p. Napier Lion.

Reconnaissance, Bombing and General Purpose variants were also offered.

DH.50

The DH.50 was a four seater and came about as a result of experience gained with the DH.9C used by the De Havilland Hire Service. Using the same engine, a 230 hp Siddeley Puma, the new design carried an additional passenger at a higher cruising speed. It was a two bay biplane with plywood covered fuselage with the pilot in an open cockpit behind the cabin.

Hubert Broad made the first night in the prototype G-EBFN 'Galatea' at Stag Lane on 10 July 1923 and only four days later Alan Cobham flew it to the International Aeronautical Exhibition at Gothenberg, Sweden. Competing against the foremost European commercial aircraft of the day, the DH.50 won first prize in the reliability trial flown daily between Gothenburg and Copenhagen from 7-12 August. Exactly a year later, on 12 August 1924, the same aircraft and pilot averaged 106 mph over the round Britain course, winning that year's King's Cup.

Cobham left Croydon on 19 September and flew 'FN to Tangier and back in 28 flying hours, covering the 920 miles between London and Madrid nonstop. After two years with the Hire Service 'Galatea' went to Northern Air Lines Ltd of Woodford and then to West Australian Airways Ltd. in 1926.

All later DH.50s had eight square, instead of sixteen circular, transparent roof lights and the second aircraft, G-EBFO, was that in which Cobham made long distance flights which earned him a knighthood.

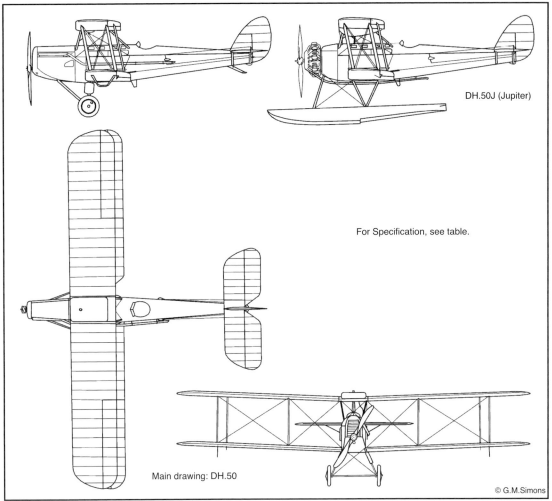

DH.50J (Jupiter)

For Specification, see table.

Main drawing: DH.50

© G.M.Simons

Fitted experimentally with full span automatic camber changing flaps and piloted by Hubert Broad, it carried Air Vice Marshal Sir Sefton Brancker, Lord Thompson and Frank Hodges 600 miles in 6½ hours to attend the Prague Aero Exhibition on 30 May 1924. The flaps reduced the landing speed by 6 mph but were removed before the 17,000 mile flight to Rangoon to enable Sir Sefton Brancker to attend a conference.

After its return, 'FO landed heavily in fog at Stag Lane at the end of a Hire Service flight with the engine breaking away from the fuselage. During reconstruction a 385 h.p. Armstrong Siddeley Jaguar radial was fitted to

give extra power needed when taking off from high altitude aerodromes. Two additional fuel tanks increasing the total capacity by 69½ gallons were fitted in the cabin and Cobham left Croydon on 16 November 1925 accompanied by his engineer A. B. Elliott and a photographer B. W. G. Emmott, arriving in Cape Town on 17 February 1926. The DH.50 landed back at Croydon on 13 March after a quick return flight and preparations were made for a similar survey flight

The first DH.50, G-EBFN, fitted with the original radiator and curved underwing fairing. *(DH via BAe Hatfield)*

Left: G-EBFO, the second DH.50, seen here fitted with full span, automatic, wing-camber changing flaps.

Below: The same machine seen at Stag Lane after being rebuilt with the Siddeley Jaguar. *(DH via BAe Hatfield)*

to Australia.

Much of this route lay over water, so the aircraft was fitted with metal floats by Short Bros. Ltd. at Rochester and the flight started from the Medway in the early hours of 30 June 1926. When 'FO returned to make its landing on the Thames at Westminster on 1 October, its Empire flights totalled 62,000 miles.

In 1929 a Nimbus engine was fitted before shipment to West Australian Airways Ltd. who later equipped it with Handley Page slots and a larger radiator.

The third DH.50, G-EBFP, was a familiar sight at Croydon for eight years, first in Imperial Airways blue and later in silver and black. In the hands of the charter section manager Captain Gordon P. Olley and others, it was in daily use for private hire and scheduled service relief until disposed of to the Iraq Petroleum Transport Co. Ltd. in 1932. Its final year of service was spent in ferrying the company's personnel from Haifa to the pumping stations along the desert pipeline.

G-EBKZ, added to the Imperial Airways fleet in 1925, was a production model known as DH.50A, with longer cabin, more splayed out centre section struts, additional radiator area and the undercarriage set more forward. Fourteen DH.50As were built at Stag Lane, nine being to Australian order, the first of which, G-AUAB, was built in 1924 for the use of the Controller of Civil Aviation, Australia. It left Melbourne on 7 August 1924 piloted by Captain Edward J. Jones on a round-Australia survey flight with the Director of Civil Aviation, Lt. Col. Horace Brinsmead OBE MC, aboard.

In 23 consecutive days flying it completed 7,658 miles, and on 8 December 1924 competed 'hors concours' in the New South Wales Aerial Derby at Richmond, Sydney and although carrying four passengers came an unofficial second. Seventeen years later, in November 1942, it was fitted with a Pratt and Whitney Wasp C radial and impressed for war service.

The first DH.50A to enter commercial service in the Commonwealth was G-EBIW/G-AUER of QANTAS, which also became the first aircraft to carry an Australian Prime Minister on an official journey when Hudson Fysh piloted The Right Honourable Stanley M. Bruce from Winton to Longreach on 30 November 1924 during his election tour. In April 1927 it was named *Hermes* and on 2 August made the first Flying Doctor flight from Cloncurry to Mount Isa piloted by Captain A. N. Evans.

In May 1928 it was renovated, re-rigged and fitted with two stretchers, a strengthened undercarriage and renamed *Victory* in order that a permanent service might be set up. The first trip was made to Julia Creek on 17 May 1928, and, based at Cloncurry, *Victory* operated for a number of years. It was disposed of to Rockhampton Aerial Services Ltd. and fell into the sea off the Queensland coast in 1935.

G-EBFO on floats with Shorts Brothers at Rochester. *(DH via BAe Hatfield)*

30 June 1926, and Alan Cobham lands G-EBFO on the Thames by the Palace of Westminster to show just how practical flying had become.*(author's collection)*

After Cobham's Australia flight, the fuselage of G-EBFO was paraded through Fleet Street, London followed by a brass band.*(DH via BAe Hatfield)*

Three DH.50As were shipped to West Australian Airways for the Wyndham - Perth - Adelaide service, and three to the Larkin Supply Co sponsored Australian Aerial Services Ltd. for the mail run between Adelaide and Sydney. The first Larkin machine, G-AUEI, was delivered at Hay, S.A., on 15 November 1924 and left on the inaugural service to Adelaide on the 18th.

Two additional DH.50As were sold to the Australian Government, the first for the personal use of Lord Stonehaven, the Governor General. This aircraft was equipped with interchangeable wheel and float undercarriage and a nine foot six inch diameter Fairey-Reed metal propeller, and was handed over at Rochester on 24 March 1926. When relegated to Royal Australian Air Force service it was allotted the serial A8-1 and left Melbourne on 28 September 1926 (some sources say the 25th) piloted by Group Captain Richard Williams DSO OBE on a survey flight up the east coast of Australia to Thursday Island, the Solomons and the Bismarck Archipelago. The seaplane returned to Melbourne without incident on 7 December having completed 10,000 miles of ocean flying. After conversion to landplane it took off from Melbourne on 21 July 1927, flown by the same pilot on a 13,000 mile internal air route survey completed on 10 September. The other Government DH.50A was G-AUAY, fitted with DH.9A type external fuel tanks under the upper mainplane and together with 'AB was in continual service for nearly 18 years until fitted with Bristol Jupiter VI. It was destroyed by enemy action New Guinea 31 January 1942. A similar aircraft supplied to the New Zealand Air Force for aerial survey was the first powered by a 300 h.p. ADC Nimbus. In 1930 it was loaned to Air Travel (N.Z.) Ltd. and piloted by Squadron Leader Malcolm C. McGregor flew a short lived Christchurch-Dunedin service. It survived until July 1933 found it working out its useful life as a DH.50J with Holdens Air Transport in New Guinea.

QANTAS found its original DH.50 a great success with such an impressive serviceability record that the DH.50A was chosen to replace the veteran DH.4 and the DH.9Cs. De Havillands were busy with Moth production so they granted a manufacturing licence to QANTAS, making available all drawings and metal parts. QANTAS produced seven DH.50As at the Longreach base. Four were Puma engined, the first - G-AUFA *Iris* - flew on 8 August 1926 and was christened by Lady Stonehaven. The other three were

Group Captain Williams (right) with Flight Lieutenant Ivor McIntyre (left) and an RAAF mechanic (centre) seen with their DH.50 A8-1 during their Pacific Islands flight in 1926.

powered by 450 horsepower Bristol Jupiter VI engines to improve both rate of climb and cruising speed. Their designation, DH.50J, first used on Cobham's Jaguar engined machine, was now applied to those with Jupiters. As a concession to primitive operating conditions, the undercarriage axles was lengthened to take an additional pair of wheels when operating from waterlogged aerodromes. All but one received mythological names, and many of their flights became milestones in Australian aeronautical history. *Iris* carried Lord and Lady Stonehaven across Australia to Darwin in 1926 and *Perseus,* piloted by Hudson Fysh, carried the first air-delivered newspapers to Normanton on the Gulf of Carpentaria on 1 July 1927. On 23 April 1929 Capt. L. J. Brain in *Atalanta* found Anderson and Hitchcock's ill-fated Westland Widgeon *Kookaburra* deep in the Australian interior, and on 27 May located the wreck of James Moir and Harold Owen's England-Australia Vickers Vellore I G-EBYX at Cape Don, N.T. Two years later, on 7 May 1931, the same aircraft and pilot inaugurated the short lived unsubsidised Brisbane to Townsville service.

The final DH.50J *Hippomenes* played a large part in the second experimental England-Australia air mail service, flying Darwin-Brisbane on 12-13 May 1931 and the return service over this section piloted by Hudson Fysh on 17-18 May. It also flew on the first regular southbound service from Darwin to Mount Isa on 19-20 December 1934. The mails were then transferred to the unnamed G-AUJS en route to Charleville. At the end of its QANTAS service, *Hippomenes* was sold to Pacific Air Transport Ltd. in New Guinea and in 1935 set up the record of fifteen round trips in one day between Lae and Wau, a total distance of 1,200 miles.

Concurrently with QANTAS production, Larkin built a single Puma DH.50A under licence and West Australian Airways Ltd. built three more. One Jupiter engined DH.50J was also built at Stag Lane to the order of the North Sea Aerial and General Transport Co. Ltd. and equipped with Fairey-Reed metal propeller,

VH-UEJ of Australian Aerial Surveys, formerly G-AUEJ, after reconstruction as a DH.50A. The aircraft carries the name *Wattle Bird* on the tail and is fitted with a Bristol Jupiter VI engine with a pair of propellers creating a four-blade unit. *(DH via BAe Hatfield)*

Left: O-BAHX was one of three DH.50As built by SABCA in 1925. The extra nose under-fairing caused by the larger radiator is clearly seen. *(SABENA)*

Below: VH-ULG , the last of the QANTAS-built DH.50s named *Hippomenes* is seen at Longreach in August 1929. *(QANTAS)*

additional fuel tanks and Short twin metal floats for a pioneer mail service along the Nile between Khartoum and Kisumu. Christened *Pelican* at Rochester on 15 November 1926, it was shipped to the Sudan and Captain Thomas A. Gladstone operated the inaugural service in the next month. It was not long before it struck

floating wreckage when taking off and was seriously damaged, forcing shipment all the way to Blackburn Aircraft's base at Athens, Greece for repairs. The service was interrupted twice more by accidents, eventually being abandoned when *Pelican* was wrecked during landing from a test flight at Kisumu on 17 October 1927.

The last British built DH.50A was G-EBQI, built for Air Taxis Ltd. in 1927 was the only DH.50A fitted with the original DH.50 type radiator. Sir Philip Richardson bought it in 1929, kept it at Brooklands and later sold it to Northern Air Lines Ltd. The major part of its career was spent as a taxi aircraft

after its return to the Brooklands School of Flying Ltd. in 1930.

The DH.50A was built under licence by SABCA (Société Anonyme Belge de Constructions Aéronautiques) in Belgium who built three, which from 1925-1928 were based at Kinshasa in the Belgian Congo and operated a regular service to Stanleyville.

Aero Tovarno Letadel of Prague built seven for the Czech Government air service, C.S.A., which had been using a single British built DH.50A since February 1925. All were powered by 240 h.p. Walter W-4 in-line watercooled engines.

DH.50J G-EBOP was named *Pelican* and operated for a brief time by the North Sea Aerial and General Transport Co. Ltd until it was wrecked on the Nile at Kisumu on 17 October 1927. *(author's collection)*

L-BAHF was one of seven DH50s built under licence for Ceskoslovenske Statni Aeroline (CSA) by Aero Tovarno Letadel. *(author's collection)*

DH.50 variants			
	DH.50A (wheels)	**DH.50A (floats)**	**DH.50A (wheels)**
Engine:	Siddeley Puma	Siddeley Puma	ADC Nimbus
H.P.:	230	230	300
Span:	42 feet 9 inches	42 feet 9 inches	42 feet 11¼ inches
Length:	29 feet 9 inches	29 feet 9 inches	29 feet 9 inches
Height:	11 feet 0 inches	11 feet 0 inches	11 feet 0 inches
Wing area:	434 square feet	434 square feet	437 square feet
Tare Weight:	2153 pounds	2800 pounds	2400 pounds
All Up Weight:	4200 pounds	4200 pounds	4200 pounds
Max Speed:	109 mph	106 mph	125 mph
Cruising Speed:	95 mph	-	105 mph
Initial climb:	605 feet per minute	-	950 feet per minute
Ceiling:	14,600 feet	10,000 feet	18,000 feet
Range:	375 miles	360 miles	380 miles

	DH50.J (wheels)	**DH50J (floats)**	**DH50J (wheels)**	**DH50J (floats)**
Engine:	AS Jaguar	AS Jaguar	Bristol Jupiter	Bristol Jupiter
H.P.:	385	385	420/515	420/515
Span:	42 feet 11¼ inches	42 feet 11¼ inches	42 feet 11¼ inches	42 feet 11¼ inches
Length:	28 feet 9 inches	28 feet 9 inches	30 feet 5 inches	30 feet 5 inches
Height:	11 feet 7 inches	11 feet 7 inches	11 feet 7 inches	11 feet 7 inches
Wing area:	437 square feet	437 square feet	437 square feet	437 square feet
Tare weight:	2532 pounds	2830 pounds	2336 pounds	2840 pounds
All Up Weight:	4200 pounds	4200 pounds	4200 pounds	4200 pounds
Max Speed:	136 mph	126 mph	132 mph	126 mph
Cruising Speed:	110 mph	110 mph	110 mph	110 mph
Initial climb:	1200 feet per minute	920 feet per minute	1250 feet per minute	1100 feet per minute
Ceiling:	20,000 feet	16,500 feet	20,000 feet	16,000 feet
Range:	660 miles	275 miles	240 miles	275 miles

DH.51

The 1923 Lympne Trials encouraged construction of low powered single seat light aircraft, but De Havillands designed a larger, more practical, touring vehicle, the DH.51. This was a serious attempt to produce a cheap aircraft using well proven constructional methods and by fitting the war surplus 90 horsepower R.A.F. 1A eight cylinder aircooled engine, available in vast numbers at ridiculous prices. De Havilland modified the engine, giving it the benefit

of dual ignition using a French-made Remy coil in addition to the standard magneto spark system.

The aircraft was a two bay biplane with a plywood covered fuselage, ball bearing controls and the standard oleo damped undercarriage. With differential ailerons on the bottom mainplane only and a spring loaded elevator instead of the traditional tail trimming gear, the DH.51 was without doubt the forerunner of the later Moth series.

The company was convinced that privately owned aircraft should be able to climb easily out of small fields

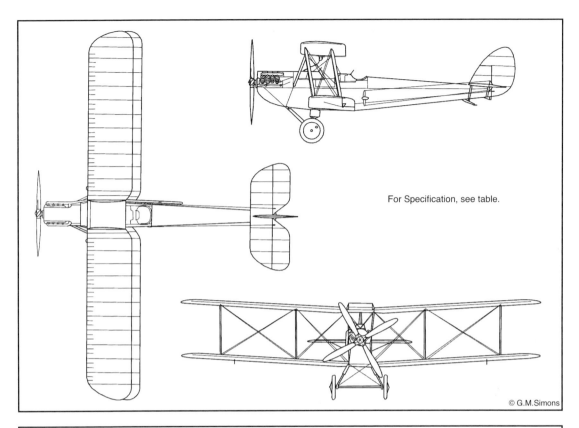

For Specification, see table.

© G.M.Simons

	DH.51		DH.51A	DH.51B
Engine:	90hp RAF1A	120 hp Airdisco		
Span:	37 feet 0 inches	37 feet 0 inches	32 feet 0 inches	37 feet 0 inches
Length:	26 feet 6 inches	26 feet 6 inches	26 feet 6 inches	29 feet 2 inches
Height:	9 feet 9 inches	9 feet 9 inches	9 feet 7½ inches	11 feet 0 inches
Wing area:	325 square feet	325 square feet	296 square feet	325 square feet
Tare Weight:	1312 pounds	1342 pounds	1437 pounds	-
All Up Weight:	2240 pounds	2240 pounds	2240 pounds	2240 pounds
Max Speed:	94 mph	108 mph	105 mph	100 mph
Cruising speed:	80 mph	-	-	-
Initial climb:	580 ft/min	960 ft/min	-	550 ft/min
Ceiling:	13000 feet	15000 feet	-	12000 feet
Range:	360 miles	-	-	-

and by fitting an eight feet nine inch four bladed wooden propeller, a rate of climb of 580 feet per minute was achieved - more than twice that of the little DH.53 flown in the Lympne Trials. The DH.51 was built as a three seater with the pilot in the rear cockpit for best possible view and two passengers in tandem in front. Ease of access to the front cockpit was achieved by leaving out the port centre section incidence wires and by raking the rear struts backward to permit the fitting of a downward hinging door, that was to become a well known feature of the Moth series. A curved sliding deck, first used on the DH.37, carried the windscreen for each cockpit and when seated, the pilot could pull it towards him to reduce draughts. In the fully forward position the adjustable decking to the front cockpit allowed for two passengers, the front one on a canvas seat and the rear with dual control. When flown as a two seater the decking slid back to form a cockpit of normal size. Fuel was carried in a 30 gallon centre section tank which gave a range of 360 miles at cruising speed.

Capt. Geoffrey de Havilland made the first flight in the prototype DH.51 on 1 July 1924 but in spite of the fact that the R.A.F. 1A engine had been a product of the Royal Aircraft Establishment, the airworthiness department of the Air Ministry would not grant a certificate of airworthiness because it had single ignition.

This was a serious flaw for although produced as an aircraft engine, the Air Ministry would not recognise the RAF 1A as suitable for use in a civilian aeroplane - even the D.H. modification to double the system did not satisfy the authorities. And even if De Havilland succeeded in getting the engine type-approved, any owner of the aeroplane so equipped would then be required to find a ground engineer to look after it who had this engine on his licence.

Clearly this was an untenable restriction and,

G-EBIM, the prototype DH.51 in flight...

...and on the ground. It was later modified into a DH51A, with single-bay wings and full-span, camber-changing flaps. *(author's collection)*

the DH.51. It was a clear-cut case against taking advantage of the cheap engine and DH had to buy and fit the Airdisco engine. While the engine gave the machine an even better performance, the higher price stifled demand and only two more were ordered. The first of these, the green and silver G-EBIQ, was delivered to Air Commodore J. G. Weir in time for the King's Cup Race of 3 July 1925.

In August 1928 the aircraft was acquired by Taxiplanes Ltd. of Clevedon, Somerset, becoming a well known joy riding machine at Brean Down near Weston-super-Mare and at other west country resorts. L. G. Anderson, bought it in June 1931 and its career came to an end at Hanworth a year of so later.

During August 1924, the prototype was

although the engines were cheap enough to acquire, De Havilland saw that access to large numbers of low-cost but non-approved engines was, while at first sight commercially attractive, would ultimately prove to be a negative move in the light aircraft business.

The alternative was the 120 hp Airdisco offering more power for a considerable weight-saving. This was a war surplus 80 h.p. Renault modernised by Maj. Frank B. Halford of the Aircraft Disposal Co. Ltd., Croydon, to incorporate redesigned cylinder heads and valve gear which raised the power output. Selecting this removed the one major selling point of

modified in order to fit the De Havilland-designed camber-changing flaps as first tried on the DH.50. These worked automatically and were spring-loaded to extend downwards when the aircraft was at rest. As flying speed increased, they would gradually retract under the load of the accelerating airflow. On landing, the reverse would occur and they would gradually go down as speeds lowered. To take this installation, the aircraft was equipped with new shorter-span single-bay wings to which the 83 square feet of flaps were attached. It was first flown in this condition as the DH.51A on 8 November 1924 and in the following year

G-EBIQ fitted with an Airdisco engine when in use by Taxiplanes. The machine is seen in its joyriding field at Brean Down, Weston-super-Mare in 1929.

was sold to Flying Officer G. E. F. Boyes. Later it was equipped with twin wooden floats and operated as the only DH.51B.

It was disposed of to the Golden Aviation Co. for pleasure flying at Mascot Aerodrome, Sydney, but in 1929 new owners A. S. Elkin and R. F. Walker fitted twin wooden floats and it flew as the sole DH.51B until engine trouble forced it to alight and overturn in Sydney Harbour in 1931.

The third and last DH.51 *Miss Kenya,* was built in 1925 for John Carberry and, devoid of its allotted markings G-EBIR, was shipped to Mombasa on 17 September 1925. After covering the last stage to the owner's property at Nyeri by ox cart it was first flown by Carberry on April 1926. His longest recorded flight was from Nairobi to Kisumu and back in February 1927 to pick up the Director of Civil Aviation, Sir Sefton Brancker, southbound from Khartoum in the borrowed Fairey IIID of North Sea Aerial and General Transport Co. Ltd.

In June 1928 Tom Campbell Black, G. Skinner and A. Hughes bought the machine and took it to Rumuriti and on 10 September it became G-KAA, the first aircraft on the Kenya register, but was not repainted until the present day system of Colonial registrations was instituted and it became VP-KAA on 3 January 1929. From 1933 until 1939 'AA was owned by G. A. G. Onslow at Kisumu but did not fly after the C. of`A. expired on 11 May 1937. During the war it was dismantled and stored at Eastleigh, Nairobi, by ground

engineer G. F. Baudet who re-erected and flew it after the war. He presented it to the Royal Air Force, but wrote off the undercarriage and inflicted other damage when landing at Eastleigh in gusty conditions at the end of the ferrying flight from Nairobi West in June 1951. The aircraft remained semi-derelict in a hangar until late 1954 when it was acquired by J. S. Le Poer Trench, who reconstructed it with the help of A.R.B. surveyor J. A. Johnstone and East African Airways. engineer A. Watkins. The veteran flew again in 1955 and was displayed statically and in the air at many local air displays. On January 7-8 January 1956 it attended the Kitale Air Display, afterwards making the longest flight of its career 220 miles nonstop home to Nairobi, where it was kept at Wilson Field, preserved with a current C. of A. as the oldest airworthy design of the de Havilland Aircraft Co. Ltd.

In July 1965 VP-KAA was airfreighted to Hatfield in an Royal Air Force Beverley and handed over to the Shuttleworth Trust for whom the airframe was stripped down and rebuilt to airworthy standards by Hawker Siddeley apprentices at Hawarden, Chester. The Airdisco engine was sent to Leavesden in 1967 for complete overhaul by apprentices at the Rolls-Royce small engine division. Carrying registration G-EBIR for the first time, it was restored to Shuttleworth trustee, Air Commodore Alan H. Wheeler, who made the first post-restoration flight at Old Warden on 15 March 1973. It remains there to this day.

DH.52

The 1922 *Daily Mail* £1,000 Gliding Competition, held at Itford on the Sussex Downs, attracted thirty five entries from home and abroad, two being De Havilland DH.52 single seat machines. Built in September-October 1922, they were wire braced monoplanes with an aspect ratio of 11 to 1, considerable ingenuity having been exercised to achieve maximum economy in weight. The fuselage was of typical De Havilland construction but miniaturised, consisting of a box structure made up of thin spruce longerons and cross struts covered with 1 mm. plywood. This was surmounted by a light cambric covered fairing round the cockpit. The triangular section decking aft of the wing was made by stretching the same material over a cable tightly

stretched between the wing mounting and the tail. Wing bracing was attached to a kingpost and differential ailerons were fitted. The designers expected elevator control to be sluggish at the low air speeds involved and gave the elevators 90 degrees of upward and downward movement using simple leather hinges. A cross axle undercarriage of light steel tubing carried small wheels and the cockpit was fitted with but one instrument—an air speed indicator calibrated down to 10 m.p.h.

Both DH.52s were finished with clear dope flying surfaces and black fuselages, the first one being test flown at Stag Lane by Capt. Geoffrey de Havilland, Hubert Broad and Alan Cobham between 5-7 October 1922. Initial trials established the landing speed at 18 m.p.h., after which the V undercarriage was replaced by a simple wheeled axle anchored to the bottom longerons by shock absorber cord, and the angle of

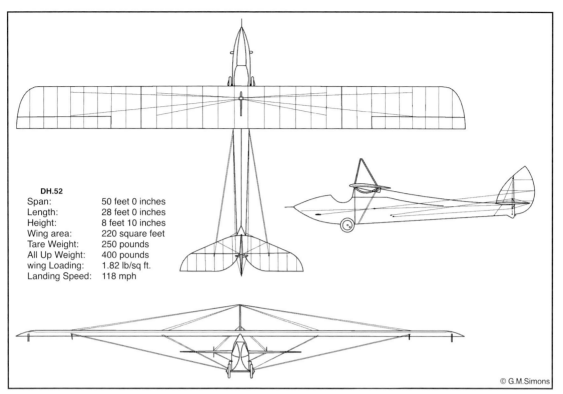

DH.52

Span:	50 feet 0 inches
Length:	28 feet 0 inches
Height:	8 feet 10 inches
Wing area:	220 square feet
Tare Weight:	250 pounds
All Up Weight:	400 pounds
wing Loading:	1.82 lb/sq ft.
Landing Speed:	118 mph

© G.M.Simons

incidence of the wing was increased. The second DH.52 was completed with both these modifications and the two machines, delivered to Itford by road on 15 October, were erected inside a large marquee. The first, *Sibylla*, entered by the de Havilland company and flown by Hubert Broad, received the competition number 4 and the second, *Margon*, entered and flown by E. D. C. Herne, was numbered 33.

Broad was catapulted from Beddingham Hill by a team of men with a rubber rope at midday on 16 October and in a flight lasting 2 minutes 18 seconds, gained a considerable altitude but damaged the glider in landing. Twenty minutes later Herne bettered this performance with a flight of 2 minutes 38 seconds but ran into a hedge and damaged the machine. Both flights revealed flexibility in the wing structure which twisted under load and neutralised the effect of the ailerons. By the 19th, Herne's aircraft had been repaired

and to obtain better lateral control in the limited time available, had been converted to wing warping. The aircraft was launched just to the north of Itford but immediately the tow rope dropped off, the wing commenced uncontrolled warping which led to its sudden failure outboard of the centre section at an altitude of 20-30 ft. Fortunately the wreck fell to earth on an even keel and the pilot escaped with a shaking but after the accident it was suggested that although the mainplane had a factor of safety of 8 it was far too flexible for ailerons, let alone warp control. There were no further flights and the two DH.52 gliders were scrapped.

In April 1923 drawings were prepared for a 37 feet 8 inches span, tandem two seat glider similar to the DH.53 Humming Bird which was to follow. This project, also designated DH.52, was not proceeded with.

Sibylla, the first DH.52 seen airborne during initial flight trials at Stag Lane with strutted undercarriage. On the original print there appears to be a pair of ropes dangling from below the aircraft, possibly the tow-rope still attached. *(DH via BAe Hatfield)*

The second DH.52 named *Margon* is seen airborne with the strutless undercarriage. *(DH via BAe Hatfield)*

DH.53 Humming Bird

The DH.53 was a small, low wing, single seat monoplane built for the *Daily Mail* Light Aircraft Trials at Lympne in October 1923 and was the first light aeroplane produced by the De Havilland Company.

The main structural features of larger machines were retained, the fuselage consisting of spruce longerons and cross struts covered with plywood while the fabric covered mainplane was of the standard two spar type but thickened at points where it was braced to the top longerons by wooden V struts.

Two identical prototypes, *Humming Bird* owned by the company and *Sylvia II* by Alan S. Butler, were piloted in the competitions by D.H. test pilot Hubert Broad and Major Harold Hemming respectively.

The 750 c.c. Douglas motor cycle engine fitted to both machines were a constant source of trouble and neither aircraft won a prize but Major Hemming's achievement in covering 59.3 miles on one gallon of petrol and Broad's loops and rolls, a feat never before performed on so small an aircraft, proved them the most practical machines present at the trials.

On its return to Stag Lane, the competition engine in *Humming Bird* was replaced by a small aero engine of proven reliability, the 26 h.p. Tomtit inverted V, two cylinder engine manufactured by Burney and Blackburne Engines Ltd. of Bookham, Surrey. The unsatisfactory bungee shock absorbers were at the same time replaced by miniature rubber-in-compression units. The standard fuel capacity of two gallons was also increased by an extra fuel tank in the form of a streamlined headrest fitted behind the cockpit to enable the machine to fly to Brussels for exhibition at the Aero Show, for which purpose it was re-christened *L'Oiseau Mouche.*

Now lettered G-EBHX, it left Stag Lane on 8 December 1923 piloted by Alan J. Cobham and after stops at Croydon and Lympne made a non-stop flight of 150 miles direct to the Belgian capital in a flying time of 4 hours with a fuel cost of just 10 shillings.

The unpainted prototype DH.53 at Stag Lane on the day of it's first flight. The engine is the 750 cc Douglas flat-twin. *(DH via BAe Hatfield)*

With the new engine it was no longer the hesitant ultra light and again piloted by Cobham, came eighth at 67.35 m.p.h. in the 1924 Grosvenor Trophy Race at Lympne and took part with varying success in all the 1925 races, in which it was joined by the second prototype, now lettered G-EBHZ. This had been sold less engine in May 1925 to a group of seven ofiicers at R.A.F. Eastchurch who flew as the Seven Aero Club. With financial help from Lord Edward Grosvenor, a 35 horsepower ABC Scorpion driving a Fairey-Reed metal propeller was fitted.

The Scorpion blew a cylinder while racing at Lympne on 1 August 1925 and 'HZ ended on its nose in a wheat field but was soon repaired and flown again at the Bournemouth Summer Meeting during 21-22 August 1926 and in the Grosvenor Challenge Cup Race at Lympne on 18 September, after which it was sold, probably as spares.

It was not long before the Air Ministry became interested in the Tomtit engined DH.53 and awarded De Havillands a contract for eight aircraft with the type name Humming Bird under Specification D. of R. 44/23. They were laid down at Stag Lane in March 1924 for communications and cheap practice flying, their permitted military load being seven pounds! One machine, J7272, was shown in the New Types Park at the Hendon Display on 28 June 1924 prior to delivery to Northolt the same evening. Three others were issued to C.F.S. Upavon, two to RAF Netheravon and two to

Farnborough for experimental use. An order for two DH.53s was placed also by the Controller of Civil Aviation, Australia, the batch of 12 being completed by one for the Avia concern in Prague and one which Alan S. Butler sent to Australia. Almost a year later a 13th machine was built to Russian order in accordance with the Soviet practice of acquiring single examples of the world's best aircraft.

The two Humming Birds for the Australian civil aviation authorities were despatched by sea in time for the Light Aeroplane Competition held at Essendon Aerodrome, Melbourne, from 29 November to 6 December 1924 in which one of them, piloted by Capt. E. J. Jones, forced landed so many times in the same field that it became known as Jones's Paddock.

The same aeroplane was flown without success by Squadron Leader Anderson in the Australian Aerial Derby held at Richmond Aerodrome, Sydney during 1925 but both machines enjoyed long careers which included service with the Aero Club of New South Wales. In the early '30s one was fitted with an ABC Scorpion engine and in 1937 was shipped to Samoa.

The purpose of the third Australian DH.53, c/n 118 remains obscure and it appears in neither civil nor R.A.A.F. records. It was acquired in wrecked condition by Dr. R. J. Coto in 1937. He rebuilt it from data, spruce, fabric and metal air-mailed by de Havillands, fitted a 40 h.p. Aeronca engine bought secondhand in England and named it *Icarus*. With a 17 gallon fuel tank behind

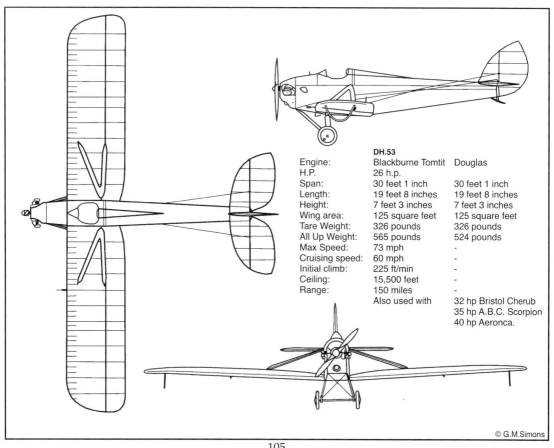

DH.53		
Engine:	Blackburne Tomtit	Douglas
H.P.	26 h.p.	
Span:	30 feet 1 inch	30 feet 1 inch
Length:	19 feet 8 inches	19 feet 8 inches
Height:	7 feet 3 inches	7 feet 3 inches
Wing area:	125 square feet	125 square feet
Tare Weight:	326 pounds	326 pounds
All Up Weight:	565 pounds	524 pounds
Max Speed:	73 mph	-
Cruising speed:	60 mph	-
Initial climb:	225 ft/min	-
Ceiling:	15,500 feet	-
Range:	150 miles	-
Also used with		32 hp Bristol Cherub
		35 hp A.B.C. Scorpion
		40 hp Aeronca.

© G.M.Simons

A delightful picture of DH.53 '12' in a two-tone paint scheme with clear doped flying surfaces at the Lympne Trials. Unfortunately, the aircraft name is not readable. *(DH via BAe Hatfield)*

the cockpit he astounded the world in May 1937 by flying 1,950 miles from Wyndham to Perth, W.A in 61 days in an airborne time of 30 hours 5 minutes. Its hulk was burned at Perth in 1964.

The eleventh production DH.53 was despatched to Prague in June 1924 where it was ably demonstrated by Hubert Broad during the flying meeting which followed the Aero Exhibition. It was then sold to the Avia company for comparative flight trials with their own, similar, Avia B.H.l6.

The first six DH.53s for the RAF, serialled J7268-J7273, made their public debut when they took off together at the start of the race between the Air Ministry Directorates at the RAF Display held at Hendon on 27 June 1925. They were thrown round the turning points of a five mile course to Mill Hill and back and it was said that the six Tomtit engines in unison sounded like desultory hand clapping. Their pilots were later to be famous, the winner being Wing Commander W. Sholto Douglas (later Lord Douglas), representing Equipment. The others in order of finishing were Air Commodore Charles Alexander Holcombe Longcroft, Personnel; Flt Lt William C. Dickson, Intelligence; Flt Lt. M. Thomas, Organisation; Flt Lt. G. M. Bryer, Training (in J7272) and Wing Commander Thomas Reginald Cave-Brown-Cave,

Research and Development (in J7273). In the following November J7272 was towed through the streets of London as part of the Lord Mayor`s Show.

The seventh and eighth Service machines, J7325-6 were specially modified for launching experiments from the airship R-33 piloted by Flt Lt Herbert Carmichael 'Bird' Irwin which left its mast at Pulham, Norfolk on 15 October 1925 carrying J7325 attached to a special trapeze. At an altitude of 3,800 feet, Squadron Leader Rollo de Haga Haig entered the cockpit from a ladder, the trapeze was lowered until the aircraft swung clear and a successful launch made. The DH.53 dived until the engine started, performed two loops and returned to the airship and hooked on. At the end of a second experiment with the same aircraft on 28 October, turbulence near the dirigible's envelope caused the airscrew to foul a supporting wire at the moment of attachment, setting up oscillations which forced the pilot to release and make a forced landing at Sarston. On 4 December the attempt was repeated by the same pilot who successfully re-engaged the trapeze in J7326 and rejoined the airship's crew.

No production DH.53s were sold by the company for private use in the United Kingdom but all eight RAF aircraft were registered as civil machines when they were struck off Service charge in 1927 and six

G-EBHX, now fitted with a Blackburne Tomtit engine of 26 horsepower and an extra fuel tank aft of the pilots seat for Alan Cobham's Croydon to Brussels flight. *(DH via BAe Hatfield)*

J7325 fitted with the airship pickup gear. It had been fitted with the rudder of its compatriot machine whilst its own was away for repair. *(DH via BAe Hatfield)*

were granted certificates of airworthiness. Several were made airworthy by P. G. N. Peters and his colleagues at the Royal Aircraft Establishment Aero Club, Farnborough. G-EBRW appeared in 1929 after `Freddy` Gough had flown it for two years at the Norfolk and Norwich Aero Club, G-EBXN was flown during 1928-32 and G-EBQP during 1927-28. 'QP had been J7326 during its airship career but was fitted with a 32 horsepower Bristol Cherub III during its civil life. This began on August Bank Holiday 1927 when Flying Officer McKenzie Richards came third in the Nottingham Air Race and ended when an unlicensed pilot stalled at sixty feet and killed himself at Hamble on 21 July 1934.

The other DH.53. which had successfully attached itself to the R-33. was acquired in crashed condition in April 1928 by Farnborough technician K. V. Wright, by whom it was rebuilt and sold to Capt. A. V. C. Douglas

at Bekesbourne in 1929.

Longest lived of the remaining DH.53s were 'RW flown at Broxbourne in 1933 by R. L. Burnett. and the Cherub engined 'XN, the last of whose seven owners was E. D. Ward at Hooton in 1938. Most flown of all Humming Birds, it was a familiar sight in its day at all the club aerodromes in the United Kingdom. The ultimate fate of many DH.53s is obscure, but it is known that one was converted into the RAE Scarab at Farnborough 1930-32, another was reconstructed as the Martin Monoplane at Denham in 1937. the year in which a third was in the possession of R. J. Coley and Co. Ltd., scrap merchants at Hounslow, Middlesex. This is thought to have been resurrected at Brooklands by students of the College of Aeronautical Engineering and flown by Capt. Duncan Davis in July 1936.

The only airworthy specimen for many years was prototype G-EBHX, which had been operated by F. J. V. Holmes of Berkshire Aviation Tours before passing into the hands of E. W. Kennett at Walmer, Kent. After a lapse of almost 20 years it was rediscovered in 1955 in the back garden of a house in Eastrey, Kent. by Sqn. Ldr. L. A. Jackson of the Shuttleworth Trust. Only the fuselage, mainplane, port aileron

Above: G-EBQP, the former J3726, was the second airship machine and was re-engined with a Cherub II.

Right: VH-UAC, the first of the Australian DH.53s with the cut-back fuselage to accomodate the 35 hp ABC Scorpion engine.*(both author's collection)*

Seen during happier times at Old Warden, G-EBHX *Le Oiseau-Mouche* awaits its turn to display. *(author)*

and the undercarriage remained but although none of the original drawings existed. the missing engine mounting, tail unit. controls and tanks were designed and built at the De Havilland Technical School. Powered by an ABC Scorpion engine. 'HX made its first flight after rebuild at Hatfield on 4 August 1960 piloted by DH. test pilot Christopher A. Capper. Handling trials, development flying and performance measurements followed, the aircraft was handed over to the Shuttleworth Trust to be housed in airworthy condition at Old Warden. Beds. It crashed at Old Warden at 0842 hours on 1 July 2012 when, according to the AAIB Bulletin: 3/2013 *'The pilot lost control of the aircraft in gusty wind conditions during a re-familiarisation flight. There was insufficient height in which to recover and the aircraft impacted the ground, causing the pilot to receive fatal injuries'.*

The aircraft wreckage was placed in store for a possible eventual rebuild. Some other DH.53 parts survive, including the fuselage of J7326, which is on display at the de Havilland Aircraft Heritage Centre.

DH.54 Highclere

In 1924 it became clear there was a need for a larger successor to the DH.34, and this was designed to Air Ministry Specification 40/22. Although structurally similar to its predecessor, the DH.54 Highclere carried the upper mainplane on centre section struts and was rigged with dihedral on the lower mainplane only, resulting in a marked reduction in gap towards the wing tips. Two crew occupied an open cockpit forward of the wings and twelve passengers were carried in four single seats on the starboard, or door, side with eight in double seats to port in the cabin. The aircraft was powered by a 650 h.p. Rolls-Royce Condor IIIA mounted as a detachable power plant with internal radiator and controlled cooling.

Talks between De Havillands, DH.34 operators and pilots led to the incorporation of several new features. Criticism having been levelled at the DH.34 on account of its high landing speed, the DH.54 was equipped with full span, automatic camber-changing flaps. The undercarriage used rubber-in-compression shock absorbers and could be jettisoned to facilitate a smooth alighting on water in the event of engine failure. The bottom of the fuselage and the cabin door were also made watertight. Large area sliding windows were retained, but the luggage was housed in a special hold underneath the pilot's cockpit to allow for a toilet to be fitted in the rear fuselage.

Hot air for cabin heating was drawn from a muff round an exhaust pipe and a Bristol gas starter was

The DH.54 fuselage under construction at Stag Lane. *(DH via BAe Hatfield)*

Hubert Broad gave passenger flights and other demonstrations at the Lympne Bank Holiday race meeting, causing considerable amusement by racing with a full complement of passengers against Alan Cobham in a Moth and just winning at an average speed of 103.4 m.p.h.

fitted to the Condor because of the impossibility of hand-swinging the fourteen foot diameter, paired four bladed, wooden propeller. The prototype, built to Air Council order, made its first flight at Stag Lane piloted by Hubert Broad on 28 May 1925. Few teething troubles were experienced and after familiarisation flights by RAE test pilots at Hendon on 25-26 June the machine made its public debut on the 27th in the New Types Park at the Hendon Display, where it was announced that it was to be evaluated on the cross Channel services of Imperial Airways Ltd. Manufacturer's trials continued during the rest of 1925 and on 31 July Captain Geoffrey de Havilland flew the Maharajah of Jodhpur and his polo team from Stag Lane to Croydon in it. Next day

After the Martlesham Heath Trials the following year the DH.54 was issued a full certificate of airworthiness but by that time Imperial Airways Ltd. had announced that in future, passengers would only be carried in multi-engined aircraft. On 7 March 1926 the DH.54 was flown from Martlesham to Farnborough, where it was allocated initially by the Acoustics Section, probably on sound locating experiments, and later for tests on its automatic wing flap mechanism. On 9 November it was transferred to Croydon for use on Imperial Airways freight services. Between 5 and 17 May Hubert Broad took it to Berck and Paris and back but

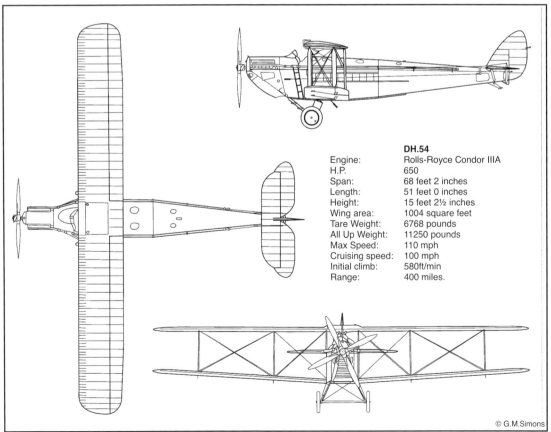

DH.54

Engine:	Rolls-Royce Condor IIIA
H.P.	650
Span:	68 feet 2 inches
Length:	51 feet 0 inches
Height:	15 feet 2½ inches
Wing area:	1004 square feet
Tare Weight:	6768 pounds
All Up Weight:	11250 pounds
Max Speed:	110 mph
Cruising speed:	100 mph
Initial climb:	580ft/min
Range:	400 miles.

© G.M.Simons

A detailled view of the engine and cockpit area of the DH.54. The height above the ground and restricted access over the exhaust into the cockpit - forcing the somewhat precarious use of a ladder and assorted hand-holds - is particularly noticable. (DH via BAe Hatfield)

forced landed at Le Touquet, and on his return flew it over to Farnborough.

A planned possible conversion to carry three twenty feet by thirteen inch diameter steel water pipes under the designation of DH.54A was considered. The door would have been enlarged to facilitate loading and three strengthened frames fitted with suitable hoists in the cabin structure were to have been installed on a strengthened floor. The conversion was never made and plans to use it as a freighter ended abruptly on 1 February 1927 when its hangar at Croydon collapsed during a heavy snowstorm. This worthy but outmoded prototype was damaged beyond repair.

DH.55

This was a design for a seven-passenger transport aircraft based on the DH.54, powered by a trio of 120 hp Airdisco air cooled engines. No detailed design has been located and the aircraft was not built.

DH.56 Hyena

The DH.56 was a two seater developed from the all metal DH.42B Dingo II to meet Army Co-Operation Specification 33/26.

It was first flown by Hubert Broad on 17 May 1925. The Hyena was similar to the Dingo and featured the well known De Havilland rudder shape, differential ailerons, ball bearing controls and rubber-in-compression undercarriage. It was powered by a 385 h.p. Armstrong Siddeley Jaguar III, two row, aircooled radial engine driving a two bladed wooden propeller equipped with Hucks starter claw. The engine was partially covered with a close fitting cowling which extended rearwards to fair it into the flat sides of the front fuselage. The unequal span wings, narrow chord lower mainplane and splayed out interplane struts of the

The prototype DH.56 Hyena J7780, fitted with the Armstrong Siddeley Jaguar III of 385 horsepower. The message hook gear is visible under the fuselage. (DH via BAe Hatfield)

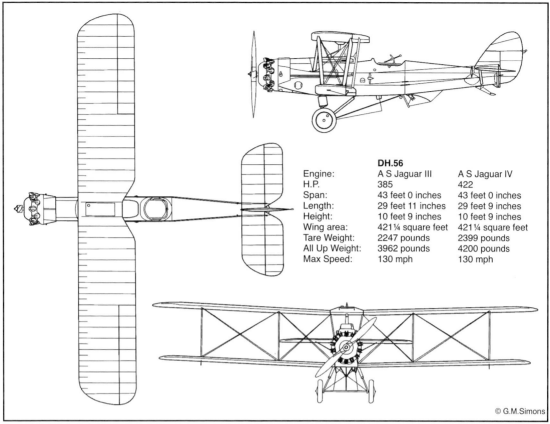

DH.56		
Engine:	A S Jaguar III	A S Jaguar IV
H.P.	385	422
Span:	43 feet 0 inches	43 feet 0 inches
Length:	29 feet 11 inches	29 feet 9 inches
Height:	10 feet 9 inches	10 feet 9 inches
Wing area:	421¼ square feet	421¼ square feet
Tare Weight:	2247 pounds	2399 pounds
All Up Weight:	3962 pounds	4200 pounds
Max Speed:	130 mph	130 mph

© G.M.Simons

Dingo were retained but partial push-rod control was introduced into the aileron circuit and over the tailplane to the elevator. Parasitic drag of wing tanks was eliminated by the simple method of carrying 100 gallons of fuel in the fuselage ahead of the pilot and raising it to the centre section gravity tank by DH wind-driven pump, or in an emergency, by hand pump. Message pick-up gear was sited below the gunner's cockpit and the Hyena was also equipped for artillery spotting, photographic reconnaissance, supply dropping and ground attack, the bombs for which were carried in a rack under the port lower mainplane. Armament

consisted of a synchronised, forward firing Vickers gun with a second gun of the same type on a Scarff mounting.

Two Hyenas were built, the first of which was shown in the New Types Park at the Hendon Display on 3 July 1926, but before it went to Martlesham, an uncowled Jaguar IV engine of 422 h.p. was fitted, complete with Bristol gas starter and a neat circular manifold with long exhaust pipes. The second Hyena, ready for test flight by 29 June 1926, was exactly similar to the first in its modified condition with uncowled Jaguar IV and long exhausts and was delivered to Farnborough by

The same aircraft. but now fitted swith the uncowled Jaguar IV engine.
(DH via BAe Hatfield)

The second prototype DH.56 Hyena J7781 fitted with the long exhaust pipes required for the Jaguar IV engine. *(DH via BAe Hatfield)*

Broad on 8 August 1926.

After competitive trials between the second Hyena J7781 and the Armstrong Whitworth Atlas, Bristol Boarhound and Vickers Vespa prototypes at the A&AEE Martlesham Heath, all four were ferried to Manston for assessment by 2 Army Co-operation Squadron. J7781 arrived on 19 August 1926, to be put through its paces by Flying Officer Alan H. Wheeler and others before being flown to the School of Army Co-Operation at Old Sarum, and later to Andover, Odiham and 4 Army Co-Operation Squadron, based at Farnborough, for Service evaluation alongside its competitors which led to the production contract being awarded to the Atlas.

Hyena J7781 operated in field exercises performed by O.T.C. cadets in camp at Tidworth Park, and in September 1927 was transferred to the RAE Engine Flight, Farnborough, where tests on its exhaust system were still in progress in May 1928.

DH.57

This was a twelve passenger, two crew airliner, similar to the DH.55, but powered by three Siddeley Puma engines of 230 horsepower each. The DH.57 would have looked similar to the DH.54 Highclere with the addition of wing engines on the lower mainplanes outboard of the undercarriage. Span 70 feet 0 inches, Length 53 feet 6 inches, Wing area 1280 square feet. All-up-weight 11,500 pounds.

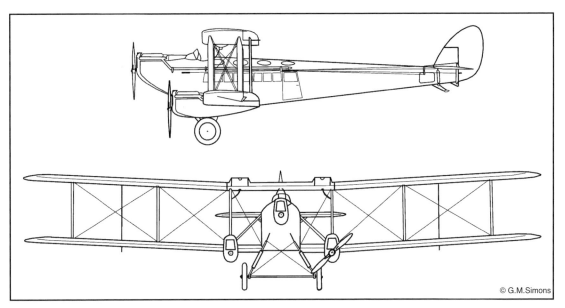

© G.M.Simons

DH.58

This type number was allocated to a transport aircraft design intended to be a scaled up version of the DH.57 for twenty passengers and two crew.

It was to be powered by three Napier Lion engines each of 450 horsepower, one in the nose, and a pair in underslung nacelles on the lower mainplanes. Span 103 feet 0 inches, Length 68 feet 6 inches, Wing area 2150 square feet. All-up-weight 21,500 pounds.

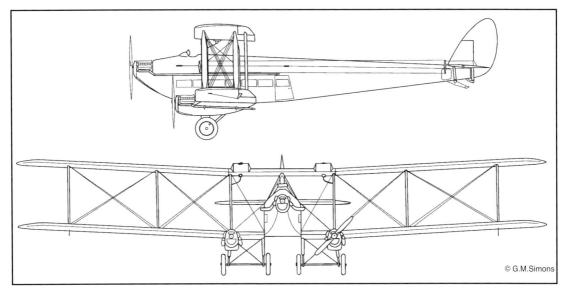

© G.M.Simons

DH.59

A designation allocated to a design study for a transport aircraft that was not proceeded with.

DH.60 Moth

After the 1923 Lympne Trials Captain Geoffrey de Havilland recognised that none of the entries from his company or any other would make the ideal club or private aeroplane of the future. Breaking completely away from contemporary concepts, the Stag Lane team built a scaled down version of the DH.51 as a two seat light biplane capable of withstanding the hard knocks of instructional work, large enough and comfortable enough for cross country flying, and powered by a reliable engine.

The result was a family of machines known the world over as 'Moths' - a type name given in deference to Geoffrey de Havilland's reputation as a lepidopterist.

The DH.60
Key to the new design was a new engine, specially designed by Major Frank B. Halford of the Aircraft Disposal Co. Ltd. using one half of the firm's 120 h.p.

Airdisco 8 cylinder V type engine, mounted on a new crank case and giving 60 h.p. for a weight of 290 pounds. The engine was christened Cirrus I and the aircraft, designated DH.60.

The simplicity of the design was a revelation. The fuselage was a plywood box built round four square section spruce longerons, with the flat sides and bottom stiffened by vertical and horizontal cross members screwed to the plywood.

Two occupants sat in tandem, the front cockpit being fitted with a generous luggage shelf under the decking. The engine was bolted to the top longerons in an elevated position where the cylinders protruded prominently from the close fitting cowling. There was no oil tank, the 1½ gallons required being carried in the engine sump. The centre section, built up of four vertical and two sloping, streamlined section hollow steel struts, supported a 15 gallon fuel tank of aerofoil section. Rear undercarriage legs of a new design were in the form of telescopic tubes sprung by rubber blocks in compression, anchored vertically below the front

The prototype DH.60 G-EBKT in flight, with unbalanced rudder, and starboard-fitted exhaust pipe and unpainted control surfaces. This famous picture shows Alan Cobham leaving Stag Lane en-route to Croydon and Zurich on 29 May 1925.
(DH via BAe Hatfield)

G-EBLV was one of the so-called DH60 Cirrus Moths, with the engine exhaust on the port side of the machine. This aircraft still survives at the time of writing. *(DH via BAe Hatfield)*

centre section struts with radius rods forward to the foot of the fireproof bulkhead. A pair of large diameter wheels with high pressure tyres were fitted to a straight steel axle.

Wing construction comprised of spindled 'I' section spruce bars with built up ribs and rounded wing tips of slightly flattened aluminium tube, the whole structure being fabric covered. A single bay layout employing wide chord interplane struts, was rigidly braced by streamline wires. For ease of hangarage, the wings folded about the rear spar to reduce overall width to nine feet eight inches, the same as the tailplane. Wing folding was via spring loaded quick release bolts in the root end fitting of the front spar and the insertion of a temporary jury strut to support the inner end of the wing cellule. Differential ailerons were fitted to the lower mainplane, the rudder was unbalanced and full dual control was installed. A tail trimming lever on the left

varied the amount of assistance given to elevator control by a spring under the rear seat. Instruments were reduced to bare essentials and twin brass household-type, tumbler-ignition switches were mounted externally.

The first flight of the Moth prototype G-EBKT was made by Capt. Geoffrey de Havilland at Stag Lane on 22 February 1925. Its performance on low power became the benchmark for light aeroplanes for several decades. Enthusiastic efforts by Sir Sefton Brancker, the Director of Civil Aviation, led to the founding of five Air Ministry subsidised flying clubs. The first club Moth G-EBLR was delivered to the Lancashire Aero Club, Woodford, by Alan Cobham on 21 July 1925 and

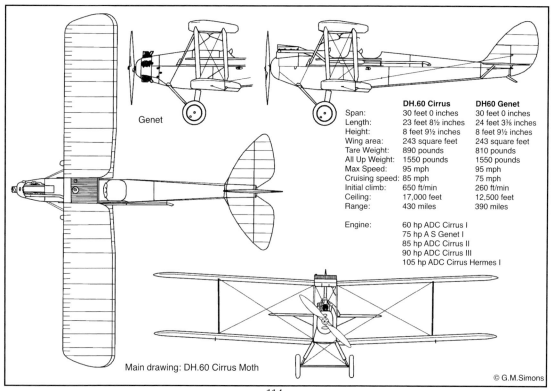

Genet

	DH.60 Cirrus	DH60 Genet
Span:	30 feet 0 inches	30 feet 0 inches
Length:	23 feet 8½ inches	24 feet 3⅜ inches
Height:	8 feet 9½ inches	8 feet 9½ inches
Wing area:	243 square feet	243 square feet
Tare Weight:	890 pounds	810 pounds
All Up Weight:	1550 pounds	1550 pounds
Max Speed:	95 mph	95 mph
Cruising speed:	85 mph	75 mph
Initial climb:	650 ft/min	260 ft/min
Ceiling:	17,000 feet	12,500 feet
Range:	430 miles	390 miles

Engine:	60 hp ADC Cirrus I
	75 hp A S Genet I
	85 hp ADC Cirrus II
	90 hp ADC Cirrus III
	105 hp ADC Cirrus Hermes I

Main drawing: DH.60 Cirrus Moth

© G.M.Simons

Right: DH60A Moth J-8031 for the RAF.
(DH via BAe Hatfield)

Left: A pair of DH60 Moth seaplanes - G-EBUJ and G-AADK - of the Singapore Flying Club. Both machines has been fitted with locally installed Hermes I engines.
(John Stride Collection)

he ferried the eighth, G-EBLV, to them on 29 August.

The London Aeroplane Club, Newcastle Aero Club, the Midland Aero Club and the Lancashire Aero Club were each allotted two Moths and two more went to the Yorkshire Aeroplane Club, the first of which was ferried to Sherburn-in-Elmet by R. W. Kenworthy during a memorable summer which saw the birth of the British flying club movement.

On 29 May 1925 the type made headline news when Alan Cobham flew 'KT 1,000 miles from Croydon to Zurich and back in a day. By the end of the year the first private Moths had been sold and evaluation orders were received from the Controller of Civil Aviation, Australia, and the RAAF. Another Moth was exported to Chile.

Twenty were built in 1925 but 1926 models, commencing with the Air Ministry's Moth J8030, were fitted with a locker behind the rear cockpit instead of the front luggage shelf. During 1926 thirty-five Moths of this type were built, including two more for the Air Ministry, fourteen for private owners and flying clubs at home, six for flying clubs in Australia, three for QANTAS, one for Japan, four for the Irish Air Corps and an company exhibition aircraft. Piloted by Hubert Broad, this, the first Moth seaplane, flew from the Medway at Rochester in November 1926 fitted with the all metal twin floats originally fitted to Short Mussel G-EBMJ. Cobham took this aircraft to the USA by sea, where arrangements were being made for Moth production. He flew the last few miles from Sandy Hook to New York, landed in the harbour and later refitted the wheels for demonstration before members of Congress. Another Moth, G-EBNX, flown in England in 1926 by parachute pioneer Leslie Irvin, also went to the USA.

For the 1926 King's Cup Race, Frank Halford produced a developed engine of 85 h.p. for Capt. de Havilland's mount G-EBNO and called it the Cirrus II.

The first production Cirrus II was later fitted to this machine for a 5,540 mile flight to India by T. Neville Stack, who, accompanied by B. S. Leete in the second prototype Moth 'KU, left Croydon on 16 November. They were the first Moths in the sub-Continent and attracted much attention.

To comply with the rules of the 1926 *Daily Mail* trials at Lympne, a special lightweight machine was fitted with a 75 h.p. Armstrong Siddeley Genet I radial. It was flown by Hubert Broad, who was disqualified, but as G-EBOU it competed in several club races.

There was a 1927 model of the Moth having reduced gap and a one foot increase in span. It was also fitted with a Cirrus II engine to improve payload and cruising speed but the thrust line of the engine was lowered to decrease drag and improve forward view by bringing the cylinder heads more into line with the fuselage decking. These modifications were first made to G-EBNP under the designation DH.60X, although production machines, commencing G-EBPM, were known simply as Cirrus II Moths, some 150 of which were delivered in 1927.

One of the first, G-EBPP, was shipped to Perth, Western Australia, by Major Hereward de Havilland who flew it across the continent to Melbourne and there rented a shed in Whiteman Street in which to assemble imported Moths. G-AUFT, supplied to the *Sydney Sun* for the distribution of pictures of the opening of the city of Canberra, was the first of eighteen erected in 1927 and was towed through the streets to be test flown at Essendon Aerodrome before delivery to the clubs, the Bush Church Aid Society, West Australian Airways and other purchasers.

The first aeroplane registered in Portugal was Cirrus II Moth C-PAAA, delivered via Croydon on 9

Seaplanes both!

Above: Hubert Broad flying the DH.60 Moth sent to the USA as a demonstrator. The aircraft, construction number 273, was fitted with twin floats from the Short Mussel at Rochester, Kent during November 1926.

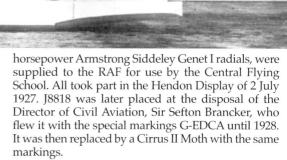

Right: A Finnish DH.60 Moth, MO-97, one of ten machines built by Valtion Leutokonetehdas, Helsinki in 1929. A further twelve were built in 1930.
(both John Stride Collection)

August 1927 to Senor Carlos Bleck, who flew it from Lisbon to Portuguese West Africa in January 1928.

The British civil market absorbed fifty Cirrus II Moths that year and the famous Moth garages could be rented from De Havillands at Stag Lane. One aircraft, G-EBQJ, originally a seaplane, was sold to D. M. M. Rooke, who left Croydon on 24 May to fly to Australia as a bet. The new model won its first laurels on 5 July when Lady Bailey established a new light aeroplane altitude record of 17,283 ft. over Stag Lane in G-EBQH. Others made pioneer long distance flights.

Six machines, numbered J8816-21, with 75 horsepower Armstrong Siddeley Genet I radials, were supplied to the RAF for use by the Central Flying School. All took part in the Hendon Display of 2 July 1927. J8818 was later placed at the disposal of the Director of Civil Aviation, Sir Sefton Brancker, who flew it with the special markings G-EDCA until 1928. It was then replaced by a Cirrus II Moth with the same markings.

United States Navy Requisition No. Aero 238 for the Fiscal Year 1927, records that 4,316 dollars were set aside for the purchase of a Moth, serialled 7564, issued to the U.S. Naval Attache in London.

VH-UMK was the ninth and last DH60 Moth built in Australia by General Aircraft Co. It was considerably different to the standard DH.60 with differing fuselage lines, rudder shape and the area surrounding the Cirrus Hermes I engine.
(via John Stride.)

Four were shipped to South Africa to Major A. M. Miller, who assembled the first, G-AUAA, on the dockside at Cape Town and took off from the esplanade to make his historic tour of South Africa, covering 2,300 miles in eight days. Three other Moths were also imported, one each for the East London, Durban and Johannesburg Light Aero Clubs.

Canada welcomed the Cirrus Moth as replacement for its forestry patrol equipment, and in 1927 the Ontario Provincial Government imported the first fitted with float and ski undercarriages and Fairey-Reed metal airscrews. They were erected in De Havilland Aircraft of Canada's first wooden hangar at Mount Dennis, Toronto along with twenty three for the Canadian Ministry of National Defence and one each for Dominion Airways and Western Canada Airways.

Four Moths were sold in the Argentine by Maj. S. G. Kingsley, former pilot of the River Plate Aviation Company and sales were also made in Finland, Germany, New Zealand, Spain and Sweden. The Italian Air Ministry bought two for test purposes, and another was sold to aircraft designer Grover Loening.

In the USA John Carberry won the Speed and Efficiency Prize in his Cirrus II Moth G-EBXP at the Los Angeles Air Meeting in August, afterwards flying north to register the machine in Canada.

More improvements were made in 1928 when the new model, fitted with a new 90 horsepower Cirrus III engine could be easily identified by a split axle - or 'X' - undercarriage. Production at the end of 1928 totalled 403 machines of all variants and by February 1929 De Havillands were building sixteen a week.

Licences were granted to the General Aircraft Co. Ltd. in Australia, the Finnish Government Aircraft Factory and to the Karhumaki Brothers, also in Finland. The Australian machines were known locally as Genairco Moths, the ninth being Hermes powered and considerably modified. Genairco later produced a number of four seat variants officially referred to as Genairco Biplanes but irreverently known as Pregnant Moths. The twenty-two aircraft built for the Finnish Air Force were originally fitted with Cirrus II engines but late production models were Hermes powered.

G-EBXG was used as the trial installation machine by Handley Page Ltd. for the development of automatic slots fitted to most of the later Moths,

Orders for the DH.60X were received from many overseas purchasers of the Cirrus II Moth. They came

G-EBWD was first registered as a DH60X Moth to Richard Ornonde Shuttleworth on 23 January 1932. It is still with the collection. *(via John Stride.)*

first and second in the 1929 Australian Aerial Derby and the Chilean Government took delivery of 24, one being reserved for the use of Senor de Salanca, Director of Civil Aviation.

The first aircraft registered in Southern Rhodesia was a DH.60X and the second, VP-YAB, was used by De Havilland agent J. H. Veasey to run an air mail service in the territory. Capt. de Havilland's original Cirrus II Moth G-EBNO, sold to Aero Material A.B. of Stockholm as SE-ABS in July 1928, was flown to Cape Town and back at the end of 1929 by Swedish pilot Captain Gosta Andree. Elsewhere in Africa G-EBZL was based at Kano, Nigeria and 'ZZ *Ashanti* lived on the Gold Coast to which it had been flown from Stag Lane by Captain R. L. Rattray. Both returned home in 1930 to continue in private and club use with other examples of the type until 1939.

With the delivery of G-AABL to the London Aeroplane Club in September 1928, the DH.60X went out of production in favour of more advanced models but a few were constructed to special order later.

DH 60G Gipsy Moth.

It was not long before Moth output was rapidly exhausting the once large stocks of war surplus Renault components. To solve the problem of supply, the De Havilland Company asked Major Frank B. Halford to design an entirely new engine. Drawings were started on 29 October 1926 and the first experimental examples rated at 135 h.p. for a weight of about 300 pounds were completed by DH engineers

Weedon and Mitchell in July 1927.

Production engines, derated for installation in the Moth, gave 85 h.p. at 1,900 r.p.m. or 100 h.p. at 2,100 r.p.m. The first, designated the Gipsy I and delivered on 20 June 1928 was installed in the company's trial installation Moth G-EBQH. Although still technically a DH.60X Moth (or if fitted with Handley Page automatic wing tip slots, the DH.60X autoslot), the Gipsy engined variety was always known as the DH.60G Gipsy Moth.

The control characteristics of earlier Moths were retained but the higher wing loading and the steerable tail skid made it easier to handle on the ground.

To publicise the new model, three of the fourteen machines competing in the 1928 King's Cup Race, G-EBQH, 'YK and 'YZ flown by Alan S. Butler, Hubert Broad and Walter L. Hope were Gipsy powered, Hope handsomely winning his second King's Cup at an average speed of 105 m.p.h.

On 25 July 1928 Capt. Geoffrey de Havilland reached a record altitude of 19,980 feet in his private Gipsy Moth G-AAAA and during 16-17 August Hubert Broad remained aloft over Stag Lane for 24 hours in G-EBWV equipped with extra fuel tanks in the front cockpit and behind the pilot's seat.

The Gipsy's final ordeal drew attention to its reliability which permitted a dramatic increase in the between overhauls life of the engine. G-EBTD, one of the company's earlier Moths, was fitted with a Gipsy I taken at random from the production line and sealed by the A.I.D., after which DH Reserve School

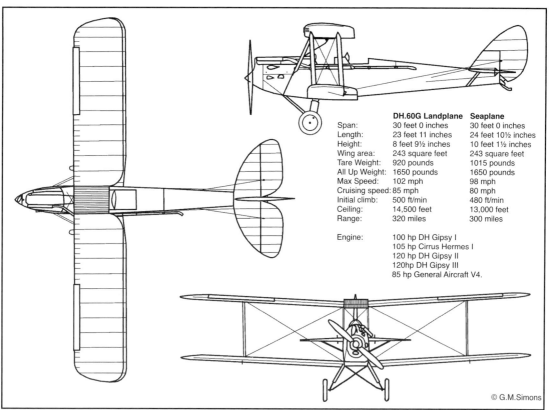

	DH.60G Landplane	Seaplane
Span:	30 feet 0 inches	30 feet 0 inches
Length:	23 feet 11 inches	24 feet 10½ inches
Height:	8 feet 9½ inches	10 feet 1½ inches
Wing area:	243 square feet	243 square feet
Tare Weight:	920 pounds	1015 pounds
All Up Weight:	1650 pounds	1650 pounds
Max Speed:	102 mph	98 mph
Cruising speed:	85 mph	80 mph
Initial climb:	500 ft/min	480 ft/min
Ceiling:	14,500 feet	13,000 feet
Range:	320 miles	300 miles
Engine:	100 hp DH Gipsy I	
	105 hp Cirrus Hermes I	
	120 hp DH Gipsy II	
	120hp DH Gipsy III	
	85 hp General Aircraft V4.	

Right: EC-AQQ was a DH.60G single seater in Spanish colours. *(author's collection.)*

Below: The well-known DH.60 Moth G-EBTD flying in the 600 hour sealed Gipsy engine reliability test of 1929. *(via John Stride.)*

three a day by the end of 1929 and licences were granted to Morane-Saulnier and the Moth Aircraft Corporation for additional production programmes in France and the USA.

Seventeen British-built Gipsy Moths were shipped to the Moth Aircraft Corporation (a subsidiary of the Wright organisation which built Gipsy engines), and some of these were sold to Canada.

An enclosed cabin version, G-AAHK, with a low racing coupé top won the Zenith Cup in France on 16 September 1929 piloted by Hubert Broad who was also first in his class in the 1929 and 1930 Challenge Internationale de Tourisme.

instructors flew it for 600 hours between 28 December 1928 and 24 September 1929. A distance of 51,000 miles was covered, during which the Gipsy received only routine attention and at the end of the test the cost of replacement parts was a mere £7 2s. 11d. These events made considerable impact on the aviation world so that the Gipsy Moth became overnight the best known of all contemporary aeroplanes.

Large numbers were shipped out to the Australian company and six, VT -AAA, 'AB, 'IE - 'IH, were sent to India for a chain of flying clubs operated by the Aero Club of India and Burma Ltd. founded by Sir Victor Sassoon in 1928. In the following year the de Havilland Aircraft Co. of India Ltd., was formed to assemble Gipsy Moths ordered for club and private use in Asia, and Major A. M. Miller formed Union Airways Ltd. with five shipped out in July 1929 to establish the first regular commercial air service in South Africa.

At £650 ex works the popularity of the Gipsy Moth was such that Stag Lane reached an output of almost

The type then took first places in the Canadian National Air Races, made fastest time and filled five out of the first six places in the Australian East-West Air Race, won the South African Aerial Derby, all the major awards at the Rotterdam International Flying Meeting, and made fastest time in the 1929 King's Cup Race, a performance repeated in 1930 by Alan Butler. It was the standard military trainer of the New Zealand Ministry of Defence, the Chilean Air Force, the Danish Flying Corps and Naval Air Service, the Rumanian Air Force, and the governments of China, India, Sarawak and Portugal.

For the training of civilian pilots the type was used by flying clubs and schools - and Gipsy Moths were flown commercially in numbers all over the world.

The name Gipsy Moth will be forever associated

G-AAIM was a Moth Coupé called Aron II, fitted with a Cirrus Hermes I *(via John Stride.)*

John Grierson aboard his Gipsy Moth seaplane G-AAJP *Rouge et Noir* at Brough before the start of his flight to Ireland on 23 July 1929. The Blackburn float mountings differed considerably from the Short Brothers version. *(via John Stride.)*

Right: John Scott Taggart's Gipsy Moth G-AADV with the Short amphibian gear.

Below: Francis Chichester gets airborne in his float equipped Gipsy Moth ZK-AKK.
(both author's collection.)

of navigation in locating and landing at the microscopic Norfolk and Lord Howe Islands during his flight back to Australia.

This historic Gipsy Moth was later wrecked taking off in a restricted waterway at Katsuura, Japan on 14 August 1931 during an attempt to fly home via the Aleutians and Canada.

with the epic flight by Amy Johnson from England to Australia in her aircraft *Jason*. Her famous flight to Australia started at Croydon on 5 May 1930 and ended at Darwin on 24 May, and although three days outside Bert Hinkler's record it was the first England-Australia solo flight by a woman.

Francis Chichester, the first male to complete the journey in a Moth, arrived at Darwin on 25 January 1930 in G-AAKK *Madam Elijah* five weeks after leaving Croydon. The aircraft was then shipped to New Zealand and a year later fitted with floats borrowed from a RNZAF Moth in readiness for his all time epic

The wooden Gipsy Moth was also built in limited numbers in Australia by de Havilland Aircraft Pty. Ltd. and the Larkin Aircraft Supply Co. Ltd.

The chief variant of the Gipsy Moth was the coupé model, the first of which was Capt. de Havilland's personal G-AAAA fitted experimentally with a light wood and fabric superstructure equipped with celluloid windows. Seven other coupé Moths with Triplex glazing were delivered in 1928 to customers, but despite the improved performance and comfort they were not popular, as the payload was reduced by twenty-five pounds; all reverted to standard.

Francis Chichester in his DH.60 Moth G-AAKK. On 31 March 1931 Francis Chichester set out from the Northern tip of New Zealand to attempt the first solo crossing of the Tasman Sea from East to West by aeroplane, in this aircraft, now fitted out as a floatplane and registered ZK-AKK. He had to island-hop to Norfolk Island and Lord Howe Island to fuel the aircraft. He landed at Lord Howe Island late on the afternoon of 1 April and moored his seaplane in the lagoon. Next morning he awoke to a gale, and the sight of his aircraft upside down. With the help of the island men and women he repaired the aircraft over a period of nine weeks, and continued to Jervis Bay, south of Sydney on 10 June. *(via John Stride.)*

The only other variants of note were the two aircraft fitted to special order with the Short amphibian undercarriage developed for that firm's second Mussel prototype, consisting of two wing tip stabilising floats and one large central float through which passed a steel shaft carrying retractable wheels. The first Moth amphibian, G-AADV, was delivered to John Scott Taggart in February 1929. The other, G-AAVC, was fitted with a Cirrus Hermes I.

In later years some aircraft were fitted with the improved 120 h.p. Gipsy II or, as with the Norfolk and Norwich Flying Club's G-AABK, with a 120 h.p. Gipsy III inverted engine. Early in 1935 a DH.60G was used to air test the prototype General Aircraft vee-four inverted 4 litre aircooled engine of 85 h.p.

The wooden Gipsy Moth continued in production

The General Aircraft inverted vee-four engine about to be air-tested in a DH.60. *(author's collection.)*

until 1934, in which year the De Havilland Technical School built two as a training exercise, bringing the total number of British-built Gipsy Moths to 595.

DH.60M 'The Metal Moth'
There was a definite need - mainly from overseas - for a strengthened version of the DH.60G with a welded steel tube fuselage. At the same time, the new version was fitted with wider cockpit doors and a larger luggage locker.

The metal fuselage - which brought with it a set of prominent longitudinal stringers as a good identification feature as well as a weight penalty of 62 pounds - was less easily damaged than the previous wooden construction, and the interior was more accessible for maintenance.

The first DH.60M, G-AAAR, was sent to Canada at the end of 1928, where as G-CA VX, it was evaluated on wheels, skis and floats by the Royal Canadian Air Force. The second, G-AACD, became the manufacturer's test aircraft, the third was sent to the Moth Aircraft Corporation in the U.S.A. and the fourth, G-AACU, became the first of several added to the strength of the de Havilland School of Flying at Stag Lane. An initial production order for fifty was placed by the RCAF in 1929 - ninety more were despatched to De Havilland Aircraft of Canada Ltd. to meet orders from all over Canada and the USA.

Many were equipped with low pressure 'doughnut' tyres, a fashion which soon ousted the old spoked wheels. Others were fitted with large, semicircular, sliding coupé tops, while floats and skis were obligatory in many areas.

Alan Butler seen leaving Heston in his special Gipsy II DH.60M G-AAXG during the 1930 Round Europe touring competition. *(via John Stride.)*

Left: K2235, a DH.60M is seen fitted with the scale Shorts Singapore force-recording float at M&AEE Felixstowe.

G-AARB, a DH.60M Moth seen flying over Brooklands racing track. *(both via John Stride.)*

Arnhold and Co. of Shanghai sold a considerable number of metal fuselaged Moths to the Chinese Air Force. One was shipped to the South African Air Force, two to the Danish Army Air Corps and eight to the Royal Australian Air Force, a repeat order for which was carried out entirely in the Sydney factory of de Havilland Pty. Ltd. Ten were also built under licence by the Norwegian Army Aircraft Factory in 1931.

Contracts were also placed by the British Air Ministry to Specifications 4/29 and 8/30 and the DH.60M saw service as a trainer with the Central Flying School and with 5 FTS, Sealand. It was issued to 24 Squadron, Hendon, to Auxiliary Air Force Squadrons and to a number of Station Flights.

One of the RAF machines was used at the M.A.E.E., Felixstowe, where in 1931 it was re-numbered K2235 and fitted with a force recording central float for taxying tests on the river with a 1:2·4 scale model of the planing bottom of the Short Singapore II flying boat hull.

Although mainly for export, over 60 of the type were sold in the United Kingdom to flying clubs, oil companies and private owners between 1928 and 1930.

There were very few modifications to the DH.60M Moth. Some of the Gipsy II engines were fitted with a revised exhaust system with the main pipe under the fuselage instead of on the port side. One special machine, G-AAXG, was built with Gipsy II engine in 1930 as a mount for Alan Butler in the Round Europe Challenge de Tourisme Internationale. A streamlined transparent canopy covered the front cockpit, entry to which was facilitated by repositioning the main centre section struts.

Standard coupé tops were fitted to special order; abnormal open models were confined to three special aircraft, G-AAKP-'KS, for National Flying Services Ltd. and an unregistered Belgian military DH.60M ordered for the personal use of Captain Chevalier Willy Coppens, Belgian Military Attaché in London and Paris, who had only one leg, was fitted with a wheel-operated rudder control.

DH.60GIII Moth Major
The next major modification to the DH.60 design was to improve the pilot's view ahead. De Havillands inverted their 120 h.p. Gipsy II engine, kept the oil in the sump by means of internal modifications based on the unspillable inkpot principle, and renamed it the Gipsy III.

When fitted to the wooden Moth airframe, a new de luxe variant known simply as the DH.60GIII Moth was created. Cowlings for the new engine faired quite naturally into the lines of the fuselage and, the cylinders being underneath, the pilot's forward view was very considerably improved. The prototype, G-ABUI, liirst flew in March 1932 after which a production line was established at Stag Lane and constructor's numbers in the 5,000 series were entirely reserved for the DH.60GIII. This conformed to the very logical block system which de Havillands adopted for all subsequent types for ease of airframe identification and simplification of production records.

Orders for the DH.60GIII Moth came from all over the world - machines were despatched to Argentina, Australia, Belgium, Egypt, Eire, India, Kenya, Lithuania, Nyasaland, the Netherlands, Portugal, South Africa, Sweden and Switzerland.

The third production aircraft, G-ABVW, was a special high performance single seater fitted with an experimental 133 h.p. Gipsy IIIA high compression engine for H. S. Broad to liy in the 1932 King's Cup Race. He came fifth but his average speed of 131-34 m.p.h. was quite exceptional for a Moth

Having conformed to Moth tradition and started its career in the fields of air racing and long distance flying, the DH.60GIII settled down to its main role as a private and club aircraft. Of the 57 built, 30 were registered to British private owners and to the Ipswich, Midland, London Transport, Leicestershire, Hull, Scottish, Edinburgh and Cinque Ports clubs, and ten fuselages were diverted to an Air Ministry contract for pilotless target aircraft as described in the chapter on the Queen Bee.

Starting with the fifty-eighth airframe in February 1934, the type name was changed to Moth Major to mark the introduction of the Gipsy Major as the standard engine. Despite the change of power plant the designation DH.60 GIII was retained, but precise identification was possible only by an inspection of the fins of the number one cylinder through the air intake. The cooling fins of the Gipsy Major tapered towards the crank case and those of the Gipsy III did not.

Following the disposal abroad of the prototype G-ACNP, production continued until May 1935, by which time 96 had been built. As before, ten fuselages were diverted to the Air Ministry Queen Bee contract and a considerable number were shipped abroad to Australia, Austria, China, Denmark, Finland, Greece, India, New Zealand, Penang, Singapore, Southern Rhodesia, Spain, Sweden and Switzerland. Twelve flown to Spain in December 1934 became Air Force trainers and one diverted from the Queen Bee contract went to the Indian Air Force with a certificate of airworthiness dated 8 January 1935.

Twenty-seven Moth Majors were to British order - seventeen British owned Moth Majors were eventually sold abroad.

DH.60 Moth Major G-ABUI. Its first owner was the Ipswich Aero Club. *(author's collection)*

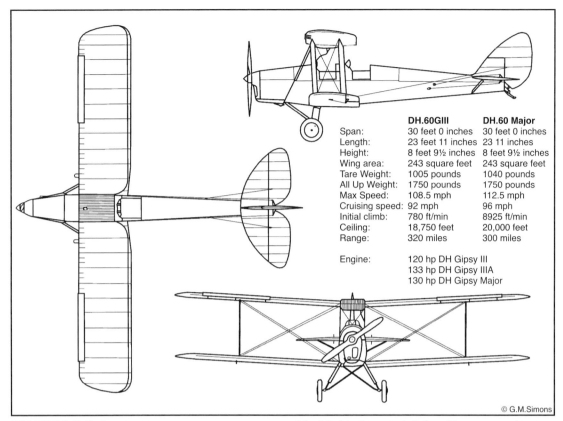

	DH.60GIII	DH.60 Major
Span:	30 feet 0 inches	30 feet 0 inches
Length:	23 feet 11 inches	23 11 inches
Height:	8 feet 9½ inches	8 feet 9½ inches
Wing area:	243 square feet	243 square feet
Tare Weight:	1005 pounds	1040 pounds
All Up Weight:	1750 pounds	1750 pounds
Max Speed:	108.5 mph	112.5 mph
Cruising speed:	92 mph	96 mph
Initial climb:	780 ft/min	8925 ft/min
Ceiling:	18,750 feet	20,000 feet
Range:	320 miles	300 miles
Engine:	120 hp DH Gipsy III	
	133 hp DH Gipsy IIIA	
	130 hp DH Gipsy Major	

© G.M.Simons

DH.60T Moth Trainer.

The DH.60 reached its ultimate development in 1931 with the DH.60M with a Gipsy II engine, extensively modified for military training as the DH.60T Moth Trainer. Intended for pilot training with full dual control, the new variant could be modified with interchangeable specialist equipment such as a camera gun, a rack for four twenty pound practice bombs under the centre fuselage, radio, or cameras. It could thus be used for fighter training, practice or offensive bombing, or for signals and reconnaissance training.

These extra loads made it necessary to strengthen the primary structure to permit an increase in maximum all-up weight to 1,820 pounds and entirely new wings, with modified section, ensured the retention of the Moth's characteristic handling, even at the extra weight. They made the stall less abrupt and slowed down any spin. To ensure ease of parachute escape from the front cockpit, the rear flying wires moved forward to the front root end fitting of the lower mainplane and the attachment of both flying wires to the same fitting formed an external recognition feature of the DH.60T.

Deeper doors were fitted to give greater freedom of exit from the cockpits and by pointing the exhaust pipe of the Gipsy II engine forward and downward under the nose, it was possible to provide doors in both sides of the fuselage.

DH.60 Moth Trainer G-ABKM on the compass platform. It was first registered to De Havillands on 20 April 1931 before passing to the Swedish Air Force as Fv.5103 *(author's collection.)*

Fv.5110 was a DH.60T dual control Moth Trainer of the Swedish Air Force. The revised anchorage for the flying wires, and 'forward facing' exhaust system is clearly visible. (*DH via BAe Hatfield*)

The Moth Trainer is regarded as the transitional type between the civilian Gipsy Moth and the Tiger Moth military trainer which appeared later that year, and although only a small number were built, the DH.60T marked a notable advance in trainer concept.

Flight trials with two prototypes under B conditions at Stag Lane as E-3 and E-4 early in April 1931, resulted in an order from Flygstyrelsen, Stockholm for ten aircraft for the Swedish Air Force, delivered by air during the summer. These were allotted local designation Sk.9, or on floats, Sk.9H.

Arnhold and Co. of Shanghai despatched a single example to the Chinese Air Force among its numerous DH.60Ms, six were supplied to the Egyptian Air Force and five to that of Iraq. After comparative trials between the trainer aircraft of seven nations the Brazilian Government placed the largest single order for the DH.60T, 40 of which were shipped to Rio de Janeiro in 1932. Fifteen were assigned to the Escola de Aviacao Militar for training purposes and the remainder to the Escola de Aviacao Navale.

DH.61 Giant Moth

In August 1927 De Havillands announced that a large single engined cabin biplane was under construction to meet an Australian requirement for a DH.50J replacement. Designed by a team led by Arthur E. Hagg in two attics in Fishermans Walk, Bournemouth during a ten week escape from Moth production at Stag Lane, the aircraft was to be powered by either Rolls-Royce Eagle, Napier Lion and Armstrong Siddeley Jaguar engines as alternatives to the Bristol Jupiter stated by the Australian order.

The pilot sat in an open cockpit aft of the cabin in the DH.61, which was similar in size and loaded weight to the DH.34. It had a structurally simple

Left: DH.61 G-EBTL *Canberra* demonstrates the reduction in span with its wings folded.

Above: a detail view of the nose of *Canberra* , showing the under-fuselage exhaust pipes and the hot air muff for heating the cabin air is seen on the port side. Also seen is the large front luggage compartment which would, as the adverts of the day stated 'take a cabin trunk or two!' (*author's collection.*)

DH.61 G-AAEV, *Youth of Britain* - the Jaguar powered machine operated by Sir Alan Cobham. *(author's collection.)*

plywood and spruce fuselage, two bay equal span, fabric covered wooden wings and strut braced tailplane. The design had standard De Havilland differential ailerons, oleo damped rubber-in-compression undercarriage, centre section fuel tank and the characteristic rudder shape and, to save hangar space, the wings were designed to fold. The undercarriage was not of the usual split type, but each wheel had its own steel axle hinged to the opposite longeron so as to cross the other diagonally. The fuselage cross section gave generous cabin space for

six passengers on curved plywood seats, or eight if the baggage load was reduced to 600 pounds. Warm air was taken into the cabin from a muff round the exhaust pipe and Triplex sliding windows were installed.

To ensure adequate view for the pilot over and around the abnormally wide cabin, the cockpit was offset to port, raised above the general lines of the fuselage and enclosed in a long streamlined fairing. Space under the cockpit was used for luggage, a second compartment for which was situated between the cabin and the engine bulkhead.

To ensure maximum take off and climb it was intended to fit a 500 h.p. Jupiter XI geared engine but none could be spared from military contracts for installation in the prototype, G-EBTL. A direct drive 450 h.p. Jupiter VI was installed instead, turning a two bladed airscrew fitted with a large boss leading smoothly into the profile of the exhaust collector

Above: Jupiter-powered DH.61 G-AAAN was owned by Associated Newspapers and named *Geraldine*. The aircraft carried an on-board office and darkroom!

Right: The second production machine G-CA0JT fitted with a Bristol Jupiter XI and installed on Short Brothers floats is launched at Rochester, Kent in June 1928.
(both author's collection.)

CF-OAK was a Canadian-built example, fitted with a 525 horsepower Pratt and Whitney Hornet engine. *(author's collection.)*

ring. Hubert Broad made the first flights at Stag Lane in December 1927 and conducted trials during January 1928. The aircraft was christened *Canberra*, and it appears that this was used as a temporary type name until 'Giant Moth' was chosen later in the year. The prototype was shipped to Melbourne and erected at Essenden by de Havilland Aircraft Pty. Ltd., test flown on 2 March 1928 and then handed over to the MacRobertson Miller Aviation Co. Ltd., who renamed it *Old Gold* for the new scheduled service between Adelaide and Broken Hill. After service with West Australian Airways in 1931 it was sold finally to Guinea Airways Ltd.

Ten Giant Moths were built and Jupiter XI geared engines were made available for installation in production aircraft. Two, G-CAJT and 'PG, were fitted with Short twin metal floats of generous proportions and the first was test flown at Rochester by Hubert Broad in June 1928. Both were used for uplifting fire fighters and their equipment, landings being made on Canada's many lakes and rivers near to the scene of

forest fires reported by patrolling Moths.

The final Giant Moth, G-CARD, first flown by Hubert Broad on 23 July 1928, visited Croydon briefly on the 28th before shipment to London Air Transport Ltd. in Ontario. It was never licensed and it is probable that components of this aircraft were used in the construction of CF-OAK, modified to take a Pratt and Whitney Hornet geared radial engine driving a three bladed Hamilton adjustable pitch metal airscrew by De Havilland Aircraft of Canada Ltd.

At the end of 1928 the Larkin Aircraft Supply Co. Ltd. and QANTAS successfully tendered for subsidised weekly air mail services over the Camooweal - Daly Waters and Brisbane - Charleville routes, three Jupiter XIF powered DH.61s were purchased at £5,340 each. G-AUHW, also named *Canberra*, was delivered to the Larkin-sponsored Australian Aerial Services Ltd. at Melbourne while G-

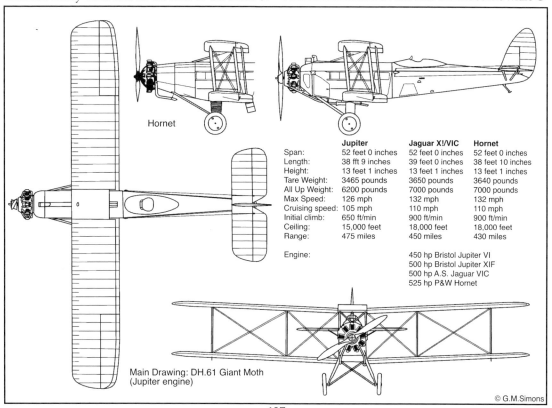

Hornet

	Jupiter	Jaguar X!/VIC	Hornet
Span:	52 feet 0 inches	52 feet 0 inches	52 feet 0 inches
Length:	38 fft 9 inches	39 feet 0 inches	38 feet 10 inches
Height:	13 feet 1 inches	13 feet 1 inches	13 feet 1 inches
Tare Weight:	3465 pounds	3650 pounds	3640 pounds
All Up Weight:	6200 pounds	7000 pounds	7000 pounds
Max Speed:	126 mph	132 mph	132 mph
Cruising speed:	105 mph	110 mph	110 mph
Initial climb:	650 ft/min	900 ft/min	900 ft/min
Ceiling:	15,000 feet	18,000 feet	18,000 feet
Range:	475 miles	450 miles	430 miles

Engine:
450 hp Bristol Jupiter VI
500 hp Bristol Jupiter XIF
500 hp A.S. Jaguar VIC
525 hp P&W Hornet

Main Drawing: DH.61 Giant Moth (Jupiter engine)

© G.M.Simons

Left: Loading luggage into nose compartments of airliners seems to fly in the face of centre of gravity stability, but many airliners had such spaces, including this one in the nose of *Canberra*.

Below: G-AUHW at Longreach, Australia en route from Melbourne to join Australian Aerial Services Ltd Camooweal to Daly Waters route.
(both author's collection.)

AUJB (initially mispainted 'JD) and 'JC were erected at Archerfield, Brisbane and named *Apollo* and *Diana* in the same mythological series as the QANTAS DH.50s. Captain P. H. Moody flew *Apollo* on the inaugural 444 mile service to Charleville on 17 April 1929 but both machines were plagued by recurring engine problems and were re-engined temporarily with the reliable 450 h.p. Jupiter VI engines with inevitable loss of performance and payload.

The Jupiter XIF's difficulties were solved in 1930 and *Apollo*, in the hands of Captain R. B. Tapp, played its part in the first Australia-England air mail run, leaving Brisbane on 25 April 1931 with 17 bags of mail to be handed over to Kingsford Smith and the *Southern Cross* at Darwin the next day. *Diana*, under the command of Captain G. U. Allan, left on the first southbound service from Darwin with 103 pounds of mail on 19 December 1934.

Production included two to British order, the first of which, G-AAAN *Geraldine*, fitted with a Bristol Jupiter XI, was delivered to Associated Newspapers Ltd. in October 1928. It was used by the *Daily Mail* for rapid news-gathering and carried a motor cycle to enable the photographer or reporter to reach the scene of interest without delay. Negatives were developed in the cabin darkroom during the return flight while the story was being typed on a folding desk. *Geraldine* was thus employed for some eighteen months, visiting all parts of Europe and the British Isles, becoming on 9

October 1929 the first aeroplane passed 'A.I at Lloyds'.

Alan Cobham Aviation Co. Ltd. took delivery of the second British Giant Moth, G-AAEV, *Youth of Britain* at Stag Lane on 14 May 1929 before a 21 week tour of towns and cities in the UK. Powered by an Armstrong Siddeley Jaguar VIC engine driving a two bladed airscrew, it was furnished as a ten seater for short haul work. In an attempt to convince local authorities that municipal aerodromes were a necessity, Sir Alan Cobham gave short flights to some 3,500 mayors and members of corporations from existing or improvised aerodromes. Through the generosity of Sir Charles Wakefield, ten thousand school children were also given free flights. The tour ended at Stag Lane on 7 October 1929 and on 10 December Cobham left for Africa to deliver the aircraft to Imperial Airways Ltd. An uneventful flight via Pisa, Tripoli, Heliopolis, Khartoum and Nairobi, brought him to the flooded aerodrome at N'dola on 1 January 1930. Although bogged for many hours he succeeded in handing 'EV over to an Imperial crew at Salisbury, Southern Rhodesia on 7 January.

In Japan the Mitsubishi company built an aircraft to the same specification powered by an Armstrong Siddeley Jaguar and designated the C.I.

DH.62

The DH.62 was a design study for an eight-seat passenger biplane with a large single fin and rudder which was powered by a pair of 240 horsepower Siddeley Puma in-line water-cooled engines. These

were mounted on the lower mainplane, protruding forward. An open cockpit with two crew occupied the nose of the aircraft. Cabin glazing was similar to that of the DH.61, and the fuel was carried in two 78 gallon tanks in the upper wing. No detail drawings have been located and the design was not proceeded with. Span: 68 feet 0 inches, length: 50 feet 6 inches.

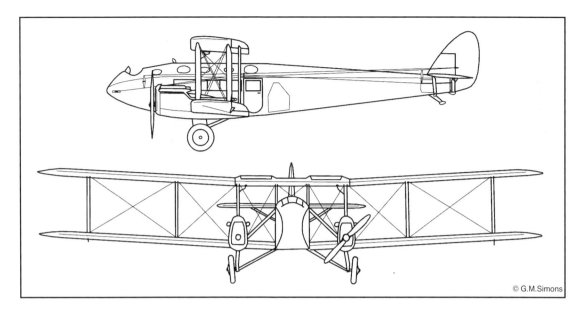

© G.M.Simons

DH.63

The DH.63 designation was allocated to a scheme for a scaled-down version of the DH.61, seating four passengers in a cabin ahead of the pilot. A single Siddeley Puma of 240 horsepower with a nose radiator would have powered the project. No detailed drawings have been located and the DH.63 was not proceeded with. Span: 45 feet 0 inches. Length: 31 feet 2 inches.

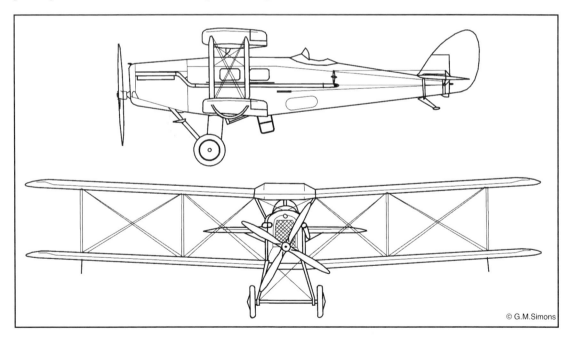

© G.M.Simons

DH.64

The DH.64 was a design designation allocated to a further investigation made in September 1926 for an enlarged, fourteen-seat passenger version of the DH.62 powered by two Armstrong Siddeley Jaguar radial engines of unspecified mark or horsepower. Span 77 feet 0 inches. Length 54 feet 9 inches. Wing area 1200 square feet. All-up-weight 11,500 pounds. Payload 2,900 pounds.

DH.65 Hound

The DH.65 Hound made its first flight at Stag Lane in the hands of Hubert Broad on 17 November 1926, as an unarmed prototype bearing the first of two allotted civil markings. Two registration reservations had been made on 15 January 1926 for G-EBNJ and 'NK. This marked the company's intention to go ahead with a high performance military aircraft that would show what could be done if designers were not hampered by Air Ministry specifications. They intended to outclass all contemporary military prototypes, which usually had everything hanging from them including the kitchen sink, and as the DH.65s were private ventures, test flying had to be done in civil guise.

By March 1926 construction was well under way, and all the lessons of the previous six years went into making the design the fastest two seat aeroplane in the world at that time. The fuselage was of standard De Havilland plywood construction with spruce longerons and cross pieces, and two bay, wooden, fabric covered mainplanes. Ailerons were fitted to the lower mainplane only. Two 74 and 52 gallon fuel tanks were carried in the front fuselage, fuel being pumped to a slim twenty gallon gravity tank in the centre section. The undercarriage used oleo damped rubber-in-compression shock legs with rear radius rods. The rudder was of traditional DH shape and the aircraft was powered by a 530 horsepower Napier Lion VIII direct drive, twelve cylinder, broad arrow, watercooled engine with frontal radiator.

The military load of 509 pounds included a DH low drag gun ring on the rear cockpit but this had not yet been fitted for the first flight. The Lion's centre row of cylinders was faired neatly into a false decking terminating in the pilot's windscreen. Insistence on clean lines and strict attention to detail allowed the Hound to carry loads considerably faster than contemporary fighters.

The Air Ministry agreed to test the Hound if the geared 540 horsepower Lion XA were fitted and made an engine available, but before the trials parts of the unfinished second aircraft were embodied, notably the metal spar wings and faired interplane struts. Nose lines were improved by fitting an underslung retractable radiator. G-EBNJ first flew with the new engine as the DH.65A on 27 February 1927 and it was flown to the A&AEE Martlesham Heath by Hubert Broad on 19 March to compete for a contract to Specification 12/26.

Although its performance outstripped those of its rivals, the DH.65 was unacceptable because equipment had to be carried externally on account of the narrow fuselage and its clean lines created too much landing float for small airfields. There must have been slight directional problems, for when the aircraft appeared at the Hendon Display on 2 July 1927 the original rudder had been replaced by one of larger area.

The DH.65A remained at Martlesham until Easter 1928 and then returned to the makers to be prepared for a series of attempts on the world's speed-with-load records. The rear cockpit was covered in and the 'load', which consisted of a number of lead bars, was attached to the lower wing and covered with fabric. The Napier Lion XA was then replaced by a Lion XI, which, although of similar power, had the type test certificate necessary for the record attempt.

The record flights were made successfully by Hubert Broad on 26 April 1928 but on the following day he flew the Hound over five circuits of a course between Stag Lane and Reading to improve on his figures and to set up the following records:

Above: G-EBNJ, the first DH.65, seen here fitted with a direct drive Napier Lion VII engine.

Left: the same aircraft after conversion to DH.65A, but before the larger rudder was fitted.
(both author's collection.)

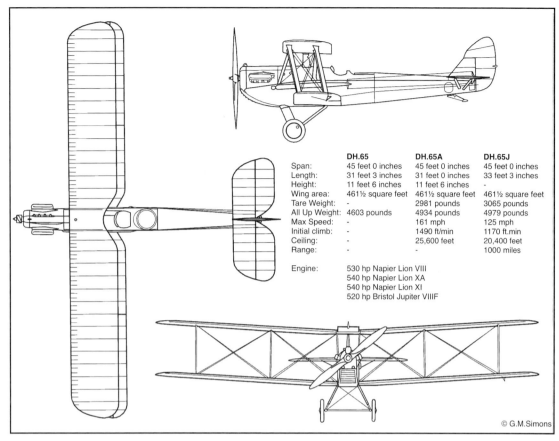

	DH.65	DH.65A	DH.65J
Span:	45 feet 0 inches	45 feet 0 inches	45 feet 0 inches
Length:	31 feet 3 inches	31 feet 0 inches	33 feet 3 inches
Height:	11 feet 6 inches	11 feet 6 inches	-
Wing area:	461½ square feet	461½ square feet	461½ square feet
Tare Weight:	-	2981 pounds	3065 pounds
All Up Weight:	4603 pounds	4934 pounds	4979 pounds
Max Speed:	-	161 mph	125 mph
Initial climb:	-	1490 ft/min	1170 ft.min
Ceiling:	-	25,600 feet	20,400 feet
Range:	-	-	1000 miles

Engine:	530 hp Napier Lion VIII
	540 hp Napier Lion XA
	540 hp Napier Lion XI
	520 hp Bristol Jupiter VIIIF

© G.M.Simons

100 km with 1,000 kg load at 162.284 mph
500 km with 1,000 kg load at 158.656 mph
500 km with 500 kg load at 158.656 mph

Afterwards the Hound received the serial number J9127 and with the Lion XA re-fitted, returned to Martlesham, where trials were resumed on 11 September 1928, but ten days later routine inspection found the plywood of the rear fuselage in poor condition. Repair would have involved dismantling the aircraft so this brought its career to an end.

As the original Hound failed to secure a production contract, an entirely redesigned version was built to

The DH.64A, fitted with a geared 540 horsepower Napier Lion XA engine prior to the record-breaking flights. *(author's collection.)*

Above: Photographs of the DH.65 Hound in flight are not that common - here Hubert Broad is seen bringing the record-breaking machine in for a low pass over Stag Lane.

Right: the DH.65J, with a 520 horsepower Bristol Jupiter VIIIF engine.
(both author's collection.)

Australian requirements. A 520 h.p. Bristol Jupiter VIIIF radial engine was fitted, along with differential ailerons on all four wings and the wide track, divided undercarriage had front, instead of rear, radius rods. The front fuselage was built of steel tubing with wire bracing but the aft section remained plywood. Wing spars were duralumin tubes of oval section with wooden ribs and steel drag and interplane struts.

The new machine was named Hound II under the designation DH.65J but no markings other than wing roundels and rudder stripes appear to have been carried After bare hull flight trials at Stag Lane, the DH.65J went to Martlesham where, with the exhaust collector ring removed but equipped with front Vickers gun, rear Lewis gun on the DH. low drag gun ring and racks for 450 Ib. of bombs under the lower mainplane, official tests were conducted between June and November 1928. Other features included dual control in the rear cockpit—which also extended into the rear fuselage to form a prone bombing position—and alternative provision for a single heavy bomb or torpedo between the undercarriage legs.

DH.66 Hercules

A fleet of new transport aircraft was required by Imperial Airways for their Middle East services, who drew up a specification which stated multi engines to minimise the risk of forced landings in the desert and ample reserves of power for tropical operation.

The design for a large two bay biplane powered by three 420 horsepower Bristol Jupiter VI radials was approved and a contract placed for five aircraft.

Although mainplane construction followed standard practice with twin wooden box spars and spruce ribs, difficulties in obtaining good quality spruce in sufficient lengths and the risk of deterioration under tropical conditions led to a fuselage of tubular steel construction with two plywood boxes forming the cabin and a rear baggage compartment of 155 cubic feet capacity suspended inside.

Two pilots sat in an open cockpit in the nose and the cabin, equipped with the usual sliding windows,

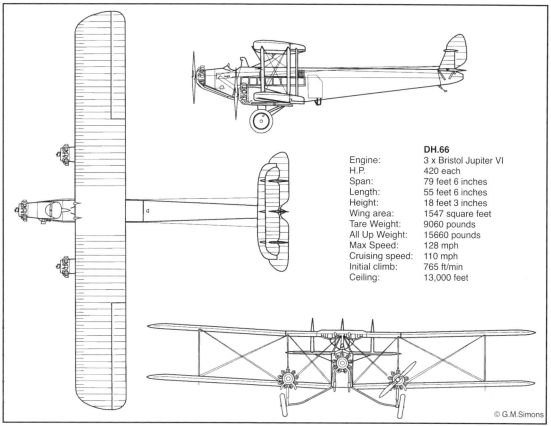

DH.66

Engine:	3 x Bristol Jupiter VI
H.P.	420 each
Span:	79 feet 6 inches
Length:	55 feet 6 inches
Height:	18 feet 3 inches
Wing area:	1547 square feet
Tare Weight:	9060 pounds
All Up Weight:	15660 pounds
Max Speed:	128 mph
Cruising speed:	110 mph
Initial climb:	765 ft/min
Ceiling:	13,000 feet

© G.M.Simons

A three-quarter front view of the fuselage structure of a DH.66 in skeleton form. The main structure was steel tube and the main cabin, luggage compartment and other areas were in the form of plywood boxes or sheet, slipped inside the main structure. The nose mount for the central engine was equally neat and simple. *(DH via BAe Hatfield.)*

had space for a wireless operator, seven passengers and up to 465 cubic feet of mail. A truly massive biplane tail unit with three fins and rudders was also fitted.

While the prototype was still under construction, a type name was chosen in a competition run in the June 1926 edition of the *Meccano Magazine* and won by E. F. Hope-Jones of Eton College who suggested *Hercules*.

The first flight of the prototype, G-EBMW occurred on 30 September in the hands of Hubert Broad. Lateral control needed to be improved, so the aircraft went back into the works to have ailerons fitted to all four wings. After acceptance trials at Croydon by Imperial Airways Superintendent Herbert G. Brackley and some crew training, it left for Heliopolis, Cairo on 18 December piloted by Captain C. F. Wolley Dod. The transfer of the desert air mail service from military to civil control was marked by an inaugural flight by the Air Minister, Sir Samuel Hoare who, with Lady Maud Hoare, left Croydon on 27 December in the second *Hercules* 'MX piloted by Capt. F. L. Barnard. On arrival at Delhi on 8 January 1927 the aircraft was named *City of Delhi* by Lady Irwin, wife of the Viceroy of India.

Before Capt. Wolley Dod left Heliopolis on the first eastbound commercial flight on 12 January the prototype was named *City of Cairo*, but for two years the service terminated at Basra, and to avoid the Persian terrain, was temporarily re-routed down the west coast of the Gulf. The delivery of the *City of*

The prototype had ailerons only on the lower wings as first but first trials revealed poor lateral control as a result of which ailerons were fitted to all four wings as here.

The difference in aircraft stance between tail skid and tail wheel is noticable. *(both author's collection.)*

Teheran at Heliopolis in March 1927 completed the Hercules contract.

1928 saw West Australian Airways Ltd. successfully tender for a new passenger and mail service between Perth and Adelaide with an express train connection to Melbourne. They received an annual mail subsidy of £70,000 and selected the DH.66 for the route. Four more were built at Stag Lane with modifications to suit Australian requirements. A cabin top with sliding windows was built over the pilot's cockpit, seating accommodation was provided for fourteen passengers in addition to mail, and a tailwheel was fitted which failed to survive rough usage and was eventually removed. Acceptance trials were conducted by Herbert Brackley at Stag Lane in March 1929 after which the four aircraft were shipped to Perth, W.A. and erected at Maylands Aerodrome ready for the first eastbound service, flown on 2 June by Major Norman Brearley in the *City of Perth,* which carried 51 bags amounting to 856 pounds of mail.

When the Imperial Airways route was extended to Delhi in 1929, a sixth DH.66 was ordered and commissioned at Heliopolis in June 1929 with the name *City of Basra.* The pilot's cabin fitted to this and all DH.66s built in 1929, was retrofitted to those built in 1926. In the following September *City of Jerusalem* stalled on approach to Jask at night and was destroyed by fire with the loss of Captain Woodbridge and two passengers, an accident which led to a replacement order. This, the eleventh and final *Hercules*, was ferried from Stag Lane to Croydon on 27 January 1930 and commissioned as the *City of Karachi.* The fleet did not remain long at full strength for a month later *City of Teheran* in the hands of Captain Foy, operating on an

Imperial Airways' DH.66 G-EBMW *City of Cairo* seen during a test flight from Stag Lane. The aircraft crashed near Koepang, Timor on 19 April 1931.*(author's collection.)*

Four aircraft were ordered as 14-seaters for use in Australia and these incorporated a number of modifications which included a closed cockpit and a large-diameter tailwheel. The first of these special machines was G-AUJO (later VH-OJO) pictured here undergoing acceptance trials in March 1929. It was flying on just two engines. *(author's collection.)*

eastbound from Gaza at night, returned with engine trouble, forced landed and broke up without casualties. As the type was now out of production, an approach was made to West Australian Airways Ltd. which led to the sale of their fourth Hercules to Imperial Airways as the *City of Jodhpur*.

Two experimental air mail services were flown for the first time in 1931 between Croydon and Melbourne. The Australian mail was picked up at Karachi by Captains R. P. Mollard and H. W. C. Alger, who left for Darwin in *City of Cairo* on 13 April 1931, ran short of fuel in appalling weather and was wrecked in a forced landing in rock strewn grassland ten miles from Koepang on 19 April. The mail was retrieved by Charles Kingsford Smith in the Fokker monoplane *Southern Cross* and flown to Darwin. Kingsford Smith returned to hand over the first Australia-England mail to Captain Alger in *City of Karachi* at Akyab on 3 May. The same Hercules flew the second eastbound mail from Karachi to Akyab on 5/6 May but a replacement for the lost prototype was needed urgently and the Australian Department of Civil Aviation granted special permission for West Australian Airways Ltd. to dispose of their third aircraft, providing it was flown to Darwin by a W.A. Airways pilot. It left Maylands, Perth on 15th May under the command of Capt. J. F. Nicholson, who handed it over to Capt. R. P. Mollard of Imperial Airways at Darwin on the 18th, Karachi

being reached on the 27th.

After overhaul it was christened *City of Cape Town*, a name which foreshadowed a southward extension of the Empire Air Route to South Africa. The survey flight for this was made by H. G. Brackley and Capt. Alger in G-AARV, the name of which was repainted for the occasion in Afrikaans as *Stad van Karachi*. Their arrival at Wingfield Airport, Cape Town on 21 December 1931 paved the way for regular services and the Hercules became well known in South Africa.

In 1934 Imperial Airways' G-AAJH *City of Basra* pioneered the aerial anti-locust campaign in Rhodesia, where G-ABCP *City of Jodhpur* was damaged beyond repair in the following year when taking off from soft ground. Two others were withdrawn from service but G-AAJH, G-ABMT and G-EBMX were sold to the South African Air Force for £775 each and delivered to the SAAF base at Swartkop in April, July and November 1934 respectively. They were serialled 260-262 and in June-July 1935 G-AAJH, now 260, returned to pest control duties when it dropped several hundred pounds of pesticide on locust swarms at Vryheid and Gollel. In the early days of the Second World War they flew military courier services to South African Forces in other parts of Africa but in September 1939 the second production aircraft 262, once G-EBMX, was reduced to spares at Broken Hill to service the other two until they too were written off in 1943.

DH.67

It is hard to decide if the DH.67 was an unbuilt project or not. The requirement came about when one of De Havilland's subsidiary companies, the Aircraft Operating Company, declared a clear demand for a specialised aircraft for use on aerial surveys.

In 1926, faced with the job of surveying the huge and inhospitable terrain of Northern Rhodesia, AOC created a specification for a purpose-built aerial survey

and photographic aircraft, the prime consideration being power and reliability, which meant the ability to stay aloft if one engine should fail. The airframe had to be rugged, which called for metal construction, and it should require little maintenance when operated in tropical, primitive conditions without organised maintenance facilities. Finally, the crew, pilot and photographer had to have above-average field of vision.

Parent company de Havilland was approached

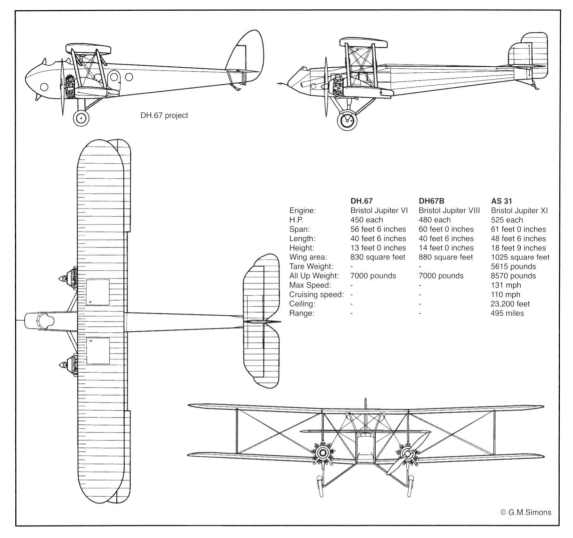

DH.67 project

	DH.67	DH67B	AS 31
Engine:	Bristol Jupiter VI	Bristol Jupiter VIII	Bristol Jupiter XI
H.P.	450 each	480 each	525 each
Span:	56 feet 6 inches	60 feet 0 inches	61 feet 0 inches
Length:	40 feet 6 inches	40 feet 6 inches	48 feet 6 inches
Height:	13 feet 0 inches	14 feet 0 inches	18 feet 9 inches
Wing area:	830 square feet	880 square feet	1025 square feet
Tare Weight:	-	-	5615 pounds
All Up Weight:	7000 pounds	7000 pounds	8570 pounds
Max Speed:	-	-	131 mph
Cruising speed:	-	-	110 mph
Ceiling:	-	-	23,200 feet
Range:	-	-	495 miles

© G.M.Simons

with this set of requirements and the design study that emerged was a scaled-down all-metal version of the DH.66 Hercules. Two 450 hp Bristol Jupiter VI engines would be provided in wing nacelles. There were facilities for an interchangeable seaplane undercarriage using two 24 ft Short metal floats. This design study was given the type number DH.67.

Pilot and navigator were housed in a side by side open cockpit under the leading edge of the centre section and the front camera operator had an open cockpit in front of and below them, giving a stepped nose. In the light of DH.66 experience, ailerons were fitted on all four wings, which were also made to fold.

By November 1927, a revised layout was produced and given the designation DH.67B. This had increased span and the DH.66 biplane tail with just two vertical surfaces. It also had more power, the engines now being the 480 hp Bristol Jupiter VIII.

In June 1929, the prototype Survey made its first flight.It was handed over to the Aircraft Operating Company on 25 January 1930 on an occasion patronised by the Secretary and Under-secretary for Air. *(via John Stride)*

The AS.31 G-AADO in flight. The extreme nose position of the cockpit is very noticable.

On 20 March 1930, piloted by Alan S. Butler, the Survey departed from Heston Aerodrome for a survey of Northern Rhodesia, covering the 7,000 miles at an average speed of 128 mph. On 11 April 1930 it reached Cape Town. *(both author's collection.)*

At this time, the De Havillands were fully stretched with the production of the Moth club/private owner machines and Hercules airliners. The survey design was thus an extra job that Stag Lane could not accommodate. A primary reason was that De Havilland's manufacturing facility to date was geared to wooden aircraft construction. The changeover to an all-metal machine merely for one order was thus both uneconomic and disruptive. Consequently, in November 1928, the entire project was offered to the Gloster Aircraft Company Ltd, with whom de Havilland had a close friendship.

The DH.67 design and project was placed in the hands of chief designer Henry Phillip Folland, who lost no time in setting about altering the DH approach to suit his company and its production methods.

Given the Gloster designation AS.31, this was to be Gloster's first twin-engined aircraft, which only superficially resembled the original design. The engines were now to be a pair of 525 hp Bristol Jupiter XIF.

The completed AS.31 was nearer to the DH.67 than to the DH.67B, having a single fin and rudder (although of typical Gloster outline) and ailerons on the lower mainplane only. It was of fabric covered metal construction throughout, employing high tensile steel wing spars, duralumin ribs and a fuselage of steel tubing.

Both pilot and co-pilot/observer had an unprecedented field of vision, their single open cockpit being situated right in the very nose where the field of view was as good as it was possible to obtain, reached via a door in the front bulkhead of a roomy cabin, and the aircraft was readily adaptable for survey, bombing, ambulance or seaplane work.

The controls received singular attention, all pivots and levers being provided with grease nipples while cables and their attendant risk of stretch were

AS.31 K2602 seen in full RAF markings. This was the second machine built. *(author's collection.)*

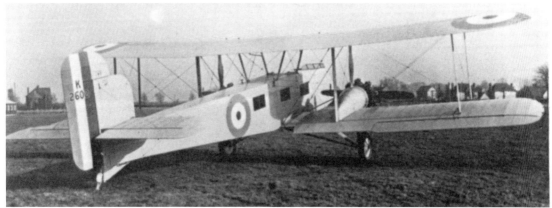

dispensed with in favour of rigid tie- and push-rods.

The special camera was an Eagle made by The Williamson Manufacturing Company Ltd of Willesden Green. It was carried on a special 'Eirie' swivelling and rise-and-fall mount that enabled it to be lowered through the bottom of the fuselage without snagging any projections on the aircraft

As specified, the aircraft could operate satisfactorily on either engine. Gloster's wrote of their aircraft: 'The fuselage is of generous dimensions, and probably never before in the history of aerial surveying has an aircraft provided such excellent accommodation for the photographer'.

Two prototypes were built, one of which, G-AADO, was equipped with three camera positions to the order of the Aircraft Operating Co. Ltd. and first flown at Brockworth in June 1929. The other, K2602,

was supplied to the Air Ministry and exhibited in skeleton form at the Olympia Aero Show of July 1929, afterwards being completed and delivered on 19 November 1931 to the RAE Farnborough for wireless telegraphy experiments. De Havilland's chairman, Alan Butler, accompanied by his wife Lois and a cameraman, delivered the Aircraft Operating Company's AS.31 to Cape Town by air, leaving Heston on 20 March 1930. Later it was flown to the scene of survey operations at Bulawayo by Maj. Cochrane-Patrick and in the course of the next year surveyed 63,000 sq. miles of Northern Rhodesia with conspicuous success. In May 1935 at the completion of a number of similar surveys in central Africa, the A.S.31 was sold to the South African Air Force with which it was still in service in 1942.

DH.68

This type number was allocated to the preliminary study for an executive transport version of the DH.67. The cabin was to have seating for six passengers with toilet facilities. The two crew sat side-by-side in an

open cockpit in the nose. The aircraft was to be powered by a pair of Armstrong Siddeley Jaguar two row radials of an undetermined mark. No detail drawings have been located. Span 58 feet 6 inches. Length 39 feet 6 inches. Wing area 845 square feet. All-up-weight 7,500 pounds.

DH.69

This was a design study in conjunction with an Air Ministry Specification for a high performance day bomber. It was to be powered by a single Rolls-Royce Falcon Mk.X water-cooled supercharged engine

driving a two bladed metal Fairey-Reed propeller. Two crew occupied tandem cockpits with forward firing guns for the pilot and a prone bombing position in the floor of the fuselage. Span: 36 feet 0 inches. Length 26 feet 6 inches.

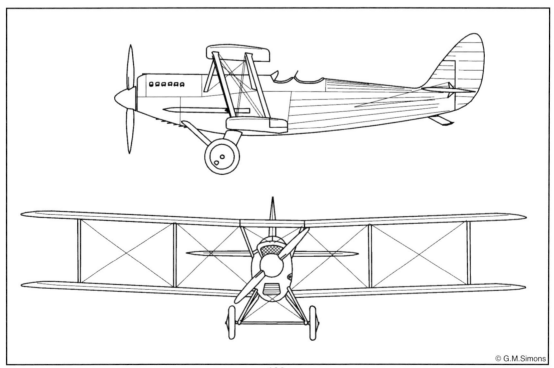

© G.M.Simons

DH.70

This type number was allocated to an Army Co-operation biplane design for the Australian Government. It was not proceeded with.

DH.71 Tiger Moth

Two tiny DH.71 aircraft were constructed in great secrecy at Stag Lane in 1927 for high speed research at reasonable cost and also to act as flying testbeds for Major Frank Halford's prototype Cirrus-replacement engines, then nearing completion.

Fuselage design followed that of the standard Moth, with stressed plywood covering, but the cockpit was tailored literally to fit test pilot Hubert Broad, making it necessary for the fuselage sides to slope outwards toward the top decking in order to accommodate his shoulders. Entry to the cockpit was only possible by dividing the adjacent decking along the centre line and allowing each half to hinge out and downwards. With the pilot in and the decking closed, the lines of the engine and of the pilot's head were continued smoothly down to the fin by means of a long tapering dorsal fillet.

The thin section, fabric covered mainplanes were built in two halves with oval tips, I section spars and wooden ribs. Aileron and elevator gaps were closed by sponge rubber strips and bracing was by means of duplicated streamlined wires, those under the wing also holding the undercarriage rigidly in place and forming the 'axle'. The undercarriage legs were plain

The pleasing lines of the diminutive DH.71 is very noticable in this view. *(author's collection.)*

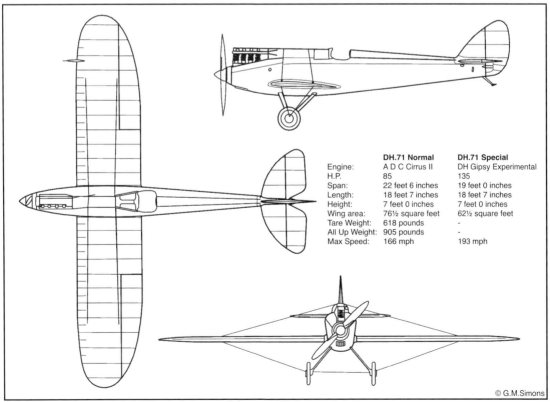

	DH.71 Normal	DH.71 Special
Engine:	A D C Cirrus II	DH Gipsy Experimental
H.P.	85	135
Span:	22 feet 6 inches	19 feet 0 inches
Length:	18 feet 7 inches	18 feet 7 inches
Height:	7 feet 0 inches	7 feet 0 inches
Wing area:	76½ square feet	62½ square feet
Tare Weight:	618 pounds	-
All Up Weight:	905 pounds	-
Max Speed:	166 mph	193 mph

© G.M.Simons

The DH.71 seen from below as it comes in for a landing.
(author's collection.)

struts, all the bungee shock absorber cord being buried inside the thickness of the wheel to cut down drag. The fuel tank of 16¾ gallons capacity conformed to the lines of the fuselage just ahead of the pilot, engine oil was cooled by finning the crankcase and making it fit snugly into the under fuselage, the rear end of which faired into a thickening at the bottom of the rudder.

The name Tiger Moth was allotted and both aircraft were entered for the King's Cup Race at Hucknall on 30 July 1927, the first, G-EBQU, with the number 16 on its fin by Lady Wakefield and the second, G-EBRV carrying the number 17 by Lord Wakefield, the pilots being C. D. Barnard and Hubert Broad respectively.

In order to check handling characteristics G-EBQU was completed with an 85 horsepower ADC Cirrus II engine and Broad made the first flight at Stag Lane on 24 June. It was then fitted with Halford's prototype engine - now known as the Gipsy and delivering 135

horsepower. Although a certificate of airworthiness was issued on the day before the race 'QU was withdrawn to be tuned for record breaking purposes. The second DH.71, Cirrus II powered throughout its life, first flew on 28 July but suffered badly with bumps during the race; the uneven ground jolted the throttle half shut and almost doubled the take off run while turbulance in the air caused involuntary hand movements which made level flight impossible. Although Broad's speed as far as Spittlegate in Lincolnshire was four miles an hour up on handicap at 166 m.p.h., he returned to Hucknall and retired.

A second set of mainplanes with reduced span of just nineteen feet was fitted to the first aircraft, enabling Broad to set up a world record on 24 August for the 100 km closed circuit in Light Aeroplane Category Class III at an average speed of 186.47 m.p.h. On the 29th an attempt was made on the world altitude record

The stripes of a Tiger! One of the two DH.71s poses for the camera at Stag Lane before the first flight. The aircraft is fitted with the original long-span wings, later exchanged for nineteen feet span units to allow an attempt on the world record.
(author's collection.)

Right: the sleek streamlining applied to the DH.71 shows up very well in this view. Springing for the wheels was contained in the hubs.

Below: the first DH.71 is prepared for the attack on the closed circuit record in August 1927. By now it is fitted with the short-span wings . *(author's collection.)*

in the same category and in 17 minutes the machine reached 19,191 feet, above which Broad could not go without oxygen even though the aircraft was still climbing at over 1,000 feet per minute!

Several light aeroplanes were exhibited in the New Types Park at the Hendon Display of 30 June 1928, one of which was the DH.71 G-EBQU in immaculate yellow finish. Unfortunately the rough surface of the airfield ruled out taking off for a flying demonstration which would have shown it to be faster than the

majority of fighters present. A year later the same aircraft was again statically exhibited, this time on the De Havilland stand at the Olympia Aero Show of July 1929. In 1930 it was shipped to Australia and flown at Point Cook by Major Hereward de Havilland but David Smith was killed in it on 17 September while practising at Mascot for the following Saturday's air racing. The engine cut on take off and the aircraft crashed into a street from a height of 150 feet.

The second Tiger Moth was withdrawn from active flying in 1928 and the engineless airframe was hoisted into the rafters of the flight shed at Stag Lane. It remained there until 1933 when, mounted on top of a notice board outside the new Hatfield factory, it formed an advertisement for that year's King's Cup Race. It then returned to its customary position in the roof, this time at Hatfield, until destroyed by a Junkers Ju 88 which bombed the factory on 3 October, 1940.

With a touch of up elevator to keep the tail firmly on the ground, Major Hereward de Havilland runs up G-EBQU at RAAF Point Cook, Victoria after its arrival in Australia duing August 1930. *(author's collection.)*

DH.72

The origins of this machine are somewhat obscure but it appears that the Air Ministry was impressed by the the DH.66s and saw in the DH.72 design a similarity to the Vickers Virginia replacement envisaged by their B. 22/27 night bomber

specification. An order was placed for one prototype to meet it and in 1928 work began on an enlarged version of the DH.66 having mainplanes of duralumin instead of wood. De Havillands were still unfamiliar with the techniques of light alloy construction and so slow progress was made in the experimental department, further delay being caused when the Ministry specified a gun position

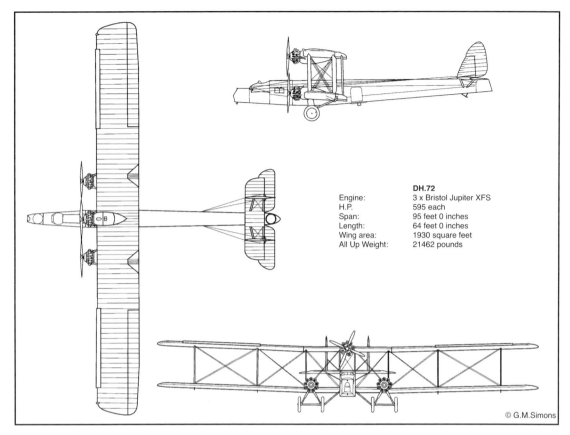

DH.72	
Engine:	3 x Bristol Jupiter XFS
H.P.	595 each
Span:	95 feet 0 inches
Length:	64 feet 0 inches
Wing area:	1930 square feet
All Up Weight:	21462 pounds

© G.M.Simons

in the nose, necessitating the transfer of the centre engine to the leading edge of the top wing.

The unfinished airframe was so long a part of Stag Lane's internal decorations that the original Bristol Jupiter VI engines were changed progressively for later marks until the Jupiter XFS was reached. The Air Ministry was eventually persuaded to move the DH.72 to Brockworth, where it was completed under an existing arrangement whereby the Gloster Aircraft Co. Ltd. undertook development of De Havilland's military designs following W. G. Carter's appointment as Gloster's chief designer.

In final form the DH.72 had a monoplane tail unit with twin fins and rudders which was almost identical in appearance with that of the projected DH.67B which Glosters had previously studied. Rows of external bomb racks were fitted under the centre part of the long, low slung fuselage, and each outboard engine nacelle was mounted above its own two wheeled undercarriage.

The aircraft was known to have been completed and flown in 1931, and also to have visited RAE Farnborough, and then to A&AEE at Martlesham Heath to be flown in competition with the Bolton and Paul P.32.

J9184, the sole DH.72 night bomber. (author's collection.)

DH.73

The design number allocated to a specialised development of the DH.67 design for high altitude survey work, a layout for which was drawn up in March 1927. It would have been powered by two 300 h.p. A.D.C. Nimbus watercooled in-line engines with frontal radiators. The scheme included a thickened lower centre section, ailerons on the lower wing only and twin vertical tail surfaces. There was also an optional cockpit layout offering either side by side or tandem seating. There were no detail drawings and the aircraft was not built. Span 51 feet 0 inches. Length (landplane) 33 feet 2 inches, (seaplane) 38 feet 9 inches Height 12 feet 6 inches. Wing area 620 square feet. All-up weight (landplane) 5,470 pounds (seaplane) 6,100 pounds.

DH.74

This was a preliminary study for a DH.50 replacement based on the DH.65A Hound. Somewhat larger than the DH.50, it carried pilot and four passengers but no engine type was specified and the design was not proceeded with.

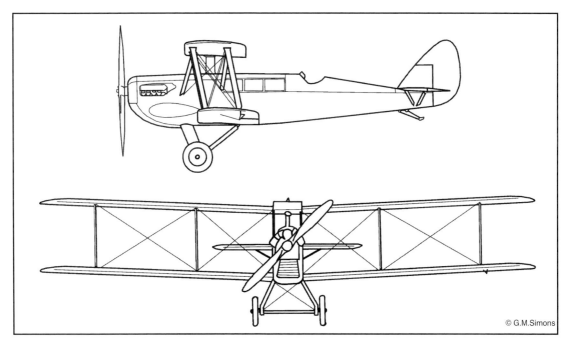

© G.M.Simons

DH.75 Hawk Moth

During 1928 Major Frank Halford reversed the birth process of the original Cirrus I by designing and bench testing a V-8 aircooled engine comprising two modern Gipsy Is mated on a common crankcase. It was a engine similar in layout to the wartime Renault but giving over twice the power at a very much lower weight. The new power unit, named the D.H. Ghost, was developed for the DH.75 Hawk Moth four seat cabin monoplane designed for light transport or taxi work overseas.

It was fabric covered, and of composite construction, features that had previously proved so serviceable under extremes of temperature. The DH.75 combined a welded steel fuselage and tail unit with a

The vee-eight air-cooled De Havilland Ghost engine developed for the DH.75 Hawk Moth.
(author's collection.)

Left: G-EBVV, the prototype Hawk Moth fitted with the 198 horsepower De Havilland Ghost engine.
(author's collection.)

wooden wing. The roomy cabin had two paired seats for pilot and three passengers with provision for dual control and luggage space in the rear. It was fitted with generous Triplex sliding windows and each pair of seats had its own door, but only on the starboard side. Fuel tanks of 35 gallons capacity were housed in the wing roots, the mainplane being built in two halves and shoulder mounted. It was braced by two streamlined tubular steel struts, the front one also forming part of the undercarriage structure of from which it could be released by a spring loaded pin for wing folding.

Hubert S. Broad first flew the prototype at Stag Lane on 7 December 1928 but it was underpowered and the performance was disappointing.

A number of Hawk Moths were built with mainplanes of increased span and sixteen inches greater chord. The first two had 240 horsepower Armstrong Siddeley Lynx geared engines which gave them a much more useful performance. At this stage the type was known for a short time as the Moth Six in order to emphasise its relationship to its smaller brother the Puss Moth, then coming on the market with the short-lived name Moth Three.

Designated DH.75A, the first two Lynx powered machines had a considerable history. One was exhibited with a wing folded, but without markings, at the Olympia Aero Show of 1929, after which the first one, G-AAFW, was demonstrated in Canada by P. C. Garrett of De Havilland Aircraft of Canada Ltd during December 1929.

Trials with this machine on skis and with the sister

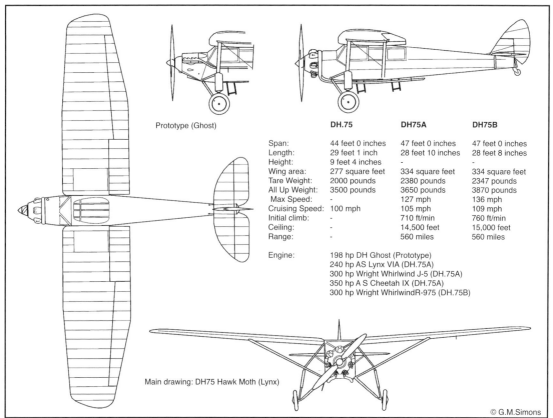

Prototype (Ghost)

	DH.75	DH75A	DH75B
Span:	44 feet 0 inches	47 feet 0 inches	47 feet 0 inches
Length:	29 feet 1 inch	28 feet 10 inches	28 feet 8 inches
Height:	9 feet 4 inches	-	-
Wing area:	277 square feet	334 square feet	334 square feet
Tare Weight:	2000 pounds	2380 pounds	2347 pounds
All Up Weight:	3500 pounds	3650 pounds	3870 pounds
Max Speed:	-	127 mph	136 mph
Cruising Speed:	100 mph	105 mph	109 mph
Initial climb:	-	710 ft/min	760 ft/min
Ceiling:	-	14,500 feet	15,000 feet
Range:	-	560 miles	560 miles

Engine:
198 hp DH Ghost (Prototype)
240 hp AS Lynx VIA (DH.75A)
300 hp Wright Whirlwind J-5 (DH.75A)
350 hp A S Cheetah IX (DH.75A)
300 hp Wright WhirlwindR-975 (DH.75B)

Main drawing: DH75 Hawk Moth (Lynx)

© G.M.Simons

144

DH.75 G-AAFW, seen here on skis in the Canadian wilderness during December 1929.

Right: G-CYVM, one of the DH.75A Hawk Moths fitted with the Armstrong Siddeley Lynx VIA as supplied to the Royal Canadian Air Force in 1930. *(both author's collection.)*

aircraft 'TX on Short floats at Rochester, led in 1930 to Contract 1907 for three Lynx engined Hawk Moths with interchangeable undercarriages for the Canadian Government. First of these, G-CYVD, temporarily reregistered CF-CCA and based at Ottawa for personal use by the Controller of Civil Aviation, was the former G-AAFW, but having no doors on the port side was not permitted to fly as a seaplane. The others, G-CYVL and 'VM, intended for Government operations, had doors on both sides and Hamilton adjustable pitch metal propellers as well as strengthened wing root fittings and cabin roof structures. They were cleared for float operation after tests at Rockcliffe by De Havilland Canada test pilot Leigh Capreol on 4

October 1930 but it was discovered that payload was limited and from then on the aircraft flew only on wheels or skis.

Several undercarriage failures occurred and after 'VL crashed during acceptance tests as a landplane at Longueil, Quebec in 1931, the others were flown only with prior permission until withdrawn from use a year or so later.

Australian markets were also aimed at and 'FX went to De Havilland Aircraft Pty. Ltd. as demonstrator in 1930. On 3 June Amy Johnson flew in it from Brisbane to Sydney after her Moth *Jason* had come to grief. Hart Aircraft Services of Melbourne used it on charter until Tasmanian Airways bought it in

From the short-lived time when the DH.75 was named The Moth Six'. Here G-AAFX wears Short Brothers floats and 'helmets' on the top three cylinders of the Lynx engine. It first flew at Rochester in this configuration on 15 October 1929. *(author's collection.)*

Looking a lot like the later De Havilland Canada Beaver, the unregistered DH.75B with a Wright Whirlwind R-975 radial engine. *(author's collection.)*

February 1934, but after serious damage in a forced landing at Brighton, Tasmania on 10 January 1935 it was rebuilt with a Wright Whirlwind J-5. It then flew with a series of owners until January 1943, when an Armstrong Siddeley Cheetah IX was fitted by the final operator, Connellan Airways Ltd. of Alice Springs.

Competition from American types killed the Hawk Moth within a year. In an unsuccessful attempt to recapture the market, one machine, designated D.H.75B, was fitted in March 1929 with the 300 horsepower Wright Whirlwind radial.

Total Hawk Moth production was eight.

DH.76

This was a DH.66 replacement design using three Bristol Jupiter geared engines. Twenty passengers were to be carried in a cabin that had seven pairs of seats along the starboard side and six single seats along the port side. A luggage hold of thirty cubic feet was located under the pilots cockpit. As far as can be ascertained, no detail drawings were produced and no weights or dimesions finalised.

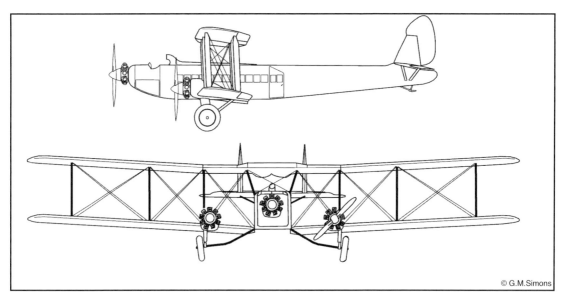

© G.M.Simons

DH.77

Air Ministry Specification F.20/27 was for an 'Interception single-seat fighter' and was issued following changes in fighter tactics which brought about the abolition of standing patrols in favour of interception by a new class of fighter specially designed to take off and climb to combat height in minimum time.

The specification called for a short range, lightly loaded type, without radio and carrying only a minimum of other equipment.

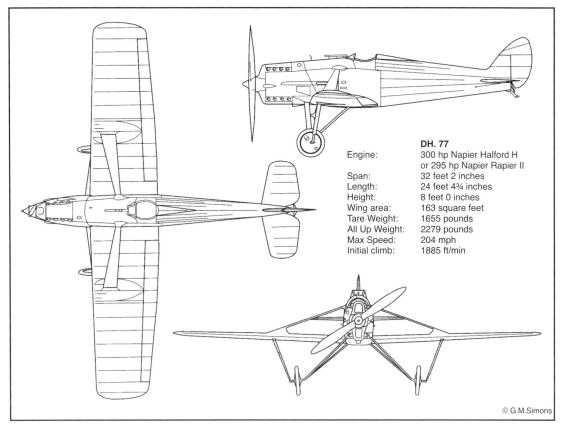

DH. 77

Engine:	300 hp Napier Halford H or 295 hp Napier Rapier II
Span:	32 feet 2 inches
Length:	24 feet 4¾ inches
Height:	8 feet 0 inches
Wing area:	163 square feet
Tare Weight:	1655 pounds
All Up Weight:	2279 pounds
Max Speed:	204 mph
Initial climb:	1885 ft/min

© G.M.Simons

The DH.77 owed a great deal to the DH.71 Tiger Moth and had almost the same performance but was 2½ times the weight and had three times the power. Furthermore its performance was almost identical with that of the contract winning Fury but on only 60% of the power. This achievement was due to the firm's understanding of aerodynamic refinement as a means of saving power and so reducing fuel load. Outstandingly clean entry resulted from close collaboration between the airframe designer Wilfred G. Carter and Major Frank B. Halford, who created a novel supercharged aircooled engine of low frontal area having four banks, each of four cylinders, driving two crankshafts geared together. Following an agreement signed in 1928, Halford engines of over 404.09 cu. in. cylinder capacity were built by D. Napier and Son Ltd. at Acton, so that it was known first as the Napier H type and later as the Rapier I. It imparted slim lines to the nose of the DH.77, which afforded superb forward view for the pilot and permitted the use of an efficient cooling system with low drag entry and exit ducts.

The fuselage was a box girder built of steel tubing and faired to oval section by fabric over wooden

J-9771 in its initial form with a Napier Rapier I engine. *(author's collection.)*

147

The sole DH.77 in its final form with a Napier Rapide II engine and semi-circular crash pylon *(author's collection.)*

formers. Tubular steel struts formed a faired-in V on each side to brace the fabric covered semi-cantilever wing to the top longeron. Large span differential ailerons were fitted and a novel form of wide track undercarriage employed slim, fabric covered rubber-in-compression legs outside the wheels and clear of the slipstream. Good spin recovery characteristics were achieved by fitting an all-moving tailplane without any fixed horizontal surface. The pilot sat above the wing with a commanding view in all directions, armament consisting of two Vickers guns under the cowlings on each side of the cockpit harmonised with a centrally mounted telescopic sight.

The DH.77 was first flown at Stag Lane by Hubert S. Broad on 11 July 1929 and proved to have a top speed approaching 200 mph with a landing speed of 60 mph. With full military load at 20,000 ft. it did 182 m.p.h. but the unladen maximum was 203 m.p.h., all on a mere 325 horsepower.

Broad carried on intensive development flying until he delivered it to Martlesham on 12 December,

Geoffrey de Havilland having flown it on 3/4 October. Broad flew it back on 8 March 1930, the machine was then purchased by the Air Ministry and allocated serial J9771, and Martlesham trials were completed in September 1930. It was shown in the New Types Park at the Hendon Display on 28 June 1930 and afterwards gave a flying demonstration which included a simulated interception climb.

It later went to Brockworth for further flight trials by Gloster Aircraft Ltd with armament removed and it completed a 100 hours Rapier engine development programme until delivered to the RAE Farnborough on 8 December 1932 for the trial installation of the Napier Rapier II in modified cowlings with external oil cooler and exhaust stacks. It also acquired oversize tyres and a crash guard in the form of a semi-circular steel tube above the windscreen, the result of years of mistrust by the the Air Council on the safety of low wing monoplanes when landing. Rapier development occupied 1933 and disposal followed the end of spinning tests in June 1934.

DH.78

A designation allocated to a design study for a transport aircraft that was not proceeded with.

DH.79

A designation allocated to a design study for a transport aircraft that was not proceeded with.

DH.80 Puss Moth

The burgeoning British private flying movement, brought about in the main by the success of the Moth and its variants, saw many pilots venturing farther afield, and beginning to demand cabin comfort and an end to the need for heavy flying clothing.

De Havillands rose to the challenge by persuading the Gipsy II engine to run upside down so that the

cylinder heads no longer lay in the pilot's line of vision, and installing it in a scaled down version of the Hawk Moth. The new aircraft was of traditional wooden construction throughout, the plywood covered fuselage accommodating the pilot in front, with a separate compartment for two side by side passengers on a bench type seat across the back of the cabin.

Entry to the interior was by two doors on the starboard side. The strut braced, folding mainplane

148

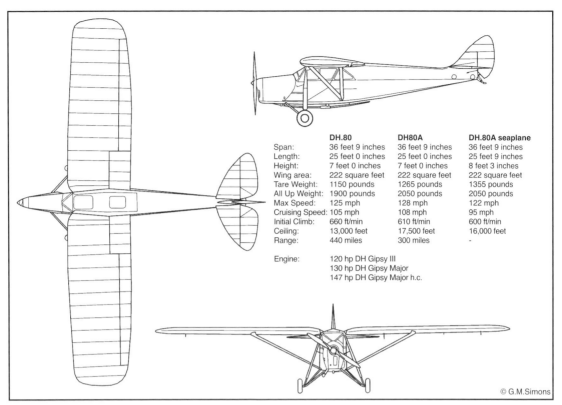

	DH.80	DH80A	DH.80A seaplane
Span:	36 feet 9 inches	36 feet 9 inches	36 feet 9 inches
Length:	25 feet 0 inches	25 feet 0 inches	25 feet 9 inches
Height:	7 feet 0 inches	7 feet 0 inches	8 feet 3 inches
Wing area:	222 square feet	222 square feet	222 square feet
Tare Weight:	1150 pounds	1265 pounds	1355 pounds
All Up Weight:	1900 pounds	2050 pounds	2050 pounds
Max Speed:	125 mph	128 mph	122 mph
Cruising Speed:	105 mph	108 mph	95 mph
Initial Climb:	660 ft/min	610 ft/min	600 ft/min
Ceiling:	13,000 feet	17,500 feet	16,000 feet
Range:	440 miles	300 miles	-
Engine:	120 hp DH Gipsy III		
	130 hp DH Gipsy Major		
	147 hp DH Gipsy Major h.c.		

© G.M.Simons

was built in two halves, shoulder mounted to cut down centre section drag, and with the main undercarriage shock absorber legs anchored to the front wing root fittings.

The DH.80 had no type name, but contemporary advertising called it the Moth Three, and at the same period the Hawk Moth was known for a short time as the Moth Six. The DH.80 flew for the first time at Stag Lane on 9 September 1929 under B conditions as E-l, but for once the designers had underestimated the effect of improved airflow over the new engine and centre section, and the machine was 7 m.p.h. up on estimated top speed. In spite of this encouraging start the DH.80 did not go into production and the truncated fuselage of the dismantled prototype was later well known as Stag Lane's Gipsy engine test rig.

Experience gained from the DH.60M showed that overseas sales success lay in metal construction and it was decided that the

Two views of the un-named DH.80 G-AAHZ in flight and on the ground showing the flat wooden sided fuselage. (*author's collection.*)

149

Above: the open starboard door, with the air brake in the 'ON' position.

Below: the neat instrument panel of an early Puss Moth, with a sloping map table below it. On the left is the tail trimming gear, and on the right the lever that works the air brake. *(both author's collection.)*

there was a need to steepen the glide, and to this end the wide undercarriage shock absorber fairings could be rotated through ninety degrees to form air brakes.

Deliveries were made all over the world via the De Havilland companies in Australia, Canada, India and South Africa. The fourth production Puss Moth was shipped to De Havilland Aircraft of Canada Ltd. for evaluation. Registered CF-AGO, it made a trans-Canada return flight from Toronto to Vancouver, a performance which proved the type well suited to Canadian conditions. It led to sufficient orders from the RCAF and civil operators for the company to establish a production line for the erection of Puss Moths from components made in England.

The British market absorbed 143 Puss Moths but on 13 October 1930 VH-UPC piloted by Capt. Nesbit crashed in Western Australia, the first of nine accidents which marred the early career of this aeroplane.

Investigations revealed structural failure of the wings and it was at first thought that this might have some connection with the rudder flutter that de Havilland Aircraft of Canada Ltd. had experienced at high speeds with their original British built machine CF-AGO and three others, CF-APE, 'CCC and 'IOL. Then on 21 May 1932 the ski-equipped Puss Moth G-CYUT crashed at Ottawa and test pilot A. L. James lived to tell the tale of the circumstances which led up to the failure of the port mainplane.

Accident investigations recorded in Report R. & M. 1699 reveal that internal damage and failure at the tips was a common feature of all accidents. Intensive investigation by the National Physical Laboratory and the RAE, who conducted flying tests at Martlesham with the Air Ministry's own Puss Moth K1824 and its eventual destruction in static tests at Farnborough in October 1932, revealed that in some circumstances, when high speed was combined with turbulent weather conditions, wing failure could occur. Wing flutter tests with mass balanced ailerons were made by Hubert Broad in January 1931 using G-AAVA fitted with a parachute seat and an emergency door.

Progressive modifications included the addition of a small stabilising stay tube connecting the forward wing strut with the rear wing root fitting, the substitution of the larger rudder developed for the seaplane variant but with mass balance and the fitting of more effective aileron mass balances. Final tests with the larger mass balanced rudder were made at the RAE in December 1932 using De Havilland's experimental

production version of the new monoplane should have a welded steel tube fuselage and carry the name Puss Moth under the designation DH.80A. The partition between pilot and passengers was deleted and the two passengers sat in staggered tandem seats, the rear one running on rails for ease of entry. Progressive development of the inverted Gipsy II culminated in the delivery of the first production engine, styled Gipsy III, on 6 May 1930 and although the power output remained unchanged, the Puss was almost 30 m.p.h. faster than the Gipsy II Moth. With such a clean design

G-ABGR of the Aircraft Operating Company in flight. This machine represents a production DH.80A, with less dihedral and a more-rounded fuselage. *(author's collection.)*

Left: G-AAYE, Maurice Jackaman's DH.80A with the original small rudder and wire wheels.

Below: The larger rudder as fitted to the Puss Moth used by the US Embassy in London from 1931 to 1935. *both author's collection.)*

Puss Moth E-8, which had an eight inch increase in sweepback on the mainplanes and a tailwheel. This aircraft reverted to standard for normal sale as G-ACYT in 1934, by which time the Puss Moth's early misfortunes had been resolved to become an outstanding machine with some of the world's greatest flights to its credit.

On 7 December 1931 Herbert John Louis 'Bert' Hinkler AFC DSM landed CF-APK, a British built Puss Moth at Hanworth, just outside London, on a flight from Madrid. This was the end of a solo trip that included the first nonstop flight from New York to Jamaica, the first British air crossing of the Caribbean Sea, the first British flight from Jamaica to Venezuela and a 22 hour South Atlantic crossing from Natal to Bathurst. Hinkler had flown from Canada to New York, then non-stop to Jamaica, then to Venezuela, Guyana, Brazil, and across the South Atlantic to Africa; this part of the journey was done in extremely bad weather, but despite a tearing gale and practically no visibility for part of the way because of low and heavy clouds, he drifted a comparatively small distance off his course. From West Africa he flew to London. For this he was awarded the Segrave Trophy, the Johnston

Memorial Prize and the Britannia Trophy for the most meritorious flying performance of the year. This was the first solo flight across the South Atlantic, and Hinkler was only the second person to cross the Atlantic solo, after Charles Lindbergh.

Hinkler ensured success by spending eight months in de Havilland's Toronto factory, supervising the erection of the aircraft and the installation of long range modifications of his own design. Sqn. Ldr. C. S. Wynne-Eaton's attempt to cross the North Atlantic in a similar long range single seater, G-AAXI, ended when the aircraft was destroyed by fire when taking off from Lester Field, Newfoundland on 6 July 1930 on a flight to the starting point at Harbour Grace.

On 15 October 1932 Jehangir Ratanji Dadabhoy Tata flew the first air mails over the 1,330 mile Karachi-Bombay-Madras route in VT-ADN. In the UK, HRH Prince Edward, the Prince of Wales, bought G-ABBS,

DH.80A G-AAVB on floats in The Welsh Harp before the record flight to Stockholm. *(author's collection.)*

'FV, 'NN and 'RR which were decorated in the red and blue of the Guards, and Amy Johnson was presented with G-AAZV *Jason II* in recognition of her solo Moth flight to Australia.

The third produciion machine, G-AAVB, was fitted temporarily with Short floats, enabling it to be flown 1,040 miles nonstop from the Welsh Harp, Hendon to the Stockholm Aero Show by Col. the Master of Sempill in twelve hours on 4 September 1930. He returned via Norway and Scotland on the 22nd and later toured the entire British coast.

Senor Carlos Bleck, who had flown a Cirrus Moth to West Africa, repeated the performance in the 100th production Puss Moth, covering 11,500 miles in the course of a return trip from Lisbon to Loanda early in 1931. His route crossed that of Mrs. Florence Wilson and Captain Marthinus C P Mostert, at that time engaged on a flight from Kenya to England via West Africa and the Canary Islands in the first of three Wilson Airways Puss Moths, VP-KAH. Their flying time was 80 hours 40 minutes.

In the U.S.A. Frenchman H. A. Darren and two friends flew from Newark Airport to San Francisco in 1934 in Gipsy Major powered G-ABEL. They crossed the Rockies at 12,000 feet with ease with three up and luggage and completed the tour via the Great Lakes in fifty hours flying time. Later the same year the Master of Sempill made a leisurely trip from England to Australia in his personal G-ABJU to attend the Centenary celebrations.

The first Puss Moth flight to Australia was made by F. R. Matthews, who left Croydon in G-ABDW on 16 September 1930 and reached Darwin in a leisurely 4 weeks 4 days.

The most remarkable flights over this route were made by Charles J. Melrose in Australian registered Puss Moth VH-UQO. After flying 8,000 miles round Australia in the record time of 5 days 11 hours during August 1934, he flew it from Darwin to Croydon in 8 days 9 hours in order to compete in the MacRobertson Race back to Melbourne! Leaving Mildenhall on 20 October he averaged 103 m.p.h. to come third in the handicap section. The Cape record also suffered at the hands of Puss Moth pilots, first with Caspareuthus and again when Peggy Salaman and Gordon Store left Lympne in G-ABEH *Good Hope* on 31 October 1931 to lower the record to 6 days 6 hours 40 minutes.

Jim and Amy Mollison were star performers on Puss Moths. The former left Lympne in a special single seat long range version, G-ABKG, on 24 March 1932 and flew via the Sahara and the west coast of Africa to reach the Cape in 4 days 17 hours 19 minutes. *The Hearts Content*, G-ABXY, was built for him with a 160 gallon fuel tank in the cabin giving a 3,600 mile range. Behind the tank lay the pilot's seat, access to which was by a small door at the rear. On 18 August 1932 he took off from Portmarnock Strand, Dublin and made the first solo east-west Atlantic crossing, landing at Pennfield Ridge, New Brunswick 31 hours 20 minutes later. *Desert Cloud* G-ACAB was then prepared for Amy Johnson and fitted with one of the first of the new 130 horsepower Gipsy Major engines. It reduced not only Mollison's Cape record by 10 hours 26 minutes but also broke that for the homeward journey. Mollison, again in 'XY, later became the first man to fly from England to South America, the first to make a solo east-west crossing of the South Atlantic and the first to cross both the North and South Atlantic Oceans, when he arrived at Port Natal in Brazil, 3 days 10 hours 8 minutes out from Lympne on 9 February 1933.

G-ABMD was specially fitted with a 147 h.p. Gipsy Major horsepower engine and modified by Airwork Ltd. of Heston for entry in the 1934 Warsaw International Touring Competition. Dr. Lachmann of Handley Page Ltd., James Martin of Martin-Baker Ltd. and Herr Hoeffner joined forces to design full span slots and wing flaps inboard of the ailerons which were rigged to droop ten degrees in flight and in conjunction with a Fairey adjustable pitch propeller, reduced the

Above: the slatted and flapped competition Puss Moth G-ABMD for W D Macpherson.

Left: G-ABXY *The Hearts Content* showing the revised cabin arrangements.

(both author's collection.)

minimum flying speed to 35 m.p.h. Extra rear windows of the type fitted to *The Hearts Content* were also provided to improve rearward vision.

The standard Puss Moth was a stable, viceless aeroplane appreciated by everyone who flew it. A number of those impressed for RAF communications duties in the United Kingdom in 1939 had been with their original owners for over eight years. Many were used by the Air Transport Auxiliary for taxi work and a number reappeared after the war.

DH.81 Swallow Moth

The DH.81 was an attempt to return to the philosophy of the true light aeroplane as demonstrated by the original Moth concept. Geoffrey de Havilland thought that the original Moth design had moved too far away from the initial goal of a cheap sporting aeroplane. It had undergone a fifty percent increase in weight and a doubling of power.

Reverting to open-cockpit layout combined with a cantilever monoplane wing, the Swallow Moth was an attempt to move in two directions at once – first to make a light plane and second to follow the gradual trend towards monoplanes.

The plywood covered fuselage was a spruce and plywood box fitted with the new Halford-designed 80 horsepower Gipsy IV inverted engine with the undercarriage shock strut attached to the top longeron, its point of attachment adjacent to the top engine mounting bracket.

The well-tapered wing featured inversely-proportioned differential ailerons which were aerodynamically mass-balanced by means of a small overhang at the tips.

On 24 August 1931, Geoffrey de Havilland took the machine on its first flight at Stag Lane in red primer dope without any markings and found that the maximum speed was 117 mph; not bad for just 80 horsepower! It was discovered that the large, tapered wing and flat-sided fuselage created a neutral directional stability and there was also a degree of wing flexibility at speed.

Changes were soon incorporated, comprising a new wing with a thicker centre-section, a reduction in aerodynamic mass-balance area of the rudder combined with a smaller fin area. At the same time the cockpits were enclosed with a hinged glazed cabin top and blending rear fuselage fairing. Now styled the DH.81A, these modifications also served to push the maximum speed up to 129 mph.

Flying continued through the autumn of 1931 and in January 1932 the aircraft was given the Class B markings E-7; no civil registration was ever allotted or applied.

A situation over which de Havilland had no control was to kill off this promising little aircraft. It co-

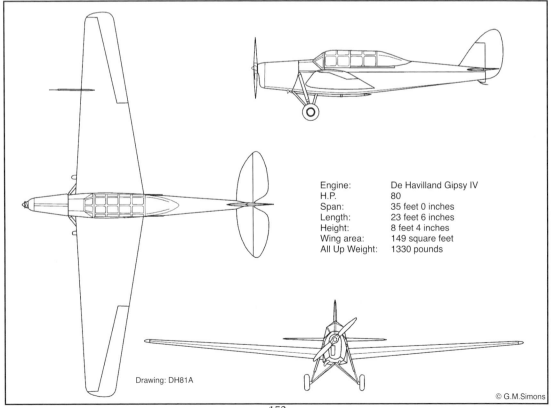

Engine:	De Havilland Gipsy IV
H.P.	80
Span:	35 feet 0 inches
Length:	23 feet 6 inches
Height:	8 feet 4 inches
Wing area:	149 square feet
All Up Weight:	1330 pounds

Drawing: DH81A

© G.M.Simons

The only known photograph of the DH.81 Swallow Moth. *(author's collection.)*

incided with the peak of the economic depression and DH soon realised that development and manufacture would be to launch out into the unknown. With manufacturing capacity fully absorbed with the DH.60 Moth it made more sense to concentrate on the aircraft production already in hand and for which a market was already established.

There was no incentive to risk capital of any sort on a new machine and so the final flight of the Swallow Moth took place on 3 February, after which the machine was dismantled and forgotten.

The Swallow Moth paved the way for the DH.94 Moth Minor of 1938, which incorporated the heavily-modified fuselage of the Swallow Moth into its prototype. In turn, the Moth Minor had some bearing on the much later DHC.1 Chipmunk.

DH.82 Tiger Moth

The origins of the DH.82 are somewhat convoluted. Clearly its origins stem from the DH.60T Trainer, which had acquired the inverted Gipsy III, with all its advantages.

All of the DH.60 series of aircraft shared one common feature: the wings were straight, with no sweep-back and stagger. This placed the upper wing directly over the lower wing. This had the advantage of providing simple wing-folding, but the down-side was that it obstructed access and exit to the front cockpit. If the occupant had to get out in a hurry it was difficult; if they were wearing a parachute, then it was a struggle. And if the aircraft happened to be in a spin at the time, escape was likely to be impossible.

Although this did not interfere with sales to

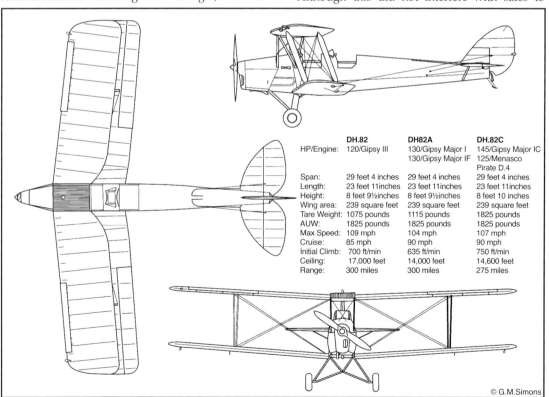

	DH.82	DH82A	DH.82C
HP/Engine:	120/Gipsy III	130/Gipsy Major I	145/Gipsy Major IC
		130/Gipsy Major IF	125/Menasco Pirate D.4
Span:	29 feet 4 inches	29 feet 4 inches	29 feet 4 inches
Length:	23 feet 11 inches	23 feet 11 inches	23 feet 11 inches
Height:	8 feet 9½ inches	8 feet 9½ inches	8 feet 10 inches
Wing area:	239 square feet	239 square feet	239 square feet
Tare Weight:	1075 pounds	1115 pounds	1825 pounds
AUW:	1825 pounds	1825 pounds	1825 pounds
Max Speed:	109 mph	104 mph	107 mph
Cruise:	85 mph	90 mph	90 mph
Initial Climb:	700 ft/min	635 ft/min	750 ft/min
Ceiling:	17,000 feet	14,000 feet	14,600 feet
Range:	300 miles	300 miles	275 miles

© G.M.Simons

Right: the new dropped down doors, staggered wings and moving of the rear lift wire to a forward point resulted in the very free passage out of the front as well as the rear cockpit.

K-2570 was one of the early production Tiger Moths showing the fabric covered rear decking of the DH.82. *(both author's collection.)*

authorities overseas, it was the one feature which the British Air Ministry found unacceptable. Despite being impressed by the success of the DH.60 in all its forms, the Ministry was adamant that were a Service instructor faced with having to jump out in an emergency, the restricted exit posed an unacceptble life-and-death situation.

Geoffrey de Havilland realised that the company was being handed information on a plate that would give them a chance to bid for the most coveted order of the age – the provision of a new training aircraft for the Royal Air Force.

How the new design came about is well known; that it was built without the benefit of drawings is undeniable. Designer Arthur Ernest Hagg and Geoffrey de Havilland's brother-in-law and works manager Frank Trounson Hearle were given a small shed and a DH.60T Moth Trainer to take to pieces and re-assemble in a suitable manner. Various wing arrangements were tried and experimental centre-section struts welded up as required. They began by moving the petrol tank, which formed the centre section, forward by eighteen inches but after discussion with Geoffrey de Havilland and Hubert Broad it was moved forward another four inches.

Slowly by trial and error the new design evolved. The centre of lift of the top wing was now too far ahead of the centre of gravity, so the wings were given a rearwards sweep by shortening the root end of the rear spars. After experimenting with three sets of rear spars it was finally settled on moving the wings nine inches rearwards as measured at the interplane struts.

Civilian Tigers! G-ADJB served with Phillips and Powis Aircraft Ltd, while many of those behind it are marked up for the De Havilland School of Flying. *(DH via BAe Hatfield.)*

S1676, one of two DH.82 Tiger Moth seaplanes evaluated by the RAF in 1932. *(author's collection.)*

thirty-five aircraft of the initial order to Specification T.23/31 were despatched to Grantham for distribution to the Central Flying School and other training units and five were used by the CFS for inverted formation flying at the 1932 Hendon Air Display. The Air Ministry ordered two more machines, S1675-6 to Specification T.6/33, which were fitted with Short twin floats prior to trials at Rochester and Felixstowe.

Unfortunately it was found that this was insufficient to bring the centre of gravity into the right position. Rather than re-make all four rear spars, the team took the simple measure of giving the top wings two inches additional sweepback. This brought the centre of gravity into the right place, and explains why the top wings of a Tiger Moth have more sweepback than the lower ones.

With the geometry defined, the first eight aircraft - G-ABNC, G-ABNI, G-ABNJ, G-ABNK, G-ABNL, G-ABNM, G-ABNY, and G-ABPH were all fitted with the inverted Gipsy III engine and the aircraft designated DH.60T, but with the name Tiger Moth.

After this trial batch was finished, a further snag arose concerning the new geometry. Moving the wings backwards also moved the wing-tip further back along the parallel line that linked main wheels to tail-skid. The tips of the lower wings were now very close to the ground and rough terrain or a mis-judged landing would surely put the wing-tip into the ground, an unacceptable situation.

The prototype DH.82 made its maiden flight at Stag Lane on 26 October 1931 under Class B conditions as E-6. It was later registered G-ABRC. Evaluation at Martlesham Heath resulted in the type being cleared for aerobatics at an all-up weight of 1,750 pounds.

Initial work was done to meet Air Ministry Specification 15/31 (some sources record this as 13/31). Following this, the

The Tiger Moth was offered in gunnery, bombing and photographic versions but only a small number of multi-purpose machines were ordered, the main demand being for ab initio and aerobatic trainers, which sold in twenty-five countries.

Production was centred at first on contracts for the RAF and foreign governments but included a number of civilian machines for the Elementary and Reserve Flying Schools, where RAF pilots were taught under the Expansion Scheme before going to the Service Flying Training Schools. Civil Tiger Moths, which did not have mass balanced rudders and ailerons, were operated by numerous flying schools.

In 1934 the Air Ministry ordered 50 examples of an improved version to Specification T.26/33 which called for the new 130 horsepower Gipsy Major engine, plywood decking to the rear fuselage in place of time honoured fabric and stringers, and a blind flying hood over the rear cockpit. In this form it was known in the

Alan Cobham's National Air Displays featured Tiger Moth flying by Geoffrey Tyson, whose speciality was to pick up a handkerchief off the ground with a flexible spike fixed to the wingtip of G-ACEZ, as seen here. *(author's collection.)*

Left: 4923, a Canadian-built DH.82C fitted with a Menasco engine for the RCAF.

Below: A17-104 was one of many Australian-built Tigers that provided ab initio training. *(both author's collection.)*

RAF as the Tiger Moth II, but outside the Service its proper designation was DH.82A Tiger Moth. In the following year further contracts were awarded to Specification T.7/35 and others were supplied to the Uruguayan Army and the Air Forces of Brazil, Denmark, Iraq, South Africa, Persia and Spain.

In 1937 production overtook military commitments, enabling Tiger Moths to replace existing flying club machines. Overseas civilian orders were also accepted from clubs and private owners, the largest customer being France which bought seventeen. In 1937 an order was placed with De Havilland Aircraft of Canada Ltd. for 25 Tiger Moths for the RCAF and a year later the firm was asked to supply 200 fuselages. By the outbreak of war 1,150 had been built at Hatfield, 227 at Toronto, one at Wellington, New Zealand and three for the London Aeroplane Club by the De Havilland Aeronautical Technical School.

Most of British and Commonwealth civil Tiger Moths were impressed into military use in 1939 when in common with their Service brethren they were fitted with Modification 112, comprising anti-spinning strakes on each side of the rear fuselage. These were first fitted to R5129, tested at Farnborough in November 1941 during an investigation into spinning troubles which were cured by removing aileron mass balances.

In 1940 all the Hatfield site was required for the Mosquito, and Tiger Moth production was transferred to the assembly line of Morris Motors Ltd. at Cowley, Oxford so that total output to 15 August 1945 exceeded 8,000 aircraft, including 3,065 built by de Havilland at Hatfield, 3,214 by Morris at Cowley while the overseas companies contributed the remainder.

An approaching invasion and a shortage of suitable anti-submarine aircraft led to the fitting of Tiger Moths in 1939-40 with under-wing racks for eight twenty pound bombs, and after release tests at Hatfield by Major Hereward de Havilland, 1,500 sets of racks were distributed to Elementary Flying Training

Light bomb racks are fitted under the fuselage of EM-836 *(DH via BAe Hatfield.)*

157

Schools in the UK where, throughout the war, RAF pilots were given ab initio instruction on Tiger Moths prior to posting to Service training schools. Later, in the Burma campaign, the Tiger again left its training role to become an ambulance carrying one casualty. The aircraft was flown from the front seat and the unfortunate patient lay under a hinged decking in what had once been the rear cockpit, the luggage locker and into the rear fuselage.

Large numbers of Australian-built Tiger Moths were shipped to Southern Rhodesia and South Africa for use under the Commonwealth Air Training Plan, which also operated in Canada, where the Tiger was redesigned and adapted to local conditions by De Havilland Aircraft of Canada Ltd. A two piece nose cowling which hinged along the centre line and opened down the front for improved accessibility housed a Gipsy Major 1C engine. By shortening the radius rods, the main undercarriage was moved forward to prevent nosing over when using the brakes which were fitted, together with a heavy duty tail wheel to improve ground handling. To combat the sub-zero temperatures of the Canadian winter, the cockpits were heated and covered by a large sliding canopy, and later, when supplies of Gipsy Majors were cut off by the Battle of the Atlantic, the American-built 125 h.p. Menasco Pirate engine was fitted. The external appearance was so changed, even the familiar wide-chord interplane struts having given place to narrow steel tubular members, that a new designation, DH.82C, was warranted. Alternative wheel, ski and float undercarriages were provided and flying training

went on all the year round. Two hundred Gipsy Major powered DH.82Cs bought by the United States Government in 1942 under the model number PT-24 were also delivered to the RCAF.

The DH.82B Queen Bee

The Queen Bee was a radio controlled target aircraft built to Specification 18/33 which although externally similar to a Tiger Moth was different under the skin. Mainplanes, undercarriage and certain detail fittings were the same, but the fabric covered metal fuselage of the Tiger Moth was replaced by a standard spruce and plywood Moth fuselage for cost and buoyancy. As it was powered by a Gipsy Major, the Queen Bee should be more correctly described as a Moth Major with Tiger Moth mainplanes, and all the early examples came from the Moth Major production line, which from 1935 was given over entirely to the building of Queen Bees.

A normal front cockpit with instruments and flying controls was retained, but a fairing was provided with which to cover it during radio controlled flying. The rear cockpit was enclosed by a section of hinged decking to form a compartment near the centre of gravity for the Farnborough-designed radio control gear, electric power for which was supplied by a wind driven generator on the port side. Extra range was obtained by fitting a 25 gallon centre section tank. The prototype, K3584, was first flown at Hatfield on 5 January 1935 and on 26 June a demonstration of take off, flying, manoeuvring and landing was given at Farnborough with the seventh production aircraft,

What goes up...

DH.82B Queen Bees were often launched by catapults powered by cordite charges.

Here K4294 '12' is seen being pushed skywards.
(both author's collection.)

...must come down! Queen Bee K5107 alights after another mission avoiding the guns. *(author's collection.)*

K4227, under commands issued by a push button control panel.

The wheeled undercarriage was fitted only for test flying or ferrying, as when operational the Queen Bee was equipped for catapulting with pick-up slings in the centre section and Short twin metal floats. After a catapult take off, usually from a ship of the Royal Navy, the Queen Bee would fly up and down a predetermined course while gunners did their best to destroy it, afterwards landing on the water to be hoisted inboard.

For initial training a Queen Bee Flight was formed at 1 Anti-Aircraft Co-operation Unit, Henlow, in May 1937 and its first operational launching was made with K8661 at Watchet, Somerset, after it was transferred there on 27 July. Anti-aircraft ranges were always sited on the coast so that in the event of a hit the Queen Bee would fall into the sea without endangering life.

DH.82Bs was built in quantity to Specification 20/35, output being 320 at Hatfield and 60 at a factory in Glasgow under the supervision of Scottish Aviation Ltd., deliveries commencing 19 October 1943 and ending on 30 September 1944. The type was operated in Britain by T to Z Flights of 1 and 2 AACU, Gosport which also supplied Queen Bees to ships of the Royal Navy. 3 and 4 AACUs at Hal Far, Malta and Seletar, Singapore were similar overseas units.

Being expendable, an unusually high number were held at Maintenance Units, but after 1942 all reserves were held by the

Pilotless Aircraft Unit at Manorbier.

After the war the Tiger Moth was used in Britain by University Air Squadrons and RAFVR schools until completely replaced by the Chipmunk in February 1955. It continued in service with the Royal Navy, which in February 1960 still had eleven airworthy examples for glider towing and use at the Royal Naval Engineering College, Plymouth.

Large numbers of surplus RAF Tigers were disposed of to military and civil authorities in France, Belgium, Holland and elsewhere from 1946 and a flood also descended on the British market in 1950. At a time when no new light aeroplanes were available, the type took on a new lease of life and every aerodrome had one or more club or private Tigers, with half dismantled specimens in the background to provide spares.

Specialised Tiger Moth conversions fell into four main categories: the addition of cabin tops, the fitting of electric starters and inverted fuel systems, the mandatory addition of large dorsal fins in Holland, and complete reconstruction as cabin four seaters.

Standard Tiger Moths spin positively to the right if the speed is reduced below 40 mph, or can be ruddered into a left hand spin, the rate of which was considerably reduced by the wartime anti-spinning

PH-UAW, one of the Dutch DH.82s modified with the outsize dorsal fin. *(author's collection.)*

Left: Thruxton Jackaroo G-AOIR comes in to land.

Below: Tigers G-AOEI at Old Warden.

Bottom: G-AMHF at rest.
(all via John Stride collection.)

strakes, later often removed. The very large dorsal fin considered necessary by the Nationale Luchtvaart School at Ypenburg made no apparent difference to spinning characteristics but nevertheless this modification was made to their entire fleet and to several Dutch private Tiger Moths. A more drastic conversion known as the Jackaroo, built at Thruxton by Jackaroo Aircraft Ltd., involved cutting the front fuselage in half lengthways and welding extension pieces in the cross members to widen the fuselage to accommodate four passengers in side byside pairs. Both the undercarriage track and centre section were also widened with a resultant increase in span and although initially powered by the Gipsy Major 1, most Jackaroos later had the 1 C engine to improve take off and climb. Nineteen were produced at Thruxton between 1957 and 1959, Mk. 1 and Mk. 3 being cabin versions, the latter e.g. G-APAO, having a metal framed canopy in place of the earlier wooden structure and also provision for brakes. The Mk. 2 was an agricultural single seater which proved unsuccessful and the only example, G-AOEY, was re-converted to Mk. 1 standard. One other Jackaroo, G-APOV, was built for the Tiger Club by Rollason Aircraft and Engines Ltd. in 1959 but was aerodynamically cleaner with widened rear fuselage and improved cowlings.

DH.82 Production

It has proved virtually impossible to decide upon the exact number of DH.82s of different marques built. However, corrolation between a number of reliable sources suggest that the following are probably the most accurate totals : between 1931 and August 1939 114 DH.82 aircraft were built at DH Stag Lane, 17 in Norway and 3 in Sweden. At the same time, 1,424 DH.82A and DH.82C machines were built comprising 1,066 at DH Stag Lane and

DH Hatfield, 227 by DH Canada, 20 in Norway, 20 in Sweden and 91 in Portugal.

Between September 1939 and August 1945, 7,253 aircraft were built, comprising 795 at DH Hatfield, 1,520 by DH Canada, 345 by DH New Zealand, 1,085 by DH Australia and by far the biggest single quantity by the types principal sub-contractor, Morris Motors Ltd at Cowley, which made no fewer than 3,508.

This makes a grand total, for all marques of DH.82 and from all sources, of 8,811 aircraft, but even this total is only an approximation based on numbers which are certain; there are suggestions that others were made which have not been accounted for and war-time records of which are lost.

The DH.82B Queen Bee, excluded from the above figures, was to account for an additional 420 aircraft comprising 210 built by DH Hatfield between 1935 and August 1939, 110 produced by the same source between September 1939 and August 1944, and 100 produced by Scottish Aviation.

DH.83 Fox Moth

By the early 1930s large numbers of short domestic and feeder airlines had sprung up all over the world. These were businesses which created a demand for a cheap and simple aircraft that could carry three people or freight between stages of around 350 miles. In general this was a market already being served in a not very satisfactory manner by the Puss Moth and other similar machines. On top of that there was a demand for a utility joy-riding aircraft with the ability to vary its fuel load according to the number of passengers carried for short-haul use

Arthur Ernest Hagg came up with an astonishingly simple solution which was to earn De Havilland a very good investment return. Hagg's answer to the problem was to take a set of standard Tiger Moth wings, tail, undercarriage and engine mounting and fit them to a new wooden spruce and plywood-covered fuselage which had an open cockpit for the pilot and an enclosed cabin that could accommodate four passengers on a short journey or three for up to 360 miles. The cabin could also be used for the transport of freight. This economical light transport machine was rendered even more attractive by using a production Gipsy Major engine.

Easy access to the passenger cabin was ensured by a large door on each side and, as in the DH.82, the routing of the lower bracing wires from the front spar root fitting only. With less stagger and sweep-back than the Tiger Moth, the wings were once more foldable. Like the '82', the lower wings had more dihedral than the upper ones but, unlike the earlier machine, slots were not fitted, automatic or otherwise.

G-ABUO, the prototype, first flown at Stag Lane on 29 January 1932, was shipped to Canada and

The prototype Fox Moth G-ABUO on trestles undergoing rigging checks prior to its first flight (*DH via BAe Hatfield*)

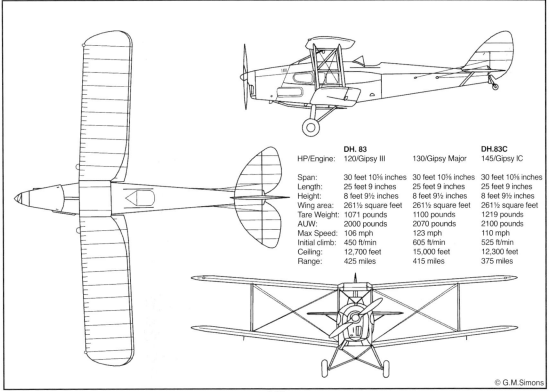

	DH. 83		DH.83C
HP/Engine:	120/Gipsy III	130/Gipsy Major	145/Gipsy IC
Span:	30 feet 10⅝ inches	30 feet 10⅝ inches	30 feet 10⅝ inches
Length:	25 feet 9 inches	25 feet 9 inches	25 feet 9 inches
Height:	8 feet 9½ inches	8 feet 9½ inches	8 feet 9½ inches
Wing area:	261½ square feet	261½ square feet	261½ square feet
Tare Weight:	1071 pounds	1100 pounds	1219 pounds
AUW:	2000 pounds	2070 pounds	2100 pounds
Max Speed:	106 mph	123 mph	110 mph
Initial climb:	450 ft/min	605 ft/min	525 ft/min
Ceiling:	12,700 feet	15,000 feet	12,300 feet
Range:	425 miles	415 miles	375 miles

© G.M.Simons

Drop, Hide or Lose of the day! Air couriers 1933 style sees packages of bicycle springs from Terry's de-luxe saddles loaded aboard Hillman Airways G-ABVK 'No.6' in this publicity picture. *(author's collection.)*

evaluated on floats and skis by Canadian Airways Ltd. So sturdy was the design that it flew as CF-API for nearly 20 years, ending its useful life with Leavens Bros. at Toronto in 1950. It was the forerunner of seven Fox Moths erected at Downsview from British built components. 98 Fox Moths were built, all except the prototype having narrow chord steel tubular interplane struts.

'Carrying pilot and, for short flights, four passengers on a single Gipsy III of 120 hp must be regarded as very economical flying indeed.' So wrote the magazine *Flight* on 18 March 1932.

The Fox Moth was an instant success, the only major change made between the prototype and production machines being the replacement of the original wide-chord wooden interplane struts by narrow, streamlined-tubular struts.

Three early examples, G-ABVI, 'VJ and 'VK, replaced the Puss Moths on the Clacton-Maylands-Ramsgate scheduled service of Hillmans Airways Ltd. As air taxis they were often in use during the flat racing season for the conveyance of jockeys and the Press around the race courses.

In July, 1932, Walter Laurence Hope won his third King's Cup Race in the second production Fox Moth, G-ABUT, at an average speed of 124.13 mph; his machine had been modified for racing with a 130 horsepower Gipsy IIIA, sliding cockpit canopy and a fuel-tank in the passenger cabin instead of in the centre section.

Most production Fox Moths had Gipsy Major engines and about one-third had sliding hoods. These were occasionally referred to as the 'Speed Model' but there was no change of designation.

Another Fox Moth, 'RU, was taken to Graham Land on the Antarctic Penninsula by the British Graham Land Expedition and flew 104 hours in three years as a sea and skiplane on survey work piloted by W. E. Hampton. Yet another, 'RK, left Rochester piloted by John Grierson on 20 July 1934 to make an outstanding seaplane flight to Iceland and over the Greenland Ice Cap to Ottawa, reached in 61 hours flying time on 30 August.

The Prince of Wales, already the owner of Puss Moths, acquired a red, blue and chromium Fox Moth, G-ACDD, early in 1933, but the acquisition of a Dragon resulted in its sale to Belgian private owner Guy Hansez as OO-ENC for participation in the Egyptian International Air Rally in December of that year.

Above: another view of G-ABUO undergoing rigging checks.

Right: the same machine, now in Canada and fited with skis.
(both DH via BAe Hatfield.)

Two uses for the Fox Moth could not be more different! Above: The Prince of Wales' Fox Moth G-ACDD.

Left: Fox Moth G-ACRU on skis as part of the British Graham Land Expedition. The aircraft was used extensively for aerial surveying reconnaissance, and depot laying.
(both DH via BAe Hatfield.)

Victor Holyman, opened the 108 mile Launceston to Flinders Island service in September 1932. QANTAS also purchased five to replace the DH.50s of the Flying Doctor service and 30 years later a sixth, VH-USJ, was still in use by the Western Australia section. Others found their way to the New Guinea goldfield service, for which they were ideally suited. At least two Fox Moths were built at Sydney by de Havilland Aircraft Pty. Ltd., one of which, later re-registered VH-GAS, saw service with Papuan Air Transport Ltd. at Port Moresby.

In 1935 it went to Air Travel (N.Z.) Ltd. as ZK-AEK, to join several other Fox Moths on the pioneer 135 mile air mail service down the west coast of South Island from Hokitika to Okuru. The Fox Moth also inaugurated serious air transport in Scotland when, in 1933, the Scottish Motor Traction Co. Ltd. and Midland and Scottish Air Ferries Ltd., both of Renfrew, bought eight and four machines respectively for frequent services to, and occasional joyriding at, remote townships in the Highlands and the Hebrides. In the south, G-ACEB pioneered the Thames air ferry between Southend and Rochester in 1934 and for six years G-ACCA and 'IG worked the Portsmouth-Ryde holiday service of Portsmouth, Southsea and Isle of Wight Aviation Ltd.

DH.83s VO-ABC and 'DE - both fitted with Fairchild floats, were used by Imperial Airways Ltd. from July 1935 for meteorological flights over Newfoundland, using moorings in Portugal Cove, St. Johns.

In Tasmania the Fox Moth *Miss Currie* flown by

During the war years Fox Moths in Britain were camouflaged and impressed, three for Air Transport Auxiliary, three for a radar trials unit at Christchurch and one each to the Royal Navy and the Blackburn company as hacks. Four were impressed by the RAAF as well as a number by the RNZAF and after the war several were still flying in Britain, Australia, New Zealand, Canada and Spain. The Spanish aircraft, then registered EC-AEI, was originally floatplane EC-VVA, delivered in April 1934, which served with the Air Force as 30-147.

Post-war demand for the machine in Canada led to the evolution of the DH.83C, built relatively cheaply at Downsview, Toronto, in 1946 using war surplus

Left: Portsmouth, Southsea and Isle of Wight Aviation Ltd's Fox Moth G-ACIG.

Below: Imperial Airways Fox Moth VO-ADE fitted with Fairchild floats seen airborne over Newfoundland in 1935. *(both John Stride Collection.)*

Canadian-built DH.82C Tiger Moth parts. These machines were fitted with normal undercarriage, skis or floats and all had the 145 hp Gipsy Major 1C, with which it was limited to three passengers. This produced a cruising speed of 96 mph and a range of 375 miles. Other modifications included wider cabin doors to allow improved freight access, refined cockpit hood, wheel-brakes and other improvements.

The Fox Moth was ideal for its purpose. It fulfilled the rôle of an economic joy-riding machine, an air taxi, a transporter of freight and an executive tourer.

Production: Ninety-eight aircraft were built, of which forty-nine appeared on the British civil register, although many were subsequently exported. Two further aircraft were assembled in Australia with seven more erected at Downsview in Canada, all from UK-made kits.

EC-VVA undergoing a float change. *(author's collection.)*

DH.84 Dragon

In the very early days of commercial aviation, the question of subsidised airlines came under discussion. In answer to a particularly pointed question, one very distinguished politician is supposed to have laid down the dictum that Civil Aviation would have to fly by itself. That single statement in many respects changed the face of civil aviation, although it took a considerable number of years before the first commercial aircraft capable of really economical operation came on the scene. This was to be de Havilland's DH.84 Dragon, a twin engined, biplane airliner.

"Hitherto the cost per passenger seat of commercial aircraft has been high, and high pay load only obtained at the expense of performance. Morever, all commercial aircraft were fitted with high power engines, and therefore high cost with the consequent adverse effects on running costs. The DH.84 combined low horse power, low first, running and maintenance costs with high performance and carrying capacity."

These are the opening words in the brochure produced by De Havilland for the launch of the DH.84 'Dragon'. The design came about with enquiries from two sources. Edward Hillman achieved very great success with his DH.83 Fox Moth services, which prompted him to ask de Havilland's for a twin engined version of this machine with which to operate his Paris route at cut prices. A request for a machine matching this description had already been received from the Iraqi Air Force, and when shown Arthur Hagg's designs, Hillman ordered four straight from the drawing board, later claiming to all and sundry that the idea for the DH.84 was his alone!

The DH.84 was a high aspect ratio, two bay biplane, accommodating six passengers in reasonable comfort in a well glazed spruce and plywood fuselage. The single pilot occupied a fully enclosed nose compartment affording good views in all directions, reached from a door in the front main cabin bulkhead.

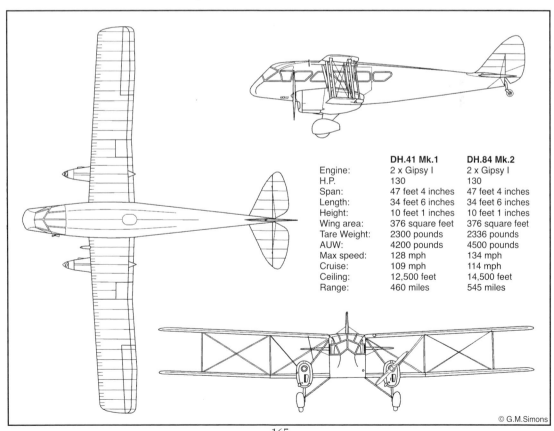

	DH.41 Mk.1	DH.84 Mk.2
Engine:	2 x Gipsy I	2 x Gipsy I
H.P.	130	130
Span:	47 feet 4 inches	47 feet 4 inches
Length:	34 feet 6 inches	34 feet 6 inches
Height:	10 feet 1 inches	10 feet 1 inches
Wing area:	376 square feet	376 square feet
Tare Weight:	2300 pounds	2336 pounds
AUW:	4200 pounds	4500 pounds
Max speed:	128 mph	134 mph
Cruise:	109 mph	114 mph
Ceiling:	12,500 feet	14,500 feet
Range:	460 miles	545 miles

© G.M.Simons

Two views of DH.84 Dragon G-ACAN before delivery to Hillman Airways. It has yet to be placed in their markings. *(DH via BAe Hatfield)*

The main cabin measured nine feet nine inches long by four feet six inches square, having a total cubic capacity of 175 cubic feet, excluding the luggage compartment. Floor space of nearly forty square feet gave an almost infinite variety of seating and furnishing arrangements, with seating for a maximum of ten passengers carried over short flights. If the aircraft was fitted out as a luxury machine just four passengers were carried in long, deep armchairs, still leaving room for a cocktail and refreshment buffet and seat for a steward, all without affecting lavatory and luggage accommodation! The cabin was fitted with a special heating device, taking warm air from the engines via ducts through the stub-planes. Fresh air was provided by vents in the roots of the upper wings.

The luggage compartment had a capacity of 35 cubic feet, and provided ample accommodation for 290 pounds of luggage. This was reduced to 25 cubic feet if a lavatory was included. With the main cabin stripped of furniture and appointments, space was available for 1300 to 1400 pounds of mail or freight.

The machine was powered by two air-cooled Gipsy Major inverted four cylinder engines, each developing 130 horsepower each. The engines were mounted on the fixed lower stub-planes, driving tractor propellers. Each powerplant, contained in a nacelle, was mounted on rubber blocks in steel tube structures to keep vibration to a minimum, with a fuel tank of thirty gallon capacity fed to the engine via duplicated fuel pumps. Underneath each fuel tank was a two gallon oil tank. With a standard fuel load the DH.84 had a range of five hours, or about 500 miles at 110 m.p.h.

A further interesting development, later refered to as the DH.84M (Military) was the ready adaptability to what was refered to as 'type colonial'. That is to say

Seven of the eight DH.84Ms ordered by Iraq line up at Hatfield for the press prior to delivery.*(DH via BAe Hatfield)*

With a shower of champagne, Amy Johnson names G-ACAN *Maylands*. Standing behind her is her husband, James 'Jim' Mollison. *(DH via BAe Hatfield)*

more, and later the whole fleet was converted to eight seaters with the removal of the luggage compartment.

Throughout 1933/4 the Stag Lane production line built DH.84's in increasing numbers, with orders from many of the smaller civil operators both within the United Kingdom and abroad. Eight of the DH.84M's were delivered to Baghdad, on 13 May 1933 for patrol duties in Iraq. A further two were delivered to Denmark, three to Portugal, whilst the Irish Army Air Corps purchased a second-hand civil example and converted it to their own requirments in 1937, flying it with the marks 'DH-18'.

Dragons replaced the Fox Moths on the routes of Midland and Scottish Air Ferries Ltd and the Scottish Motor Traction Co. Ltd, with one machine kept on permanent readiness for ambulance work in the Western Isles. Aberdeen Airways operated from Dyce with three aircraft. Northern and Scottish Airways Ltd founded with just one Dragon flew between Renfrew, Campbeltown, Islay and the Outer Hebrides, while Highland Airways, founded by Captain Ernest Edmund 'Ted' Fresson on 3 April 1933 purchased four, and inaugurated its service between Dyce and Orkney with G-ACIT on 17 May 1934. Some DH.84s were privately owned. Member of Parliament W L Everard eventually purchased two G-ACEK *Leicestershire Vixen II* and G-ACKU, the latter appearing in silver and yellow livery.

Overseas operators included Indian National Airways with VT-AEK and 'AEL leaving Heston on delivery on 2 November 1933. Automobiles Fernandez SA bought EC-W14, later registered EC-TAT, G-ACIE/OK-ATO was used for executive travel by the BATA Shoe Co of Czechosolvakia. Misr. Airwork in Egypt flew SU-ABH, 'ABI and ABJ opening up a Cairo to Alexandria service in August 1933, along with routes to Mersa, Matruh, Port Said, Luxor and Aswan. Canadian Airways purchased two, the first of which CF-APJ carried Mail between Moncton NB and Charlottestown for nearly ten years. Wilson Airways of Nairobi, Kenya acquired two for services to Mombassa, Zanzibar and Dar-es-Salaam.

an aircraft that could be used for the normal carriage of passengers or freight, but could also be used to discipline unruly tribes in case of need. This development entailed an extension of the main cabin space to include the luggage bay, the fitting of a gunner's platform with gun ring to the roof of the cabin with an alternative gun position in the floor, a fixed gun firing forward from the cockpit, the fitment of bomb racks, release gear and sights, wireless and rough seating for troops or police. Following airworthiness tests, the dorsal fin was extended to cure a instability problem. In either the airliner or military role, it was found that the Dragon could easily accomodate stretcher cases, and as the machine was fitted with split-axle undercarriaqe, leavinq the underside of the fuselage completely clear the aircraft was an ideal aircraft for aerial mapping, survey and aerial photographic work. The maximum speed at sea level was in the neighbourhood of 130 mph, cruising at about 110 m.p.h. The take-off performance was sprightly for the time, clearing a height of 145 feet just 546 feet from the start of the roll. The all-up-weight was 4,200 pounds, a tare weight being 2,285 pounds giving a disposable load of 1,915 pounds.

The prototype was flown from Stag Lane under class 'B' marks of 'E-9' by Captain Hubert Broad on 24 November 1932, and was found to surpass the performance of the Fox Moth. Following Certificate of Airworthiness trails at Martlesham Heath the type C of A was issued on 16 December 1932. The aircraft was delivered to Hillman's in their blue silver and white livery, registered by now as G-ACAN. The aircraft was christened *Maylands* at Hillman's Maylands aerodrome, Romford Essex on 20 December by Amy Johnson. The remainder of Hillman's order of four aircraft were delivered in time for the inaugural Romford - Paris service on 1 April 1933. Encouraged by the early success of the Dragon Hillman orderd two

Long distance record attempts

Already famous for making long-distance flights, Jim Mollison and Amy Johnson decided in 1933 to make

Railway Air Services G-ACPX loads another group of passengers.*(DH via BAe Hatfield)*

an attempt on the world's long distance record. The Mollisons decided to attempt the record together, and elected to fly from New York to Baghdad, hoping for a flight of 6,000 miles. At the same time they also wanted to be the first to fly the North Atlantic in a westerly direction before positioning in New York. They commissioned a special DH.84 with three overload tanks in the main cabin carrying a total of 600 gallons. Two 15 gallon oil tanks were installed in the engine nacelles, replacing the standard fuel tanks. The Dragon was cleaned up aerodynamically, increasing its speed by 5 mph under normal conditions. Better fuel economy was obtained by raising the compression ratio of the two Gipsy Major engines. Additional modifications included covering the passenger glazing and strengthening the undercarriage to carry the loaded weight of 7,334 pounds.

The aircraft, registered in Amy's name as G-ACCV, was named *Seafarer* and doped Titanine black overall, with a Union Jack on the fin.

The flight was scheduled to start from Croydon Airport on 5 June 1933. But due to bad weather on the day the flight was postponed until 8 June. Last minute checks were made on the Dragon, which was loaded with 400 gallons of fuel. Just before 6.00 am the aircraft was taxied beyond the boundary of the airfield and onto rough ground to take full advantage of the 1,200 yard take-off run, but the machine hit a bump, then another. One undercarriage leg collapsed followed almost immediately by the other. The Dragon tipped almost onto its nose, then slewed around before slumping onto its belly The Mollisons escaped shaken but unhurt.

The same could not be said for *Seafarer*. All four wings were damaged, the propellers bent, engine mounts strained, and undercarriage smashed.

Seafarer was repaired and was ready again at the end of June. While repairs were taking place the Mollisons decided to make their next attempt from the three mile stretch of smooth, hard sand at Pendine on the South Wales coast. On 3 July the Dragon was positioned at Pendine to await suitable weather. 7 July brought new dangers when the tide rose with

unexpected speed and reached the parked aircraft before volunteers pushed it to safety. Alarmed by this incident the Mollisons flew the Dragon to Cardiff's Pengam Moors Airport next day to await favourable weather reports.

On 22 July the Dragon re-positioned at Pendine and loaded with 420 gallons of fuel ready to go. At noon Jim took 1,000 yards to unstick, heading for New York, and on the following day at 16.32 hrs local time they were sighted over Bar Harbour, Maine. Almost the entire sea crossing was in poor conditions with fog and low cloud obscuring the sea. Bad weather and fatigue had made the Dragon's course erratic, wasting much fuel, so much so that within 100 miles of New York they realised they were not going to make Floyd Bennett Field where 25,000 people awaited their arrival. There was no alternative but to land at the small aerodrome of Bridgeport, Connecticut.

Bridgeport switched on every available light and sent up another aircraft to guide *Seafarer* in, but Jim, exhausted after 39 flying hours, reportedly made a downwind landing, overshot the airfield and crashed into a swamp. The Dragon turned over twice, flinging Mollison out through the windscreen. Amy was able to crawl out of the wreckage, and by the time help arrived was found crouched over her badly cut and unconscious husband. Within hours souvenir hunters had stripped *Seafarer* of everything removable.

Once out of hospital the Mollisons received a typical New York welcome, bandaged but cheerful. Jim had more than 100 stiches to his cuts, Amy had injured an arm and ankle. By September both had recovered and remained in Amercia to attend a ceremony at Bridgeport, which on 4 August was named Mollison Airport in their honour.

Both were keen to make a second attempt, and thanks to the generosity of Lord Wakefield a new airframe was purchased, being fitted out with the engines and tanks salvaged from *Seafarer*. Registered G-ACJM and named *Seafarer II*, this machine was painted black overall again, but with red and orange fuselage cleat lines. The completed aircraft was shipped to Canada aboard SS *Duchess of York*, and at

Jim Mollison and Amy Johnson pose for the camera in front of *Seafarer* as the aircraft is fuelled, apparently through the roof! (*DH via BAe Hatfield*)

Wasaga Beach, Ontario on 3 October 1933 a second attempt was made. Loaded with 608 gallons of fuel the Dragon ran the full three miles of the beach without lifting. On the third attempt it rose a few feet, but refused to lift any further before crashing back onto the sand, badly twisting the undercarriage. The aircraft was loaded to a weight of 7,334 pounds, more than twice the permissible weight of a standard Dragon.

In May 1934 G-ACJM was sold to James R Ayling and Captain Leonard Reid, with little more being heard of it until the early evening of 9 August, when it landed at Heston, having made the first non-stop flight from Canada to England. The aircraft had been purchased with the express purpose of making a private attempt at the record. Named *Trail of the Caribou*, the Dragon had set off from Wasaga Beach at 5.10 Toronto time, taking nearly a mile to take off. Throttle problems had caused the fuel calculations to be estimated a 16 gallons per hour, making the Baghdad possiblity very slim so the crew decided to make for London upon crossing the Irish Coast, covering the 3,700 miles in 30 hours 50 minutes. When the contents of the tanks were checked at Hatfield next day they were found to still contain 200 gallons, more than enough to reach Baghdad. The problem was eventually diagnosed as carburettor icing, giving faulty throttle settings and therefore causing an error in the fuel consumption calculations.

Commencing with the 63rd airframe, G-ACMO of Jersey Airways Ltd, an improved version came off the production line during September 1933. Individual framed windows and faired undercarriage denoted the Mk II in physical appearance, but not seen was a 500lb increase in the all up weight. Series production began with airframe no. 6062, and 53 were built. The first to fly was G-ACKU for W L Everard in November 1933, which was flown to victory in the Oases Circuit race in Egypt by W D Macpherson a month later.

The closing of the Stag Lane production line and the ensuing move to Hatfield leaves uncertainty about which was the last Dragon to leave Stag Lane. It is known however, that G-ACNI was first flown there on 22 March and that the move was completed by May.

The airlines loved the DH.84. Jersey Airways Ltd was founded on 9 December 1933 by Mr W L Thurlgood, proprietor of the Peoples Motor Services Ltd, Ware. His first Dragon, Mark I G-ACMJ was delivered on the 15th. The aircraft was followed at intervals by seven Mark IIs. By 1934 his Channel Isles service had developed to where eight would fly the route from Heston in formation.

Norman Edgar (Western Airways) Ltd, formed in 1933 using G-ACJT, was later re-named Western Airways after the take-over by Whitney Straight's Straight Corporation. The company operated several on its Weston super Mare to Cardiff Pengam Moors service, extended to Bournemouth on 17 May 1934 and to Le-Tourqet/Paris from 3 May 1935. The Weston to Cardiff route was at one time the busiest air route in the world.

Another big-time Dragon operator was recently formed Railway Air Services, who's sole Mk I G-ACHV was joined by nine Mk II's for its Birmingham - Cardiff - Haldon - Plymouth and Birmingham - Bristol - Isle of Wight services.

Two Mk. II,s arrived in Canada; CF-AVD went to Quebec Airways Ltd in February 1935 and then to Canadian Airways in August for its West Coast and Maritime routes, either on skis in winter or floats during the summer months. The aircraft was fitted with Canadian Fairchild floats and the extended dorsal fin of the DH.84M to compensate for the aerodynamic effect of the floats.

The second machine, CF-AVI, was operated by Consolidated Mining and Smelting at Trail BC for two years before passing to North Shore Airways Ltd of Toronto from December 1937. They operated it on floats until the aircraft was torn from its moorings and swept over a dam at Godbout PQ during a storm on 13 January 1941.

Two decidedly non-standard Dragons! Right: ZS-AEI of the Aircraft Operating Company with 'porthole' windows.

Below: G-ADFI *The Silver Ghost* of Aberdeen Airways with a locally made landing light in the nose. (*Author's collection*)

Australia proved to be the almost perfect environment for the rugged machines. VH-URF and *G were equipped with Williarnson 'Eagle 4' cameras for photographic surveys of the Kalgoorlie Goldfields by the Western Mining Corporation of Australia. Three other examples flew the 2,252 mile Perth to Daly Waters route for MacRobertson-Miller Aviation Co. Ltd. Sister aircraft operated with Butler Aviation over the Charlesville to Cootamundra section of the England to Australia Air Mail.

East Coast Airways became the first NZ operator of any twin-engined aircraft when they took delivery of ZK-ADS and 'ER for the four times a day Napier to Gisborne route opened on 15 April 1935. Both these aircraft were later impressed into the Royal New Zealand Air Force at the outbreak of the war.

De Havilland's South American representative, W. T. Ballantyne, flew PP-SPC to Brazil with his wife as passenger on delivery to VASP. The Dragon was fitted with extra tankage for the long crossing of the South Atlantic. A special DH.84 was built for Smiths Instruments and equipped as a flying showroom for their products, and became well known around the skies of Europe.

Closer to home, EI-ABI *lolar* (*The Eagle* ex G-ACPY of Blackpool and West Coast Air Services) became famous as the aircraft which inaugurated the first Aer Lingus return service between Dublin and Bristol. At 09.00hrs, following a short religious service and a blessing by the Irish Air Corps Chaplain, the aircraft lifted off the grass runway at Baldonnel Military Aerodrome near Dublin, on 27 May1936. Aer Lingus had been formed a month before, with an authorised capital of £100,000, a staff of twelve, a single aircraft, and it is said, a biscuit tin full of aircraft spares!

The production of Dragons ceased in May 1937, the last two airframes being sold to Portugal as DH84M's and were used amongst other things for photographic survey work.

CF-AVD shows the framed windows of the Dragon Mk.II and the twin float undercarriage designed by the Canadian Fairchild company. Note also the extended dorsal fin. (*DH via BAe Hatfield*)

One of the two DH.84s sold to the Portugese Air Force. *(DH via BAe Hatfield)*

With the outbreak of war in September 1939 all civil flying ceased and came under the control of the National Air Communications. organisation, although several airlines were allowed to continue services, if the routes were thought to be of 'national importance'.

Between April and October 1940 some seventeen machines belonging to many companies were impressed into the RAF and allocated serials in place of their civil registrations. X9345, ex G-ACIU of Surrey Flying Services, was abandoned at Mourmelon, France in April 1940, but the remainder were used for training parachutists at numbers 6 and 7 Anti Aircraft Co-operations Units at Ringway and Castle Bromich. Five continued in civil use, although flown in camouflage operating in Scotland and on the Lands End - Scillies route of Channel Air Services Ltd until G-ACPY, the former *'Iolar'* was shot down by a German Fighter on 3 June 1941.

Abroad, eleven civil machines in Australia were impressed into the RAAF with the 'A34' prefix. There was a very urgent need for Radio and Navigation Trainers in Australia, and this was met in a very convenient manner by De Havillands Pty Ltd of Banksdown by using existing drawings and jigs shipped out to Australia from Hatfield. The Dragon had been preferred to the higher powered DH.89 Dragon Rapide as Gipsy Major engines were already available from General Motors Holdens Ltd who were at that time building them in Melbourne for the Australian DH.82 Moth contract. A34-12, the first Australian built example first flew on 29 September 1942, some 87 examples being built and delivered to the Royal Australian Air Force between October 1942 and June 1943. These aircraft were used to supplement the 11 impressed civilian examples. All were strictly

DH.84 Dragon 1414 of the South African Air Force, formerly ZS-AEH.

ZK-AXI of the Auckland Flying School Ltd. *(both Author's collection)*

utility machines, with unframed windows similar to the Mark I.

The three DH84s purchased by the Ministry of National Defence for Turkey were still in existance as late as 1943, although information is still very sparse. However, it is known that they were used for liason and training duties with the TuAF.

By far the largest collection of survivors in the immediate postwar period was in Australia where those remaining after the war were put- up for disposal in 1946-47, when forty-six appeared on the Australian Civil register for many charter companies.

Over the years the few survivors have been lovingly restored to probably better than original condition and displayed to the public.

DH.85 Leopard Moth

The DH.85 was a full three seater designed for luxury private travel in 1933 incorporating refinements made possible by the use of the higher powered Gipsy Major engine. A saving in structural weight came about by abandoning the welded steel fuselage in favour of a spruce-and-plywood box structure in which the pilot was seated centrally in front of two side by side passengers. Major external differences between the Leopard Moth and its predecessor included a folding mainplane with swept back leading edge forming a tapered wing; an externally braced and adjustable tailplane; and main undercarriage legs which were anchored to the rear of the engine mounting instead of to the top longerons. This permitted wider opening of the door for easier access to the cabin. Bendix wheel brakes were also fitted and the undercarriage shock leg fairings could be rotated through ninety degrees, to

form an air brake which steepened the gliding angle from 1 in 12 to 1 in 9.

Piloted by Capt. Geoffrey de Havilland and bearing the Class B marking E-l, the prototype G-ACHD made its first flight at Stag Lane on 27 May 1933. It was 4 m.p.h. up on estimate and 9 m.p.h. faster than the Puss Moth. Six weeks later, on 8 July, with mass instead of the original horn balanced ailerons, it carried 'D.H.' to victory in the King's Cup Race at Hatfield, averaging 139.51 m.p.h.

Orders came from all parts of the world to Stag Lane, but it was not long before the works was transferred to Hatfield when the old aerodrome closed on 5 January 1934.

In three years 132 Leopard Moths were built, of which 71 were sold on the home market. The first 30 aircraft had flat sided fuselages but thereafter a slightly rounded effect was obtained by means of a fabric covering stretched over external wooden stringers. The

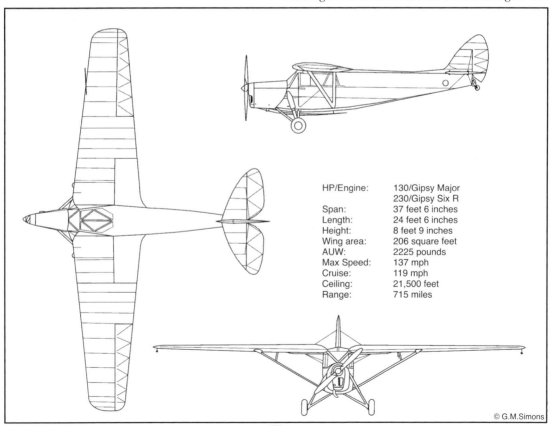

HP/Engine:	130/Gipsy Major
	230/Gipsy Six R
Span:	37 feet 6 inches
Length:	24 feet 6 inches
Height:	8 feet 9 inches
Wing area:	206 square feet
AUW:	2225 pounds
Max Speed:	137 mph
Cruise:	119 mph
Ceiling:	21,500 feet
Range:	715 miles

© G.M.Simons

The all-wood DH.85 luxury three-seat tourer. *(DH via BAe Hatfield)*

type was very popular with private owners such as Nigel Norman, founder of Heston Airport, who secured the registration G-ACNN, featuring his initials, and applied it to the Leopard Moth in large chromium plated letters.

Companies such as Olley Air Services Ltd., which used G-ACLM and 'PK; and Air Taxis Ltd. which had G-ADWY, found them ideal for taxi work, as did the Heston based firms Air Commerce Ltd., British American Air Services Ltd. and Birkett Air Services Ltd. all of whom operated a considerable number of Leopard Moths. Several of these, including Birkett's G-ADCO, were chartered by newspapers to cover the Abyssinian War of 1936.

A number of long distance flights were made in Leopard Moths, the first by T. Neville Stack and F. E. Clifford who left Heston on 15 March 1934, flew to Bathurst and into Senegal, recording their experiences by dictaphone in the air with the intention of writing a book on their return.

That same month Bernard Rubin and Ken Waller flew 'LX to Australia to survey the route which the former's Comet would fly in the MacRobertson Race

and succeeded in breaking the record for the return journey by arriving at Lympne on 1 May in a time of 8 days 12 hours. On the engineering side the prototype Leopard Moth made a valuable contribution to the success of the Comet racers when it became a flight development vehicle for the Gipsy Six R engine with variable pitch airscrew under the designation DH.85A. Both Hamilton and Ratier airscrews were tested. Flight tests begun by Geoffrey de Havilland Jnr. on 23 October 1933 ended when the engine was granted type approval in the following August.

M. Christian Moench, president of the French Aero Club de l'Est, took delivery of Leopard Moth F-AMXA in March 1934, and later flew it from Marseilles to Madagascar in seven days. On 10 October a red machine without markings landed at Heston to clear Customs for Paris on delivery to Portugal, piloted by Lt. Humberto del Cruz with Carlos Bleck as passenger. This aircraft was fitted with extra fuel tanks in the cabin and left Lisbon with the same crew on 25 October to visit all the Portuguese possessions overseas and arrived at Dili, Timor on 7 November. The flight was sponsored by the Lisbon daily paper *O Seculo* and the DH.85 completed the journey of 43,495 miles by crossing Africa to visit the Cape Verde Islands before returning home to be handed over to the Portuguese Air Force. The last great Leopard Moth flight ended at Lympne on 3 May 1937 when H. F. 'Jimmy' Broadbent landed in

Above: OO-NAD was one of the original flat-sided fuselage DH.85s.

Right: BD-148 in wartime impressment colours. The aircraft was formerly G-ACMA of the National Benzole Company *(John Stride Collection)*

One of the few Leopard Moths to survive - G-ACMN in flight. *(DH via BAe Hatfield)*

VH-AHB, only 6 days 8 hours 25 minutes after leaving Darwin. The special cabin fuel tank giving a 1,500 mile range was later removed at Hanworth and the aircraft sold to Sam Harris as G-AFDV.

Sixty Leopard Moths were sold overseas, many to wealthy owners in France and Switzerland. One went to Algiers, others were exported to Argentina, Australia, Austria, Belgium, China, the Congo, Egypt, Germany, Holland, India, Japan, Kenya, Poland, South Africa, Southern Rhodesia and Spain.

Forty-four British Leopard Moths were impressed at the outbreak of the European War for communications duties in camouflage with the RAF and ATA. Several in India formed part of the Delhi Communications Flight, and others were 'called up' in Southern Rhodesia, South Africa and elsewhere. Very few survived to re-enter civilian life and a handful of Leopard Moths returned to use overseas.

DH.86 Express Air Liner

Over the years, and with a high degree of justification, a popular myth has built up that De Havillands always built wonderful aeroplanes. Whilst it is true that many of their designs were daringly innovative, which eventually evolved into perfectly safe, economic and very successful machines, it took a lot of hard work and risks to make them so.

The DH.86 design came about as the result of a requirement from the Australian Government in collaboration with Imperial Airways for a fast, multi engined airliner to operate in safety on the Singapore - Darwin - Cootamundra section of the England to Australia Air Service, operating across the Java and Timor seas. About the same time de Havilland's submitted a proposal for a four-engined airliner with a high margin of safety in the event of an engine failure. It was evident that this new design not only met the requirements laid down in the tender, but would exceed the performance handsomely!

A contract was placed with De Havilland's by Imperial Airways on behalf of QANTAS Empire Airways, and used by them as basis for their tender to the Australian Government. One of the prime requirements for the tender was that all aircraft submitted had to have a valid Certificate of Airworthiness by the closing date for tenders.

The DH86 was designed and built in just four months. It was during construction that Major Frank B Halford produced the six cylinder version of the four cylinder Gipsy Major, to be known as the Gipsy Six. The first set of these engines were rushed through Air Ministry type approval tests in time for installation in the prototype DH.86, E-2, later G-ACPL. The aircraft

Captain Hubert Standford Broad, MBE, AFC (*b.* 1897 *d.*1975) at the controls of the prototype DH.86 during a demonstration flight. *(DH via BAe Hatfield)*

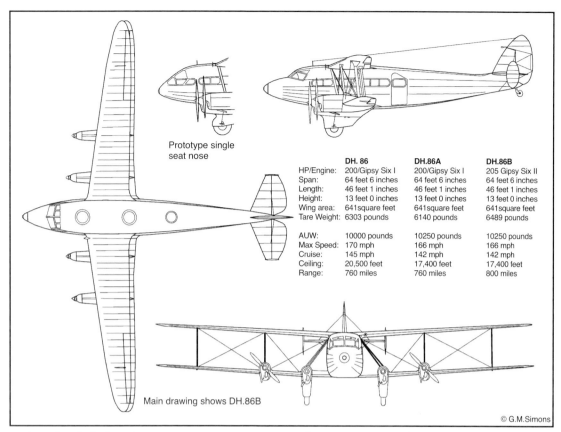

Prototype single seat nose

	DH. 86	DH.86A	DH.86B
HP/Engine:	200/Gipsy Six I	200/Gipsy Six I	205 Gipsy Six II
Span:	64 feet 6 inches	64 feet 6 inches	64 feet 6 inches
Length:	46 feet 1 inches	46 feet 1 inches	46 feet 1 inches
Height:	13 feet 0 inches	13 feet 0 inches	13 feet 0 inches
Wing area:	641 square feet	641 square feet	641 square feet
Tare Weight:	6303 pounds	6140 pounds	6489 pounds
AUW:	10000 pounds	10250 pounds	10250 pounds
Max Speed:	170 mph	166 mph	166 mph
Cruise:	145 mph	142 mph	142 mph
Ceiling:	20,500 feet	17,400 feet	17,400 feet
Range:	760 miles	760 miles	800 miles

Main drawing shows DH.86B

© G.M.Simons

made its first flight from Stag Lane on 14 January 1934 in the hands of Captain Hubert S Broad, the aircraft being passed on to the Aircraft and Armament Experimental Establishment at Martlesham Heath for trials the following week, resulting in a Certificate of Airworthiness being issued on 30 January, just one day before the Australian Government's time limit for submissions of contracts ran out.

The type was structurally interesting at the time as it departed from the usual de Havilland practice in that construction of the fuselage was an internally unobstructed plywood box with Spruce stiffening members and soundproofing on the outside. This gave clear walls, floor and roof, allowing the best use of the available space, with the average height of the cabin ceiling to be 6 foot 3 inches. Sheet 'Elektron' guards were fitted over the outside corners of the fuselage, serving to give better shape and remove the need for the fabric to pass round a sharp corner. It was as a result of this that the

The prototype DH.86 in flight in Class B markings. Note the single-seat nose and the curved underarriage 'trousers'. *(DH via BAe Hatfield)*

E-2 - later to become G-ACPL gets airborne from Stag Lan on 14 January 1934 in the hands of Hubert Broad.
(DH via BAe Hatfield)

fuselage had a slightly rounded appearance.

The aircraft was equipped to carry ten passengers, and was flown with a single pilot in the nose, assisted by a Navigator/Radio Operator sitting on the starboard side behind him with full radio and navigation equipment. The tail surfaces were of typical De Havilland design and construction for the period, the tailplane adjustable in flight by cables from the cockpit via a square cut screw to counteract changes in trim. The fin was also adjustable in flight, again by cables from the cockpit via a screw, allowing it to be offset to either side, thus counteracting any unbalanced thrust in the event of engine failure.

The mainplanes were sharply tapered, especially the outer sections, being RAF.34 modified aerofoil section, with a high aspect ratio of 12.3:1. As the aircraft was a two-bay biplane, the wings comprising top stub, top extension, bottom stub, bottom intermediate and bottom extension planes. All had 'I' section spruce spars, apart from the bottom stub planes which were of tubular steel, with a tubular steel centre section spar running under the fuselage.

All four engines were installed in structures forward of the lower mainplanes. Each undercarriage 'leg' consisted of a trousered unit with integral fuel tanks fitted behind. Each fuel tank contained 38 gallons. An auxiliary tank containing 33 gallons was fitted in each bottom stub plane. A three and a half gallon oil tank was fitted at the rear of each engine nacelle. Later aircraft were fitted with 'Dowty' hydraulically operated flaps on the upper mainplanes. These were operated via a hand-driven pump in the cockpit. They were intended for operation at an airspeed of 80 to 90 mph. It is interesting to note that in an early handbook describing maintainance on the type special mention was made that *'A drip tray was fitted to the floor of the Pilot's cockpit under the flap operating ;pump to catch any leakage or overflow from the pump. This tray should be cleaned out regularly to ensure that spilt fluid does not accumulate'.*

Five different interior main cabin layouts were offered to potential customers. The 'Long Distance Luxury Air Liner' was equipped with just eight seats, whilst the eight berth 'Sleeping Car Model' was also offered. The most popular interior was one fitted for ten passengers, but a sixteen seat 'Air Ferry Model' was available. At least one aircraft, G-ADVK of Blackpool and West Coast Air Services, was

A not often seen rear view of the DH.86, showing the thickened lower stub planes containing the auxiliary fuel tanks.
(DH via BAe Hatfield)

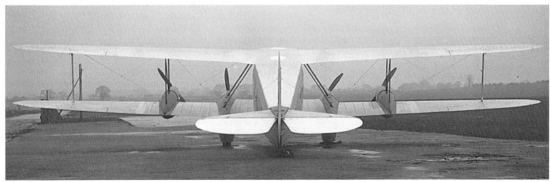

Left: one of a number of different interior configurations.

Below: the single seat cockpit.
(both DH via BAe Hatfield)

equipped with eighteen seats.

It is known that a lower powered version fitted with four Gipsy Majors instead of the Gipsy Sixes was to be offered by De Havilland's, with a lower all-up-weight of only 8,800 pounds against that of 10,000 pounds for the Gipsy Six powered machine. This variant would have had a 20 m.p.h. lower speed. There is no evidence to suggest that any DH.86 was ever equipped with Gipsy Majors.

Early proving flights were undertaken by the newly created Railway Air Services Ltd, formed as an associate company to Imperial Airways on 21 March 1934 to operate internal air services within the United Kingdom in conjunction with the four principal railway companies. It was with G-ACPL in the red, green and silver colour scheme of RAS that the presentation of the first internal Air Mail Pennant was made by the Postmaster General, Howard Kingsley Wood at Gatwick on 16 May 1934. The aircraft had already been fitted with revised undercarriage fairings, and temporarily fitted with metal propellers. G-ACVY *Mercury* and G-ACVZ *Jupiter* were the only other DH.86s built for single pilot operation, and 'CVY inaugurated RAS's trunk route between Croydon, Castle Bromwich, Barton, Belfast and Renfrew on 20 August 1934.

For long haul work the Australian Government called for an increase in fuel carried to 183 gallons. There was also to be side-by-side seating for the Pilot and First Officer. To meet this the prototype was returned to the makers at Hatfield to be fitted with an elongated two seat nose. It emerged in the Imperial Airways colour scheme, named *Delphinus* during the following August.

1935 saw Imperial Airways placing their first DH86, G-ADFF in service.The type was to be called the 'D', or *Diana* Class. Along with eleven others, *Dione* flew the European routes. April saw the beginning of the Paris - Marseilles -Rome - Brindisi twice weekly mail service, connecting with the flying boats for the Trans - Mediterranean sector. The Khartoum - Accra service was opened by G-ADCN *Daedelus* on 13 February 1936 whilst G-ACUD *Dorado* opened the

Hong Kong - Saigon - Penang shuttle on 23 March.

Imperial Airways (Far East) Ltd had been formed in August 1935, and G-ACWD *Dorado* was sent out to make six survey flights, the last two making connection with the Australian service at Penang. The first fully scheduled run was on 23 March 1936, placing Hong Kong within ten days of London. *Dorado* was joined by G-ACPL *Delphinus*, G-ADCN *Daedalus* and G-AOC *Delia*. All four aircraft were painted with large Union Jacks as a warning to Japanese forces which occupied much of the coastline along these routes. This didn't however stop them from being fired upon - or attacked by fighters at various times. A traffic arrangement between Britain and Siam in late 1937 allowed a change in route, shortening the service by about one and a half days. The terminus then was moved from Penang to Bangkok. It was at Bangkok that G-ADCN *Daedalus* was accidentally lost when destroyed by fire on 3 December 1937.

Hillman's Airways had purchased three DH86s the

VH-UUA of QANTAS Empire Airways in flight. It was originally ordered as G-ACWE for Imperial Airways but was diverted to QANTAS to make up for the losses. *(DH via BAe Hatfield)*

first was G-ADEA, which was named *Drake* by Lady Cunliffe-Lister on 20 June 1935, but the airline was taken over by British Airways in 1936. The aircraft were used to supplement British Airways own fleet of four aircraft on Day Passenger/Night Mail flights between Gatwick and the Continent.

The problem with DH.86s...

QANTAS Empire Airways were successful in their tendering for the section of the Empire Air Route with the DH86, and their first aircraft, VH-USC arrived in Brisbane on 13 October 1934 after a long flight from Croydon. This was not the first of the type to arrive in Australia. VH-URN, the first production machine had already been shipped out to Holyman's Airways Pty. This aircraft was not to survive for long, as it vanished off Wilson's Promotory on 19 October with Victor

Holyman, Gilbert Jenkins as the co-pilot and ten passengers. There was speculation that the accident had been caused by the pilots changing over in the confined single pilot cockpit, but as the machine was never located, no-one knew for sure.

This tragedy was soon followed by the crash of QANTAS Empire Airways VH-USG, flown by Captain R A Pentergast, an experienced Imperial Airways pilot at Barradale, near Longreach, Queensland at the end of its ferry flight from the UK on 15 November killing the pilot and three others on board. With this happening so soon after the loss of VH-URN an extensive enquiry took place, but again, the cause was never fully established. Two theories were put forward, but never proven. One was that the machine had been loaded with the centre of gravity outside the operating limits, the other that the fin post had given

Imperial Airways' G-ADUE *Dardanius* and G-ADUF *Dido* at Gatwick in 1936. *(DH via BAe Hatfield)*

way, causing the aircraft to enter a spin. Although the fourth aircraft was flown out, the second and third machines were despatched by sea, awaiting the results of investigations by the Australian Department of Civil Aviation and trials by de Havilland's with VH-USF, both at Hatfield, and with the Air Ministry at Martlesham Heath with both one and two engines out on the same side. QANTAS strengthened the fin post fittings on its remaining aircraft, and paid special attention to the load

Structural tests were also conducted at Hatfield, and although these revealed no weaknesses, several modifications were embodied as a precautionary measure, including the removal of the rudder servo tab and strengthening of the fin. The QANTAS Empire Airways contract had been completed by diverting G-ACWE as VH-UUA. All five of these aircraft were known as the Commonwealth Class, and named after Australian State Capitals. QANTAS were not yet ready to use the aircraft on the Singapore -Darwin sector, so arranged for Imperial Airways to fly two of their DH.86s from England for use on this leg.

William 'Bill' Cash was directly involved. *'After VH-USG belonging to QANTAS Empire Airways crashed near Longreach on 15 November 1934 they insisted that Imperial Airways should not only deliver the next aircraft, but fly it over the Darwin-Singapore route for a while. Captain Alan B H Youell was chosen and the rest of the crew - all volunteers - were Flying Officer Allen, an Australian, Engineer Tug Wilson and myself as Wireless Operator. We left Croydon in VH-USF on 7 January 1935 and it soon became apparent that something was wrong with the fuel system. The gauges indicated a heavy consumption on one side, so it was decided to throttle back the inboard engine on that side only and apply fin bias. However, after about forty minutes into the flight the gauges indicated a reversed situation, so the procedure too was reversed. When we got to Baghdad Capt Youell decided to ignore the gauges, a decision proving to be very wise.*

We reached Singapore on 20 January where F/O Allen and Tug Wilson were dropped and I continued on with Capt Youell, arriving in Darwin on the 24th. The day after we were told that the aircraft was grounded. The AID (Aeronautical Inspection Directorate) surveyor had arrived from Sydney and informed us that the cause of the crash of VH-USG had been determined.

Fin bias was operated by a transverse wormscrew under the forward end of the fin. In order to convert linear movement along the worm to a circular movement the king-

post of the fin had a slotted fitting under it. This fitting had been wrongly installed at the factory so that no movement along the slot was possible; instead the bottom of the post was forced forward and, with fin bias used, it eventually fractured just above the fitting. The inspector drew a pencil line on the fin which indicated some distortion of the finpost, but he gave permission for the aircraft to be flown to Singapore without passengers on condition that no fin bias was used. All DH.86s were to be inspected, and it is possible that others were similarly affected.

Whilst VH-USF was grounded in Singapore two services were operated by Armstrong Whitworth AW15s which normally operated the Karachi-Singapore sector until 'USF re-entered service on 18 February.

The problems encountered with the fuel gauges were traced to the addition of 'slipper' tanks in the bottom centre-section feeding into the main system by gravity. Unfortunately this did not always happen simultaneously on both sides. The fuel gauges had been re-calibrated to include these tanks and any failure to drain gave a greatly exaggerated rate of consumption because the readings during the early part of the flight referred to two tanks. Later the idiosyncrasies of the fuel system were accepted as a fact of life and discrepancies were ignored during the first half hour or so of each flight. Many pilots distrusted the aircraft, this

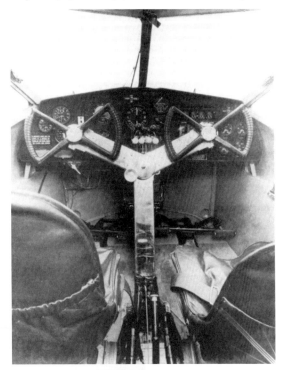

Above: the two-seat cockpit version of the DH.86.

Left: VH-USC during test-flying at Hatfield.
(both DH via BAe Hatfield)

179

Allied Airways. G-AETM *The Norseman* at the start of the first service to Stavanger from Aberdeen. *(via Peter V Clegg)*

eventually becoming something of a phobia.

Pilots in those days seemed intent on doing 'three point' landings. These were easy enough in the DH.84, but inadvisable on the faster DH.86 which had a built-in skittishness near the ground. During the bounce that often resulted the aircraft acquired a drift which could result in a swing to port uncontrollable by rudder alone. The answer was to roll the aircraft on with the tailwheel about a foot or two above the ground. On take-off the swing could he corrected by leading with the port outer throttle partly opened, ready to respond. Some aircraft never swung; for instance Railway Air Services G-ACVY, 'CVZ and 'CPL even when the latter was converted to two pilot operation.

This story is backed up by amendment A.S.9 DH86 I.M.I. dated 15.4.35 in a DH.86 *Manual of Instructions for Operation, Maintenance and Rigging of the de Havilland 4-engined Express Air Liner (Type DH86).*

The amendment stated that *"When the Empennage is rigged and the Fin Bias Gear completely assembled a small clearance of 0.06 inches should exist between the front of the eyebolt and the front of the slot in the screwed traversing sleeve when the fin is in neutral, that is the central position. It will be readily appreciated that in this position the Front Bottom Fin Attachment is in its most forward condition and as the Fin is wound from side to side, the Attachment will travel backwards in its slot. The Bias Gear should be operated to its full extent in either direction to ensure that there is clearance between the eyebolt and the ends of the slot at the extreme lengths of the travel".*

This was by no means the end of the story for, on 2 October 1935, VH-URT *Loina* of Holyman's Airways crashed into the sea off Flinders Island in the same area and under similar circumstances to VH-URN the previous year. The aircraft had been on a flight from Essondon to Launceston via Flinders Island. Piloted by Captain Norman Evans, the last message heard was

Left: EI-ABT Sasana of Aer Lingus.

Below: *'The Night Mail is about to depart for Stockholm...'* British Airways' G-ADEB about to leave the Beehive Terminal at Gatwick in 1935. *(DH via BAe Hatfield)*

The interior of an unidentified two-seat cockpit DH.86. Noe the thickness of the fuselage walls!

The 'zulushield' enplate fins on the tailplane of Railway Air Services 'WR. (*via John Stride*)

that the machine was approaching Flinders Island and on course. Wreckage was found floating in the sea. Two months later, on 13 December 1935, VH-USW of Holyman's was *en route* from Launceston to Melbourne when movement was detected in a wing strut fairing. Capt A M Bayne believed that a strut collapse was imminent, and fearing a major structual failure elected to make a crash landing on Hunters Island in the Bass Strait. Damage to the aircraft was serious, but none of the eight people on board were injured.

On the other side of the world on 22 October 1935 Imperial Airways lost G-ADCM *Draco* when it crashed at Zwetti, Austria. Ten months later there was more trouble. British Airways lost G-ADEB on 12 August 1936 at Altenkirchen, Germany followed by G-ADYF on 15 September when it crashed on take-off from Gatwick at night.

Investigations were called for. The Air Ministry decided to take action and requested in a letter 489643/36/RDA6 dated 1 October 1936 that Martlesham Heath conduct more trials on DH.86 G-ADYH following the adverse criticism of that machine's handling qualities by its operators British Airways. In the light of data gained from

these tests, the Air Ministry was forced to take action long before Report No.M/636,b/C.A was issued during December 1936.

It was discovered that 'DYH's handling was so bad that the trials were not completed. The ailerons were light at low speeds, but became increasingly heavy as the speed increased. Between 110 and 120 mph there was an appreciable delay between movement of the control wheel and response of the aircraft that got less

G-ADEA is named *Drake* by Lady Cunliffe-Lister at a ceremony on 20 June 1935 (*DH via BAe Hatfield*)

as the speed increased, but this was erratic and not proportional to the movement of the wheel. When the ailerons were moved coarsely in bumpy weather there was a marked twisting of the wings. The rudder also suffered from excessive lag before the aircraft responded and was inefficient at low speeds. Also in the 110 to 120 mph speed range the same problem occurred with the elevators, which allowed up to four inches of control movement before any response was felt from the aircraft. All the controls lacked harmony and were difficult to co-ordinate.

When an outer engine was shut down the aircraft developed a swing that was difficult to check, so much so that should an outer engine fail to take-off temporary loss of control could result.

The machine was difficult to control in disturbed air. It was thought that many of these problems were caused by the aircraft being rigged out of true, but careful re-rigging showed no improvement.

No dive or stall tests were completed, nor were handling trials conducted with the centre of gravity on the forward limit. No night landings were considered advisable. The report concluded that the aeroplane was only safe to fly in calm air and for the gentlest of manoeuvres, for otherwise the aircraft became nearly unmanageable. It recommended that the Certificate of Airworthiness be withdrawn for all aircraft that displayed these flying qualities pending modification.

In view of this somewhat startling report, the Air Ministry arranged for two pilots from Martlesham Heath to fly two DH.86s at Croydon Airport on 27 October. It was discovered that G-AEAP suffered the same problems, but they were slightly less marked whilst G-ACVY (which had been recently flown by A&AEE pilots and therefore of known handling) was satisfactory. Further tests were later conducted at Croydon and Gatwick on a number of 86s which were then split into two groups.

In Group One were all those aircraft that were considered unsafe, and were to be grounded immediately. Group Two contained aircraft that were considered safe as long as the following conditions were applied:
1. The spring loading was removed from the elevators.
2. They were not flown at night.
3. They were only to carry passengers by day when flown by pilots with at least 50 hours experience on the type. The division was as follows:

Group One

G-ADUH	Imperial Airways
G-ADYC	British Continental Airways
G-ADYE	British Continental Airways
G~ADYG	British Airways
G~ADYH	British Continental Airways
G-ADYI	British Airways

Group Two

G-ADFF	Imperial Airways
G-ADUE	Imperial Airways
G-ADUF	Imperial Airways
G-ADUG	Imperial Airways
G-ADUI	Imperial Airways
G-ADVK	Blackpool & West Coast Air Services
G-ARAP	Imperial Airways
G-AEFH	Imperial Airways
G-AEIM	Wrightways

All were flown as close as possible with the same weights and conditions, but discrepancies appeared. It was discovered that British Airways rigged the elevators differently from the method recommended by the makers, whilst Imperial Airways evolved its own method of rigging ailerons that appeared to give better control. To see if differences in physical dimensions could be at fault a series of chord, thickness and perimeter measurements of the wings were taken, but all appeared within manufacturing tolerances.

In the meantime De Havilland had evolved a further variant - the DH.86B. This machine had additional end-plate fins (commonly known as 'Zulu Shields') fitted to the extremities of the tailplane, which was increased in area. These fins were slightly off-set

Seen at Hatfield prior to delivery is SU-ABV of Misr. *(DH via BAe Hatfield)*

St Catherines Bay - Jersey Airways G-ACZN, seen at Portsmouth in 1936. *(John Stroud)*

to counteract any tendency to swing during take-off. The upper and lower surfaces of the tailplanes were covered with 1.5 mm 3-ply and the elevators were fitted with a modified form of spring-loading.

The handling quality changes were remarkable. When SU-ABV (tested with the Class B marks of E-2) was flown, the instability problems had disappeared. The controls were now harmonised and the aircraft was now no longer tiring to fly.

Nevertheless, the A&AEE still called attention to the fact that slightly higher gearing was needed on the aileron control circuit, there was still insufficient tail trimming range, the pilot's rudder bar could be fouled by the second pilot when he operated the flaps and the undercarriage which was still considered to provide insufficient shock absorption and rebound damping. The aircraft was, however, cleared for normal passenger carrying operations.

These small modifications to outward appearance resulted in a dramatic change in the aircraft's handling characteristics. The end-plate fins themselves were slightly offset to starboard to counter any swing that might develop on take-off. A small increase in tailplane area also helped matters. Modifications were also made to the elevator spring loading and both wing extensions were covered with plywood.

The reports issued from Martlesham Heath in December 1936 and March 1937 were of a very different tone. Aileron control was now effective at all speeds, as was the rudder, although still heavy in operation. The elevators were light and effective at all speeds. The aircraft in general was now stable at high speed, with neutral stability at low speeds. Some small faults were noticed however. There was not quite enough elevator trim, the undercarriage was still harsh, minor problems were noted with the windscreen and rudder pedals, but a C of A was granted.

As a result of these successful modifications, all surviving DH.86As were brought up to the DH.86B standard. The last ten 86Bs were further modified with increased tailplane chord at the tips and higher gearing on the aileron circuit. The problem with the undercarriage was never solved.

Although no mention is found in the A&A.EE Test Reports, one suspects that the increase in fuselage area with the lengthened and widened two-seat nose fitted for QANTAS requirements lay at the heart of the stability problems, putting the entire aircraft 'out of balance'. However, in direct contradiction to this, Union Airways of New Zealand and later the Royal New Zealand Air Force operated three DH.86As without the end-plate fins for many years without any untoward problems!

After the official investigations, subsequent aircraft were all built as DH.86Bs, commencing with G-AENR of Blackpool and West Coast Air Services. British Airways standardised its fleet on the Lockheed 10A Electra and sold off it's DH.86 fleet. Two machines went to Wearne Aircraft Services, G-ACYF as VR-SBD, and G-ADEA as VR-SBC for use linking Singapore with Kuala Lumpur and Penang. Two went to

N6246 away from home! The aircraft is seen here at RAF Hal Far, Malta. *(John Hamlin Collection)*

The ultimate DH.86 shape - G-AEJM of Wrightways was a DH.86B. *(DH via BAe Hatfield)*

Primeras Lineas Uruguayas de Navegacion Aerea (PLUNA) of Uraguay for internal services connecting Montevideo with Artigas and Riveria. The four others were passed onto the Air Ministry, two becoming VIP transports with 24 Sqdn RAF, G-ADYG becoming N6246 and G-ADYI AX795. The other two Air Ministry aircraft were modified to comply with specification 28/37 and used as 'flying classrooms' for wireless operator and Navigator training.

Misr Airwork of Egypt purchased four aircraft, to be used on services between Alexandria, Assuit, Cairo, Haifia and Cyprus. Jersey Airways bought six to replace the DH.84 Dragons on the Channel Isles - Eastleigh - Heston service. Three machines were shipped to New Zealand for use with Union Airways of New Zealand Ltd. These three aircraft flew over 1,250,000 miles before flying ceased at the outbreak of World War II, when they were impressed into Royal New Zealand Air Force use.

Railway Air Services, lost one of their early aircraft, the 'single pilot' G-ACVZ *Jupiter,* at Elsdorf, near Cologne on the night of 15/16 March 1937 whilst being flown by Captain George Holmes. On board was Captain Charles Wolley Dod OBE, manager of the European area of Imperial Airways Ltd. Much mystery still remains as to why a RAS internal route machine was flying over Germany, with such an important member of Imperial Airways staff on board.

Allied Airways (Gandar Dower), Devlet Hava Yollari, the Turkish State Airline also bought new aircraft, whilst the last three built went to W.R. Carpenter and Co. of Australia. The last of these three was to be the last DH86 built, but was to crash in New Guinea on 15 March 1940.

DH.87 Hornet Moth

The DH.87 came about as an experimental design project to investigate the possibility of replacing the Gipsy Moth with a side-by-side cabin biplane. Pilots of De Havilland light cabin types traditionally sat away from the passengers so that his attention might not be distracted, but this was to change with the Hornet Moth a practice that was to revolutionalise *ab initio* instruction.

The DH.87 bore a resemblance to the Leopard Moth, employing the same type of rear fuselage construction, but the front fuselage was built of welded steel tubing. The undercarriage fairings rotated to form air brakes and the tapered wood and fabric mainplanes, easily spread or folded by one man, were

E-6, the prototype Hornet Moth, showing the original rounded wingtips. *(DH via BAe Hatfield)*

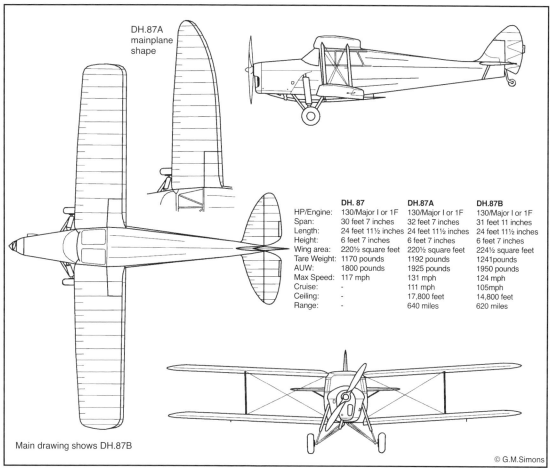

DH.87A mainplane shape

	DH. 87	DH.87A	DH.87B
HP/Engine:	130/Major I or 1F	130/Major I or 1F	130/Major I or 1F
Span:	30 feet 7 inches	32 feet 7 inches	31 feet 11 inches
Length:	24 feet 11½ inches	24 feet 11½ inches	24 feet 11½ inches
Height:	6 feet 7 inches	6 feet 7 inches	6 feet 7 inches
Wing area:	220½ square feet	220½ square feet	224½ square feet
Tare Weight:	1170 pounds	1192 pounds	1241 pounds
AUW:	1800 pounds	1925 pounds	1950 pounds
Max Speed:	117 mph	131 mph	124 mph
Cruise:	-	111 mph	105 mph
Ceiling:	-	17,800 feet	14,800 feet
Range:	-	640 miles	620 miles

Main drawing shows DH.87B

© G.M.Simons

reminiscent of its larger relative, the DH.86. Full dual flying controls were provided, the stick being mounted in the centre between the seats, with two handles extending over each of the two seats. A welded aluminium fuel tank of 35 gallons capacity located behind the pilot's seat gave a standard range of nearly 600 miles and the space above it formed a rack for two large suitcases. A cruising speed of 111 m.p.h. on the power of one Gipsy Major made the Hornet Moth an attractive touring aircraft.

Geoffrey de Havilland made the first flight in the prototype, E-6, at Hatfield on 9 May 1934 and in accordance with the company's usual proving and publicity techniques, flew it in the King's Cup Race as G-ACTA on 13 July, only to be eliminated in the heats

after averaging 127 m.p.h.

De Havilland was still smarting from the problems that had beset the Puss Moth and, more recently, the DH.86 airliner and were in no mood to see a repetition of these embarrassments. Before the Hornet Moth went to the open market, then, it was to be exhaustively tested, a procedure that was not common at that time. Although the prototype (carefully described in *Flight* as 'an experimental machine') handled perfectly well, there were considered to be a number of teething problems which needed sorting out before full-scale production could begin.

Two further Hornet Moths, E-1/G-ADIR and G-ADIS were then built to assist the prototype in a flight test programme which lasted a year and eradicated a number of teething troubles before

G-ADIS was the second production DH.87 showing the pointed wingtips of the DH.87A *(DH via BAe Hatfield)*

P6785, with square cut wingtips - a DH.87B. This was one of four supplied to the Air Ministry on Fairchild floats. *(John Stride Collection)*

construction began on any scale. The production model, designated DH.87A, had more sharply tapered mainplanes which, although 2 feet greater in span, were of the same area. The front fuselage side panels were larger and the tankage was increased.

The first production batch left the factory in August 1935. During the three years up to May 1938, 165 Hornet Moths were built, 84 for the British market. It was soon discovered that in certain circumstances the DH.87A demanded more skill than that possessed by the average A Licence pilot, and early in 1936 mainplanes of new design to eliminate wing drop at the stall were fitted to the third machine, G-ADIS.

In February 1936, the Hornet Moth appeared with a new wing that was now only very slightly tapered and which had more square-cut wing-tips. This was styled the DH.87B. While its performance was slightly inferior to the DH.87A in regards maximum and cruising speeds, it was a far safer, more docile machine to fly. At Martlesham Heath it was recorded that four distinct variants of the machine were submitted for evaluation, the first in July 1934 and the last in March 1936.

The new model gave no trouble whatever and owners were invited to trade in their original mainplanes so that eventually only a few DH.87As remained in the Dominions and five in Britain.

During its brief prewar career the Hornet Moth became a popular aircraft in the private, club and executive fields both at home and overseas but aspired to none of the record breaking epics of its older relatives. The largest single fleet, numbering ten,

formed the equipment of a chain of flying clubs operated in Southern England by the Straight Corporation, while others served with the Border, Lancashire, London, Norfolk and Norwich, RAF, Scottish and Yorkshire clubs.

The type shared the popularity of its forebears and secondhand specimens found a ready market overseas where they kept company with new Hornet Moths shipped out from the Hatfield works.

Overseas the De Havilland companies assembled imported Hornet Moths: seventeen for South Africa , eleven for Canada, seven in Australia and four for India. At the same time others were delivered by air and sea to Austria, Belgium, Denmark, Egypt, Eire, France, Greece, Hong Kong, Java, Kenya, Northern and Southern Rhodesia, Singapore, Spain, Sweden and Switzerland.

De Havilland Aircraft of Canada Ltd. designed and constructed a seaplane undercarriage which used Fairchild metal floats and one Hornet Moth seaplane, CF-AYJ, became the personal aircraft of P. C. Garrett, Managing Director.

Four others were supplied to the British Air Ministry for evaluation as seaplane trainers and after extensive tests at the MA&AEE, Felixstowe, were restored to wheels and despatched to Lee-on-Solent in June 1939. Two survived the war to reappear in 1946 at White Waltham where, stripped of camouflage, they were reconditioned before joining the fleet of Hornet Moths at that time used by the West London Aero Club.

The vast majority of British registered Hornet Moths were relatively new in 1939 and, being ripe for

G-ADKC was a DH.87B, and first flew for Kenneth Crossley in 1936. *(John Stride Collection)*

Hornet Moth G-ADKW overflies Panshanger sometime in the post-war years. *(author's collection)*

impressment, were snapped up rapidly by the RAF as communications aircraft and for the calibration of early radar installations. Hornet Moth OY-DOK even succeeded in escaping from German-occupied Denmark and was taken over by 24 Squadron in December 1941 as HM498.

A high proportion survived to fly again as civil aircraft, notably with the London Aeroplane Club at Panshanger.

DH.88 Comet

In March 1933 a wealthy Australian philanthropist, Sir McPherson Robertson, decided to sponsor a 12,300 mile race from England to Australia to commemorate the centenary of the founding of the State of Victoria. He offered prize money totalling £15,000. This became known as the 'MacRobertson' Race: the name stuck and entered the history-books.

Almost inevitably it was expected that all the aircraft in such a formidable speed trial would be of American origin.

It was through the personal enthusiasm of Geoffrey de Havilland, supported by his key staff, that the DH.88 Comet was planned as Britain's entry. The Comet would be more than an entry, though: it would be the winner and it was up to the de Havilland Company to see that the finest technology it could muster would be employed. Besides being the fastest machine the company had ever designed, it would also be the first to have a retractable undercarriage and controllable-pitch airscrews.

Although nobody had money to throw around, especially in the immediate years following the Depression, de Havilland heavily subsidised the aircraft, offering the machine, ready to fly, for £5,000. A conservative estimate of the actual development costs puts the necessary selling price nearer to 50 percent greater.

Planned as a 200 mph racer and designed by A E Hagg, the news of the venture was advertised to alert potential competitors but its actual specification was to remain a closed secret. The project was given considerable publicity in the Australian and British press but the announcement also stipulated that orders must be placed by February 1934. The offer was accepted and with only nine months to go before the start of the race, three aircraft were ordered straight from the drawing board by Jim and Amy Mollison, racing motorist Bernard Rubin, and Arthur O. Edwards, the managing director of the Grosvenor House Hotel in Park Lane, London.

Success depended on the designer's ability to combine small field performance with high cruising speed and long range, a requirement brilliantly met by the imaginative use of a thin wing, split trailing edge flaps and variable pitch propellers. A crew of two, essential when flying long stages, was seated in

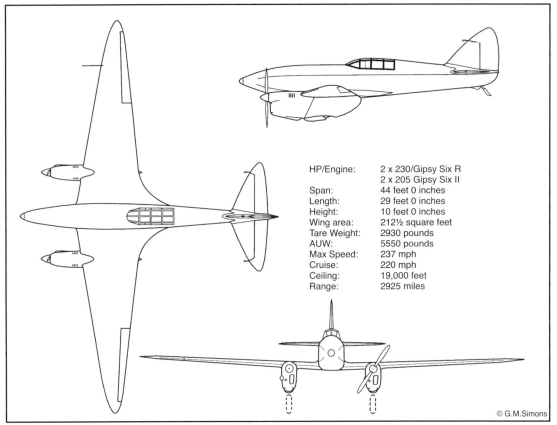

HP/Engine:	2 x 230/Gipsy Six R
	2 x 205 Gipsy Six II
Span:	44 feet 0 inches
Length:	29 feet 0 inches
Height:	10 feet 0 inches
Wing area:	212½ square feet
Tare Weight:	2930 pounds
AUW:	5550 pounds
Max Speed:	237 mph
Cruise:	220 mph
Ceiling:	19,000 feet
Range:	2925 miles

tandem to reduce frontal area.

The design of the all-wooden aircraft was surprisingly conventional although the solution to many of the detail problems was radical. The fuselage comprised four spruce longerons built up to form a perfectly streamlined section using transverse bulkheads and laminated planked skinning. Fuel was entirely contained in the fuselage with almost the entire available cubic capacity forward of the cockpits given over to tanks. The nose contained two large tanks of 128 gallons and 110 gallons both placed in front of the pilot's cockpit. A further tank with a capacity of 20 gallons was placed behind the cockpit and could also be used to alter the aircraft's trim.

The thinnest-possible cantilever wing was designed around RAF 34 section that allowed only 11 inches as the greatest depth of the wing. Construction was centred on an internal structure comprising three spruce and plywood box spars with built-up ribs and stringers. This was then given added strength by being covered using layers of narrow diagonal planking, each spruce strip applied individually. Four laminations at the root provided a covering 9/16-inch thick that tapered to two having a total thickness of 1/8-inch at the tips. Finally a top coating of the finest Irish linen aircraft fabric was doped on. The whole airframe was treated in the same manner.

Two wing-mounted nacelles housed the engines and retractable undercarriage. The motors were special high-compression Gipsy Six 'R' engines built to Frank Halford's design. By using a modified cylinder head, valve rocker gear and piston set, the compression ratio was increased from the normal 5.25 to 6.5 while at the same time the overall height of the engine was reduced. The normal running speed of the motor was increased to 2,350 rpm while at the maximum of 2,400 rpm, 224 hp was produced for take-off.

Originally it had been planned to fit American-made Hamilton controllable-pitch airscrews but in the end these could not be ready in time so French-made Ratier automatic two-pitch airscrews were fitted. These allowed the pilot to select one change of pitch (from take-off to cruise) after which the propeller's compressed-air reservoir had to be recharged on the ground using a bicycle pump.

The Comet's retractable undercarriage operated by turning a handwheel in the cockpit which turned a shaft to rotate the radius-rod locking arm. Because it was worked by a screw-jack, it was claimed that the assembly was strong enough to allow a landing with a partially-lowered leg. Dunlop wheels provided with Bendix brakes combined with Dowty shock-absorbers to make a simple and practical landing gear. The tailskid was both sprung and pivoted to allow tracking on the ground.

It was the first large British aeroplane to be fitted with Schrenk-type landing flaps. These extended between the engine nacelles and under the fuselage.

The Comets were built in great secrecy at Stag Lane and after trial erection the components were taken by

Hubert Broad brings DH.88 E-1 in for a landing. *(DH via BAe Hatfield)*

road to Hatfield for final assembly and test. Even the owners were not allowed to see them but De Havillands were as good as their word and the first Comet, actually the Mollisons' G-ACSP, flew at Hatfield under B conditions as E-l piloted by Hubert Broad on 8 September, just six weeks before the race.

Each Comet boasted distinctive racing colours, the Mollisons' *Black Magic* G-ACSP was black and gold; Bernard Rubin's G-ACSR, flown by Owen Cathcart-Jones and Ken Waller was green; and G-ACSS, named *Grosvenor House* and flown by Charles W. A. Scott and Tom Campbell Black was scarlet and white.

After intensive test flying, fuel consumption tests and crew training, all three Comets checked in at Mildenhall on 14 October but on the 18th Cathcart-Jones damaged 'SR by landing from a test flight with the undercarriage only partially lowered. Damage was done to undercarriage fairings and to the Ratier airscrews but the latter were straightened by the Fairey

Aviation Co. Ltd. after which fanatical repair work had the machine back in the air just twelve hours before the start of the race.

The MacRobertson Race started from Mildenhall at dawn on 20 October 1934 and by the end of the first day the Mollisons, Scott and Black had covered the 2,530 miles to Baghdad. The Mollisons made it nonstop but 'SS refuelled at RAF Kirkuk and Cathcart-Jones and Waller lost their way, making a forced landing at Dizful in the Persian desert, 240 miles to the south east. Nevertheless they overtook the Mollisons at Allahabad, where 'SP had retired from the race with engines damaged by the use of commercial motor spirit.

Scott and Black managed to stay ahead of the KLM Douglas DC-2 and arrive first in Melbourne to win the speed prize in an elapsed time of 70 hours 54 minutes 18 seconds.

Cathcart-Jones and Waller arrived fourth in 108

The Mollison's at Mildenhall with G-ACSP before their departure. *(DH via BAe Hatfield)*

hours 13 minutes 30 seconds, collected news reels and press photographs of the finish and took off at once for England. They arrived at Lympne on 2 November, 13 days 6 hours 43 minutes after leaving Mildenhall, and set up a new out-and-home record.

On 20 December the same machine, now named *Reine Astrid,* left Evere, Brussels, piloted by Ken Waller and Maurice Franchomme carrying Christmas mail to the Congo. They arrived back from Leopoldville on the 28th having completed a 8,000 mile round trip, after which the Comet returned to Hatfield for overhaul and sale to the French Government as F-ANPY. In the course of delivery from Croydon to Le Bourget on 5 July 1935 Hubert Broad established a new inter-capital record time of 52 minutes. The Comet was purchased for experimental work in preparation for a projected high speed South Atlantic air mail service.

A fourth DH.88, F-ANPZ, constructed to French Government order to assist in this work, was fitted with DH./Hamilton variable pitch airscrews and a mail compartment in the nose and thus did not have the landing light. It was the first aeroplane with airframe, engines and propellers all DH built and was delivered from Croydon to Le Bourget by Hugh Buckingham in 59 minutes.

The Portuguese Government had similar mail-carrying ideas and acquired *Black Magic* for a projected proving flight from Lisbon to Rio de Janeiro. Now named *Salazar*, it was ferried from Hatfield to Lisbon on 25 February 1935 by Senor Carlos Bleck and Lt. Costa Macedo, who covered the 1,010 miles nonstop in 6 hours 5 minutes. A return trip was made in the following September and in 1937 Macedo again brought the aircraft back to Hatfield for overhaul and made a return flight to Lisbon in 5 hours 17 minutes in July.

A fifth Comet, G-ADEF *Boomerang*, was built for Cyril Nicholson, who planned a series of attempts on major long distance records. Piloted by Tom Campbell Black and J. C. McArthur, it made a record Hatfield-

Cairo nonstop flight of 2,240 miles in 11 hours 18 minutes on 8 August 1935 during the first stage of an attempt on the Cape record. This was abandoned through oil trouble and the machine returned non-stop in 12 hours 15 minutes and established a new out-and-home record to Cairo. Although entered in the King's Cup Race of 7 September 1935, *Boomerang* failed to start and left a fortnight later for a second attempt on the Cape record, but propeller trouble over the Sudan on 22 September compelled the crew to abandon the aircraft by parachute.

Official interest in the Comet resulted in *Grosvenor House* being shipped back from Melbourne, taken over by the Air Ministry and sent to Martlesham for trials during which enlarged air intakes were fitted to replace those damaged when the undercarriage failed to lock down on 30 August 1935. It appeared with this modification as K5084 at the Hendon Display on 26 June 1936 but the undercarriage failed again on 2 September during landing tests at an all-up weight of 5,000 pounds and it was put up for disposal as scrap. 'CSS was saved by F. E. Tasker, who had it rebuilt by Essex Aero Ltd. at Gravesend, fitting a pair of Gipsy Six series II engines driving DH/Hamilton variable pitch propellers. Painted pale blue and renamed *The Orphan*, G-ACSS came fourth in the 1937 Marseilles-Damascus-Paris race piloted by Arthur E. Clouston and George Nelson.

Then, just as now, advertising played an important part in financing record attempts, so that when Clouston and Mrs. Kirby Green left Croydon to break the out-and-home Cape record on 14 November, the veteran G-ACSS had been renamed *The Burberry*. The record was successfully lowered to 15 days 17 hours for the round trip, and adorned with yet another name - *Australian Anniversary* - it left Gravesend for Australia on 6 February 1938, but an eventful flight terminated in Cyprus with a collapsed undercarriage. Temporary repairs enabled it to be flown home for one last historic flight. With Clouston and Victor Ricketts as crew, 'SS took

The original DH.88 G-ACSP now in Portuguese markings as CS-AAJ *Salazar. (author's collection)*

School restored it to the original *Grosvenor House* condition for display at the 1951 Festival of Britain Exhibition. Later, still with only one engine installed, the historic aircraft which provided so much data for the DH.98 Mosquito was preserved in the showrooms of the De Havilland Engine Co. Ltd. at Leavesden. On 30 October 1965 it was handed over to the Shuttleworth Trust and taken to Old Warden, where overhaul to flying condition commenced in 1976.

off from Gravesend on 15 March, reached Sydney in 80 hours 56 minutes and then crossed the Tasman Sea to Blenheim, New Zealand in 7½ hours. After an overnight stop the Comet set off on the return journey and when it touched down at Croydon on the 26th, 26,450 miles had been covered in 10 days 21 hours 22 minutes to create a new record. It returned to Essex Aero Ltd. at Gravesend, where it donated an engine to Alex Henshaw's long distance Mew Gull G-AEXF, afterwards remaining under tarpaulins for thirteen years until students of the de Havilland Technical

Although it was one of the lowest-powered machines in the MacRobertson Race, the Comet was the fastest British civil aircraft ever produced apart from the Schneider seaplanes.

DH.89 Dragon Six / Rapide

There was an undoubted need for a faster and more comfortable Dragon and work commenced late in 1933, resulting in a scaled down, twin engined version of the high performance DH.86, employing a similar type of fuselage construction, tapered mainplanes, nacelles and trousered undercarriage. Designated DH.89, it was powered by two Gipsy Six engines which at once suggested Dragon Six - a name that was

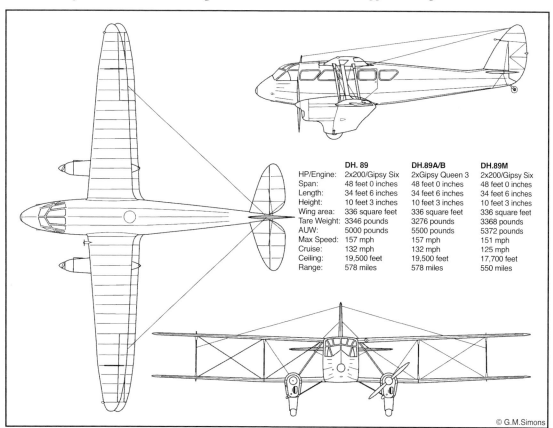

	DH. 89	DH.89A/B	DH.89M
HP/Engine:	2x200/Gipsy Six	2xGipsy Queen 3	2x200/Gipsy Six
Span:	48 feet 0 inches	48 feet 0 inches	48 feet 0 inches
Length:	34 feet 6 inches	34 feet 6 inches	34 feet 6 inches
Height:	10 feet 3 inches	10 feet 3 inches	10 feet 3 inches
Wing area:	336 square feet	336 square feet	336 square feet
Tare Weight:	3346 pounds	3276 pounds	3368 pounds
AUW:	5000 pounds	5500 pounds	5372 pounds
Max Speed:	157 mph	157 mph	151 mph
Cruise:	132 mph	132 mph	125 mph
Ceiling:	19,500 feet	19,500 feet	17,700 feet
Range:	578 miles	578 miles	550 miles

© G.M.Simons

E-4, the prototype DH.89 'Dragon Six' seen at Martlesham undergoing official tersting. *(DH via BAe Hatfield)*

initially used. When series production began at Hatfield the type name became Dragon Rapide, a design that became a mainstay of world commercial aviation for so long that it became known everywhere simply as the Rapide. During the ten years it was in production, 728 were built and it is true to say that just like the ubiquitous Douglas DC-3, no real replacement has ever been found.

The prototype, E-4m first flew at Hatfield in the hands of Hubert Broad on 17 April 1934 and was sold as CH-287 to the Ostschweiz Aero Gesellschaft at St. Gallen for transporting winter sports enthusiasts from Zurich to St. Moritz.

Hillmans Airways Ltd., first operators of the Dragon, were also the first British purchasers of the Rapide, their first aircraft, G-ACPM, making a public debut at Hatfield on 13 July 1934 when Hubert Broad flew it in the King's Cup Race and averaged 158 m.p.h. before retiring with hail damage. Railway Air Services Ltd. also bought Rapides for trunk routes between Croydon, Speke, Renfrew and Belfast and for summer services between Speke, Whitchurch, Eastleigh and Shoreham. Another purchaser was Jersey Airways Ltd.

The 1936 Rapide, commencing G-ADWZ, had a nose landing light, thickened wing tips and cabin heating and was cleared for take off at 5,500 pounds all up weight.

In 1937, commencing with G-AEOV, small trailing edge landing flaps were fitted under the lower mainplane, a modification which gave rise to the amended designation DH.89A. Many earlier machines had these retrofitted during overhaul.

Specification G.I 8/35 for a Coastal Command General Reconnaissance aircraft was met by modifying a standard Rapide with a Mk. V Vickers gun on the starboard side of the nose, a bomb bay for two 100 pound and four 20 pound bombs under the cabin floor, one Lewis gun Mk. Ill on a patent DH. gun mounting on top of the rear fuselage in place of the rear escape hatch, extra cabin windows and a long curved dorsal fin. The crew of three, comprising pilot, wireless operator/gunner, and navigator/bomber were provided with a Youngman dinghy in the top centre section. The single prototype, K4227, designated DH.89M, was passed over in favour of the Anson but the design effort was not wasted as three modified DH.89Ms were delivered to the Spanish Government in December 1935 for police duties in Morocco. A Vickers E gun was fitted in the nose, a Spanish

An early DH.89 Dragon Rapide instrument panel. This varied very little over the years, apart from possibly the fitting of linear rather that rotary oil pressure gauges. *(DH via BAe Hatfield)*

Luxury (left) and airline standard (right) interiors of the DH.89. (*DH via BAe Hatfield*)

designed bomb sight was built into the floor and twelve 27 pound Spanish Government standard bombs were carried in a rack under the fuselage. The mid-upper gunner was provided with a Vickers F gun and a second fired downwards through the floor. When the civil war began in 1936 they were formed into Grupo 40, commanded by Capt. J. A. Anslado, and operated on the Nationalist side as 40-1 *Capitan Pouso*, 40-2 *Capitan Vela* and 40-3 from bases at Logiono,

Burgos and Saragossa. In 1936 two further DH.89Ms were built for the Lithuanian Government.

A standard Rapide, K5070, was added to the strength of 24 Squadron, Hendon in 1935 as an Air Council VIP transport, and was housed with King Edward VIII's red, blue and silver Rapide G-ADDD. In 1938 P1764 and '65 were acquired for communications duties to Specification 21/38 and three trainers, R2485-'87 for 2 Electrical and Wireless

DH.89 interior layouts - 1
From top to bottom:

Convertable European Branch Liner. Six/eight seater. A separate radio compartment could be installed without reducing the number of seats if smaller armchairs were specified.

International Passenger Liner or Charter Vehicle. Five seater, plus lavatory and luggage space. Toilet bulkheads were detachable for quick conversion to eight seater.

International Passenger Liner or Charter Vehicle. Alternative to previous. As with all these variants, two 18-gallon auxilliary fuel tanks could be fitted under central seats.

Private Cruiser. Four seater, plus fold-down seat for attendant. The starboard side seats could be extended to convert into a divan bed.

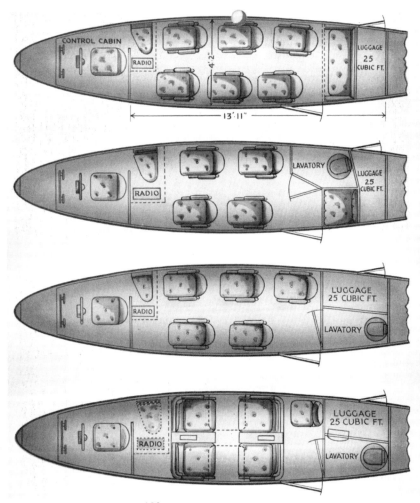

(*DH via BAe Hatfield*)

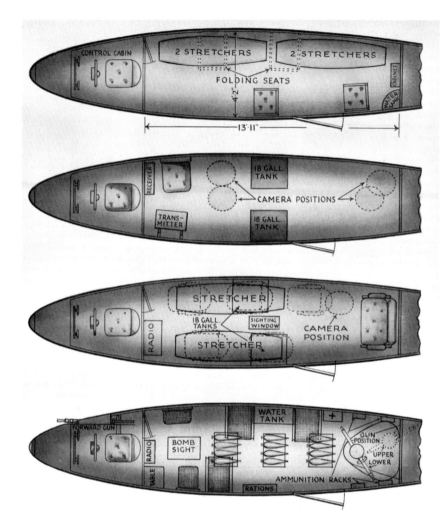

DH.89 interior layouts - 2

From top to bottom: **Air Ambulance.** Two De Havilland light alloy stretchers on the starboard side, with two attendant folding seats on the port side.

Air Survey Vehicle. Four alternate camera positions, with options for radio operators positions and auxillary fuel tanks with seats above if required.

Oilfield type Utility. Fully equipped for air ambulance, survey freight or passenger duties.

Military general Purpose machine. Equipped with bomb racks, bomb sight, one forward gun operated by pilot, one upper and lower gun for alternate use, racks for ammunition drums, optional camera in place of lower rear gun. Separate flare, first aid and ration stowages. Water tank, radio equipment, four folding seats and radio operators table.

(DH via BAe Hatfield)

School to Specification T.29/38.

A single Rapide, A3-1, was supplied to the RAAF for survey work and this survived the war and many years of outback work as VH-UFF.

ZK-ACO, *Tainui*, was purchased by the New Zealand Melbourne Centenary Air Race Committee and in the hands of J. D. Hewett and C. E. Kay, finished fifth in the MacRobertson Race in 13 days 18 hours 51 minutes and later went into airline service in New Zealand and Australia. Another early example went to Lineas Aereas Postales Espanolas in Spain, one to the Italian airline Ala Littoria and three to the Asiatic Petroleum Co. Ltd. for oil prospecting in Netherlands New Guinea. Private sales were also made and several were despatched to de Havilland Aircraft of Canada Ltd., the first of which, CF-AEO, was equipped with Fairchild floats and the long dorsal fin before delivery to Canadian Airways Ltd. Four others were ski-equipped for the Rimouski-Hannington service of Quebec Airways Ltd.

As one of the world's most widely used pre-war transports, the Rapide also flew in the colours of literally hundreds of airlines. The last civil delivery before the outbreak of war was the 205th aircraft, VT-

Four Canadian DH.89s on ski undercarriage. Most Canadian machines had dual doors for safety. *(DH via BAe Hatfield)*

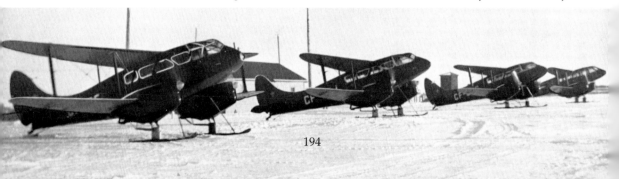

Not often seen is this shot of a pair of Romanian DH89Ms at Hatfield just prior to delivery. *(DH via BAe Hatfield.)*

ALO, for Tata Airlines Ltd., Bombay.

British owned Rapides ranged far over Europe and the Near East in the service of charter firms such as Olley Air Service Ltd., whose G-ACYR was chartered by autogiro pioneer Juan de la Cierva and newspaperman Luis Bolin and flown to Las Palmas, Canary Islands, by Capt. Charles W H Bebb to pick up the Governor, General Franco, and fly him to Tetuan in Spanish Morocco to assume command of the Spanish forces at the beginning of the civil war. It arrived on 19 July 1936 after a night stop at Casablanca, returned to England and saw service on the internal air routes during the Second World War. It was presented to Franco as a souvenir in 1953.

A considerable number of Rapides were used as flying classrooms at the Shoreham and Perth air navigation schools of Airwork Ltd. In May-June 1940 nine were lost while ferrying supplies to the British forces in France, after which the majority were impressed for duty with Air Transport Auxiliary and the air forces and navies of Britain and the Commonwealth. Fourteen were camouflaged to continue in a civil capacity under the National Air Communications banner, with blanked off windows, on essential services in Scotland, and a number of others performed similar duties in New Guinea, India and New Zealand.

To supplement impressments, production was increased at Hatfield and the Rapide became the DH.89B Dominie Mk. 1 navigation and W/T trainer or Mk. 2 communications aircraft, the former externally identified by the roof-mounted D/F loop.

A number of civilian examples were impressed into the Fleet Air Arm which, between 1940 and 1945, also took delivery of 63 Dominie Mks. 1 and 2. Remaining production was for the RAF, ATA and USAAF units in Britain. In 1941 one Dominie was taken on charge at Hatfield as a works 'hack'

Two views of the RAF's DH.89M K4772, both in flight and showing the upper gun position and draught protector for the gunner. *(DH via BAe Hatfield.)*

195

Above: DH.89s operated on floats in Canada, as seen here with CF-BBH of Canadian Airways operating the Vancouver - Victoria service.

Left: A small number of Luxury Rapides were built. G-ACTT was flown for a short time by HRH Prince Edward the Prince of Wales. *(both author's collection)*

under B conditions as E-0228.

By 1942 output had reached 185 machines a year but as all Hatfield factory space was required for the Mosquito the Dominie line was transferred to Brush Coachworks Ltd at Loughborough, where a further 346 were built between 1943 and 1945.

The last 100 production aircraft, built too late for military service, were furnished to civil standards by the de Havilland Repair Unit at Witney and disposed of as normal Rapides.

They formed the initial postwar equipment for many concerns, including Koninklijke Luchtvaart Maatschappij N.V., (KLM) the Anglo Iranian Oil Co. Ltd., Iraqi Airways Ltd., Jersey Airways Ltd. and the Danish ambulance service, while others were despatched to the Lebanon, Brazil, Portugal, Sweden and Transjordan.

Eight were shipped to Peru and assembled in a Government factory at Callao. The first three were climbed to 17,000 feet so as to overfly the Andes en route to their base in the hinterland and two others were put on DH Canada floats. After acceptance tests on the first one at a naval base near Lima, the second was flown to the jungle city of Iquitos and there equipped with floats for use on the Amazon River.

Hundreds of surplus Dominies were disposed of after the war, among which were found a considerable number of pre-war civil Rapides. With roughly daubed civilian marks they flew away from Maintenance Units for conversion by the purchaser, or via de Havilland's Witney refurbishment line, which assembled two additional aircraft from spares in 1947. There were far too many for British requirements and the large surplus was sold in almost every country of the free world. An attempt was also made to re-use and extend the Dominie mark numbers, the six passenger version

A number of DH.89s were operated by the 27th Air Transport Group of the USAAF, as shown here by X7454 which is known to have carried the name *Wee Wullie* on the port side of its nose. *(author's collection)*

Island Air Services operated pleasure flying trips over London out of London's Heathrow Airport - its owner, Monique Agazarian, a former ATA girl, took place in the first ever thousand movements a day from there. G-AGJG survives to this day in pristine condition owned by David and Mark Miller. *(Monique Agazarian)*

with pilot and radio operator being Mk. 2 as in Dominie days, while Mk. 3 denoted the alternative version for pilot and eight passengers. These designations were seldom used in practice.

One of the largest Rapide fleets ever formed flew on the Scottish, Scilly and Channel Islands routes of British European Airways Corporation, which in 1950 grouped the survivors into the Islander Class.

The RAF's last remaining Dominies were declared obsolete in June 1955 and disposed of by public tender and in their declining years were used for communications by major British aircraft manufacturers and for pleasure, charter or feeder line flying all over the world.

Although the Dominie had long since disappeared from the RAF, there were still fourteen on Admiralty charge in 1961 which were kept in airworthy state, mainly for cadet flying.

Almost every postwar DH.89 was powered by the surplus RAF Gipsy Queen 3 engine but a Mk. 4 aircraft fitted with Gipsy Queen 2s driving constant speed propellers had long been suggested. This conversion was not made until 1953, when Flightways Ltd. of Eastleigh made the prototype installation in G-AHGF and promptly sold it in New Zealand.

With these engines the Rapide was cleared for take off at an increased weight of 6000 pounds and had a worthwhile improvement in climb, cruising and single engine performance. Many Rapides were thus modified and could be identified by their large

spinners and healthy take off roar.

A one-off conversion made by De Havillands to one of its communications Rapides, G-AHKA, in 1948, was known as the Mk.5, with manually operated variable pitch airscrews fitted to special Gipsy Queen 3 MVP engines. Ten years later the X5 fixed pitch metal airscrew was specially developed for the Rapide by the Fairey Aviation Co. Ltd, which gave an improved performance similar to that of the Mk. 4 but without the increased cost and maintenance of variable pitch mechanisms. Rapides modified in this way were

One of the last military operators of the DH.89 was the Fleet Air Arm, which flew NR782 out of Culdrose in the 1960s. *(author's collection)*

Dominies together! Not a common sight by any means, here DH.89 Dominie G-AJHO (ex NR747) is seen in formation with DH.125 Dominie XS735. *(author's collection)*

known as Mk. 6, the first of which was G-APBM, produced by Air Couriers of Croydon in 1958.

In 1962 cigarette company Rothmans of Pall Mall Ltd. provided the Army Free Fall Parachute Association with Rapides G-AGTM, G-AJHO, G-AKIF and G-ASRJ, painted in silver and blue and emblazoned with the sponsor's crest. One was stationed in Germany and the others at Netheravon, where they operated for many years, undergoing the indignity of interiors wrecked by parachutists boots, with wing trailing edges suffering the same fate.

It was around this time that the value of the aircraft reached rock bottom. I was part of a team that purchased G-AJHO as a write off from Norwich Union Insurance for one pound after it was allegedly taxied into a fence, suffering minor wing damage.

Slowly, the world's population of airworthy Rapides began to increase as more and more neglected airframes entered long-term restoration. With the popularity of Captain Mike Russell's Russavia pleasure flying operation at Duxford, the delights of bumbling around a Rapide began to be appreciated more and more by the public so that now more and more are used for pleasure charters.

DH.90 Dragonfly

The DH.90 Dragonfly was a tapered wing, five seat, luxury tourer appearing to be a scaled down DH.89, but it was totally different structurally as the fuselage was a monocoque shell of pre-formed ply with light spruce stringers, a construction technique similar to that of the Comet racers and the Albatross airliners.

Improved performance and ease of access to the cabin came about by removing all struts and wires from the inner wing bay through the use of heavy duty spars built into the lower centre section. It was thus possible to use cantilever undercarriage units

The second production DH.90, YI-HMK *The Golden Eagle* for King Fiesal of Iraq, undergoes engine runs at Hatfield before delivery. *(DH via BAe Hatfield)*

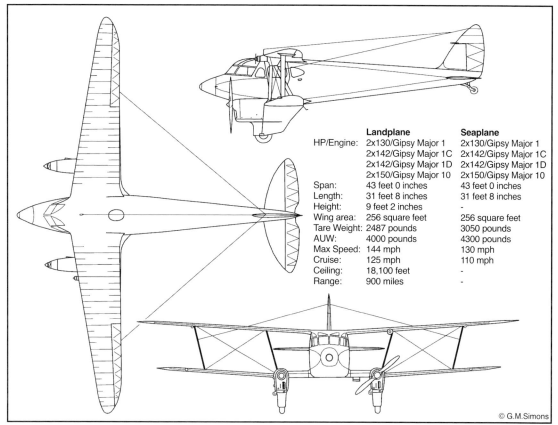

	Landplane	Seaplane
HP/Engine:	2x130/Gipsy Major 1	2x130/Gipsy Major 1
	2x142/Gipsy Major 1C	2x142/Gipsy Major 1C
	2x142/Gipsy Major 1D	2x142/Gipsy Major 1D
	2x150/Gipsy Major 10	2x150/Gipsy Major 10
Span:	43 feet 0 inches	43 feet 0 inches
Length:	31 feet 8 inches	31 feet 8 inches
Height:	9 feet 2 inches	-
Wing area:	256 square feet	256 square feet
Tare Weight:	2487 pounds	3050 pounds
AUW:	4000 pounds	4300 pounds
Max Speed:	144 mph	130 mph
Cruise:	125 mph	110 mph
Ceiling:	18,100 feet	-
Range:	900 miles	-

© G.M.Simons

built integral with Rapide-type nacelles housing two Gipsy Major engines.

Fuel for 900 miles was carried in two thirty-gallon tanks in the thickened lower centre section and a third holding twenty-five gallons was located at the rear of the cabin. When flying with full load, fuel was reduced to give a range of 625 miles.

Dual control was provided in the two front seats and there was a double seat in the rear with a fifth occupant in the centre of the cabin.

The maiden flight of the prototype, E-2/G-ADNA, took place at Hatfield on 12 August 1935 and a second

aircraft G-AEBU, powered by Gipsy Major IIs with provision for variable pitch propellers, flew as the DH.90A demonstrator in February 1936. It was the first of 66 production aircraft built.

As was now almost traditional, the prototype was on the starting line of the King's Cup Race at Hatfield on 10 July 1936 and in the two days' racing piloted by Capt. Geoffrey de Havilland and his son Geoffrey, averaged 143.75 m.p.h. and came eighth.

The Dragonfly achieved maximum performance on low power by the use of new construction methods, which brought about a high sales price of £2,650, so

The prototype DH.90 G-ADNA showing clean shape and lines of the machine in flight. *(DH via BAe Hatfield)*

A somewhat unusual three-quarter-rear view of the prototype DH.90 G-ADNA in flight. *(DH via BAe Hatfield)*

that initial sales on the British market were relatively low at just twenty-one. Nevertheless, a number were purchased by wealthy private fliers, and still more went to the London Aeroplane Club, who acquired one for which the dual instruction charge was £5 10s. per hour and another was used as a navigation trainer by Air Service Training Ltd., Hamble.

Similar sales occurred overseas, the second production DH.90 YI-HMK, was furnished for the personal use of King Feisal of Iraq, and was later joined by YI-OSD. Wealthy French owners Baron L. de Armella, Baron Jules de Koenigswater, Jacques Duprey and Gustav Wolf took delivery of four in 1936-7 while others were supplied to QANTAS; Wearnes Air Services Ltd., Singapore; Rhodesia and Nyasaland Airways; PLUNA of Uruguay; Divisao dos Transportes Aereos (DTA) in Angola; Linile Aeriene Romane Exploatate en Statui (LARES), Rumania; Misr Airwork Ltd., Egypt; Ala Littoria, Italy; the Turkish State Airline; and the Swedish and Danish Air Forces. Others were built for private ownership and taxi work in Argentina, Belgium, Holland, India, Italy, Kenya, New Zealand, Nigeria and South Africa.

De Havilland Canada were responsible for conversion to Edo floats and CF-BFF was so equipped for Gold Belt Air Services Ltd. The Royal Canadian Mounted Police used four Dragonflies to combat rum-running off the Nova Scotia coast.

Only two Dragonflies were the subject of major modifications, the first being one of the company's 'hack' aircraft on which the pilot's windscreen and canopy were improved by large double curvature front panels, enlarged 'eyebrow' windows and

Above: Canadian Dragonfly CF-BFF on Edo floats.

Left: G-AECW operating as De Havillands communications aircraft in July 1940, with roundels and camouflage/yellow paint scheme *(both John Stride Collection).*

An intriguing scene inside the finishing shop at Hatfield. Apart from the two DH.90s, S-23 and S-24, for the Danish Air Force, there are plenty of other machines to interest the eye! *(DH via BAe Hatfield)*

lowered side panels. The other was VP-KCA, supplied to Wilson Airways Ltd., Nairobi in September 1936, which had one starboard window deleted and a small freight door cut in the side.

The DH.90 proved suitable for commercial operation and many machines eventually drifted away from private ownership.

Production ceased in 1938 and in June 1940 the Dragonfly jigs were used to build a road block on the Barnet by-pass. During the Second World War six Dragonflies, including three of the RCMP machines, were impressed into the Royal Canadian Air Force as 7623-7628, and VH-UXS was commandeered by the RAAF as A43-1. Fifteen

Dragonflies which suffered a similar fate in England became industrial 'hacks' - one of them, the former London Aeroplane Club machine, retained its civil status to serve as de Havilland's communications aircraft throughout the war.

With spares non-existent and repairs to monocoque fuselages difficult, they were progressively struck off charge until, with the return of peace, only one Canadian and one British impressee survived. A number of other machines which entirely evaded war service were in daily use until the 1960s.

Slowly the worldwide population dwindled, until only two machines survived.

VP-KCA for Wilson Airways is seen at Hatfield in September 1936; the aircraft has a freight door, and non-standard windows. *(DH via BAe Hatfield.)*

DH.91 Albatross

The DH88 Comet, specially designed for the MacRobertson Air Race, may have won the competition to Australia, but it only just beat the metal Douglas DC2 airliner. Foreign operators were beginning to use the Douglas machine, and it was realised that British Airlines faced tough competition on the air routes, with a serious loss of prestige. To overcome the threat de Havilland's sought finacial assistance from the Air Ministry to build a 200 mph monoplane airliner powered by four engines. After protracted discussions the company secured an order, dated 21 January 1936, for two experimental transatlantic mail-planes to Air Ministry Specification 36/35 capable of carrying 1,000 pounds of mail at 210 mph for a distance of 2,500 miles against a continuous headwind of 40 mph.

Allocated the design number DH.91 and type name 'Albatross', the machine was designed by Arthur Hagg. Construction was mainly of wood and fabric, embodying lessons learned from the DH.71, 77 and 88. The low position cantilever wing was built along the same lines as the Comet, in one piece with a dihedral of 5° and an incidence of 1.5°. The structure consisted of a central box of stressed skin to which was attached the plywood leading and trailing edges. The central girder was built up of two box spars interconnected

with spruce girder ribs over which was laid a number of spruce longitudinal stringers supporting the skin which was two layers of spruce slatting laid diagonally at 20° to the spar and bound with casein glue. All was finally covered with a layer of Tago, cemented cedar three-ply.

The differentially operated Frise ailerons were of welded steel construction covered with fabric, each being built in two parts with separate mass balances to simplify the alignment of bearings. Controllable

Two views of one of the DH.91s under construction. The fuselage was built almost as a complete single unit in a jig.

As was common with the later DH.98 Mosquito, the one piece wing was built 'upside down'.
(both DH via BAe Hatfield.)

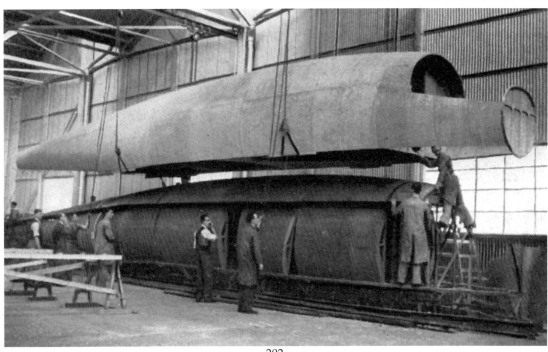

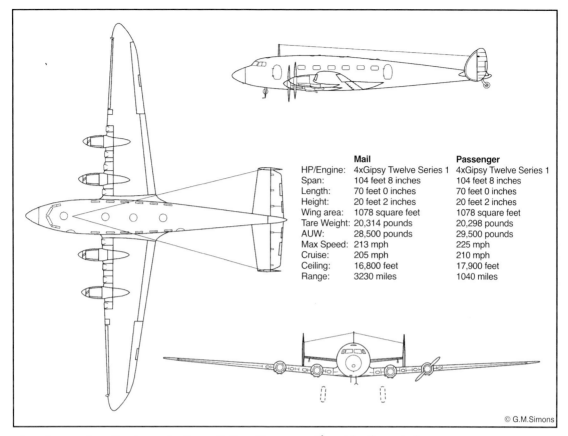

	Mail	Passenger
HP/Engine:	4xGipsy Twelve Series 1	4xGipsy Twelve Series 1
Span:	104 feet 8 inches	104 feet 8 inches
Length:	70 feet 0 inches	70 feet 0 inches
Height:	20 feet 2 inches	20 feet 2 inches
Wing area:	1078 square feet	1078 square feet
Tare Weight:	20,314 pounds	20,298 pounds
AUW:	28,500 pounds	29,500 pounds
Max Speed:	213 mph	225 mph
Cruise:	205 mph	210 mph
Ceiling:	16,800 feet	17,900 feet
Range:	3230 miles	1040 miles

© G.M.Simons

trim-tabs were later fitted to each aileron. Split trailing flaps were fitted to the prototype, but subsequent aircraft were fitted with Handley Page slotted flaps.

The long, tapering fuselage, so asthetically beautiful, was a circular monocoque structure comprising an outer and inner layer of double camber Port Oxford cedar plywood with a sandwich of balsa in between. The layers were cemented under pressure on a retractable jig, allowing the whole fuselage to be lifted off in one piece. Four fuel tanks were installed in the fuselage, each of 330 Imperial gallon capacity, two on either side of a central gangway.

By the time that the prototype appeared in May 1937 for extensive engine and taxi-trials at Hatfield it was clear that this design bore no family resemblance to any previous De Havilland designs. Problems were encountered with the new untried 525 horsepower Gypsy 12 inverted vee type engines designed by Major Frank Halford, who had united two Gipsy Six engines onto a common crankcase. It was thought that all four engines would have to be changed before the scheduled maiden flight, but careful inspection

The fuselage of one of the mailplane DH.91s is about to be mated with its one-piece wing. *(DH via BAe Hatfield)*

Above: The prototype mailplane E-2/G-AEVV in flight, showing it's original inset fins and rudders.

Left: the fuel tanks inside the main cabin, extending the range of the mailplane version. *(both DH via BAe Hatfield)*

revealed that just one unit was at fault.

When R G Waight and G D Tucker took the prototype in Class B marks 'E-2' into the air for the first time at 06.55 hrs on 20 May in front of an audience of company officials and workers it was clear that Waight was still taking no chances with the engines, for they were operating at only half throttle. Some problems were encountered with the undercarriage during this flight, for the demonstration took place with the wheels partially retracted.

The prototype appeared at the 1937 Hendon Air Padgent on 26 June, but did not taken part in the rehersal, with only fast and slow taxi runs permitted before the spectators. Two days later E-2 made a semi-public appearance at Hatfield for the SBAC show, held on 28 and 29 June.

De Havillands went to great lengths to explain the aerodynamic and economic advantages of the Albatross: *'The objective achieved in the evolution of the Albatross has been to combine the high factors of safety, comfort and practical operation which are necessary in a transcontinental liner with a purity of aerodynamic form hitherto unattained in aircraft of any category, civil or military, and so to secure high speed with a lower power expenditure than has ever before been possible for the same paying load. In that way a new level of economy is established together with the advantages of swift transport.'*

The company went on to state that with its engines delivering 1,300 horsepower, or only 62 per cent of their take-off power, the Albatross carried its load and fuel at a normal cruising speed of 210 m.p.h. If it were perfectly streamlined for instance if its weight and its 4,000 square feet of exposed surface were represented as a pane of glass of negligible thickness towed edgewise through the air by the same thrust horse

Armchair comfort! The clean, uncluttered flight deck of this DH.91 suggests almost luxury. *DH via BAe Hatfield)*

With its four Gipsy Twelves turning, G-AFDJ *Falcon* appears ready to depart on another service. *(DH via BAe Hatfield)*

power, it would travel only 49 m.p.h. faster. Its speed was 81 per cent of what it would be if ideally streamlined.

This purity of form was reflected directly in the figure of ton-miles of payload transported per gallon of fuel consumed, which, given an aircraft of moderate first cost and upkeep charges, is the most significant factor in the overall cost of operation. The fully equipped Albatross passenger liner with a crew of four and enough fuel for a normal range of 600 miles transports 2.4 tons of paying load 210 miles in one hour for a fuel expenditure of 83 gallons, thus yielding a power-economy factor hitherto unequalled in any air liner of comparable speed and payload, no less than 6.07 ton-miles of payload per gallon.

The aerodynamic cleanness or speed efficiency of the Albatross has been obtained by the combination of several outstanding features and was possible largely because the aircraft, engines and airscrews were produced by one company possessing a wealth of experience in all three fields of development.

In the first place the Gipsy Twelve power unit, logically developed by Major Halford from the Gipsy Six and Gipsy Major in-line engines, has an exceptionally low frontal area (1.75 square inches per horse power) and is enclosed in a clean and circular cowling measuring in cross-section only 30 per cent of the diameter of its geared airscrew. This means that only one-tenth of the area of the airscrew disc is occupied by the power plant. And although the wing is exceptionally thin no less than 55 per cent of the frontal area of all four power installations is absorbed in the depth of the wing. The

How low can you go? A truly dramatic picture of a head on pass from an unidentified DH.91. *(DH via BAe Hatfield)*

Right: a detail view of one of the Gipsy Twelve engine installations in its extremely neat cowling. Such streamlining gave the DH.91 mailplane remarkable performance for its power. The fuselage fuel tanks are visible through the cabin windows.

Below: how the reverse flow cooling systrem worked on the DH.91. (both *DH via BAe Hatfield*)

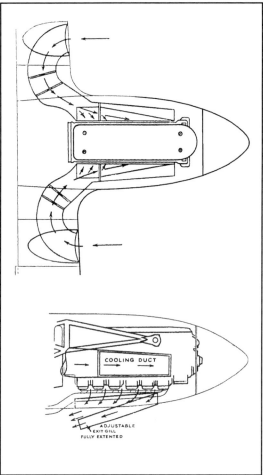

COOLING DUCT

ADJUSTABLE
EXIT GILL
FULLY EXTENTED

pure bullet shape of the installation is not impaired by an airscoop; instead the engine is specifically designed for cooling from the rear by ducts which deliver air at controlled pressure and flow rate from orifices which are incorporated in the leading edge of the wing in such a way that lift and drag are not materially affected.

In brief the Gipsy Twelve has a cleaner entry and is believed to have a lower cooling loss than any other engine in production.

Special structural methods were adopted to create an aircraft of fine lines to take full advantage of the low drag of the power units. Indeed, design of aircraft and engine were closely co-ordinated and proceeded side by side.

The wing of the Albatross is of wooden stressed-skin construction, a single box girder of robust scantlings in which the reduction of thickness in relation to span can, without excessive weight, be carried further than is possible in metal construction. The thickness is only 2.1 per cent of the span. This thin wing of large span affords a relatively high lifting capacity together with the valuable feature of low drag.

The fuselage is of circular cross section, has an admirable aerodynamic shape and is of a special carapace or lobster-claw construction, comprising a double stress-bearing shell of double curvature in which parallelism of the inner and outer walls, in both planes, is preserved by an interlayer of light stabilising material. The structure of the shell is hermetically sealed by films of synthetic resin embodied in the preformed stress-bearing walls.

This form of structure has been the subject of extensive research by the De Havilland Company and is patented. It has a remarkably high ratio of strength and stiffness to weight and, besides advantages of vibration damping and sound absorption, ease of maintenance, etc., it provides a surface free from rivets and lap joints on which any desired *degree of smoothness can be easily obtained.*

Wing-root interference is low and excrescences have been remarkably eliminated. The tailplane is a pure cantilever of similar construction, clean to a degree. Doors and windows fit flush. The undercarriage is completely retracted and faired while in flight. Close fitting cowling joints avoid wasteful drag-creating air leaks around engine nacclles and undercarriage units.

Following the death of R G Waight , killed while flying the experimental TK4 on 1 October, his place in the test programme was taken by Geoffrey de Havilland Jnr. Data gained during the early flights show that the inset strut-braced fins and rudders gave poor longitudinal stability when the aircraft was climbing at full throttle and low airspeeds, so a completely new cantilever tail was designed and built to overcome this defect with end-mounted fins carrying unbalanced rudders. The fins and dihedral tailplane were of two spar construction covered with plywood while the rudders, elevators and trimming tabs were of Alclad frames covered with fabric. This new tail was first flown on E-2 during January 1938.

In Air Ministry contract 458574/35 two Royal Air Force serials were allocated for the mailplanes, K8618 and K8619, but these were never taken up and on 3 March 1938 both machines were given the civil registrations G-AEVV and G-AEVW, being nominally registered to the Secretary of State for Air.

Further indications of a problem that was to plague the Albatross thoughout its service appeared on 31 March 1938 when with four others on board Geoffrey de Havilland discovered that the undercarriage failed to lower correctly; luckily he was able to make a safe landing with only minor damage to the airframe. Repairs were completed during April and the machine was flying again in May, by now painted with the marks G-AEVV.

The second machine was flown unpainted during July, suffering a serious accident whilst undergoing overload take-off trials at Hatfield with Geoffrey de Havilland Jnr at the controls during the evening of 27 August. These trials were scheduled for three take-offs and landings to be made with a 3000lb overload weight, but during the third circuit of the airfield the ballast shifted, causing the Albatross to fly in a distinct tail-down manner. There was no hope in shifting the ballast forward, and a landing in the present condition and weight would be impossible, so Geoffrey circled the airfield using up fuel, eventually bringing the aircraft in to land. As expected, the tail down atitude made a landing on the mainwheels impossible, the tailwheel touching down heavily with the fuselage snapping in half aft of the trailing edge of the wings. The nose jerked into the air running across the field leaving the rear fuselage and tail behind. The broken halves were returned to the shops and placed back into the jigs, being repaired by a interior strengthening band, said to only add 12.5lbs to the AUW. The repaired machine re-emerged during early October to take up test flying with the Class B marks E-5. The cost of each mailplane appears to be £30,875.

From the outset Imperial Airways Ltd had shown a strong interest in the passenger carrying variant. This was to have a radio operator,s compartment behind the cockpit bulkhead, followed by a galley on the port side with luggage bay on the port side of a central gangway. A door in a further bulkhead led into the passenger saloon, divided into three compartments with the main entrance door, toilet and additional luggage space aft. Four emergency exits were provided in the roof, and all the main cabin windows could be pushed out if required. Normal accomodation was for 23 passengers, although this was convertable to a night sleeper with 22 day seats and 12 berths at night.

G-AFDJ is seen at Croydon Airport, with the Air Ensign flying. *(via John Hamlin)*

On 29 July 1938 Imperial Airways Ltd placed an order for five machines, each costing £30,953, to be allocated their type classification of 'F' class, the first of these being flown unpainted before delivery as E-2 but with the fleet name *Frobisher* under the port cockpit windows only along with the inscription 'Imperial Airways London'. This aircraft was finally delivered to the airline during November 1938. The remaining four aircraft off the production line were all initially flown in natural finish, possibly with, Class B registrations carried for test flights.

It was hoped to make the first experiamental mail flight across the Atlantic using the Air Ministry sponsored mailplanes during September 1937, but the prototype had not completed its official tests. Later a similar flight from Hatfield to New York was planned with intermediate stops at Shannon, Hattie's Field, Newfoundland and Montreal for November 1938 as soon as 100 hours of test flying was completed. Captains E R B White and A C P Johnstone of Imperial Airways Atlantic Division were chosen to make the trip, but that also fell though. Imperial Airways were not too keen on the idea, for they were planning to use their new Short S.30 Flying boats on a non-stop service with the aid of air to air refuelling. The two mailplanes were used therefore by IAL for crew training at Hatfield for the remainder of the 'F' Class fleet.

Captain Alan B H Youell flew *Frobisher* on its official proving flight from London to Brussels on 18 November 1938, covering the 200 mile distance in 66 minutes. Frobisher flew the London to Paris route in the hands of Captain J T Percy with 18 passengers, 810 pounds of baggage, 372 pounds of freight and 506 pounds of mail on 25 November in 53 minutes at an average speed of 222 mph, therefore allowing the claim

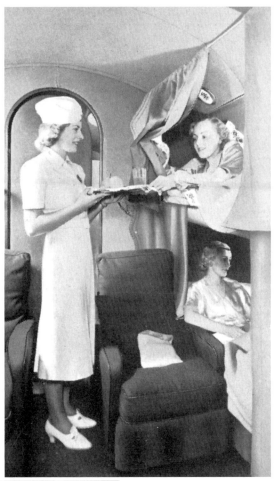

Above: The interior of the Night Liner. This is known to be a De Havilland publicity photograph, the air hostess wearing the company 'house' uniform.

Left: the same interior, this time configured for day use. (both *DH via BAe Hatfield*)

Almost certainly a posed image, G-AFOI *Frobisher* at Croydon. *(via John Hamlin)*

of a new record time.

The first 'F' Class airliner flights outside Europe occured the week before Christmas 1938, when both *Frobisher* and *Falcon* were taken off the European routes, each making a return trip to Egypt with heavy loads of mail. Weather across Europe was poor, but both aircraft made flying speeds averaging 219 mph to Alexandria.

Most of the 1938 route schedules were re-arranged in 1939 as a result of the Government's policy to amalgamate Imperial Airways and British Airways into one corporation. This led to replanning of the European routes to eliminate competitiveness. With joint BAL/IAL services in operation on the London/Paris route from 16 April 1939 the 'F' class were operating eight services a day in the week, with an additional five on Sundays. This summer peak gradually diminished as August drew closer.

In the meantime *Fortuna* had appeared outside the flight-shed at Hatfield during October 1938, and was later used by De Havilland's for the experiamental installation of three-bladed propellers, designed with a better pitch range, for it was found that the two-bladers were inadequate at the cruising height of 11,000 feet. It was not possible to obtain maximum engine rpm's for the propellers were at fully coarse pitch for the last half of the throttle quadrant. The results were not as good as expected, for *Fortuna* was delivered to Imperial with two-blade propellers. IAL continued these trials with *Frobisher* when a complete set were installed during January 1939. Following close to the news of *Frobisher's* record breaking flights was news of its accident at Croydon on 17 January 1939. Heavy rain had fallen before the

arrival of the flagship at 12.20hrs from Paris, making the airfield very slippery. The grass surface offered very little resistance, so when the brakes were applied for turning onto the concrete apron the port undercarriage leg contacted the concrete edge with the whole weight of the Albatross behind it, forcing it to give way inwards. The starboard leg now took the full weight of the turn, resulting in it breaking and folding sideways. Both wingtips hit the ground in turn, breaking both wing spars outside the outboard engines. *Frobisher* had previously skidded at Orly Airport, luckily without damage, but IAL withdrew the three machines in service for four days, pending investigation into the cause of the Croydon incident. *Falcon* returned the type to service, taking the evening dinner flight to Paris, but unfortunately suffered a very similar accident at Croydon on 17 May 1939.

The Albatross was a pleasant aircraft in which to fly, although the large dihedral of the mainplanes gave passengers the impression that the aircraft was flying one wing low, a sensation that could only be dispelled by looking out of the opposing window! In bumpy weather the wings flexed noticeably, causing the fuselage to twist about its longitudinal axis, which could be felt in the cockpit and could be unpleasant for the passengers. The passenger cabin was criticised for noise and vibration, with the general seating arrangements regarded as cramped compared to the standards set by other earlier airliners still in service.

Commemoration of the 30th Anniversary of M Bleriot's flight across the English Channel took place on 25 July 1939 when Captain Youell took *Fiona*, the seventh and last Albatross built, on a special flight from Le Touquet to Croydon, but instead of flying

Franklin in full RAF camouflage. *(author's collection)*

at the normal operating height Youell brought the aircraft down considerably lower, crossing the Channel from Barraques to Dover Castle. Each of the eighteen passengers received a specially signed certificate from Captain Youell to record their presence on the flight.

With the clouds of war gathering, plans for evacuating Croydon were put into effect on 29 August. All continental flights had ceased by the 31st with all aircraft being dispersed to Whitchurch and Coventry. A day before, *Fortuna* had left for Karachi with eleven senior Army Officers on board, a flight which must be regarded as the longest to date made by any Albatross. Soon after the return to the UK *Fortuna* left Shoreham on 22 September to start wartime service in Alexandria, flying important documents between the Middle East and the UK.

Operations within the UK transferred to Heston, and once the initial panic of the outbreak of war had subsided the Paris services resumed on 11 October, the 'F' class operating twice daily in each direction. A further route to Lisbon was opened on 4 June 1940 when *Fingal* started to twice weekly service with a refuelling stop at Bordeaux.

During the latter half of 1939 the two mailplanes G-AEVV and G-AEVW were placed on loan to BOAC, involving the conversion to passenger carrying, at a cost estimated at £15,000 each. Both

were registered to the Corporation during 1940 with the fleet names *Faraday* and *Franklin* respectively. During the conversion the tare weight was increased from 20,314 pounds to 21,215 pounds in G-AEVV, G-AEVW being 1000 pounds more because of its superior type of flap. It appears that BOAC made little use of these converted mailplanes before they were handed back to the Air Ministry on 1 September 1940, receiving compensation of only £20,000. Delivery to the Royal Air Force did not occur until 24 October, when *Franklin* was taken on charge of 271 (Transport) Squadron. *Faraday* had been delayed at Hatfield because of a fire that had occured at Whitchurch during the night of 12/13 October, causing considerable damage to the cabin roof, extending forwards to the after-end of the cockpit. Later investigations revealed that the fire had been deliberately started by person or persons unknown from within the aircraft using carbide powder. Luckily the main structure was undamaged, but the cost of repair was still around £2,000.

This was not the only machine damaged in this way for, on 20 October 1940, a former Imperial Airways employee, who bore a grudge against the company after being sacked for stealing, visited the airfield to extract revenge. He cut a hole in the rear fuselage near the tail of *Frobisher* and inserted a

G-AFDK in camouflage, with the wartime National Air Communications markings. (author's collection)

210

package of carbide powder on which he then poured water. When the mixture started to bubble, he put a match to the gas, which ignited. *Frobisher* burned for at least two hours. Following the court case, which established that he had also caused the fire in G-AEVV, he was sentenced to a four year prison term. Interestingly, Royal Air Force records state that this aircraft was destroyed by enemy action on 20 October 1940.

Meanwhile *Fingal* met with an equally ignominious fate. With the outbreak of World War Two the aircraft was flown to Whitchurch airfield, Bristol. The aircraft took off from Whitchurch on a flight to Bramcote for storage on 5 October 1940 with Captain E R B White in command and a crew of two plus nine BOAC engineers as passengers. At a height of 1,000ft, south east of Pucklechurch all four engines cut out. The pilot attempted a forced landing, lowering the undercarriage and touched down 30 yards from a hedge. The aircraft bounced, slid down a slope, collided with a cottage, finishing up with its nose over a lavatory seat. The remains were sold to C J Packer for scrap, the centre section being used as a storeroom at his garage at Chippenham, Wilts until chopped up towards the end of 1946.

The three survivors maintained the various shuttles until *Fortuna*, piloted by Capt. G. P. Moss, crashed on mud flats near Shannon in July 1943 with most of the BOAC board on board. Spares non-existent, *Fiona* and *Falcon* were broken up a few months later.

DH.92 Dolphin

The DH.92 was built in the experimental shop at Hatfield in the spring of 1936 to incorporate the firm's many ideas for the so-called 'modernising' of the previous DH.89 Rapide design. The nose was reshaped in the style of the DH.86A with a flight deck for two pilots seated side-by-side with dual control and featured the hinged nose cone of the DH.90 Dragonfly to give access to a forward baggage compartment. A door in the port side, with retractable step, led into a Rapide-style cabin with rear toilet while a third door, in the starboard side, opened into the main luggage compartment in the rear fuselage.

The mainplanes were of unequal span as on the Dragonfly, with ailerons on the upper wing only, but were rigged with greater sweep-back in the manner of the DH.86. The strengthened bottom centre section of the Dragonfly was made even thicker and stronger to house a forty gallon internal fuel tank in each side and,

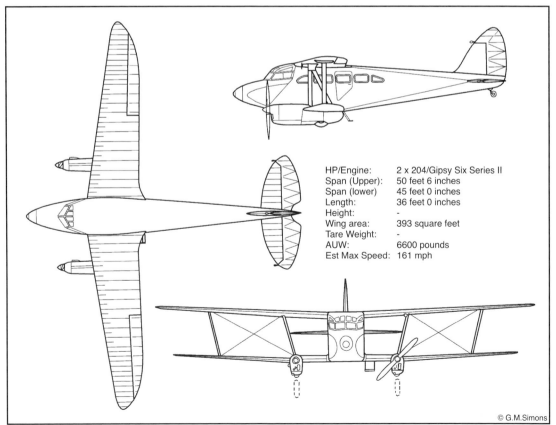

HP/Engine:	2 x 204/Gipsy Six Series II
Span (Upper):	50 feet 6 inches
Span (lower):	45 feet 0 inches
Length:	36 feet 0 inches
Height:	-
Wing area:	393 square feet
Tare Weight:	-
AUW:	6600 pounds
Est Max Speed:	161 mph

© G.M.Simons

There are only three known pictures of the DH.92 Dolphin, and none show the complete aircraft. Left is E-3 in its original form with trousered undercarriage. *(DH via BAe Hatfield.)*

after the trial installation of a faired and unfaired fixed undercarriage, carried one of a new design which retracted electrically into enlarged nacelles similar to those of the DH.88 Comet racer.

The Dolphin's wing cellule used the Dragonfly's bracing system with 'I' struts outboard and inverted Vees inboard, while for ease of loading, all bracing wires were eliminated from the inner wing bays. A two-piece trailing edge flap passed right under the fuselage between the nacelles, the tail unit being similar to that of the Rapide but larger, all movable surfaces being mass balanced.

Despite its external similarity to three previous De Havilland types, most of the Dolphin's main assemblies were of entirely new design. Power was provided by two 204 h.p. de Havilland Gipsy Six series II engines intended to carry variable pitch propellers, but for test purposes the prototype was completed and flown with fixed pitch wooden propellers.

Although the civil registration G-AEMX was

Two views of the Dolphin E-3, now fitted with retractable undercarriage - this was its final configuration. *(DH via BAe Hatfield.)*

issued on 27 August 1936, with the aircraft recorded in the Air Ministry files as a 'three seater biplane' - ready for the aircraft to participate in the Schlesinger Race from Portsmouth to Johannesburg in the following month, as far as is known, it was never used. Geoffrey de Havilland Jnr.'s flying log books record that he flew it twice only, first on 9 September 1936 and again on 21 November. It was found to be structurally overweight and no more examples were built, the prototype's short life being spent in undercoat with Class B marking E-3.

Flight dated 10 September 1936, on the decision to discontinue the type: *'The South Africa Race will be poorer by one entry, and a most interesting entry at that, for the De Havilland Company announces that the design of the DH.92 is to be discontinued, and that this experimental type will not be put into production.'*

It is stated the development of the four-engined Albatross, important contracts contributing to the expansion of the Royal Air Force, and other urgent activities impose a heavy load on certain sections of the Company's organisation, making it impossible to devote the personnel and time necessary for the early production of the Dolphin - the type-name chosen for the ninety-second De Havilland design. The manufacture and technical development of the Dragonfly, the Dragon Rapide, and the DH.86A will, of course, be continued at any rate of output required to meet the demands air transport operators, and the development of new commercial types will follow the completion of the Albatross.'

No three view drawings have been located but enough component drawings and three detail photographs survive to form the basis of the accurate reconstruction three view to be made. There is however, some conflict as to the span of the DH.92. Some sources claim that the span was 50 feet 6 inches. whereas a contemporary press release quoted 53 feet 7 inches.

DH.93 Don

The DH.93 was a three seat, low-wing, general purpose trainer with retractable undercarriage built to Air Ministry Specification T.6/36. It was of wooden stressed skin construction with side by side dual controls for pilot instruction, generous cabin space for radio training and a rotatable dorsal turret for gunnery practice.

Power was supplied by a twelve cylinder De Havilland Gipsy Twelve aircooled supercharged engine driving a constant speed metal propeller as in the DH.91 Albatross airliner. This engine, given the name Gipsy King 1 by the Air Ministry, was cooled by air ducted from intakes in the leading edge of the mainplane in a similar manner.

The prototype, E-3/L2387, first flew at Hatfield on 18 June 1937 and was flown at the Hendon Display on the 26th of that month by Flight Lieutenant. E. R.

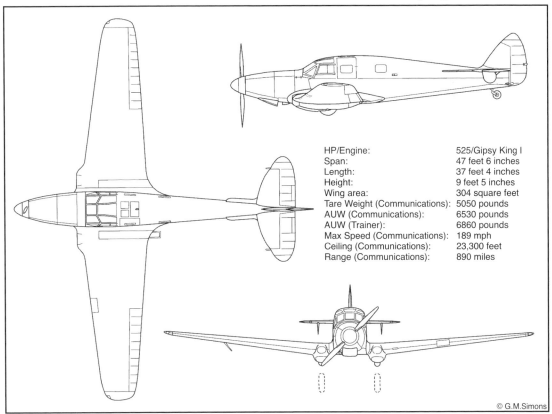

HP/Engine:	525/Gipsy King I
Span:	47 feet 6 inches
Length:	37 feet 4 inches
Height:	9 feet 5 inches
Wing area:	304 square feet
Tare Weight (Communications):	5050 pounds
AUW (Communications):	6530 pounds
AUW (Trainer):	6860 pounds
Max Speed (Communications):	189 mph
Ceiling (Communications):	23,300 feet
Range (Communications):	890 miles

© G.M.Simons

The prototype DH.953 Don outfitted as a turreted general purpose trainer.

L2391, the fifth Don, converted for communications duties. The aircraft had auxilliary fins under the tailplane and reduced rudder horn balance area.(*both DH via BAe Hatfield.*)

Symonds and exhibited there at the Society of British Aircraft Companies Show during the following week. Initial flight trials dictated the fitment of small auxiliary fins under the tailplane before the prototype was sent to Martlesham. Production then commenced at Hatfield. However, before deliveries commenced official policies changed and the order was cut back from 250 to 50 aircraft.

An early production Don was used by the manufacturers in 1937 to test a two bladed reversible pitch airscrew for holding down speed in a dive. Officially inspired 'improvements' were then made on such a scale that structural weight became excessive and the turret and other heavy equipment was removed to convert the Don for communications duties. The first such conversion was made to L2389, the third airframe, and after this had been submitted to Martlesham, communications Dons were issued in small numbers to 24 Squadron, Hendon and to the Station Flights at Abingdon, Andover, Brize Norton, Eastchurch, Mildenhall, Netheravon, Northolt, South Cerney, Upavon and Wyton.

Total deliveries amounted to thirty aircraft and another twenty delivered unassembled or as engineless airframes. Their Service lives were short and by 1940 they had been relegated to Schools of Technical Training or to Air training Corps Squadrons as ground instructional airframes.

DH.94 Moth Minor

For many years the De Havilland company had considered the introduction of a low wing successor to the Gipsy Moth that would have no rigging problems, be easier to build, but would have superior performance on less power.

Part of this thinking came about when the Gorell Committee's report on private flying appeared, one of its proposals was that in due course all privately-owned machines would be free from the necessity of possessing a normal Certificate of Airworthiness, being allowed to fly on a basis of regular maintenance. That this never came to pass can be viewed as a mixed blessing but it did open the door for a cheaply-built, low-maintenance aircraft that could operate within this proposed relaxing of legislation.

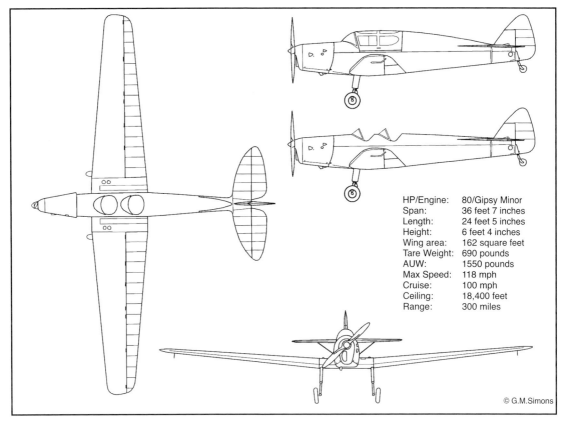

HP/Engine:	80/Gipsy Minor
Span:	36 feet 7 inches
Length:	24 feet 5 inches
Height:	6 feet 4 inches
Wing area:	162 square feet
Tare Weight:	690 pounds
AUW:	1550 pounds
Max Speed:	118 mph
Cruise:	100 mph
Ceiling:	18,400 feet
Range:	300 miles

© G.M.Simons

The first result was the DH.81 Swallow Moth of 1931, a two seat, open cockpit monoplane powered by an 80 h.p. Gipsy IV engine. Some development work was done, including the fitting of a cabin top, but it was shelved because in a time of trade depression, full productive capacity had to be concentrated on old favourites such as the Puss Moth, biplane Moths and Dragon derivatives.

Nevertheless Capt. Geoffrey de Havilland personally kept the scheme alive, brought it to fruition five years later as the DH.94 Moth Minor and made the first flight in the prototype, in Class B marks E-4, at Hatfield on 22 June 1937.

He shared the test flying with son Geoffrey and John Cunningham, during which the last mentioned pair parachuted from a Moth Minor which refused to recover from a spin during CG aft limits trials.

Power was supplied by a 90 h.p. Gipsy Minor engine specially designed for it by Major Frank B. Halford. The airframe was the product of a design team led by J. H. Phillips and J. P. Smith, who married the spruce and plywood box-style fuselage of the original wooden Moth to a high aspect ratio plywood covered mainplane built on similar lines to those of the

DH.94 Moth Minor ZS-ARE, the South African demonstrator machine in flight. *(author's collection.)*

DH.94 production under way at Hatfield in 1939.

Below: The perforated air brake flap which extended across the centre-section had intermediate settings to stretch or shorten the approach to landing.
(both DH via BAe Hatfield.)

Comet and Albatross. The wing folded outboard of the centre section, in the root ends of which space was provided for suitcases or extra fuel tanks. Tail surfaces were fabric covered, ailerons and rudder were mass balanced and a spring loading device corrected trim when changing from powered to gliding flight. Cantilever undercarriage legs were anchored to the front spar of the centre section and wheel brakes and a tail wheel were fitted as standard. The aircraft was flown from the front seat and provided with a large perforated air brake under the centre section to steepen the glide and shorten the landing run.

By June 1939 production in the Hatfield '94 shop' had already reached eight aeroplanes a week. They were priced at £575 ex works and to initiate the sales drive one Moth Minor was sent to each of the Australian, Canadian, Indian and South African companies while British flying clubs, eager for modern equipment and cheaper flying, ordered a considerable number to be used on subsidised Civil Air Guard training. A few were acquired by private owners.

Over one hundred Moth Minors had been built by the outbreak of war in September 1939 but early in 1940 production in the UK was abandoned because all the Hatfield factory space was required for the war effort. All the Moth Minor drawings, jigs and tools, along with stocks of finished and unfinished airframes were then shipped to Australia, where construction

was completed in the Bankstown factory of de Havilland Aircraft Pty. Ltd. At least forty were supplied to the Royal Australian Air Force as an interim trainer until the Tiger Moth was available in quantity. A considerable number survived the war and served Australian light aviation for many years. Thirty-two Moth Minors impressed by the British Air Ministry were used for a wide variety of purposes but many were issued to Station Flights and became Commanding Officers' personal mounts. One British civil Moth Minor, G-AFPJ, was at Almaza, Cairo at the outbreak of war and was almost certainly that procured by the USAAF and flown in the Near East

Moth Minor G-AFPT of the West London Aero Club in flight.
(Simon Peters collection.)

A delightful image of Moth Minor E8 in flight against a dramatic cloudscape. *(Simon Peters collection.)*

during the war as 42-94128 *Sand Fly.*

A number of Moth Minors were fitted with hinged coupé tops, the first of which flew in the summer of 1938. One coupé was modified by the De Havilland company as a long range machine for an attempt on the light aeroplane long distance record by John Cunningham, who hoped to reach Baghdad. This was first flown by Geoffrey de Havilland Jnr. as E-2 on 31 March 1939 and by his brother John on 8 April 1940, by which time war had stopped the attempt. It was the first of an experimental trio, the next, fitted with a tricycle undercarriage and canopy over just the rear seat, being flown by John de Havilland as E-6 on 29 April 1940. The last was a cabin model, E-14/G-AGAO, with hand operated variable pitch propeller. De Havilland also supplemented its two communications Hornet Moths with the camouflaged open cockpit Moth Minor G-AFTH which had been previously been evaluated for basic trainer suitability at Boscombe Down in December 1939, and with the coupe 'OJ. From 1942 the latter flew as E-0236 (later E-1) and after the war was acquired by the London

The tricycle Moth Minor E-0226 showing the somewhat strange open front cockpit and enclosed rear one. *(DH via BAe Hatfield.)*

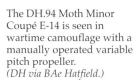

The DH.94 Moth Minor Coupé E-14 is seen in wartime camouflage with a manually operated variable pitch propeller. *(DH via BAe Hatfield.)*

Moth Minor A21-18 of the RAAF at Point Cook Victoria in 1940 in a yellow trainer scheme.
(Simon Peters collection.)

VH-AAM, seen at Moorabbin sometime in 1955, with advertising for Aspaxadrene asthma medication. The aircraft was finally withdrawn from use in 1958.
(Simon Peters collection.)

Aeroplane Club.

Sixteen Moth Minors came up for disposal after the war, most of which were used privately with great success, and several were raced as single seaters with the front or rear cockpit faired in according to taste. Seven which survived in the United Kingdom included G-AFNG and NI, originally open models but converted into the standard cabin type at Panshanger

in 1954.

All who flew the aircraft were impressed with its ease of handling and its performance on the Gipsy Minor engine. The Moth Minor did not really come into its own as a civilian light aircraft until after the war, by which time only a handful had survived. By all accounts it was a safe and docile aircraft offering a first-class view for the pilot, who flew from the front seat.

DH.95

The twin-engined all-metal stressed-skin monoplane that was being designed and built at Hatfield in 1938 marked more than purely a simple change of philosophy at De Havilland Aircraft Company. It marked the start of a new era that had to prove itself as rich as that which it replaced.

This, the first all metal aircraft built by the De Havilland company it was designed by Ronald E. Bishop and named Flamingo by Capt. de Havilland. The Flamingo was a shoulder-wing cantilever monoplane powered by two 890 horsepower Bristol Perseus XIIC sleeve valve radials and was equipped with such up to date refinements as De Havilland hydromatic three bladed propellers, split trailing edge flaps, hydraulically retractable undercarriage and a low slung fuselage affording the ease of entry and loading necessary for short haul work.

The four-piece cantilever wing was of modified RAF.34 section and comprised two stubs attached to follow-through spars in the fuselage, and two outer panels. The stubs were built around a lattice-girder

main-spar of extruded aluminium alloy. The auxiliary spars were Wagner beams with a light-skin D-section spar. Four fuel tanks having a total capacity of 402 gallons were mounted in the wing stubs, two per side.

The aileron hinge-brackets and outer sections of the split trailing-edge flaps were supported on stronger ribs having solid shear webs. Each of the outer wings was covered with fabric aft of the spar. Detachable metal wing-tips were fitted. Differentially-controlled fabric-covered ailerons were built around Alclad D-section torsion nose spars and pressed Alclad ribs. Hydraulically operated Handley Page slotted trailing edge flaps extended from each side of the fuselage as far as the ailerons. Each of the flaps was made in two halves so as to allow for flexure and were built the same way as the ailerons.

The fuselage was built in two sections, the front portion extending from the nose to the bulkhead behind the pilot's cabin being detachable. In order to minimise damage in the event of a wheels-up landing the bottom of the fuselage was reinforced with stout keel members and strengthened ring frames.

Each of the retractable undercarriage legs comprised a single Lockheed cantilever compression

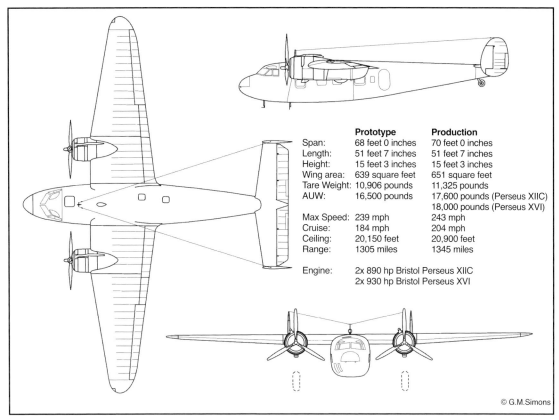

	Prototype	**Production**
Span:	68 feet 0 inches	70 feet 0 inches
Length:	51 feet 7 inches	51 feet 7 inches
Height:	15 feet 3 inches	15 feet 3 inches
Wing area:	639 square feet	651 square feet
Tare Weight:	10,906 pounds	11,325 pounds
AUW:	16,500 pounds	17,600 pounds (Perseus XIIC)
		18,000 pounds (Perseus XVI)
Max Speed:	239 mph	243 mph
Cruise:	184 mph	204 mph
Ceiling:	20,150 feet	20,900 feet
Range:	1305 miles	1345 miles
Engine:	2x 890 hp Bristol Perseus XIIC	
	2x 930 hp Bristol Perseus XVI	

© G.M.Simons

strut operated by Dowty hydraulic gear. For ease of maintenance and spares-holding, each unit was interchangeable. Dunlop wheels with Bendix brakes were fitted and retracted backwards into the rear halves of the engine nacelles; however, the tailwheel was non-retracting.

Passenger accommodation was arranged for twelve, fourteen or seventeen passengers and a twenty-seat cabin was described as available to order. The fully-upholstered Rumbold seats were arranged in rows three-abreast, two to the starboard and singles to the port with a fourteen-inch gangway between. Each seat was individually adjustable.

The normal crew comprised Captain, First Officer and radio operator. Novel for the pilots was the provision of segmented control 'wheels' that emerged from the instrument panel. Commonplace in years to come, this was a great curiosity at the time and drew much comment.

Prototype trials commenced at Hatfield with the

The Flamingo was the first all-metal passenger aircraft to be produced by de Havilland and the first not to have a DH-made engine. It was also the first effort from the drawing board of Arthur Hagg's replacement as chief designer – Ronald E Bishop. The central fin was added as a temporary measure after the first flight and pending the manufacture of replacement fins and rudders of increased area. This central fin was fixed, and had no moving parts. [DH via BAe Hatfield]

Factory pictures of the stages of manufacture of the DH.95 Flamingo taken at Hatfield in the summer of 1938.

Above left: The nose assembly of the fuselage revealing its simple jigging.

Above right: Assembling the framework of thin frames and stringers for the fuselage prior to skinning.

Left: The large aeroplane rapidly taking shape in the late autumn of 1938. The changeover from wood to all-metal construction marked a turning point in the manufacturer's history. [all DH]

first flight of the unmarked prototype on 22 December 1938 piloted by Geoffrey de Havilland Jnr. and George Gibbins, and included the temporary fitment of a third, central, fin. This was removed when enlarged fins with horn balanced rudders of greater area were fitted.

So comfortable did de Havilland feel with the machine that the moment the unmarked aircraft left Hatfield's turf he retracted the undercarriage.

34-year old Ronald Bishop had produced a masterpiece for the company with the DH.95. Cruising speed was ten mph greater than the machine's American rival – the Lockheed 14H.

At Martlesham Heath for its C of A trials in July 1939, it was reported that the prototype easily met all performance criteria and was exceptionally good on one engine. The dashboard-mounted control columns were innovative and were generally liked. However, there were criticisms. The special single instrument that produced read-outs for revolutions, cylinder-head and oil-temperatures was singled out for universal condemnation, in particular as in order to read the function required it was necessary to operate a switch. In addition the Exactor engine cowl flaps were imprecise and were included in the four items requiring improvement (Report No 745 dated July 1939).

Registered G-AFUE, the prototype was loaned to Guernsey & Jersey Airways Ltd for proving flights on their routes from Heston and Eastleigh to Guernsey and Jersey. British Overseas Airways Corporation also ordered eight machines. Production aircraft incorporated several important changes. First the wing span was increased by twenty-four inches and with it

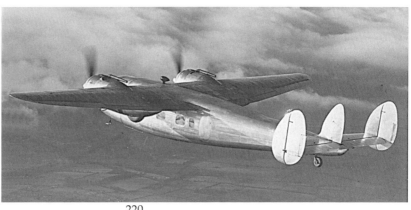

A somewhat unusual threequarters rear view of the unmarked prototype DH.95 in flight, showing the partially protruding wheels from the nacelles.
(DH via BAe Hatfield.)

The unmarked prototype DH.95 lands back at Hatfield. *(DH via BAe Hatfield.)*

the span of the ailerons by two feet per side. To match this the flap area was reduced by 4 sq.ft.

Other basic changes included a reduction in dihedral from three to one degrees. The rudders on the prototype had static balances: now the fins and rudders were increased in area and the rudders given larger horn balances. At the same time, wings and tail-surface leading edges were fitted with Goodrich inflatable de-icing boots. The fifth Flamingo, flown as E-16, and all subsequent aircraft were powered by the 930 horsepower Perseus XVI engine. This test-bed first flew on 7 April 1940 and later became G-AGAZ.

Between September 1940 and April 1941, seven Flamingos were delivered to BOAC at Bramcote, where their wartime temporary base was situated. These were fully camouflaged but bore their civilian registrations. Known to the operator as 'K' Class, they were all named after kings of England.

In July 1939 Gordon Olley announced that in the New Year he would have Flamingos and that he expected to start taking delivery 'shortly', but no record has been found of Olley's order.

The career of this fine aircraft was not to be as planned, though, and with the outbreak of war all were pressed into service with the Royal Air Force.

The military version, the 22-seat de Havilland Hertfordshire, was designed to Air Ministry Specification 19/39 dated 2 September 1939 and was

Below left: Something of a sensation was caused by the Flamingo's cockpit, for it was the first British passenger aircraft that used instrument-panel-mounted control wheels, leaving an unobstructed floor. The view from the 'office' was extremely good. Below right: Thought to be an interior mock-up photograph, this shows the layout of the twelve-seater DH.95, The toilet is on the starboard side and the stewardess is in the doorway to the rear baggage room. *[DH]*

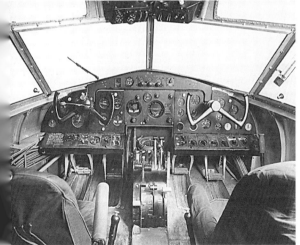

No, not the Hertfordshire, but AE444 (c/n 95005) carrying De Havilland 'Class B' marks E-16 undergoing single engine testing. It was an engine and propeller test bed. *(DH via BAe Hatfield.)*

for a two-crew machine capable of carrying eighteen troops. It was very similar to the civil version except that the large cabin windows were replaced by small circular portholes. An order for thirty was cancelled and only the prototype, R2510, was built.

Another Specification (20/39) was dated 9 Setpember 1939 for a communications version to carry two crew plus wireless operator and a fitter and accommodation for eight passengers. A VIP Flamingo was the subject of Specification 21/39 and two were delivered during September 1940 (R2764 and R2765) while a third, R2766, was attached to the King's Flight and civil registered G-AGCC for a while.

With the Expansion Scheme at its height, the remarkable performance of the all metal Flamingo attracted Air Ministry interest as a future military transport, and serial number T5357 was allotted to, but not carried by, the prototype during official evaluation in March 1939. Civil orders were placed by the Egyptian Government and by Guernsey and Jersey Airways Ltd., with whom the prototype went into service on loan in May 1939 for proving flights between Guernsey, Jersey, Eastleigh and Heston. Before the two Flamingoes ordered by this company could be delivered, war had broken out and they joined the prototype as VIP transports with 24 (Communication) Squadron at Hendon for the use of Mr. Winston Churchill and his advisers when making urgent trips to France during the pre-Dunkirk period.

Throughout the period of hostilities the Flamingos were used extensively for communications and essential airline work. Five survived the war and were flown to Redhill for refurbishment by British Air Transport Ltd. Work progressed for a while but then the cash dried up. After several years of uncertainty they were broken up.

In all twenty aircraft were laid down of which fifteen were originally on the British Civil Register, two of which were not taken up leaving a total of

Finally with enlarged fins and rudders the Flamingo shows off its practical lines in flight. It was, however, so close to the outbreak of war that it was already destined for an uncertain future. War broke out within weeks and aircraft ordered by operators were impressed into military service. *(DH via BAe Hatfield.)*

G-AFYH

DH95 Flamingo R2765 Lady of Hendon was first flown as E-10. It is seen here in the service of 24 Squadron being being scrapped in 1944. *(Simon Peters Collection.)*

thirteen registrations. The rest were cancelled.

During the war, De Havilland Aircraft made one further and final attempt to revive the design. This time it was pitched as being a direct rival to the Douglas DC-3 Dakota as a 22-seat troop transport and as a 19-20 passenger post-war airliner. On 1 August 1943 the company published a document the cover of which was marked 'SECRET'. This was for the Flamingo Mark II project and concerned developments that pre-empted the recommendations of the Brabazon Committee and might well have taken the design into the realm of a post-war airliner.

The project, which was characterised by having a single, Mosquito-like vertical tail, was stillborn.

The Flamingo was Britain's first real challenge to the growing tide of American airliner imports. It was a sane and sensible aircraft that was easy and safe to fly and had no vices. The Mk.II project was estimated to be better than both the Lockheed Fourteen and the Lodestar, while it was comparable to the Douglas Dakota. It was thus the first of many DC-3 replacement designs. We were deprived of the opportunity to beat the Americans at their own game!

DH.96

As far as ca be traced, this type number designation was allocated to two completely separate designs. The first was a layout made in 1938 for a twin-engined

transport aircraft based on the DH.91 Albatross. No detailed drawings have been located, and later the type number was transferred to a two-seat low wing monoplane to Air Ministry Specification T.1/37 and similar to the Miles Magister.

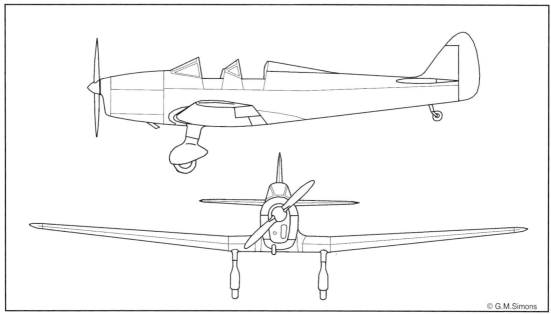

© G.M.Simons

DH.97

This was the last number allocated to a transport

design project before the Second World War broke out. It was not proceeded with.

DH.98 Mosquito

Experience in the design and construction of wooden aircraft of high performance convinced De Havillands that it was possible to build an unarmed bomber that could out-perform all contemporary fighters. Initial ideas in 1938 suggested a miniature Albatross powered by two Rolls-Royce Merlin engines and having sufficient range to carry a worthwhile bomb load to Berlin, but in October of that year the project was turned down by the Air Ministry, who were incapable of seeing any virtue in unarmed wooden aircraft.

Nothing further was done until 29 December 1939 when, through the foresight and enthusiasm of Sir Wilfred Freeman, Air Council Member for Research, Development and Production, a detailed design was sanctioned for a light bomber having a

range of 1,500 miles and able to carry a bomb load of 1,000 pounds. It was to be equally suitable for unarmed reconnaissance or as a long range fighter.

Design work was done at Salisbury Hall, London Colney, by a team headed by Ronald E. Bishop and on 1 March 1940, after much official reluctance, a contract for fifty aircraft W4050-W4099 was placed to Specification B.1/40.

Designated the DH.98 Mosquito, it was an all wood cantilever monoplane with a circular section, tapering fuselage built of laminations of cedar ply separated by a layer of balsa wood. To simplify the installation of controls, wiring and pipelines, the port and starboard halves of the fuselage were made separately, and the one piece, stressed skin mainplane was built round the radiators and ten fuel tanks of 539 gallons capacity. The low drag nacelles for the 1,250 h.p. Merlin 21 engines housed the retractable undercarriage for which the DH system of rubber - in - compression shock absorbers was revived to speed production, to which end light alloy castings were used instead of forgings.

The Mosquito prototype was built secretly in a small hangar at Salisbury Hall and flew for the first time in the hands of Geoffrey de Havilland Jnr. at Hatfield on 25 November 1940, less than eleven months from the start of design work.

Above: Mosquito prototype W4050 comes together in the small hangar at Salisbury Hall 'sometime in 1940'.

Right: the same machine, marked as E0234, undergoes engine runs. At this time the aircraft is still missing the undercarriage doors.
(both DH via BAe Hatfield.)

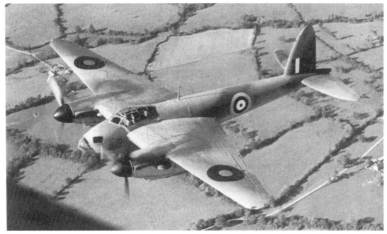

Left: W4051. The fuselage originally intended for this aircraft was used to replace W4050's which had been fractured at Bascombe Down, and so W4051 received a production fuselage instead.

Below:W4052, the fighter prototype, differed from the bomber prototype in having two uprated Merlin 21s of 1,460 horsepower, and a flat bullet-proof windscreen. Constructed at Salisbury Hall, it was flown out of a field adjacent to the assembly hangar on 15 May 1941 by Geoffrey de Havilland Jr. *(DH via BAe Hatfield.)*

Performance during the first two flight tests, made in B conditions as E-0234, astounded even the manufacturers and its fighter-like manoeuvrability and upward rolls from ground level on one engine at last attracted active official interest. The prototype was re-serialled W4050 for further flight tests and for three months of official trials which began on 19 February 1941 and established it as the world's fastest operational aircraft, a distinction it enjoyed for the next 2½ years.

In order to save a month of dismantling and re-erection time, W4052, the Mosquito II night fighter prototype to Specification F.21/40, was flown out of a field at Salisbury Hall by the same pilot on 15 May 1941. It had strengthened wing spars so that it could be thrown about in combat and was equipped with four 20 mm. Hispano cannon under the floor, four .303 inch machine guns in the nose, a flat bullet-proof windscreen and the then secret AI Mk. IV radar.

Entry was by a door in the starboard side of the cockpit instead of through a trapdoor in the floor as in other versions. W4052 was also used for the development of night fighter tactics, which included fitting a pneumatically operated segmented air brake round mid fuselage. Last of the three prototypes, the photo reconnaissance Mosquito I W4051, made its first flight on 10 June 1941 and was handed over to the Photographic Reconnaissance

Left: The idea of fitting a turret to the Mosquito was considered. W4050 went back into the shops to have the mock-up of an upper turret fitted for drag-tests during July 1941. Right: The first fighter was W4052, shown here with one of a number of versions of the Youngman frill air-brake, extended in the open position. By this time the air-brake had been modified with a cut-out in the top section, possibly to improve the airflow over the fin and rudder when the brake was deployed. *[both DH BAe Hatfield]*

Above: a half-shell in its vertical jig - some of the equipment, including the instrument panel has been fitted.*(DH via BAe Hatfield.)*

Left: This view shows just how easy it was for workers to gain access to all sections of the fuselage to install items of equipment. *(DH via BAe Hatfield.)*

Below: Twenty Mosquito B.XX bombers undergoing final assembly at De Havilland Canada's Downsview factory. *(National Aviation Museum of Canada)*

The cockpit of the fighter prototype.
(DH via BAe Hatfield.)

with dummy turrets, on 14 September and 5 December 1941 respectively. A considerable drag penalty combined with the good results obtained with the fixed gun fighter variant ended the experiment.

Both bombers and fighters were operational by May 1942 and from then on all three versions were developed to suit the changing military situation, becoming ever faster, heavier and increasingly difficult to intercept. The first production bomber was the B. Mk. IV series 1 with increased tankage, ten of which were delivered after prototype trials with W4072, first flown on 8 September 1941. It was discovered that if bomb vanes were cropped it was possible to carry four 500 pound bombs instead of the intended 250 pounders - doubling the Mosquito's hitting power before it even went into service. Initial deliveries included 263 B. Mk. IV series 2 machines identified by longer nacelles projecting aft of the wing and dividing the wing flaps. The first operation by B. Mk. IVs was a daylight attack on Cologne on 31 May

Unit at Benson in the following month. W4054 and W4055 followed it and these were the first Mosquitoes taken on RAF charge. The first operational flight, a high altitude sortie to photograph enemy harbours at Brest and Bordeaux, was made by W4055 on 20 September.

A scheme to produce Mosquito turret fighters was short lived. The first flight of W4050 with a mock-up turret on 24 July 1941 was followed by an order for two more, W4053 and W4073, built at Salisbury Hall and flown out of its small field, also

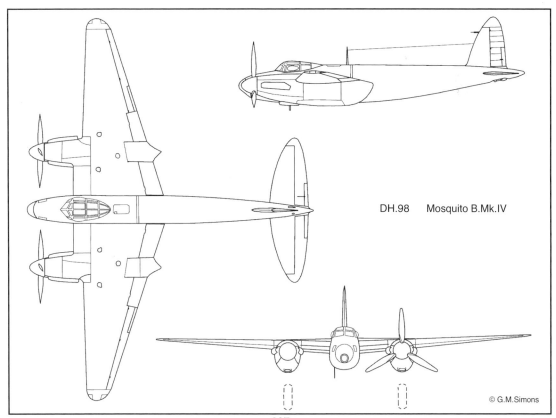

DH.98   Mosquito B.Mk.IV

© G.M.Simons

227

1942 by four aircraft of 105 Squadron, Marham which in company with the second Mosquito bomber squadron, 139, later carried out low level precision attacks all over Europe. These included the destruction of Gestapo HQ at Oslo on 26 September 1942, a feat resulting in a communique making public mention of the Mosquito for the first time. Modifications were then made to 26 aircraft for the carriage of a 4,000 pound bomb, plus 50 gallon drop tanks under the outer wing panels, enabling Mosquitoes to reach and bomb Berlin for the first time on 30 January 1943. Several trials aircraft included DZ594 with the first bulged bomb bay, DZ714 with H2S radar, DK290 with cut away bomb bay for dropping trials in connection with the Wallis 'Highball' bouncing bomb, and LR495 with the wing mounted S.C.I, smoke curtain installation.

Bomber development was via the single B. Mk. V with strengthened wing to carry two 500 pound bombs or 100 gallon drop tanks, to 25 examples of the Packard Merlin 31 powered B. Mk. VII built by de Havilland Aircraft of Canada Ltd., the first of which, KB300, flew at Downsview on 24 September 1942. Starting with LR495 was a batch of 54 British built B. Mk. IXs with 1,680 horsepower Merlin 72 engines, the prototype being a converted B. Mk. IV DZ540. Two additional 500 pound bombs were carried under the wings and in 1944 some were equipped with bulged bomb bays to accommodate a single 4,000 pound 'blockbuster' while others were fitted with Oboe radar and diverted to pathfinding duties. Fifty-four production B. Mk. IVs were also modified to carry the 4,000 pound bomb. For night intruder operations by the eleven Mosquito

squadrons of 8 Group, a development of the B. Mk. IX, designated the B. Mk. XVI, was built with a pressure cabin and Marshall blower to permit full use of high altitude Merlin 72 engines which gave a ceiling of 37,000 feet. A special Merlin 60 powered aircraft, MP469, the first pressurised Mosquito, flew in November 1943 and was the forerunner of 1,200 B. Mk. XVIs, many of which carried the 4,000 pound bomb and auxiliary fuel tanks.

Canadian production progressed from the B. Mk. XX with American equipment via the Packard Merlin 69, arabic-mark-numbered, B. Mk. 23 project to the B. Mk. 25, 400 of which were produced with the Packard Merlin 225 operating at boost pressures up to 18 pounds per square inch. When production ceased in October 1945, supposedly 1,134 Mosquitoes had been built in Canada, many of which established record times for the Atlantic crossing during routine delivery flights to the United Kingdom by the Northern Route, the best time of 5 hours 30 minutes made in April 1945. The

Right: Long range fuel tanks in the bomb-bay of the later P.R. variants gave fuel sufficient for nine hour sorties. One of the holes in the fuselage for a camera can be seen towards the top of the picture.

Below: W4051 is prepared for a test-flight at Hatfield. With its proven speed at altitude performance, it is not surprising that the P.R. Mosquito was given priority. (both DH via BAe Hatfield.)

final bomber variant was the Airspeed-built B. Mk. 35, the prototype of which flew on 12 March 1945. Powered by one Merlin 113 and one 114 with power take-off for the cabin blower, it was faster than, but otherwise similar to, the B. Mk. XVI and although too late for the war, formed the postwar equipment of 109 and 139 Squadrons at Hemswell.

The Mosquito's fighting career began when the first of 466 N.F. Mk. II aircraft entered Home Defence service with 157 Squadron at Castle Camps in January and 23 Squadron at Ford in July 1942. Later 23 Squadron took part in the defence of Malta and in operations over Italy. N.F. Mk. II DD723 was equipped experimentally with underslung radiators and a Turbinlite in the nose. The F. Mk. II day fighter was dropped but a single example, A52-1001, was flown in Australia in 1942 and thereafter fighter variants were produced only in the fighter-bomber or night fighter category, the first and most widely used being the F.B. Mk. VI, 1,218 of which were built by the parent company, 1,200 by the Standard Motor Co. Ltd. and 300 by Airspeed Ltd. The prototype F.B. Mk. VI, a converted Mk. II HJ662, first flown in February 1943, was followed by 300 Merlin 21 or 23 powered F.B. Mk. VI series 1 which, in addition to full fighter armament carried two 250 pound. bombs in the bomb bay and two others under the mainplane. Subsequent aircraft, known as the F.B. Mk. VI series 2, were fitted with Merlin 25s, and strengthened to carry 500 pound instead of 250 pound bombs and were fitted for long range tanks.

The Mosquito was the natural enemy of hostile shipping and to further this propensity a Mk. VI, HJ732, was fitted with a 57 mm Molins quick firing gun, weighing nearly a ton, to become the prototype F.B. Mk. XVIII, first flown on 25 August 1943. Twenty-seven were built and first saw action on 4 November 1943; one also shelled and sank a U-boat near the French coast on 25 March 1944 and another was supplied to the United States Navy.

The gun was an adaptation of a weapon designed originally for naval use, with the addition of an automatic feed. It was designed and manufactured by Molins Machine Company, one of the world's leading manufacturers of cigarette-making, packing and handling equipment. Desmond Molins had already done work on the automatic feed, which was to store rounds in groups of four or five, with an electrical drive to move the next group into position over the breech feed. The magazine took up relatively little space, and allowed the heavy shells to be fed automatically into the weapon without the use of case links. While working on the gun's feed unit, Molins found that the gun needed modification to allow the recoil mechanism to operate the magazine. In time this gun became known as the 'Molins Gun' or, in official parlance, the 'Airborne Six-Pounder Class M Gun'.

Recoil problems ended the experiment in favour of a rocket projectile installation first made to HJ719 early in 1943, eight 60 pound rockets being equivalent to a broadside of six inch naval guns.

Above: the oft-shown picture of an armourer holding a 6 pound shell under the nose of a Mk.XVIII Mosquito. This shows the business end of a Mk.XVIII with the four machine guns for aiming and a certain amount of protection and the end of the 57mm barrel sealed over to keep the draught out of the fuselage.

Below: the 'magazine' that was also the auto-feed mechanism holding 22 shells. The firing rate on 'full auto' was one shell every one and a half seconds. *(both Molins Machine Co. Ltd, via author)*

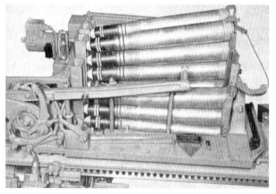

Projected Mosquito F.B. Mks. X with Merlin 72 and XI with Merlin 61 engines were never built and the next types ordered in quantity were the Merlin 21 or 23 powered N.F. Mks. XII and XIII. These were fitted with AI Mk. VIII radar but in common with all later night fighting Mosquitoes, except the N.F. Mk. XV, all carried four 20 mm. cannon instead of nose machine guns. The 97 N.F. Mk. XIIs were converted Mk. IIs but the 270 Mk. XIIIs, the first of which flew in February 1944, were new production aircraft, 100 Mk. IIs also being converted to N.F. Mk. XVII standard by the installation of AI Mk. X radar. Both the N.F. Mk. XVII and the N.F. Mk. XIX, 220 of which were built, were identified by an outsize bulbous nose housing the scanner, the newer mark having Merlin 25s and operating at the increased all-up weight of 21,750 pounds.

To combat high flying reconnaissance by the Junkers Ju 86P, the pressurised prototype MP469 was converted for high altitude interception in seven days. Work began on 7 September 1942 that included the removal of 2,300 pounds of armour and equipment, the fitting of extended wings, small wheels and four machine guns in the nose. John de Havilland flew it to 43,500 feet and although it was never used in action, five B. Mk. IV aircraft were

similarly converted to carry AI Mk. VIII radar and a four gun pack below the fuselage under the designation N.F. Mk. XV. Three examples of the F.B. Mk. 21, based on the F.B. Mk. VI and powered by the Packard Merlin 31 or 33, were built in Canada and followed by two F.B. Mk. 24s with Merlin 301s, and 338 examples of the F.B. Mk. 26 with Merlin 225s. The next major developments were the T.Mk.29 fighter/bomber trainer (50 converted from F.B. Mk. 26), and the Merlin 76 powered N.F. Mk. 30, over 230 of which were built at Leavesden in 1945. RK955 was completed as the first N.F. Mk. 36 and flown in May 1945 had Merlin 113 engines, total production being 266. British AI Mk. IX radar replaced the American AI Mk. X in the last fighter variant, the N.F. Mk. 38, the first of which flew at Leavesden on 18 November 1947. The last 81 were built at Hawarden, where the first machine flew on 30 September 1948 and the last, VX916, in November 1950.

Photographic reconnaissance Mosquitoes achieved ever higher operational altitudes through the use of specially developed Merlin 72 engines with two-stage superchargers, first fitted to Mk. IV DZ385, to make the first of five Mosquito P.R. Mk. VIIIs which were followed by 90 examples of an

An attack on shipping in Sandefjord, Norway on 2 April 1945 by 143 Squadron. *(DH via BAe Hatfield.)*

BOAC Mosquito G-AGFV, - note how the civilian registration is outlined in silver and underlined with red, white and blue on both the fuselage and upper surfaces of the wings as an aid to show that this was a civilian aircraft.

Right: How the lucky travelled - a priority passenger in the converted bomb bay, with his own oxygen supply and an intercom to the crew. *(both DH via BAe Hatfield.)*

astrodome-equipped photo-reconnaissance variant of the Mk. IX, fitted with Merlin 72 engines and designated P.R. Mk. IX. The first of the type flew on 6 May 1943 and thereafter Benson-based P.R. Mosquitoes of the RAF and F-8 Mosquitoes of the 8th USAAF - forty of which had been supplied from the Canadian B. Mk. XX production line - kept the whole of Europe under daily surveillance. The type also went into service in the Far East and during 1944 made an aerial survey of Burma and photographed all enemy seaports in Malaya and the Dutch East Indies.

Even more operational height was obtained when the pressure cabin came into use and a converted B. Mk. XVI, MM258, became the prototype P.R. Mk. XVI, 432 of which were built and carried the main P.R. responsibility until the end of the war. Additionally five aircraft were lightened and fitted with extended wing tips, which increased the span of 58 feet 10 inches and with Merlin 113

engines flew under the designation P.R. Mk. 32. A final version , the P.R. Mk. 34, was a very long range aircraft for use with South East Asia Command, had a range of over 3,500 miles, obtained by fitting a large overload fuel tank in the bomb bay and doubling the size of existing wing tanks to raise the total fuel to 1,255 gallons. Powered by the Merlin 113 and 114 and equipped with four F.52 vertical cameras and one F.24 oblique camera, the first production P.R. Mk. 34 flew on 4 December 1944. Fifty were built at Luton by Percival Aircraft Ltd. before contracts were cancelled. They saw service

A PR.XVI of 87 Squadron RAAF taxies out for take-off at Coomalie Creek, northern Australia in 1945. *(John Stride)*

with the postwar RAF and some were modified to take Merlin 114A engines, improved Gee equipment and redesigned undercarriage retraction gear as the P.R. Mk. 34A. Final variants designated P.R. Mk. 35 and TT Mk. 35 were conversions of the B. Mk. 35 for flashlight reconnaissance at night and target towing by civilian Anti-Aircraft Co-operation Units. The P.R. Mk. 35s emanated from Leavesden but T.T.Mk.35 conversions were all made by Brooklands Aviation Ltd. They were of two types, a few early models with external M.L. Aviation Type G winch, and a much larger number with the winches inside modified bomb bays.

Of the grand total of 7,781 Mosquitoes built, 24 became British civil aircraft, commencing with a Mk. IV and six Mk. VI machines converted at Hatfield and Bramcote respectively in 1943 for the carriage of diplomatic mail, newspapers and magazines on the BOAC wartime Leuchars-Stockholm route. On return trips bomb bays were filled with urgently needed ball bearings and the service operated in daylight despite determined attacks by German interceptor fighters. After Capt. Gilbert Rae was shot up by a Focke Wulf Fw 190 and made a forced landing in Sweden, the route was flown only at night and occasionally important passengers were also carried, locked in the bomb bay with a supply

of refreshments, reading material and oxygen. Three extra aircraft replaced losses in 1944 but so hazardous was the undertaking that only five survived when the service ceased in 1945.

The last operational Mosquitoes were those of 81 Squadron in Malaya, where the final sortie was flown by P.R. Mk. 34A RG314 on 15 December 1955.

The Mosquito N.F. Mk. 36 with A.I. Mk. 10 radar was the only all-weather fighter available to the RAF before the arrival of Meteors and Vampires in 1951-52. The last RAF Mosquito sortie in Britain was probably the disposal flight of RL201 of 23 Squadron from Coltishall to West Raynham on 30 May 1952.

A dual control trainer version first flown on 30 January 1942 and known as the T.Mk.III, was produced in small batches in 1943, at first by the conversion of F. Mk. II airframes, and others were built in 1948-49 and remained in service with 204 Advanced Flying School and with the Operational Conversion Units of Bomber Command until 1953. A similar aircraft built in Canada with Merlin 33s was designated T.Mk.22 and later, with Packard Merlin 225s, the T.Mk.27. Fourteen T.Mk.III airframes destined for the RAAF as A52-1002 to A52-1015, were shipped to Australia, where Mosquito production began at Bankstown in 1942 using drawings, jigs and tools from the parent company

Above: LR359, the modified FB.Mk.VI that was the first twin-engined aircraft to land on a carrier, piloted by Captain Eric Brown, The upper surfaces were naval grey/green and the undersides yellow.

Right: LR387, folding wings, cannon and torpedo - a Sea Mosquito TR.Mk.33 converted from an FB.Mk.VI in 1945. *both DH via BAe Hatfield.)*

Loading a 4,000 pound bomb aboard a Mosquito with the bulged bomb-bay; this was the heaviest single item the aircraft was to carry.

The TT.39 nose conversion of the B.XVI with optically flat glazing for observation of gunnery results, produced to meet Royal Navy Specification Q. 19/45. The work was done by General Aircraft Ltd of Hanworth.
(both DH via BAe Hatfield)

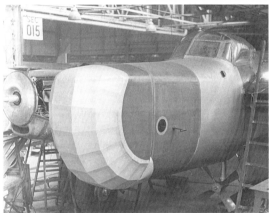

and De Havilland Aircraft of Canada. These used mark numbers in the 40 series, first of which was the F.B. Mk. 40 based on the Mk. VI, the first 100 aircraft being fitted with Packard Merlin 31s and the remaining 112 with Merlin 33s. The first machine, A52-1, first flew at Sydney on 23 July 1943 and later under De Havilland supervision, the RAAF

converted five F.B. Mk. 40s to P.R. Mk. 40 by replacing the armament with five vertical and oblique cameras. The first P.R. Mk. 40, flew on 26 May 1944 and the fleet was used while the Japanese were being cleared from New Guinea in 1944.

Chronologically the next Australian type was the T.Mk.43, similar to the British T.Mk.Ill but converted from the RAAF F.B. Mk. 40 and the first, A52-1050, flew on 27 June 1946. The last twenty undelivered F.B. Mk. 40s and eight others selected from random from storage, were fitted with Packard Merlin 69 engines and full P.R. Mk. 40 camera installation as the P.R. Mk. 41, the first being A52-300, delivered on 29 May 1947. This variant was used for an aerial survey of Australia completed in 1953. A single F.B. Mk. 42 was made, created by the installation of Packard Merlin 69s in F.B. Mk. 40 A52-90 but no further conversions were made and the aircraft became the prototype P.R. Mk. 41 A52-300.

The varied career of the Mosquito included service at sea with the Royal Navy to Specification N.I 5/44. To prove feasibility, Mosquito F.B. Mk. VI LR359 was fitted with arrester gear and became the

The crew of Spartan Air Services B.Mk.35 adjust their equipment before taking out CF-HML on another survey flight. Note the non-standard nose glazing and the conversion of the hinged escape hatch into an entry hatch. To operate the specialise survey equipment, a third crew member was carried.
(John Stride Collection)

G-AJZE, the former WG231, was one of a pair of British European Airways's Gust Research Unit machines, seen here at Cranfield. *(via John Stride.)*

first British twin engined type to land on an aircraft carrier when Lt. Cdr. Eric M. Brown M.B.E., D.S.C. put it down on H.M.S. *Indefatigable* on 25 March 1944. Further trials were conducted at Boscombe Down with TS446 and TS449, but the first real Sea Mosquito with folding wings and nose radome was the former F.B. Mk. VI LR387, equipped with large diameter four bladed propellers. The first production aircraft, TW227, designated T.R. Mk. 33, first flew at Leavesden on 10 November 1945. Folding wings were fitted from the 14th aircraft, TW241, which also had long travel Lockheed oleo legs in place of the rubber-in-compression units. All 50 production aircraft were equipped to carry an 18 in. torpedo and two 50 gallon drop tanks which could be exchanged for the 30 gallon type if it was desired to carry two rocket projectiles. The type saw little service and merely replaced the Fleet Air Arm F.B. Mk. VI shore based aircraft of 811 Squadron during 1946-47. The Royal Navy also took delivery of six examples, commencing VT724, of the T.R. Mk. 37, recognised by an enlarged nose accommodating the scanner of the British A.S.V. radar.

The ultimate Mosquito derivative was the T.T.Mk.39 shore-based naval target tug to Specification Q.I 9/45, produced by the conversion

of B. Mk. XVIs at Hanworth by General Aircraft Ltd. who allotted their own type number G.A.L.59 to the work. This included lengthening the nose to provide glazed accommodation for a cameraman who recorded shell bursts; installing an electrically driven winch in the bomb bay and fitting a dorsal observation cupola for the winch operator. Powered by two Rolls-Royce Merlin 72/73 or 76/77 engines, it was equipped to tow the 32 and 16 foot span targets or a small drogue.

After the cancellation of the Miles E.24/43 (Miles M.52) research aircraft, Vickers pilotless, rocket propelled models were carried beneath modified Mosquito B. Mk. XVI PF604 and dropped into the Atlantic off the Scilly Isles in 1947-48 for transonic research purposes by the Royal Aircraft Establishment

In March 1948 two P.R. Mk. 34s owned by the Ministry of Supply were based at Cranfield on loan to the BEA Gust Research Unit as G-AJZE and 'ZF and for two years flew the length and breadth of Europe investigating clear air turbulence in readiness for the introduction of new turboprop and turbojet transports.

Several American F-8 Mosquitoes were entered for postwar races under United States civil marks

Something of an oddity - the former B.Mk.25 KA997 was obtained by Dianna Bixby for a round-the-world record attempt which started on 2 April 1950 and was painted not only with a sharks mouth artwork on the nose, but also on the droptanks, N1203V is seen before the start of the round-the-world record attempt. *(via Stuart Howe)*

DH.98 Mosquito Specifications

Mark:	PR.Mk.I	F.Mk.II	T.Mk.III	B.Mk.IV
Span:	54 feet 2 inches	54 feet 2 inches	54 feet 2 inches	54 feet 2 inches
Length:	40 feet 6 inches	40 feet 6 inches	40 feet 6 inches	40 feet 6 inches
Height:	12 feet 6 inches	12 feet 6 inches	12 feet 6 inches	12 feet 6 inches
Wing area:	454 square feet	454 square feet	454 square feet	454 square feet
Tare weight:	12,824 pounds	13,431 pounds	13,104 pounds	13,400 pounds
AUW:	19,670 pounds	18,547 pounds	16,883 pounds	21,462 pounds
Max speed:	382 mph	370 mph	380 mph	380 mph
Cruise:	255 mph	255 mph	265 mph	265 mph
Ceiling:	35,000 feet	36,000 feet	37,500 feet	34,000 feet
Max range:	2,180 miles	1,705 miles	1,560 miles	2,040 miles

Mark:	FB.Mk. VI	PR.Mk.VIII	PR.Mk.IX	NF.Mk.XII
Span:	54 feet 2 inches	54 feet 2 inches	54 feet 2 inches	54 feet 2 inches
Length:	40 feet 6 inches	40 feet 6 inches	40 feet 6 inches	40 feet 6 inches
Height:	12 feet 6 inches	12 feet 6 inches	12 feet 6 inches	12 feet 6 inches
Wing area:	454 square feet	454 square feet	454 square feet	454 square feet
Tare weight:	14,344 pounds	14,800 pounds	14,569 pounds	13,696 pounds
AUW:	22,258 pounds	21,395 pounds	22,000 pounds	19,700 pounds
Max speed:	378 mph	436 mph	408 mph	370 mph
Cruise:	255 mph	258 mph	250 mph	255 mph
Ceiling:	33,000 feet	38,000 feet	38,000 feet	36,000 feet
Max range:	1,855 miles	2,550 miles	2,450 miles	1,705 miles

Mark:	NF.Mk.XIII	NF.Mk.XV	B.Mk.XVI	PR.Mk.XVI
Span:	54 feet 2 inches	62 feet 6 inches	54 feet 2 inches	54 feet 2 inches
Length:	40 feet 6 inches	44 feet 6 inches	40 feet 6 inches	44 feet 6 inches
Height:	12 feet 6 inches	12 feet 6 inches	12 feet 6 inches	12 feet 6 inches
Wing area:	454 square feet	479 square feet	454 square feet	454 square feet
Tare weight:	15,300 pounds	13,746 pounds	14,635 pounds	14,635 pounds
AUW:	20,000 pounds	17,600 pounds	23,000 pounds	22,350 pounds
Max speed:	370 mph	412 mph	408 mph	415 mph
Cruise:	255 mph	230 mph	245 mph	250 mph
Ceiling:	34,500 feet	43,000 feet	37,000 feet	38,500 feet
Max range:	1,860 miles	1,030 miles	1,485 miles	2,450 miles.

Mark:	NF.Mk.XVIII	NF.Mk.30	TR.Mk.33	PR.Mk.34
Span:	54 feet 2 inches	54 feet 2 inches	54 feet 2 inches	54 feet 2 inches
Length:	40 feet 6 inches	44 feet 6 inches	40 feet 6 inches	40 feet 6 inches
Height:	12 feet 6 inches	12 feet 6 inches	12 feet 6 inches	12 feet 6 inches
Wing area:	454 square feet	454 square feet	454 square feet	435 square feet
Tare weight:	13,224 pounds	13,400 pounds	14,850 pounds	14,180 pounds
AUW:	19,200 pounds	21,600 pounds	23,850 pounds	22,100 pounds
Max speed:	370 mph	407 mph	376 mph	425 mph
Cruise:	255 mph	250 mph	262 mph	300 mph
Ceiling:	36,000 feet	38,000 feet	30,100 feet	43,000 feet
Max range:	1,705 miles	1,300 miles	1,625 miles	3.340 miles

Mark:	B.Mk.35	NF.Mk.38	TT.Mk.39	FB.Mk.40
Span:	54 feet 2 inches	54 feet 2 inches	54 feet 2 inches	54 feet 2 inches
Length:	40 feet 6 inches	41 feet 2 inches	43 feet 4 inches	40 feet 6 inches
Height:	12 feet 6 inches	12 feet 6 inches	12 feet 6 inches	12 feet 6 inches
Wing area:	454 square feet	454 square feet	454 square feet	454 square feet
Tare weight:	14,635 pounds	16,000 pounds	15,980 pounds	14,344 pounds
AUW:	23,000 pounds	21,400 pounds	23,000 pounds	22,258 pounds
Max speed:	415 mph	404 mph	299 mph	378 mph
Cruise:	276 mph	-	-	255 mph
Ceiling:	42,000 feet	36,000 feet	-	33,000 feet
Max range:	1,955 miles	-	-	1,855 miles

Mark number	Engine
Mk. I, II, III, IV, VI, XII, XIII, XVII:	two 1,460 horsepower Rolls-Royce Merlin 21
Mk. I, II, III, IV, V, VI, XII, XIII, XVII:	two 1,460 horsepower Rolls-Royce Merlin 23
Mk. VI, XVIII, XIX, 33, 37:	two 1,635 horsepower Rolls-Royce Merlin 25
Mk. VII, XX, 21, 40, F-8:	two 1,460 horsepower Packard Merlin 31
Mk. XX, 21, 22, 40, 43:	two 1,460 horsepower Packard Merlin 33
Mk. 33:	two 1,705 horsepower Rolls-Royce Merlin 66
Mk. XIV:	two 1,705 horsepower Packard Merlin 67
Mk. 23, 41, 42:	two 1,750 horsepower Packard Merlin 69
Mk. VII, IX, XIV, XV, XVI, 30, 39:	two 1,680 horsepower Rolls-Royce Merlin 72 and 73*.
Mk. XV, XVI, 30, 39:	two 1,710 horsepower Rolls-Royce Merlin 76 and 77*.
Mk. 30, 32, 34, 35, 36, 38:	two 1,690 horsepower Rolls-Royce Merlin 113 and 114*.
Mk. 34A	two 1,710 horsepower Rolls-Royce Merlin 114A
Mk. 25, 26, 27:	two 1,620 horsepower Packard Merlin 225
Mk. 24:	two 1,620 horsepower Packard Merlin 301

* Merlin 73, 77 and 114 engines had cabin blowers and were not fitted to Mk. XII, IX, 30 and 36

but the civil Mosquito's chief postwar occupation was in the field of aerial survey. A number of P.R. Mk. 34As were converted for civil operation at Hatfield in 1955-56, some of which were delivered to Fotogrametric Engineers Inc. in Los Angeles via the North Atlantic route while others went to the IREX Survey Co. for oil prospecting in Tripoli. The largest fleet was that of the Ottawa-based Spartan Air Services Ltd., which bought 15 Mosquito P.R. Mk. 35s in 1954, some of which were cannibalised and eventually broken up at Hurn, Hants. The five airworthy machines then performed high altitude photographic missions in Canada, the USA, Mexico, Colombia, British Guiana, the Dominican Republic and Kenya.

After the war the ageing Mosquito still had considerable military potential and a large number of surplus machines were acquired at low cost by many nations.

It is a remarkable fact that the first prototype Mosquito W4050 survived the war to be exhibited at the Radlett S.B.A.C. Show of September 1947. Five years later it was rediscovered in a shed at Chester and through the enthusiasm of a number of historically minded people in the industry, it was restored to its original condition, painted in wartime colours and provided with a specially built hangar at Salisbury Hall, its birthplace.

DH.99

This type number covered proposals made to the Ministry of Aircraft Production in November 1941 for a scaled-up Mosquito night bomber with two high altitude Napier Sabre N.S.8SM engines cruising at 300 m.p.h. and having a range of 2,200 miles and operating at 27,000 feet with a bomb load of 18,000 pounds.

Development was envisaged with Sabre N.S.19 SIM two-stage, three speed engines driving 15 foot diameter contra-rotating propellers to increase the full load cruise to 328 m.p.h. at 32,000 feet.

In December 1941 the twin Sabre project was renamed the DH.101 and the DH.99 number was re-allotted to designs for a light, twin engined civil aircraft which J. P. Smith and the Moth Minor team had been working on at the outbreak of war, and which, due to military commitments, did not materialise.

DH.100 Vampire

Designed to Specification E.6/41, and given the code-name 'Spider Crab', the prototype Vampire single seat interceptor jet fighter LZ548/G was first flown at Hatfield by Geoffrey de Havilland Jnr. on 29 September 1943, sixteen months after the commencement of detail designs. It was an all metal aircraft except for the Mosquito style plywood and balsa cockpit section. The engine, a 2,700 pound static thrust Goblin 1 turbojet designed by Major Frank B. Halford and manufactured by the De Havilland company, was fitted behind the pilot in a short nacelle. Consequently the tail unit was mounted on twin booms and for compressibility reasons the tailplane was set high on tall pointed fins. As propeller clearance was now a thing of the past, the aircraft sat low to the ground on a short legged retractable nose wheel undercarriage.

Two further prototypes, LZ551/G and MP838/G, the second of which carried the standard armament of four 20 mm. Hispano cannon, quickly joined the development trials and on 13 May 1944 a contract was placed for 120 (later increased to 300) Vampire F. Mk.

LZ548/G was the prototype DH.100 Vampire and is seen here at Hatfield a few days before its first flight on 29 September 1943. It carries the original pointed fins. *(via John Stride.)*

Is to be built by English Electric Co. Ltd in the Preston works.

Production aircraft commencing TG274/G, first flown at Samlesbury on 20 April 1945, were the first fighters of any nation with a top speed above 500 m.p.h. and were identified by square cut vertical tail surfaces. Many of the initial batch of forty were used for test purposes. The 41st Vampire F. Mk. I, TG314, and subsequent aircraft were powered by the 3,100 pound static thrust Goblin 2 and equipped with Mosquito slipper tanks. Cockpits were pressurised from the 51st aircraft, TG336, and equipped with one-piece canopies commencing TG386 in January 1946.

Vampires were too late for the Second World War but from 1946-51 were used by the Second Tactical Air Force in Germany and the Odiham-based Vampire wing of Fighter Command, their public debut being the fly-past over London by 247 Squadron during the victory celebrations of 8 June 1946. Replacing Mosquitoes of 605 (County of Warwick) Squadron at Honiley on 3 July 1948, the Vampire became the first jet aircraft issued to the Royal Auxiliary Air Force.

TG276, TG280 and TX807 were experimentally fitted with Rolls-Royce Nene I engines to Specification F.11/45, were identified by 'elephant ears' intakes on top of the nacelle, which fed air to the double sided

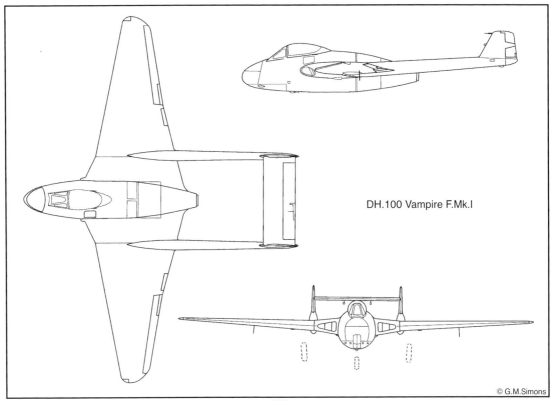

DH.100 Vampire F.Mk.I

© G.M.Simons

Above: TG/278 in flight.

Right: Three of 54 Squadron's Vampires become the first jet aircraft to cross the Atlantic for a goodwill tour of the USA and Canada during July 1948.
(both via John Stride)

impellers. They were used for performance and engine trials under the designation Vampire II. Boulton Paul Ltd. later modified TX807 to dispense with the dorsal intakes and shipped it to Australia, where as A78-2 it served as the development vehicle for the Nene powered F. Mk. 30.

The third production aircraft, TG278, with a four foot extension to each wing tip and special hood, flew on 8 May 1947 as a testbed for the de Havilland Ghost turbojet and for high altitude trials in the course of which John Cunningham established a new World's altitude record of 59,446 ft. on 23 March 1948. It was later fitted with a Mk. 3 tailplane during development of a Ghost engined production version that was initially designated Vampire Mk. 8 but was eventually built as the DH.I12 Venom.

The fuselage pods of TG283 and TG306 were used for the DH.108 programme, the special nose section for which was flown on Vampire TG281 and the high speed canopy for TG306 on TG443. One Vampire F. Mk. I was supplied to the RCAF and another, TG372, went to Canada for winterisation trials. Swiss needs were met by fitting TG433 with a 3,300 pound static thrust Goblin 3 with modifications, as the prototype Vampire F.B. Mk. 6 prior to a Swiss Government purchase of four Vampire F. Mk. Is and seventy-five F.B. Mk. 6s. The Swedish Air Force also re-equipped with 70 Vampire F. Mk. Is, the first of which was

TG276, the prototype Vampire Mk.II, fitted with the Rolls-Royce Nene engine and 'elephant ear' intakes. *(via John Stride.)*

delivered in March 1946. They were allotted the Swedish designation J28 and some had Swedish-built Goblins. A number of drop tank experiments with TG275 led to the standardisation of the 100 gallon pylon-mounted, cylindrical type, but no matter the size and position all had an adverse effect on the machine's longitudinal stability. This was overcome by increasing tailplane chord by 4½ in., reducing that of the elevator by 1½ in. and fitting acorns to the fin and tail junctions. Tests showed that tailplane position did not affect compressibility, so to simplify manufacture the tailplane was lowered thirteen inches to a position still clear of the jet efflux.

Vertical tail surfaces were changed to the standard DH shape, a long range wing increased total internal tankage to 326 gallons and provision was made for 100 or 200 gallon drop tanks. In this form it became the prototype Vampire F. Mk. III, first flown on 4 November 1946, but in accordance with the new

policy to use arabic type numbers, production was to Specification F.3/47 as the Vampire F. Mk. 3. The new mark then replaced the Vampire F. Mk. I both in Germany and the U.K., six aircraft of 54 Squadron, Odiham being the first jet fighters to fly the Atlantic. Together with two Mosquitoes, they reached Goose Bay via Iceland and Greenland on 14 July 1948 to take part in displays and exercises in Canada and the USA.

At the end of April 1948 VV190 was used as a flying testbed for the Goblin 4 and Vampire F. Mk. 3 VG703 completed fifteen months weathering and tropical trials in Singapore, the Philippines and Khartoum on 21 October 1949. Four were delivered by air to the Royal Norwegian Air Force, 83 equipped four RCAF fighter squadrons and Vampire F. Mk. I TG431 was sent to Australia as A78-1 for evaluation. Vampire IV was the designation allotted to the Vampire III airframe with Rolls-Royce Nene engine but none were built in Britain and the type was

'242' of the South African Air Force. *(via John Stride.)*

TG278, the Ghost engined high-altitude Vampire in which John Cunningham (below) reached 59,446 feet on 23 March 1948. The aircraft had a strengthened canopy and extended wingtips. *(DH via BAe Hatfield)*

developed in Australia as the F. Mk. 30, eighty examples of which were constructed by de Havilland Aircraft Pty. Ltd. and powered by Australian built Rolls-Royce Nene 2-VH engines. The prototype, A79-1, was first flown by test pilot Brian Walker on 29 June 1948.

Trials with Vampire F. Mk. I TG444 with the wing clipped to a 38 feet span and first flown on 29 June 1948 preceded the introduction of the Vampire F.B. Mk. 5, a ground attack variant with the wing strengthened for carrying bombs or rocket projectiles and having square cut tips to reduce the span by two feet. The heavier airframe also called for a long stroke undercarriage. The first production F.B. Mk. 5 flew on 23 June 1948, the type being operated with the Far East Air Force against Malayan terrorists and replacing earlier marks in the UK and Germany. One, VV465, was sent to Australia where, as A78-3, it was the forerunner of 29 F. Mk. 30s reworked to F.B. Mk. 5 standard as F.B. Mk. 31s. All Mk. 30 and 31 aircraft were later modified with belly air intakes as the cockpit canopy interfered with the airflow to the original 'elephant ear' intakes.

Following John Derry's demonstration of VV218 at the Farnborough SBAC Show in September 1948, overseas interest was aroused and the prototype F.B. Mk. 51 export fighter VV568 was despatched to France for Nene development along with 30 ex RAF aircraft for L'Armee de 1'Air. VZ253 was sold to the Italian Government, an export version designated F.B. Mk. 50 satisfied the second and third Swedish contracts and the F.B. Mk. 52, based on the F. Mk. 6, was supplied to Egypt, Finland, Iraq, Lebanon, Norway

and Venezuela. Standard F.B. Mk. 5s were also delivered to the Indian Air Force and to the SAAF.

A large number were built under licence including 85 F. Mk. 6s by Swiss factories; 80 F.B. Mk. 52As in Italy by Macchi and Fiat; 67 Goblin powered F.B. Mk. 5s assembled in France from British built components by SNCA du Sud-Est, the first of which flew at Marignane on 21 December 1950; and 183 Goblin powered Vampire 5s preceding 250 F.B. Mk. 53s built by the same firm as the SE-535 Mistral. The Mistrals were fitted with French-built Nene engines but differed from the Australian F. Mk. 30 and the projected French Nene powered F.B. Mk. 51 equivalents because the 'elephant ear' intakes

F.Mk.1, TG330 was built by English Electric. *(John Stride Collection)*

240

A Vampire Mk. 5 is demonstrated at Bretigny Airfield near Paris by John Derry. A large number of this Mark were supplied to France while French Vampire production was organised. *(DH via BAe Hatfield)*

were replaced by enlarged wing root ducts developed by Boulton Paul Ltd. The first Mistral flew on 2 April 1951; one was used as a testbed for the SNECMA reverse thrust system in 1952; and Mme. Auriol broke the Women's World Speed Record in another on 12 May 1951 by averaging 515 m.p.h. round a 100 km. course between Istres and Avignon.

Experience with the Vampire F.B. Mk. 5 in the Near and Far East led to the production of a tropical version termed the F.B. Mk. 9 with cockpit air conditioning and refrigerating equipment in the mainplane, which led to the sole recognition feature, an eight inch increase in the length of the starboard wing fillet. It was the last single seat Vampire used by

the RAF and when production ceased with WX260 in December 1953.

When replaced by Venoms in 1954/55, Vampire F.B. Mk. 5s were handed over to Flying Training Command as ground attack and rocket firing trainers. Experiments included in manufacturer's and R.A.E. test programmes comprised afterburning tests with an extended tail pipe and Mk. I tail unit on VV454; transonic speed tests with models on a wing sleeve fitted to F. Mk. 3 VF343; and boundary layer suction research by the RAE and Cambridge University using F. Mk. 3 VT858 in 1953-55.

The Royal Navy expressed early interest in the Vampire and at the Christchurch factory the second

VT141 and VT143, a pair of Vampire F.Mk.20s of the Royal Navy. The arrestor hook can see seen stowed on top of the jet pipe. *(via John Stride.)*

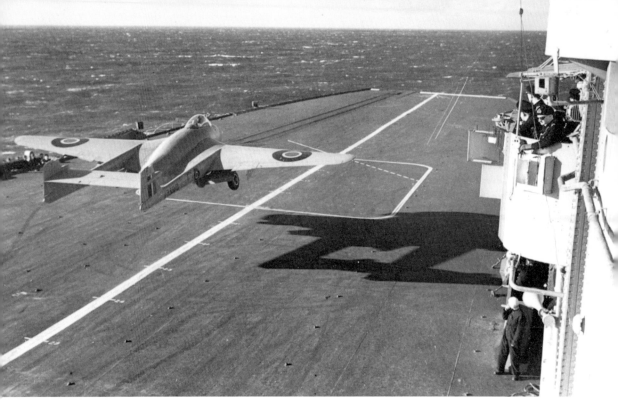

The Vampire was the first jet aircraft to be flown from an aircraft carrier when the second prototype, LZ551 was modified and landed in HMS Ocean by Lt Cdr Eric 'Winkle' Brown on 2 December 1945. *(via John Stride.)*

prototype, LZ551, was given a 40% increase in flap area by continuing them under the booms, long travel oleo legs and an arrester hook for deck landing trials which commenced on HMS. *Ocean* on 3 December 1945. Redesignated Sea Vampire 10 and piloted by Lt. Cdr. Eric M. Brown R.N.V.R., it was the first pure jet aeroplane ever to operate from a carrier.

The second 'hooked Vampire', a conversion of the 91st production F. Mk. I TG426, was followed by two fully navalised prototypes, VF315 and TG328, and a batch of 18 production Sea Vampire F. Mk. 20s, the first of which, VV136, flew in October 1948 and the last, VV165, in June 1949. They were navalised adaptations of the F.B. Mk. 5 with clipped wings strengthened for accelerated take off, enlarged dive brakes and flaps and long travel oleo legs, with an 'A' frame arrester hook in its housing above the jet pipe. Sea Vampires

were used for the Royal Navy's jet familiarisation programme, which culminated in the delivery of two seat Sea Vampire T.Mk.22s.

At least three Sea Vampire F. Mk. 21s, including the former F. Mk. I TG286 and F. Mk. 3 VT802, were given strengthened undersides for experimental landings with undercarriage retracted on rubberised decking on HMS *Warrior* early in 1949 and on the dummy rubber deck at Farnborough up to 1953, to test the feasibility of undercarriageless shipborne aircraft.

Vampires held at least one record, when on 31 August 1947 John Cunningham raised the Class C.l/1 100km. closed circuit speed record to 496.88 m.p.h. in F. Mk. I VF332.

DH.100 Powerplants	
Mark	Engine
Prototypes:	one 2,700 pounds static thrust De Havilland Goblin 1
Mk.1, 3, 5, 10, 20:	one 3,100 pounds static thrust De Havilland Goblin 2
	one 4,400 pounds static thrust De Havilland Ghost 2/2
Mk.II, IV:	one 4,500 pounds static thrust Rolls-Royce Nene 1
Mk.6, 9, 50, 51, 52:	one 3,350 pounds static thrust De Havilland Goblin 3
Mk.30:	one 5,000 pounds static thrust Commonwealth Aircraft Corp Nene 2-VH
Mk. 50, 53:	one 5,500 pounds ststuc thrust Hispano-Suiza Nene 102B
Mk.52A:	one 3,100 pounds static thrust De Havilland Goblin 2

DH.100 Vampire Specifications

Mark:	F.Mk.1	F.Mk.3	FB.Mk.5	FB.Mk.6
Span:	40 feet 0 inches	40 feet 0 inches	40 feet 0 inches	38 feet 0 inches
Length:	30 feet 9 inches	30 feet 9 inches	30 feet 9 inches	30 feet 9 inches
Height:	8 feet 10 inches	8 feet 10 inches	8 feet 10 inches	8 feet 10 inches
Wing area:	266 square feet	266 square feet	262 square feet	262 square feet
Tare weight:	6,372 pounds	7,134 pounds	7,253 pounds	7,283 pounds
AUW:	10,480 pounds	11,970 pounds	12,360 pounds	12,390 pounds
Max speed:	540 mph	531 mph	535 mph	548 mph
Ceiling:	-	43,500 feet	40,000 feet	-
Max range:	730 miles	1,145 miles	1,170 miles	1,220 miles
Mark	**FB.Mk.9**	**F.Mk.20**	**FB.Mk.30**	**FB.Mk.53**
Span:	38 feet 0 inches	38 feet 0 inches	38 feet 0 inches	38 feet 0 inches
Length:	30 feet 9 inches	30 feet 9 inches	30 feet 9 inches	30 feet 9 inches
Height:	8 feet 10 inches	8 feet 10 inches	8 feet 10 inches	8 feet 10 inches
Wing area:	262 square feet	262 square feet	262 square feet	262 square feet
Tare weight:	7,283 pounds	7,623 pounds	7,600 pounds	7,656 pounds
AUW:	12,390 pounds	12,660 pounds	11,000 pounds	12,628 pounds
Max speed:	548 mph	526 mph	570 mph	568 mph
Ceiling:	-	43,500 feet	49,000 feet	44,000 feet
Max range:	1,220 miles	1,140 miles	-	-

DH.101

Known as the Twin Sabre Bomber, formerly designated the DH.99 but re-numbered the DH.101 in December 1941. Air Ministry Specification B.11/41 was written around them, but on 4 April 1942, De Havillands were told that Napier Sabre engines would not be available and that Rolls-Royce Griffons should be considered instead. In view of the expected reduction in performance, the project was terminated.

DH.102

The layout was similar to the DH.101 but was a lower powered night bomber to Specification B.4/42. It was termed the Mosquito replacement and was to have been fitted with two Rolls-Royce Griffon or Merlin engines and carry a 5,000 pound bomb, load but at a lower speed that the DH.98. Construction began, but ceased in December 1942 when the DH.103 came into being.

DH.103 Hornet/Sea Hornet

The operational success of the Mosquito led to the idea of a scaled down single seat version capable of meeting single engined Japanese fighters in combat among the islands of the South Pacific. Very long range had therefore to be added to normal medium altitude fighter characteristics and perfected streamlining would contribute largely to its success. To this end Rolls-Royce closely collaborated with De Havilland to develop special Merlin power plants of minimum frontal area. These permitted an exceptionally sleek installation which was a feature of the mock up shown to Ministry of Aircraft Production officials at Hatfield in January 1943. So the Hornet was born, but permission to build was not given until June 1943

The DH.103 Hornet prototype RR915 made its first flight from Hatfield on 28 July 1944 piloted by Geoffrey de Havilland Jnr. *(DH via BAe Hatfield)*

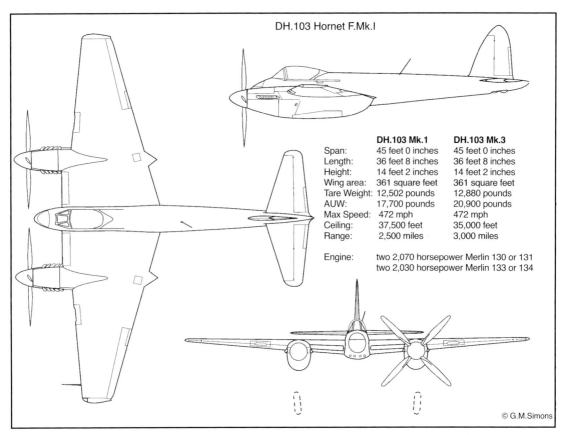

DH.103 Hornet F.Mk.I

	DH.103 Mk.1	DH.103 Mk.3
Span:	45 feet 0 inches	45 feet 0 inches
Length:	36 feet 8 inches	36 feet 8 inches
Height:	14 feet 2 inches	14 feet 2 inches
Wing area:	361 square feet	361 square feet
Tare Weight:	12,502 pounds	12,880 pounds
AUW:	17,700 pounds	20,900 pounds
Max Speed:	472 mph	472 mph
Ceiling:	37,500 feet	35,000 feet
Range:	2,500 miles	3,000 miles
Engine:	two 2,070 horsepower Merlin 130 or 131	
	two 2,030 horsepower Merlin 133 or 134	

© G.M.Simons

RR919, the second prototype Hornet is seen at Hatfield with a pair of bombs on the under-wing hardpoints in November 1944. Note also how the rear of engine nacelles form part of the flaps.
(DH via BAe Hatfield)

when the Hornet ceased to be a private venture and Specification F.I 2/43 was written round it.

Although resembling the Mosquito, the Hornet was an entirely new design. The fuselage was the same as the Mosquito in construction, but the one piece, two spar, cantilever laminar flow mainplane, designed to high strength factors consisted of a composite wood and metal internal structure with a stressed birch ply double upper skin and an undersurface of reinforced Alclad. The Hornet was the first type of aircraft in which wood was cemented to metal, a unique method of construction only possible by using the revolutionary new Redux adhesive. Four bladed de Havilland Hydromatic propellers driven by a Rolls-Royce Merlin 130 in the starboard nacelle and a Merlin 131 in the port

were inward rotating to eliminate swing on take off and landing. Cooling was by leading edge radiators in the centre section and the aircraft represented the ultimate in propeller driven fighter design. Armament consisted of four 20 mm. Hispano cannon beneath the pilot, who sat in the extreme nose under a sliding canopy with a truly wonderful view.

Piloted by Geoffrey de Havilland Jnr., the first prototype, RR915, flew from Hatfield for the first time on 28 July 1944, just thirteen months after the start of detail designs. Design performance was more than met, climb and manoeuvrability were exceptional, the prototype reaching 485 mph, a speed probably never

244

The sleek, svelte lines of the DH.103 Hornet are particularly noticable in this view of PX396. *(DH via BAe Hatfield)*

exceeded by any other production aircraft powered by piston engines. In the first sixty days' trials by Geoffrey de Havilland and Geoffrey H. Pike, fifty hours were flown and a second prototype, RR919, was completed with two 200 gallon drop tanks under the wings, which gave a range of over 2,500 miles when cruising at 340 m.p.h. at 30,000 feet.

Production of the Hornet F. Mk. 1 began at Hatfield late in 1944 and the first aircraft, PX210, was delivered to Boscombe Down on 28 February 1945, but the war with Japan was over before any reached the Pacific. Production Hornets were only marginally slower than the prototype and one gave an unprecedented display of air to ground firing at Boscombe Down in the following August. On 29 October the Hornet was shown publicly for the first time when PX237 attended the RAE At Home display.

The Hornet's intended alternative role in the Pacific was photographic reconnaissance, and prototypes of the P.R. Mk. 2, PX216, PX220 and PX249, with rear fuselage mounted cameras, followed naturally. Five other P.R. Mk. 2s were produced but the rest of the order was cancelled and they were scrapped.

Hornet F. Mk. 3s were equipped with wider tailplanes, larger elevator horn balances and two 200 gallon underwing tanks which could be removed for the carriage of two 1,000 pound bombs. Internal tankage was increased from 360 to 540 gallons to give the Hornet a 40% increase in range. The public debut of the F. Mk. 3 was made by PX366 at an exhibition organised at Farnborough in June 1946, after which the type remained in production at Hatfield until the jigs were moved late in 1948 to Chester. The first Chester-built Hornet flew in March 1949 and at the completion of the last contract in June 1952, a total of 211 Hornets had been delivered to the RAF. Production F. Mk. 3s were fitted with a curved dorsal fin, later retrospectively fitted to all Hornets to improve stability at high speeds.

64 Squadron, was the first Hornet-equipped squadron, took part in the Victory Fly Past over London on 8 June 1946 from its base at Horsham St. Faith, just outside Norwich. 19 Squadron formed with Hornets at Church Fenton in the following October. 41 and 65 Squadrons were equipped later, those of 65 being chosen to fly to Uppsala on 20 May 1948 for an official visit to the Swedish Air Force. They returned on the 27th after a formation flight over Stockholm.

On 15 September 1949 one of two Hornets detailed to participate in Battle of Britain celebrations at

PX219, the first Sea Hornet to fly with full naval modifications, including folding wings and arrestor hook under the rear fuselage. *(DH via BAe Hatfield)*

TT191, A F.Mk.20 Sea Hornet parked on a somewhat snowy Hatfield. *(DH via BAe Hatfield)*

Gibraltar, was flown out from Bovingdon by F/Lt. H. Peebles at an average speed of 357.565 m.p.h. to establish a British point to point record. On the return journey on 9 September Gp. Capt. A. C. P. Carver flew to Bovingdon under strict cruise control at the tropopause in 2 hours 30 minutes 21 seconds, and landed with 15 minutes fuel left in his tanks, setting up a new record at 435.871 m.p.h.

The RAF declared all early Hornet F. Mk. 1 aircraft obsolete in 1950 but in 1951 most of Fighter Command's F. Mk. 3s were despatched to Malaya for use by the Far East Air Force. They were then equipped with underwing rails for eight rocket projectiles or racks for two 1,000 pound bombs for highly successful attacks against jungle terrorists and were the last piston engined fighters to see active service in the RAF. The final batch was twenty-three aircraft, the last twelve being fitted with a F.52 vertically mounted camera under the designation Hornet F. Mk. 4. In reality they were F. Mk. 3 aircraft with the sixty gallon top fuel tank replaced by a smaller one holding forty six gallons in order to make room for the camera.

Sea Hornet

During the early stages of the Hornet project, the possibility of carrier based action against the Japanese was considered and for this reason opposite handed engines and the high drag flaps needed for power-on approach had been incorporated in the design. Late in 1944 prototypes of a Fleet Air Arm version were put in hand and three early production Hornet F. Mk. Is were selected for naval modification to Specification N.5/44. Design work was done by the Heston Aircraft Co. Ltd., which produced a wing with Lockheed hydraulic power-folding similar to that of the Sea Mosquito, a forged steel arrester hook on a flush fitting external V frame, tail down accelerator pick-up points, and

Above: VR851, one of three F.Mk.20 Sea Hornets loaned to 806 Squadron FAA for exhibition flying at New York in 1948. It is seen flying over Toronto Harbour with one prop feathered. Note the camera port forward of the roundel in the rear fuselage.

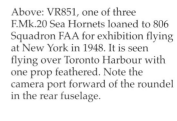

Left: a trio of F.Mk.20 Sea Hornets of 728 Fleet Requirements Unit, Hal Far, Malta in 1954. *(both author's collection)*

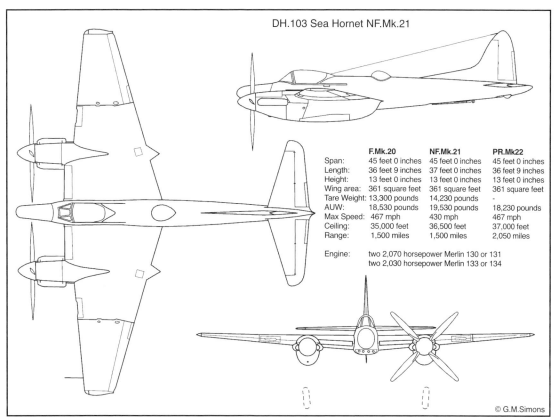

DH.103 Sea Hornet NF.Mk.21

	F.Mk.20	NF.Mk.21	PR.Mk22
Span:	45 feet 0 inches	45 feet 0 inches	45 feet 0 inches
Length:	36 feet 9 inches	37 feet 0 inches	36 feet 9 inches
Height:	13 feet 0 inches	13 feet 0 inches	13 feet 0 inches
Wing area:	361 square feet	361 square feet	361 square feet
Tare Weight:	13,300 pounds	14,230 pounds	-
AUW:	18,530 pounds	19,530 pounds	18,230 pounds
Max Speed:	467 mph	430 mph	467 mph
Ceiling:	35,000 feet	36,500 feet	37,000 feet
Range:	1,500 miles	1,500 miles	2,050 miles

Engine: two 2,070 horsepower Merlin 130 or 131
two 2,030 horsepower Merlin 133 or 134

© G.M.Simons

mountings for specialised naval radar and radio equipment. De Havilland supplied Airdraulic undercarriage legs to replace the existing rubber-in-compression units, which were unable to absorb the high rate of descent usual in deck landings. The weight penalty of these modifications totalled 550 pounds.

The first prototype, PX212, flew on 19 April 1945 and like the second aircraft, PX214, was just a hooked Hornet with a standard non-folding mainplane. Both were shown to the public for the first time at a Press Show at Heston on 2 October but PX219, the first to fly with full naval modifications and folding mainplane, had already commenced trial landings on the Light Fleet Carrier HMS *Ocean* on 10 August. A production order was then placed for the Royal Navy's first twin engined, long range escort strike fighter, designated Sea Hornet F. Mk. 20. The first production aircraft, TT186, with slotted flaps, flew at Hatfield on 13 August 1946 and went to Lee-on-Solent with several others for service trials with 703 Squadron. Armament was similar to the RAF counterpart, consisting of four 20 mm. Hispano cannon in the nose, two 1,000 pound bombs under the wings and alternative provision for eight 60 pound rocket projectiles. Camera windows were built into the rear fuselage for optional F.R. Mk. 20 capability. During deck landing trials it was found that side loads on the undercarriage caused torque link trouble which necessitated the fitting of redesigned main legs, tests with which began on HMS *Illustrious* on 11 October 1948.

801 Squadron re-formed at Ford with Sea Hornets on 1 June 1947 and later moved to Arbroath before embarking in HMS *Implacable* in 1949. Sea Hornets remained in service until 1951 and three machines were attached to 806 Squadron to form a composite naval group which embarked in the Light Fleet Carrier HMCS *Magnificent* on 25 May 1948. After completing eight weeks training in Canada they went to New York to give flying demonstrations at the International Air Exposition held from 21 July to 8 August.

A Sea Hornet F. Mk. 20 was sent to Australia for Royal Australian Navy evaluation but although intended to be serialled A83-1, it retained the Royal Navy serial TT213.

Sea Hornet F. Mk. 20 TT193 flew with the FAA in the UK and with the RCAF at Edmonton, Alberta before being acquired by Spartan Air Services Ltd., the Mosquito-equipped Ottawa survey company. On 28 June 1951 it was issued with a restricted certificate of airworthiness as a three seat civil photographic aircraft. Registered CF-GUO, it operated at a higher all-up-weight, and the following April was sold to Field Aviation, another aerial survey company. It was scrapped after an engine failure and lack of spares.

Production of the Sea Hornet F. Mk. 20 ceased on 12 June 1951 with the delivery of WE247. The type was relegated to second line duties and served with 728 Fleet Requirements Unit at Hal Far, Malta, until 1955.

An urgent naval requirement for a high performance, night fighter or strike navigator, was met by converting the Sea Hornet F. Mk. 20 into a radar equipped two seater. Design responsibility rested with the Heston Aircraft Co. Ltd., who produced the first trial installation aircraft to Specification N.21/45. Conversion was done to Hornet F. Mk. 1, PX230, without the folding wing but equipped with Merlin 133/34 power plants; increased tailplane span; heated radar-navigator's cockpit over the trailing edge with one piece canopy and separate K type dinghy; an ASH radar scanner installed in a thimble radome in the nose and flame damping exhaust manifolds were fitted. Designated the Sea Hornet N.F. Mk. 21, it first flew on 9 July 1946 and was followed by a second prototype in the shape of former Hornet F. Mk. 1 and Sea Hornet F. Mk. 20 PX239. This not only had power folding wings but also the very considerable dorsal fillet which later became a retrospective modification on all earlier marks. In spite of the parasitic drag of additional equipment, the N.F. Mk. 21 was only 5 m.p.h. slower than its predecessor.

Production aircraft commencing VV430 were built in the Hatfield factory but towards the end of 1948 the jigs were moved to Hawarden Chester, where further Sea Hornets were built. The 78th and final Sea Hornet N.F. Mk. 21 was VZ699, and total production of Sea Hornets of all marks amounted to 198 machines. Satisfactory tests by the Service Trials Unit and the Naval Air Fighting Development Unit at Ford resulted in 809 Squadron being re-formed with the type at

Culdrose on 20 January 1949. It was the only front line squadron so equipped and in 1950 embarked in HMS *Vengeance,* which in October of that year was steaming off Gibraltar. When certain of 809 Squadron's aircraft were recalled to Lee-on-Solent, the Royal Navy was given an opportunity of matching the RAF Hornet flights of the previous year. On 16 October four Sea Hornets flew in formation at 18,000 ft., nonstop from Gibraltar to Lee, covering the 1,040 miles in 3 hours 10 minutes at an average speed of 330 m.p.h. On 24 November a fifth aircraft covered the distance in only 2 hours 45 minutes.

The two seaters were relegated to second line squadrons and radar training duties in 1954 and continued in limited service until most were broken up at Yeovilton two years later. Forty-three examples of a photographic reconnaissance version known as the Sea Hornet P.R. Mk. 22 were also delivered to the Fleet Air Arm, closely resembling the F. Mk. 20 but fitted with two F.52 cameras for day reconnaissance or one Fairchild K.19B for night use. It could also carry standard underwing armament and was virtually a navalised version of the RAF's Hornet P.R. Mk. 2. The prototype was TT187, and one of the first production aircraft, VZ658, was exhibited with three vertical cameras installed at the S.B.A.C. Show at Farnborough in September 1948.

DH.104 Dove/Devon

De Havilland's first postwar civil machine was a twin Gipsy aircraft , designed by Ronald E Bishop's team as an interpretation of the Brabazon Committee's Type 5B to replace the DH.89 Rapide. It was an all metal, low wing, cantilever monoplane with semi-monocoque fuselage, with pneumatically retractable nosewheel undercarriage, and two D.H. Gipsy Queen 70

supercharged engines driving three bladed D.H. hydromatic feathering and reversible pitch propellers. It was the first British transport fitted with braking props. Built to Air Ministry Specification 26/43 and appropriately named the Dove, the prototype G-AGPJ was piloted by Geoffrey H. Pike on its first flight at Hatfield on 25 September 1945 - the 25th anniversary of the founding of the company.

Development flying was followed by Farnborough trials which included a public demonstration on 29

The Dove production track - closes to the camera is a machine for Central African Airways. *(DH via BAe Hatfield)*

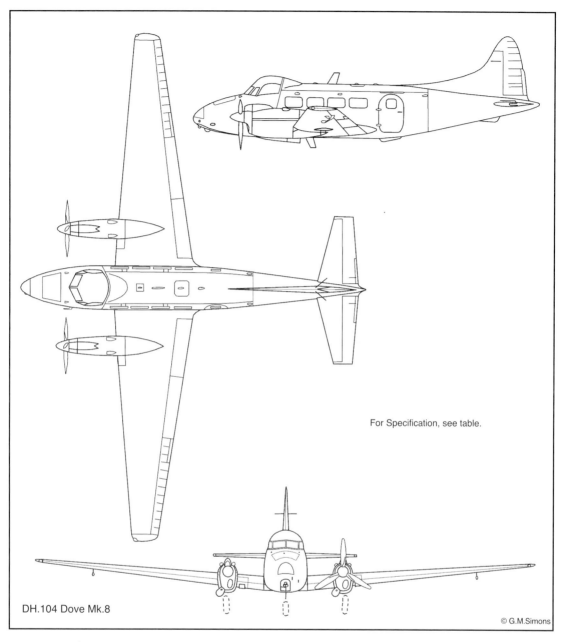

DH.104 Dove Mk.8

For Specification, see table.

© G.M.Simons

October and then 'PJ returned to Hatfield to be fitted with an enlarged dorsal fin for improved control when flying on one engine. The fin was remodelled later into the now familiar curve. In the following May the aircraft was handed over to the Ministry of Supply in whose service it had a long career as a development vehicle, terminated with a tyre research programme by the Dunlop Rubber Co. Ltd. as WJ310 at Baginton in 1952-53. Forerunner of over 500 production models, it flew later in Portuguese colonial service as CR-CAC.

Despite superiority over the Rapide in both cruising speed and single engine performance, the Dove's high purchase price and greater operating costs were beyond the means of most of the struggling

charter firms of the period.

Initial deliveries were to airline operators around the world; a number were also despatched to de Havilland Aircraft of Canada Ltd., including the first production aircraft, CF-BNU, and the 15th, CF-DJH, which in 1947 became the sole example flown with a twin float undercarriage. Fourteen went into airline or business use in Canada and others were sent south to the USA, Mexico and Venezuela.

Increasing demand saw the assembly line transferred to larger premises at Hawarden in 1951, the output from which made a valuable contribution to the export drive.

Although initially offered as a light transport with

The prototype Dove seen at the end of 1945 with the fitted with the first revision of the dorsal fin. *(John Stride Collection)*

seating for eight passengers, or as an eleven seater with reduced baggage space and no toilet, the Dove began a long association with the business world when the six-seat Dove 2 executive version was introduced in 1948. The first Dove 2, Vickers-Armstrongs Limited's G-AKSV, demonstrated at the Farnborough SBAC Show in September of that year, foreshadowed purchases by the English Electric Co. Ltd., David Brown and Sons (Huddersfield) Ltd., Helliwells Ltd., Enfield Rolling Mills Ltd., Short Bros. and Harland Ltd., the Dunlop Rubber Co. Ltd., the Shell Refining and Marketing Co. Ltd., Ind Coope and Allsop Ltd. and Ferranti Ltd. Executive Doves were operated on strict airline schedules and found a ready market overseas, being used by such firms as Williamson Diamond Mines Ltd. in Tanganyika and the Anglo American Oil Co. Ltd. of South Africa. They served as personal aircraft of distinction, 'CGG with the Governor General of the Belgian Congo; VT-CEH, 'VA and 'DBG with the Maharajahs of Baroda, Bikaner and Jaipur; and VT-COV with the Governor of Assam.

The Dove 3 was a projected high altitude survey model with oxygen and remote controlled vertical camera, and one airframe, completed to Specification C.I 3/46 as the prototype military communications version, was known as Dove 4. This had two crew and seven passengers achieved by removing the front starboard seat to make way for a J Type dinghy. An initial batch of thirty aircraft, VP952-VP981, was supplied to the RAF in 1948 under the designation Devon C. Mk. 1 and formed the equipment of 31 (Metropolitan Communications) Squadron, Hendon, and of Headquarters Communications Flights. Devons were stationed at foreign capitals such as Teheran and Buenos Aires under civil marks as Dove 4s for the temporary use of the Air Attaches. Devons were also supplied to the air forces of the Belgian Congo, Ceylon, Egypt, Eire, India, Iraq, the Lebanon, New Zealand, Pakistan and South Africa. In Sweden they were designated Tp46.

Airline Doves were also transferred to military status in Ethiopia, Iraq and Jordan. A small number of Devons were employed by the RAE and the Empire Test Pilots' School, Farnborough. In 1955 ten aircraft, XJ319-324 and XJ347-350, were delivered to the Fleet Air Arm under the designation Sea Devon C. Mk. 20 for operation by part of 781 Squadron at Lee-on-Solent as the Southern

The interior of one of the 'airline' Doves. *(John Stride Collection)*

Left: Devon C1 VP971 on the ground. Compare this picture to the one below of Devon VP952 at RAF Woodvale. The perspex roof to the cockpit has gone, and the engine cowlings have many more 'lumps and bumps'. *(both John Stride Collection)*

Communications Squadron. Three more were added in January 1956 for scheduled services to naval air stations and special flights abroad. When replaced by Sea Herons in May 1961 some were disposed of on the civil market.

During the first fifteen years of the Dove's production life, the only airframe modification of note was the fitting of an asymmetrical elevator to eliminate buffeting, and all the major Dove variants resulted from the development of the Gipsy Queen engines. In its basic form with fuel injection and giving 330 horsepower at take off, this engine was known as the Gipsy Queen 70 and from 1948 was the standard power plant of the Dove 1 and 2 in developed form as the Gipsy Queen 70-3. From 1952 the 340 horsepower Gipsy Queen 70-4 was available as an alternative amending the designation to Dove 1B and 2B respectively. Designations Dove 1A and 2A and all subsequent marks with suffix 'A', were reserved for custom-built models for the American market. When the 380 horsepower Gipsy Queen 70 Mk. 2 was introduced the next year, allowing an increase in all-up weight to 8,800 pounds, the corresponding designations became Dove 5 and 6. The single Dove 6B G-AMRN resulted from fitting these engines in an early production aircraft returned from South Africa.

Few Mks. 1 and 2 remained in service in the 1960s, the majority of existing Doves, and some Devons, having been fitted with uprated engines during overhaul. Secondhand Doves found a ready sale in almost every country of the globe.

To satisfy a renewed interest in business flying in 1960, the Dove was remodelled in two versions. The Dove Custom 800, furnished to purchaser's requirements by Horton & Horton of Fort Worth, Texas, was for United States and South American markets which absorbed more than one hundred air-delivered Doves for feeder line service or executive use. This work entailed the aircraft being outfitted with removable bulkheads, and various custom interiors were available, including airliner-orientated configurations. The British version, also a six seater and known as the Dove 8, was available with standard furnishings and demonstrated an improvement over older models resulting from the installation of two 400 h.p. Gipsy Queen 70 Mk. 3 engines. Earlier marks were indistinguishable externally, but the Dove 8 was recognised by enlarged oil cooler intakes above the spinners and exhaust thrust augmentor tubes under the engines to reduce cooling drag and maintain a positive flow of air through the cowlings. Five inches of extra headroom were provided for the crew by fitting a domed roof as used on the Heron. This resulted in deeper side windows to the cockpit, which had the radio controls transferred to the roof and an improved one piece instrument panel.

The float-equipped Dove 1 CF-DJH seen flying over Toronto in 1947. *(John Stride Collection)*

A 'second stage' Riley Dove conversion is seen here on F-BGOA, fitted with Lycomings and a swept fin. The aircraft was supplied to Cie de Pont-a-Mousson at Nancy, France in 1967.
(John Stride Collection)

The first Dove 8 delivery took place at Hatfield on 24 January 1961, when G-ARJB was handed over to J. C. Bamford (Excavators) Ltd.

An eight to eleven passenger transport version of the Dove 8 was offered under the designation Dove 7, two being delivered to the Royal Malayan Air Force on 6 September 1961 and one to the United Arab Republic on the following day.

The 542nd and final Dove, G-AVHV, was delivered to Dowty Group Services Ltd. at Staverton on 20 September 1967 but was destroyed when it crashed into houses while landing at Wolverhampton just three years later, on 9 April 1970.

Modifications and moderisations

In 1965 eight Devons were re-engined to Dove 8 standard with the Gipsy Queen 175 by Hawker Siddeley and at RAF Maintainance Units. Initially they retained the original Dove cockpit canopy, but the raised Mk. 8 type was installed later when they were redesignated Devon C. Mk. 2.

Only limited success attended American efforts to modernise the Dove. The first type of conversion, intended for the executive market and offered by the Riley Aeronautics Corp located at the Executive Airport in Fort Lauderdale, Florida as the Riley Turbo Executive 400, featured two 400 horsepower Lycoming IO-720-A1A flat-eight piston engines, a better flight deck, restyled cabin and swept fin, the prototype was demonstrated in Britain in 1965. At least seventeen were produced in the USA. A number of similar conversions were undertaken in Britain by McAlpine Aviation Ltd. at Luton.

A more ambitious conversion for third level operators, the Carstedt CJ-600A Jet Liner, was first flown in the USA on 18 December 1966. Carstedt Inc, of Long Beach, California, fitted an eighty-seven inch fuselage stretch that enabled eighteen passengers to be carried on the power of two Garrett 605 ehp TEP-331 propeller-turbine engines. Carstedt also offered the CJ600F stretched cargo conversion of a Dove 1 fitted with TPE331 turboprops.

The Carstedt CJ600F N4921V, with fuselage extension, turboprops and tail stand. *(John Stride Collection)*

Mark number	DH.104 Powerplants
	Engine
Prototype:	two 330 horsepower De Havilland Gipsy Queen 70
Dove 1 and 2:	two 330 horsepower De Havilland Gipsy Queen 70-3
Dove 1B and 2B:	two 340 horsepower De Havilland Gipsy Queen 70-4
Dove 5 and 6:	two 380 horsepower De Havilland Gipsy Queen 70 Mk.2
Dove 7 and 8:	two 400 horsepower De Havilland Gipsy Queen 70 Mk.4
Devon C.Mk.1:	two 330 horsepower De Havilland Gipsy Queen 71
	two 340 horsepower De Havilland Gipsy Queen 70-4
Devon C.Mk.2:	two 400 horsepower De Havilland Gipsy Queen 175
Sea Devon Mk.20:	two 340 horsepower De Havilland Gipsy Queen 70-4
Riley:	two 400 horsepower Lycoming IO-720-AIA

DH.104 Dove/Devon Specifications				
Mark:	**Dove 1 & 2**	**Dove 1B/2B Devon/Sea Devon**	**Dove 5 & 6**	**Dove 7 & 8**
Span:	57 feet 0 inches	57 feet 0 inches	57 feet 0 inches	57 feet 0 inches
Length:	39 feet 4 inches	39 feet 4 inches	39 feet 4 inches	39 feet 4 inches
Height:	13 feet 4 inches	13 feet 4 inches	13 feet 4 inches	13 feet 4 inches
Wing area:	335 square feet	335 square feet	335 square feet	335 square feet
Tare weight:	5,650 pounds	5,650 pounds*	5,725 pounds	6,580 pounds
AUW:	8,500 pounds	8,500 pounds	8,800 pounds**	8,950 pounds
Cruise:	165 mph	179 mph	179 mph	162 mph
Ceiling:	20,000 feet	20,000 feet	20,000 feet	21,700 feet
Max range:	1,000 miles	1,000 miles	1,070 miles	1,175 miles

* Devon 5,780 pounds   ** Dove 6B 8,500 pounds

DH.105

This type number was allocated to designs for a three seat low wing primary trainer wityh a fixed undercarriage and 'bubble' canopy in 1946 to Specification T.23/43 The production contract was eventually awarded to Percival Aircraft with their Prentice and so the DH.105 was not built.

DH.106 Comet

It was clear to all at De Havillands in 1943 that the Allies were likely to win the war, and that with the jet engine there was a very strong possibility of eliminating the wartime lead in transport aircraft from the Americans. A team led by Ronald E. Bishop made a number of design investigations to meet the Brabazon Committee's Type Four specification. During 1944 a number of configurations were studied, one with twin booms and three Goblin turbojets, a rear engined canard with Ghosts and a tailless type with swept wing and short fuselage. However, the new DH.106 transport crystalised into something more orthodox. The name Comet was revived and construction took place at Hatfield amid much secrecy.

Great attention had been given to handling characteristics at both ends of the speed range by providing generous flaps and employing Lockheed Servodyne hydraulically assisted power controls. Four crew occupied a flight deck in the nose, the all-weather visibility from which had been carefully determined by means of flight trials with a repeatedly modified Airspeed Horsa glider towed by a Halifax. The tricycle undercarriage was equipped with large single main wheels which retracted outward into bulges in the under surface of the wings.

Piloted by John Cunningham with a crew of three, G-5-1/G-ALVG, first of two prototypes ordered by the Ministry of Supply to Specification 22/46, made its first flight from Hatfield on 27 July 1949. The aircraft was a thirty-six seater with a circular section fuselage mounted above a thin, moderately swept wing with four De Havilland Ghost 50 engines buried in the wing-roots.

The first public demonstration at Farnborough in September 1949 was followed by a number of overseas flights to measure fuel consumption under simulated airline conditions, starting with a return trip to Castel Benito in Libya at an average speed of 448 m.p.h. by John Cunningham on 25 October.

A 5½ hour endurance flight was made round the UK, followed on 21 February 1950 by the first flight with the cabin pressurised to maintain a cabin altitude at 8,000 feet when cruising at 40,000 feet. Some 324 hours flying was completed in eleven months of almost trouble free trials that included out and back

The windscreen rain clearance capabilities of the new design were tested 'in the real world' by putting a mock-up nose on the front of a Airspeed Horsa glider flown from Hatfield during the bitter winter of 1946. *(DH Hatfield)*

This strange looking vehicle was built from a 3-ton truck chassis. A pair of transverse I-beams at the front held a pair of Mosquito main undercarriage units as outriggers and a Comet nosewheel leg with tanks of scrap metal on either side to simulate the loads on the nosewheels. The gentleman in the trilby is Sir Geoffrey himself. *(DH Hatfield)*

inter-capital records early in 1950 between London and Rome, Copenhagen and Cairo at average speeds above 420 m.p.h. The Cairo record was established on 24 April 1950 while carrying eleven technicians to tropical trials at Khartoum and Nairobi.

The second Ministry of Supply Comet, G-5-2/G-ALZK, flown at Hatfield by John Cunningham and Peter Bugge on the anniversary of the first flight of the prototype, was delivered to the BOAC Comet Unit at Hurn on 2 April 1951 to start a 500 hour route proving and crew training programme. Techniques of fuel economy, holding and descent were evolved during twelve proving flights to Johannesburg, Beirut, Delhi, Singapore and Djakarta.

A production line was established at Hatfield for the construction of ten Comet Is to be delivered to the state airline starting, with G-ALYP on 8 April 1952 and ending with 'YZ on 23 September. Small multi-wheel bogie undercarriage units which lay flush with the under surface of the mainplane when retracted were standard on all production Comets.

BOAC began simulated passenger schedules to Johannesburg carrying freight in January 1952 and the world's first pure jet flight with fare paying passengers was made to that city by G-ALYP on 2 May 1952. A regular day-and-a-half scheduled service over the 10,200 mile route between London and Tokyo was inaugurated on 3 April 1953. The Comet Is proceeded to cut flying times by half and to eclipse all contemporary schedules and block speeds.

The Comet reached a peak of fame and popularity when Queen Elizabeth the Queen Mother, Princess Margaret, Sir Geoffrey and Lady de Havilland made a Royal request flight round Europe on 23 May 1952, and in the following year G-ALYW carried the same Royal passengers to the Rhodes Centenary celebrations at Salisbury, Southern Rhodesia.

CF-CUM, first of two Comet 1As for Canadian Pacific Airlines, placed on static display at Farnborough in September 1952, instigated the first of ten overseas sales. Equipped as forty-four seaters and operating at a higher all-up weight of 110,000 pounds, the Comet 1As were powered by Ghost 50 Mk. 2 engines using water-methanol injection and were equipped with extra bag tanks in the outer wings to increase total fuel capacity to 7,000 gallons for use on longer sectors.

5301, first of two similar aircraft ordered by the Royal Canadian Air Force to equip 412 Transport Squadron, became the first jet transport to cross the Atlantic on its delivery flight to Ottawa via Keflavik and Gander on 29 May 1953. Three others, F-BGSA-'SC, were delivered to Union Aeromaritime de Transport, (UAT) the first of which made its first proving flight from Paris to Dakar via Casablanca on 27 December 1952. Three further Comet 1As, F-BGNX-'NZ, were acquired by Air France, whose first Paris-Rome-Beirut jet service was flown by 'NY on 26

An overall view of the Comet assembly shops at Hatfield.*(DH Hatfield)*

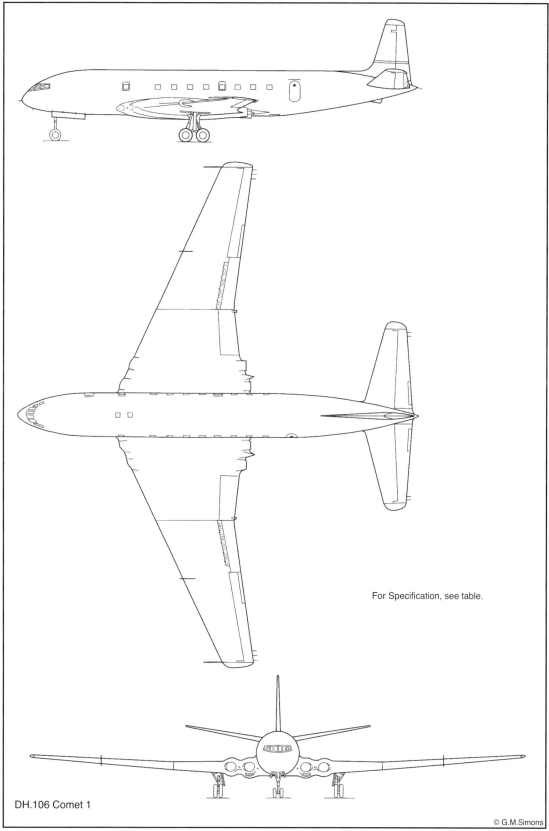

For Specification, see table.

DH.106 Comet 1

Above: The very first hop at 9.50am on 27 July 1949. Three more hops were made that day before the first proper flight. Note the square cabin windows and single mainwheel undercarriage.
Below left: De Havilland's always captioned the picture on the left as *'6.17pm on July 27. The first take off'*. Given that the undercarriage is retracted, it is more likely John Cunningham's flyby at the end of the flight. What is not in doubt is the other picture *'6.48pm. The first landing'*. (all DH Hatfield)

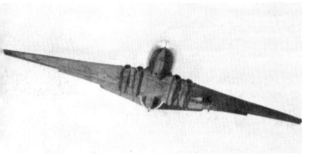

An original print of the first Comet in flight - a print that has been signed by test pilot John Cunningham. *(DH Hatfield)*

Above: the 'waving off' party as Comet Yoke Peter leaves London Airport for the inaugural flight to Johannesburg.

Left: Captain Geoffrey de Havilland (left), John Cunningham and members of the BOAC and De Havilland Boards 'see away' from London's Heathrow Airport, the world's first jet airliner passenger service.
(both DH Hatfield)

August 1953.

CF-CUN, named *Empress of Hawaii*, the second of the Canadian Pacific Comets, had been involved in a take off disaster at Karachi on 3 March 1953 while on its delivery flight to Sydney, Australia to start the company's first trans-Pacific service to Vancouver. Its sister aircraft was then disposed of to BOAC and converted to into a Comet 1 as replacement for G-

ALYZ which was damaged beyond repair in a take-off incident at Rome on 26 October 1952. These accidents showed that if the nose was held too high on take off, the aircraft would not reach flying speed, so the Comets were then fitted with drooped leading edges.

These problems were the start of a series of widely publicised incidents that were painstakingly investigated. G-ALYV was destroyed with the loss of forty-three lives while climbing westbound out of Calcutta on 2 May 1953; Yoke Peter plunged into the sea from a height of 26,000 feet near Elba with a loss of thirty-five lives just after take off from Rome on 10 January 1954; and Yoke Yoke crashed off Stromboli with twenty-one passengers, also after take off from Rome, on 8 April.

As a result, all Comets were grounded, but examination failed to reveal any mechanical or structural defect. Instrumented flight trials with G-ANAV coupled with ground fatigue testing of G-ALYR and 'YS and water tank pressure testing of G-ALYU at Farnborough were used in conjunction with a microscopic examination of the salvaged wreck of 'YP which accurately pinpointed the failure of one corner of the rear ADF 'window', a panel in the roof.

The first prototype Comet, used as a testbed for de Havilland Sprite rocket motors, made its first assisted take off on 7 May 1951 and after performing at the 1952 SBAC Show was handed over to the RAE for structural testing. The focus then switched in the direction of the development of a Transatlantic Comet with more power and more fuel. This was the Comet 2 with a three foot fuselage extension, tankage increased to 7,000 gallons and fitted with Avon 502 axial flow jet engines. The trial Avon installation was made to Comet 1 G-ALYT during manufacture and the aircraft first flew at Hatfield as the Comet 2X on 16 February 1952. On completion of tropical trials with this aircraft

in May of the following year, an order was placed for twelve 44 seat Comet 2s for BOAC service to South America. The first, G-AMXA, which had first flown on 27 August 1953, was shown at the SBAC Show in the following month and concluded flight trials with a demonstration of long range characteristics when John Cunningham covered the 3,064 miles from Hatfield to Khartoum nonstop in 6½ hours on 22 January 1954. As a result of the Comet 1 investigation all Comet 2 fuselage pressure shells were rebuilt at Chester in heavier gauge metal with rounded openings, and the engine jet pipes were 'swept out' to reduce fuselage buffeting. RCAF Comet 1As also were rebuilt and returned to service as Comet IXBs on 26 September 1957. Two surviving Air France Comet 1As, acquired by the Ministry of Supply in 1954, were similarly modified for use at the RAE in 1958.

A number of overseas orders were received for the Comet 2 and additional production facilities were established at the Chester works and at Short Bros. and Harland Ltd.'s Belfast factory but trials showed that although the range was now adequate for the South Atlantic it was still not sufficient for nonstop operation over the northern route. As modification was only possible at the expense of increased tare weight, only eighteen Comet 2s were completed and only fifteen of

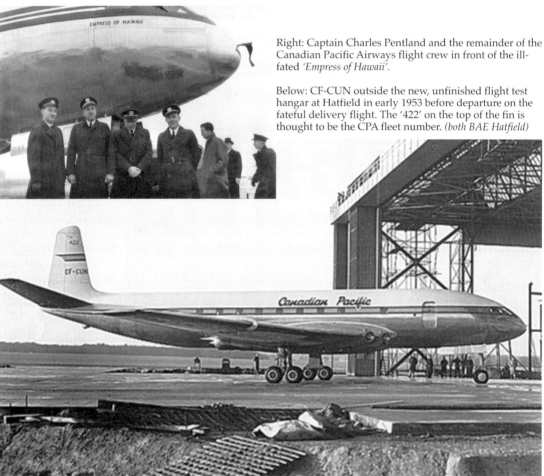

Right: Captain Charles Pentland and the remainder of the Canadian Pacific Airways flight crew in front of the ill-fated 'Empress of Hawaii'.

Below: CF-CUN outside the new, unfinished flight test hangar at Hatfield in early 1953 before departure on the fateful delivery flight. The '422' on the top of the fin is thought to be the CPA fleet number. (both BAE Hatfield)

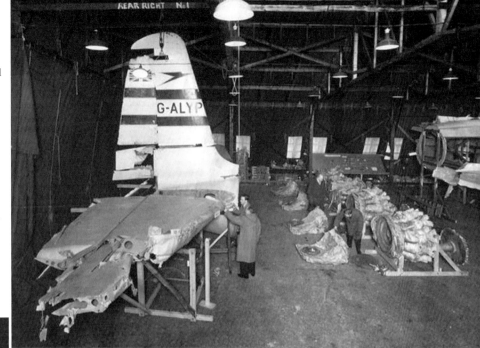

The wreckage of G-ALYP was cleaned and then assembled inside a canvas hangar at Farnborough.

All four engines had been recovered - as had many large sections of the aircraft, which were mounted on specially constructed wooden trestles in their correct relative positions.

these actually flew. A few were fitted with Avon 118s for use by the RAF on 'unspecified' duties. These machines emerged as the R.2 variant. The Comet R.2 ELectronic/SIGnal INTelligence (SIG/ELINT) aircraft were delivered to 51 Squadron at RAF Wyton in 1957, the flight-deck crews having been trained by 216 Squadron. Conversion work was carried out by Marshalls of Cambridge and continued until the aircraft were rolled out in February 1958. The aircraft were supplied without engines but with a guaranteed minimum fatigue life. The engines now installed in them were Rolls-Royce Avon 504s rated at 7,330 pounds of thrust each.

The decision to equip Comets as SIGINT platforms goes back to a US/UK ELINT conference of December 1952. An English Electric Canberra was soon delivered but the Treasury dragged its heels on Comet for about a year. Three airframes were converted at CSE Watton by the Special Radio Installation Flight (SRIF). Work began in the spring of 1957 but one airframe was destroyed in a hangar fire on 3 June 1959. Two years elapsed before GCHQ could persuade the Treasury to release funds to replace it.

The first two examples were delivered to 192 Squadron at RAF Watton which was soon re-numbered 51 Squadron and moved to RAF Wyton. Eventually seven Comet R Mk 2s were delivered and took over the ELINT role from the venerable Lincoln and RB-29A Washington. With four jet engines, the performance of the Comet was considerably better than its piston engined predecessors.

The Comet R Mk 2 was frequently deployed on so-called 'ferret' sorties over the Barents Sea north of Norway, along the Baltic and even detached to Cyprus where it could easily monitor activity along the border of the Black Sea – an area of particular interest. These activities were described as 'Radio Proving Flights', the purpose of which was to allow the intelligence community to build up a picture of Soviet air defences, upon which RAF Bomber Command could then base their operational plans.

The flights all took place over friendly or neutral territory or over international waters, no penetration of Warsaw Pact airspace was involved. The Prime Minister was sent a copy of the proposed monthly programme of flights for his approval. Once this was obtained, Ministry of Defence and Foreign Office officials carefully planned each individual flight and final authorisation rested with the Secretary of State for Defence.

The principle rules governing RAF 'radio proving flights' were that the aircraft approached no closer than 30 nautical miles to Soviet or Satellite territory. Except in the case of West Germany, aircraft were not permitted to overfly the territory or territorial waters of friendly or neutral countries whilst engaged in these operations without the concurrence of the competent authorities in the countries concerned. No more than four aircraft were used together in the same operating area. Daylight operations were limited to single aircraft

XK659 had first flown on non-passenger carrying proving flights in BOAC colours, but was later converted into a Comet 2R. It was never converted to oval windows and thus would never fly with pressurisation. It is seen above with assorted 'lumps and bumps' under its fuselage, including one aerial that looks suspiciously like some form of sideways looking radar!

At some point in the aircraft's career whilst at RAF Wyton it gained this smoke-ejecting duck emblem - clearly a variation of 51 Squadrons 'droopy goose' badge - on its vertical fin, the meaning of which has been lost in the mists of time. *(both Warrant Officer Paddy Porter BEM)*

and single aircraft operating by day or night were not permitted to make a direct 'provocative' approach to the coast or border and had to fly broadly parallel to the coast line. Operations involving more than one aircraft at night had to be normally flown in conditions of at worse 'half moonlight', but preferably total darkness'.

The American intelligence community also ran their own electronic intelligence gathering operations using, during the same period, the RB-47. The American government submitted a monthly list in advance to the British government detailing when an RB-47 intelligence gathering flight was planned to operate from a British base, such as Brize Norton.

RAF flights were usually conducted with two aircraft, a Comet R.2 and a specially equipped Canberra, also from 51 Squadron. Typically, the Canberra would fly a profile that would attract the attention of the Warsaw Pact radar defences, allowing the Comet to record the transmissions. This would usually involve the Canberra flying at low-level below radar cover towards the target area and then, as the aircraft neared the minimum distance from the Warsaw Pact boundary, it would suddenly climb rapidly into radar cover alerting the air defence radars. Meanwhile the Comet would sit back at higher altitude, flying parallel to the boundary, listening in

and recording the frequencies and transmissions of the radar and radios used by the air defence forces. Direction finding equipment onboard the Comet would also enable the location of the radar and transmitters to be determined.

Flights were conducted throughout in strict radio silence, to maintain an element of tactical freedom and surprise whilst concealing the identity of the aircraft from the Russian defences. Radio silence was only broken in an emergency or to recall the aircraft. As far as it can be ascertained, no RAF aircraft conducting a 'radio proving flight' was ever lost, although a number of American aircraft were shot down whilst engaged in these activities.

In addition to the front crew of two pilots, two navigators and a flight engineer, up to ten specialists were carried in the main cabin of the Comets, where they operated the monitoring and recording equipment, much of which was manufactured in the USA. Because of a long-standing agreement to share intelligence, the Comet R Mk 2 often operated in conjunction with USAF RB-47s.

The decision to replace the Comets was made perhaps as early as 1961. A secret group, the Technical Committee of London Signals Intelligence Committee began looking into future ELINT research in November 1961. This group had been behind the development of the 'Airborne Rafter' programme hunting for KGB agent's radio transmissions over Britain. The committee reported that tactical ELINT collection over the Eastern Bloc borders was a future need and in 1962 Plessey was awarded a development contract for a 'experimental sideways-looking ELINT system'. This system was covered under Air Staff Requirement 817 'Sideways Looking Airborne Search Reviewing System.' It has been claimed by some sources that this was the offical start of the what became the Nimrod R.1 programme. The Comet R.2s were replaced by three Nimrod R.s in 1974.

Eventually most of the other Comet 2s were modified for transport duties with 216 Squadron, Lyneham, XK669 and 670 being equipped for training under the designation Comet T.Mk.2 and delivery of eight others with strengthened freight doors for scheduled runs to the Far East, Australia and Christmas Island as C. Mk.2s, commenced on 7 June 1956. The two training aircraft were later brought up to C. Mk.2 standard and three additional ex-civil Comet 2s, XK655, 659 and 663, were modified for signals duties by Marshalls at Cambridge and served with 192 and 51 Squadrons. The first Comet produced at Chester was also the last C. Mk.2, XK716. After continuous test flying which ended with de-icing tests with an Avon 524 in the starboard outer position, the original Comet 2X G-ALYT made a last twelve minute flight on 28 May 1959 to Halton where John Cunningham landed on the 3,800 ft. grass strip and handed it over to 1 School of Technical Training as an instructional airframe. This was not the first time he had landed a Comet on grass, for on Wednesday, February 1952 he made an unscheduled landing at 27 Luton Airport in G-ALYP when its base at Hatfield became smog-bound.

The Comet 2 was succeeded by G-ANLO, a single example of a stretched version known as the Comet 3 with Avon 502 engines, large pinion tanks at two-thirds span and maximum accommodation increased to 78. It was flown for the first time by Messrs. Cunningham and Bugge on 19 July 1954 and in the course of a long development programme, the same crew left Hatfield on 2 December 1955 and flew round the world via Australia, New Zealand, Fiji, Vancouver and Dorval, arriving home on the 28th. The Comet 3 averaged 501 m.p.h. to lower the Perth-Sydney record to four hours

six minutes and was the first jet airliner to cross the Pacific and the first to circumnavigate the globe. It was later re-engined and first flew with Rolls-Royce Avon 523s on 25 February 1957.

The Comet 4, proposed in 1955 with Avon 524s and still greater fuel capacity, at last satisfied BOAC's North Atlantic requirements and nineteen aircraft G-APDA-'DT were ordered in 1957 and the first flew at Hatfield on 27 April 1958. Route proving trials were conducted with two machines, G-AMXD and 'XK, with Avon 524s in the outboard nacelles and Avon 504s in the inner under the designation Comet 2E. To build up Avon experience, simulated services were flown throughout 1957 between London, Beirut and Calcutta and from May 1958 the Comet 2Es also turned westward over the North Atlantic. During its final certification trials they were joined by the first Comet 4 G-APDA, which between dawn and sunset on 14 September was flown by John Cunningham and crew 7,925 miles from Hong Kong to London in a flying time of 16 hours 16 minutes. Three days later the same aircraft lowered the London-Gander record to 5 hours 47 minutes and on successive days made Montreal-Vancouver-Mexico City-Lima-Buenos Aires nonstop flights. The world's first Transatlantic jet flights with fare paying passengers were made simultaneously on 4 October by G-APDC (Captain Roy E Millichap) westbound and 'DB (Captain Tom B Stoney) eastbound. Comets took over all London-New York 'Monarch' flights in the following month and during 1959 were used on the Ceylon, Australia, Tokyo and Johannesburg routes. In 1960 Comet services were opened to the Caribbean, Chile, Canada and Persia and in their first two years of operation the nineteen BOAC Comet 4s flew 27,000,000 miles, carried 327,000 passengers in a total flying time of 68,500 hours.

First fruit of demonstrations in Latin America was an order from Aerolineas Argentinas for six Comet 4s with which jet operations commenced over the Andes between Buenos Aires and Santiago on 16 April 1959. Services across the South Atlantic to Europe started on 19 May and the New York service was opened shortly afterwards. The last three Argentine Comets were fitted with thrust reversers.

In July 1956 American interest had crystallised into an order from Capital Airlines for four long distance Comet 4s and ten special Comet 4As to operate short

Yes, it DID happen! The scaffolding around the Tower in the background dates this picture to 1952 when John Cunningham made an unscheduled landing at Luton with Comet G-ALYP - the aircraft that later flew the world's first ever jet passenger service. (*via John Stride collection*)

Left: The Comet at Rio seen through an archway of the terminal building at Galeao Airport. The Comet covered the 5,850 miles from London in 15 hours 49 minutes flying time. The outward and return flights were completely 'snag-free'.

Below: Light at the end of a dark tunnel - Comet 2E G-AXMD in the foreground with the sole Comet 3 G-ALNO in flight behind.

and medium stage lengths at a reduced cruising altitude of 23,500 feet. They were to have forty-inch fuselage extensions, accommodate up to 92 tourist passengers and have wing span reduced by seven feet to permit higher cruising speeds at the lower altitude. These orders were cancelled for financial reasons but in April 1958 British European Airways Corporation ordered a shorthaul version to suit its own requirements as the Comet 4B. This was stretched thirty-eight inches to seat a maximum of ninety-nine passengers, the span was reduced and the pinion tanks deleted. To speeed up their entry into service, a flight test programme was conducted with Comet 3 G-ANLO which, with shortened wing span and thrust reversers, flew under the designation Comet 3B on 21 August 1958. It was then demonstrated in BEA livery as *RMA William Brooks* at Farnborough in the following month. The first BEA Comet 4B, G-APMA, commenced certification trials in June 1959 and deliveries commenced in the following November. On 19 July 'MA covered the Northolt-Le Bourget stage of the *Daily Mail* London-Paris air race in 27 minutes.

The first scheduled services were operated on 1 April 1960, using 'MB between Tel Aviv and London; 'MD operating in the reverse direction; 'MA was operated to Nice and 'MF flew the inaugural service to Moscow. Within two months the fleet was achieving a daily average utilisation of 7½ hours and by mid 1961 the Comet 4B fleet had increased to fifteen. Early in 1960 four Comet 4Bs equipped to carry 22 first class and 64 economy class passengers, were delivered to Olympic Airways, Athens, who in consortium with B.E.A.C. linked Athens with Istanbul, Tel Aviv, Nicosia, Beirut, Cairo, London and the chief European capitals.

Resulting from the astonishing field performance of Comet 4 G-APDA at Mexico City Airport at a height of 7,340 feet above sea level, in hot weather from an 8,200 feet long runway, on 21 September 1958, a specialised version known as the Comet 4C was ordered by Cia. Mexicana de Aviacion for its 'Golden Aztec' services linking Mexico City with Havana, Chicago and Los Angeles. This was a compromise having the same wing, fuel capacity and all-up weight of the Comet 4 but the large capacity fuselage of the

The delivery of Comet 4s to BOAC was a great event.
Right: Notables on a notable occasion! On 30 September when the first two Comets were formally delivered, Sir Gerard d`Erlanger, Chairman of BOAC, shakes hands with Sir Geoffrey de Havilland, as he alights at London Airport. To the right of Sir Geoffrey are Mr. Basil Smallpeice, Managing Director of BOAC, Mr. W. E. Nixon. Chairman of De Havilland Holdings Ltd., and the De Havilland Aircraft Co. Ltd., and Mr. Aubrey Burke, Deputy Chairman and Managing Director. Mr. A. S. Kennedy, De Havilland Financial Director, is between Sir Gerard and Sir Geoffrey. On the left are Sir George Cribbett, Deputy Chairman of BOAC, Mr. John Cunningham, De Havilland Chief Test Pilot, and Mr. C. T. Wilkins, De Havilland Chief Designer. *(both DH Hatfield)*

Comet 4B. The first Comet 4C, G-AOVU, flew at Hatfield on 31 October 1959 piloted by W. P. I. Fillingham and by May 1960 orders had been received for 50 Comet 4s, 4Bs and 4Cs. In addition to the Hatfield- and Chester-built specimens already mentioned, three Comet 4s were delivered to the East African Airways Corporation; seven Comet 4Cs to United Arab Airlines for services from Cairo to Beirut and London; and four others to Middle East Airlines for routes radiating from Beirut to Europe and India. Guest Aerovias also operated two Comet 4Cs on lease

from Mexicana.

In September 1960 an increase in all-up weight to 160,000 pounds was authorised for Comet 4s and 4Cs, which from that time onwards were fitted with the 4B stub wing which eliminated the tare weight penalty and so increased the range to 3,225 miles. During the 1961 SBAC Show, orders were received for a Comet 4C for the personal use of King Ibn Saud of Saudi Arabia and for five Comet C. Mk. 4s for RAF Transport Command. Equipped with 94 rearwards- facing seats, but easily convertible for ambulance duties to carry

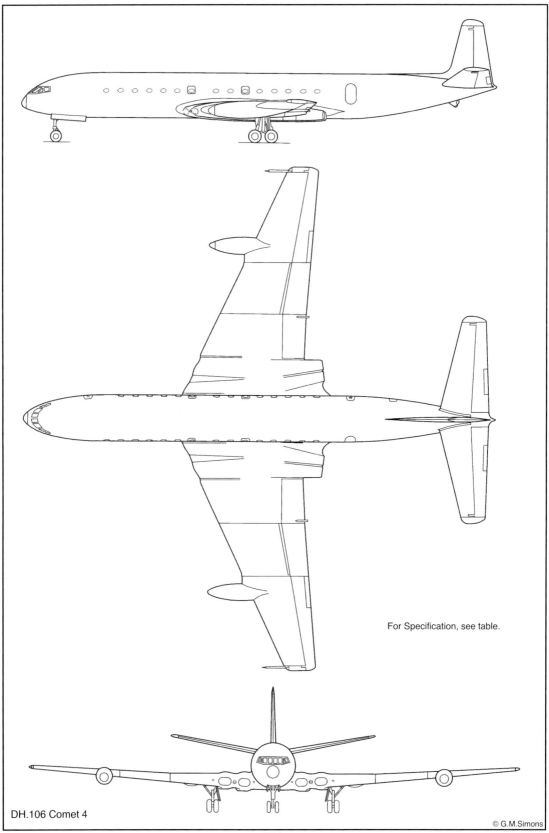

For Specification, see table.

DH.106 Comet 4

Kuwait Airways' 9K-ACE seen in flight. *(BAe Hatfield)*

twelve stretchers, 47 sitting cases and six sick berth attendants, the first Comet C. Mk. 4 XR395 made its maiden Chester-Hatfield flight on 15 November 1961.

Plans were also in hand for a further development of the Comet 4 as a new jet for BOAC. This was the Comet 5, of which BOAC appeared to be initially in favour. A number of studies were made, one of which was for a stretched Comet 4 with an all-up-weight of 226,000 pounds powered by four Rolls-Royce Conway 10 engines of 16,000 pounds thrust each. These were to be mounted in the wing as with the earlier machines, which now had a sweepback at one quarter chord of thirty degrees and also featured a swept fin.

Seating would have been for 105 passengers and the maximum cruising speed would have been 563 mph at 30,000 feet, Development costs were put at

DH.106 Comet 5 design sketch

© G.M.Simons

beween 8 and 10 million pounds and the company went on record saying that it needed orders of at least thirty aircraft in order to proceed. The airliner would have been available for delivery in 1962/3. BOAC tentatively suggested that they might be interested in around twenty but their interest soon waned, and the project was stillborn.

As a contribution to future developments in commercial aviation and to make ready for the entry into service of the DH.121 Trident and the Vickers VC10, Comet 3B G-ANLO, now XP915, joined the RAE at Bedford on 21 June 1961 for use by the Blind Landing Experimental Unit and the aerodynamics department. Comet 2E G-AMXK was also used at Hatfield by Smiths Aircraft Instruments Ltd. for development work on their own automatic landing system. On 18 November 1966 it was delivered to the RAE Bedford for further trials as XV144.

The last Comet service out of Heathrow, flown by Sudan Airways on 11 November 1972, heralded the decline of the type as a major transport. Hawker Siddeley Dynamics' test bed XM823, once G-APAS, flew to Colerne in May 1973 for preservation and the 51 Squadron C. Mk. 2s became instructional airframes at St. Athan, Halton, Cosford and Topcliffe. XK697, once G-AMXJ, went to the Wyton Air Scouts as a clubroom and XK695/G-AMXC, flew to Ringway on 13 May 1974 to be dismantled and re-erected near the Manchester Ship Canal as a café. Comet 3 XP915/G-ANLO was used at the RAE Bedford for non-flying runway foam arresting tests in 1973 but on 22 August was despatched by road to Woodford as an additional Nimrod trial installation airframe.

To increase its spares backing, Dan-Air Services Ltd, which already operated a considerable number of Comets, acquired East African Comet 4s 5H-AAF, 5X-AAO and 5Y-AAA, which were flown from Nairobi and dismantled at Lasham in 1971. Aerolineas Argentina's LV-AHN and 'HS met the same fate after their arrival in December that year, followed by Middle East Airlines' Comet 4C OD-ADT, ferried via Gatwick on 3 October 1973. Mexicana's Comet 4 XA-NAP, once XA-NAZ/G-APDR, flew back to Stansted via Goose Bay on 25 June 1971 as spares for Channel Airways Ltd. and went to the Fire school when the company ceased operations in 1972. Channel's ex-Greek Comet 4Bs, G-APYD and 'ZM, were sold to Dan-Air which acquired others from BEA Airtours.

Overseas, the former RCAF Comet 1XB, N373S,

and the AREA Comet 4 HC-ALT, once G-APDI, were derelict at Miami in September 1973, but Mexicana's newer Comet 4Cs XA-NAR, 'AS and 'AT, were acquired by Westernaire Inc. and flown to Albuquerque, New Mexico in May 1973 as N888WA, N999WA and N777WA.

When the last Airtours Comet service, flown by G-ARJL, landed at Gatwick from Paris on 31 October 1973, Dan-Air became the only major Comet operator, with 11 Mk. 4Bs in 109 seat configuration and three Mk. 4Cs. Their Mk. 4s were withdrawn progressively, the last Comet 4 service being flown Newcastle-Alicante-Teesside by G-APDB on 13 November 1973.

A landmark event occurred on 12 February 1974 when G-APDB was delivered from Lasham to Duxford the home of the famous aviation museum. Delta Bravo was the second aircraft off the Comet 4 production line and, when it entered service with BOAC, was the first of the Comet aircraft to fly the Atlantic. By the time it had completed its service with Dan-Air, it had flown 36,268 hours with 15,733 landings. Tom Walters, who had flown DB in its earlier years with BOAC and was now the Chief Training Captain on the Dan-Air Comet fleet, took the aircraft from Lasham to Duxford via Hatfield, where the aircraft was built. Here he made two low passes down the runway in a final salute before flying on to Duxford. The aircraft was then handed over to the safe keeping of the East Anglian Aviation Society. Dan-Air

retained the title to the aircraft but the Society had undertaken to maintain it in good condition and to keep it in Dan-Air's livery. The aircraft is still there to this day, although the Imperial War Museum has now taken over the responsibility for the Museum; they have also put it back into BOAC colours, despite the original agreement.

After the defence cuts in 1975, the five Comet C. Mk. 4s of 216 Squadron, XR395 to XR399, were delivered from Leconfield to Lasham for Dan-Air and put into commercial use as Comet 4Cs G-BDIT to 'IX.

Further to implement its policy of flying Comets as a long-term operation, the company also bought up Sudan Airways' Comet 4Cs ST-AAW (which had been in long-term storage at Teesside) and ST-AAX; as well as the former Egyptair 4Cs SU-ALM, 'MV and 'NC. These were re-registered as G-ASDZ, G-BDIF, G-BEEX, 'EY and 'EZ respectively. Most were ferried into Lasham, where they languished for a while, donating items every now and then to keep the others flying. Eventually, almost all were broken up.

By the mid- 1970s the Comet was beginning to reach the end of its useful life. Nevertheless, it says much for the skills and expertise of the engineers at Lasham, for they obtained a contract from the Ministry of Defence to partially modify one of the fleet, G-APDP, into a test-bed aircraft for the Nimrod Airborne Early Warning (AEW) machine. This aircraft, now serialled XX944, was delivered to the Royal Aircraft

The Comet 4 paint shop. Here are aircraft for Aerolineas Argentinas, BEA, Mexicana and Middle East Airlines (MEA)

G-APYC - later to be registered SX-DAK *Queen Frederica* - is seen on a pre-delivery test flight. *(DH via BAe Hatfield)*

Establishment at Bedford during June 1973.

These newer acquisitions were brought up to civil standards by the engineers at Lasham and quickly placed into service along with three ex-Egyptair machines, allowing some of the earlier aircraft to be retired. With the so-called fuel crisis it could be expected that the Comet would be retired in favour of more economic aircraft, but with the book value written down to practically zero and adequate spares backing available, the type still retained its appeal to the airline. It says much for the passenger appeal of the Comet to the public and the part the aircraft played in the story of the airline that one source quotes that during the 1979 IT season, 30% of all British holiday-makers carried overseas used Dan-Air Comets!

As the Comet became increasingly more expensive to operate Dan-Air gradually started replacing Comets with other newer types such as Boeing 727s. 1980 became the last Comet season with four ex-RAF machines maintaining passenger services, until most finally retired in late October.

Captain Arthur Larkman was Operatons Director

for Dan-Air: *'We were forced to end our Comet flights as operating costs were now prohibitive. Some 'last flights' on the Comet were advertised and were quickly filled. The final commercial flight was on a 4C, 'India Whisky', on 9 November 1980, which was chartered by a group of enthusiasts. The aircraft was commanded by Captain John Kelly, with Captain Simon Searle as Co-pilot and Gordon Moores the flight engineer. Val Barnett, the Fleet Stewardess and my daughter Sue, who was a Comet Number One, were in charge of the cabin crew.*

Flight number DA8874 had been chartered by John Hunt of Ian Allan Ltd. Before moving, John had been reservations manager with Dan-Air and was determined that the Comet was to go out in a blaze of glory. 119 passengers boarded with others waiting up to seven hours for the possibility of a standby seat! The aircraft made low flypasts of the airfields at Lyneham, Heathrow and Brize Norton before landing back at Gatwick.

Thus the era of Dan-Air's Comets passed, but a commercial concern could not become sentimental. The Comet design had come to a premature twilight of its years as a fuel thirsty and expensive-to-operate jet, so it was time again to consider the future. With the demise, someone within the Company calculated that during the fleet's life, the legendary Comet had flown a

Above: Comet SU-ALD, part of the United Arab Airline conglomorate, with Misrair titles.

Right: Mexicana's XA-NAS poses for De Havilland's flight test department's staff photographers. *(Both DH via BAe Hatfield)*

267

C.4 XR399 of 216 Squadron. The early colour scheme was for a highly polished underside, but this was later replaced with light grey paint when polishing was found to damage the skin. *(BAe Hatfield)*

total of some 238,000 hours in Dan-Air service, which equated to a distance of 95,400,000 miles!

Nimrod - the Mighty Hunter!

The search for an aircraft to replace the fleet of Avro Shackletons in what was then RAF Coastal Command began with objectives set out in Air Staff Requirement 381 during 1958, which laid out six tasks, of which the most important was the ASW role — to detect, fix and destroy submarines either on the surface or submerged, and whether conventional or nuclear. The others included search and rescue, wide-area surveillance, detecting and shadowing enemy surface units and forces, with the ability to make limited air-to-surface strikes against individual vessels, and trooping in case of emergency.

The required performance called for an aircraft having a large fuselage capacity, a long range/endurance, a high maximum speed in order to be able to reach search areas far off-shore in the minimum time and good handling and 'ride' characteristics at low speed and altitude during the search. As with any other aircraft design exercise, meeting these requirements called for an assessment of possible trade-offs and decisions on the precise points at which to pitch compromises, and Hawker Siddeley set about a series of design feasibility studies. As the Manchester Division (originally Avro) had been

responsible for the Shackleton, the design activity for ASR381 was naturally centred there.

The deciding factor became the ability of the aircraft to survive the failure of one of the engines. Calculations showed that a version of the Comet re-engined with the then new Spey turbofans in place of the original Avon 500s would normally start its patrol at a weight at which a positive rate of climb could be maintained on two engines, and in the course of a long patrol this would go down to the point where climb away on one engine would be possible.

Thus, it was possible to suggest an operational procedure in which the aircraft made a high speed dash to the search area on all engines, and then stopped one engine and retained a second at flight idle power for immediate response in the event of failure of one of the other two engines. Then, when the critical weight for single-engined climb was reached, the 'flight idle' engine could also be stopped, both engines being re-started for the high speed cruise back to base.

The Comet was suited to this kind of operational procedure, since the engine location was close inboard in the wing roots and few problems arose in the case of asymmetric power. The relatively low wing loading of the Comet represented a good compromise between the needs of high-speed cruise and low-speed search, and it had the added, somewhat fortuitous, advantage of providing a comfortable ride and good

G-BDIT - the former RAF C.4 XR395 climbs out after maintenance at Dan-Air's Lasham facility. The aircraft is in the final Dan-Air scheme worn by the Comets. *(Kurt Lang)*

Three RAE Comets in formation on 4 April 1972. *(DH via BAe Hatfield)*

controllability at low speeds and altitudes. Its size was adequate for the mission requirements of crew, equipment and weapon load and the aircraft fitted into available RAF airfields without any problem. The Spey engine could be installed in place of the Avons with only the minimum of engineering changes.

De Havillands were bought by Hawker Siddeley in 1960, but kept as a separate company until 1963. It became the the de Havilland Division of Hawker Siddeley Aviation and all types in production or development changed their designations from 'DH' to 'HS'.

With the Manchester design office designation HS.801, the maritime Comet took shape during 1964. The version of the Spey adopted was a military equivalent of the civil Spey 25 used in the BAC One-

Eleven and Trident, the principal modifications being concerned with anti-corrosion treatment for operation in a salt-laden atmosphere, the elimination of some magnesium components for the same reason, and a change in the accessory gearbox to drive the larger alternators needed for the extensive avionic fit in the aircraft. The increased mass flow of the Spey over that of the Avon resulted in larger air intakes and exhausts being required.

The basic structure of the Comet was retained for the maritime version, and the problem of how the weapons could be accommodated in an airliner was elegantly solved by adding an un-pressurised ventral pannier for almost the whole length of the fuselage, fairing forward and upward round the nose to provide

XW626, the former BOAC G-APDS - nicknamed by some as the 'ComRod - after modification at Woodford for Nimrod AEW.3 test work. It is seen here on final approach to RAE Farnborough. *(BAe Hatfield)*

DH.106 Powerplants	
Mark number	Engine
Comet 1:	four 4,450 pounds static thrust De Havilland Ghost 50 Mk.1
Comet 1A:	four 5,000 pounds static thrust De Havilland Ghost 50 Mk.2
Comet 1XB:	four 5,500 pounds static thrust De Havilland Ghost 50 Mk.4
Comet 2:	four 7,300 pounds static thrust Rolls Royce Avon 503
	four 7,300 pounds static thrust Rolls Royce Avon 118
Comet 2E	two 7,330 pounds static thrust Rolls Royce Avon 504 and
	two 10,500 pounds static thrust Rolls Royce Avon 524
Comet 2X:	four 6,600 pounds static thrust Rolls Royce Avon 502
Comet C.Mk.2:	four 7,300 pounds static thrust Rolls Royce Avon 117
Comet 3	four 10,000 pounds static thrust Rolls Royce Avon 502
	four 10,000 pounds static thrust Rolls Royce Avon 523
Comet 4 and 4B:	four 10,500 pounds static thrust Rolls Royce Avon 524
Comet 4C:	four 10,500 pounds static thrust Rolls Royce Avon 525B
Comet C.Mk.4:	four 10,500 pounds static thrust Rolls Royce Avon 350

a housing for the ASV 21 radar scanner. The basis for the HS 801 design was the Comet 4C, this being the final version of the commercial jetliner, but the fuselage length reverted to that of the earlier Comet 4, which was six feet shorter. Most of the fuselage windows were eliminated, and the size of the pilots' windscreens was increased, with the addition also of an eyebrow window each side.

Magnetic Anomaly Detection (MAD) equipment was provided in a conventional 'sting' fairing at the rear of the aircraft, and Electronic Countermeasure - also called Electronic Support Measures - was located in a fairing on top of the fin. The extra side area of the weapons bay pannier had an adverse effect on directional control, so a small dorsal fin was designed for the maritime Comet - that was increased to have a

larger area after prototype flight testing. The starboard pinion tank, a feature of the original Comet 4, provided a convenient housing for a 70-million candlepower Strong Electric searchlight, controlled directionally by joy-stick at the co-pilot station, and two wing strong points were introduced to allow for the carriage of air-to-surface missiles on pylons. With the gross weight increased from the Comet 4C's 162,000 pounds to a maximum of 177,500 pounds, a stronger undercarriage was called for, and a Rover APU was provided for engine-starting. The entire cabin was, of course, laid out for the maritime role.

By the end of 1964 the maritime Comet was the favoured solution to ASR381, and in June 1965 its selection as a Shackleton replacement was formally confirmed when an Instruction To Proceed was issued

DH.106 Comet Specifications				
	Comet 1	Comet 1A	Comet 2	Comet 3
Span:	115 feet 0 inches	115 feet 0 inches	115 feet 0 inches	115 feet 0 inches
Length:	93 feet 0 inches	93 feet 0 inches	96 feet 0 inches	111 feet 0 inches
Height:	28 feet 4 inches	28 feet 4 inches	28 feet 4 inches	28 feet 6 inches
Wing area:	2,015 square feet	2,015 square feet	2,015 square feet	2,121 square feet
AUW:	107,000 pounds*	115,000 pounds**	120,000 pounds***	145,000 pounds
Cruise:	490 mph	475 mph	490 mph	500 mph
Cruise Altitude:	35,000 feet	40,000 feet	40,000 feet	40,000 feet
Max stage length with full pax load:	1,750 miles	1,750 miles	2,100 miles	2,500 miles
Passengers:	36-44	36-44	36-44	58-78

lower passenger figure represents all First Class, the higher alternative all Tourist Class seating
* G-ALVG 102,000 pounds, G-ALZK 105,000 pounds **Comet 1XB 117,000 pounds ***Comet 2X 108,000 pounds

	Comet 4	Comet 4A	Comet 4B	Comet 4C
Span:	114 feet 10 inches	107 feet 10 inches	107 feet 10 inches	114 feet 10 inches
Length:	114 feet 6 inches	114 feet 1 inches	118 feet 0 inches	118 feet 0 inches
Height:	28 feet 6 inches	28 feet 6 inches	28 feet 6 inches	28 feet 6 inches
Wing area:	2,121 square feet	2,059 square feet	2,059 square feet	2,121 square feet
AUW:	160,000 pounds	152,500 pounds	2,059 square feet	2,121 square feet
Cruise:	503 mph	522 mph	532 mph	503 mph
Cruise Altitude:	42,000 feet	23,500 feet	23,500 feet	39,000 feet
Stage length with full pax load:	3,225 miles	2,730 miles	2,500 miles	2,650 miles
Passengers:	60-81	70-92	72-101	72-101

lower passenger figure represents all First Class, the higher alternative all Tourist Class seating (Dan-Air fitted more)

to Hawker Siddeley. The requirement was for thirty-eight aircraft, plus two prototypes which were to be converted from Comet airframes. This was a convenient arrangement, not only because an extremely tight schedule was established by the RAF to achieve an Initial Operational Capability only forty-eight months from the instruction to proceed, but also because two Comet 4C airframes remained unsold from the Chester production line, where the jigs were still intact although commercial orders had dried up with the delivery of the 75th Comet 4. While these jigs were being refurbished and the final assembly line for the HS801 was being set up at Woodford, Cheshire, modification of these two Comets proceeded at Chester.

Thus started the story of the Nimrod, which, having the 'HS' appelation, is to be told elsewhere.

DH.107

This type number was not used, in order to avoid confusion with the Handley-Page HP.107 project, which itself was never proceeded with.

DH.108

The DH.108 was a single seat research aircraft without horizontal tail surfaces built to investigate the behaviour of swept wings and to provide basic data for the DH.106 Comet jet transport and the DH.110 fighter. Design work began in October 1945 and three prototypes were built to Specification E.I 8/45 using standard fuselages taken from Vampire production.

A completely new wing was attached to the existing pick-up points and was of all metal construction with a moderate sweep back of 43 degrees and was 15% greater in area than that of the Vampire. Control was obtained by using a conventional rudder in conjunction with elevons which combined the duties of elevator and ailerons and were fitted outboard of the split trailing edge flaps.

The first prototype, TG283, was completed in the spring of 1946 and although the Under Secretary of the Ministry of Supply referred to it as the Swallow, it was not the maker's practice to bestow names on research aeroplanes, and the DH.108 was no exception. After completion at Hatfield, TG283 was taken by road to Woodbridge, Suffolk, where on 15 May 1946 Geoffrey de Havilland Jnr. made a few preliminary hops on the 3,500 yard emergency runway and afterwards made a normal take off and uneventful first flight of 30 minutes duration.

Previously RAE Farnborough had warned the design team led by Mr. Ronald E. Bishop of the possibility of dutch rolling, or dropping a wing with complete loss of control at low speeds, in aircraft of this configuration. The DH.108 was therefore, fitted with Handley Page slots fixed in the open position, and anti-spin parachutes in cylindrical containers at each wingtip. As it turned out, none of these problems

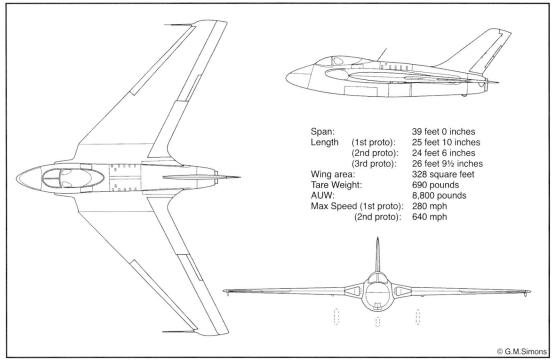

Span:		39 feet 0 inches
Length	(1st proto):	25 feet 10 inches
	(2nd proto):	24 feet 6 inches
	(3rd proto):	26 feet 9½ inches
Wing area:		328 square feet
Tare Weight:		690 pounds
AUW:		8,800 pounds
Max Speed (1st proto):		280 mph
	(2nd proto):	640 mph

© G.M.Simons

TG283, the first prototype DH.108, seen at Hatfield on 30 May 1946. The aircraft had fixed Handley Page leading edge slots ands anti-spin parachutes on its wingtips. *(author's collection)*

developed, and the pilot even succeeded in flying slowly enough to formate on a Dove and to pose alongside a Proctor for air to air photography. Later, Geoffrey Jnr flew to Hatfield to indulge in dog fights with a Mosquito.

Starting on 16 September 1948 TG283 made several test flights with dihedral on the wing, but this was soon removed and when full trials were complete and the aerodynamic characteristics of the swept wing had been fully investigated, the aircraft was transferred to the RAE Farnborough in October 1948. Here it continued stability, control and landing trials which led to the fitting of a long stroke Sea Vampire undercarriage. Landings at higher angles of attack without risk of striking the tail pipe on the runway were made in February 1950 at a much reduced touch-down speed of 95 knots. Sadly, the career of this machine ended in

a crash at Hartley Wintney during stalling trials on 1 May 1950, Squadron Leader George E. C. Genders AFC DFM being killed.

The first DH.108 was built as a subsonic aircraft solely for the purpose of solving swept wing control problems, but the second prototype, TG306, was a much modified and potentially supersonic version built to assess the high speed characteristics of such a wing. It was therefore fitted with Handley Page automatic slots which could be locked by the pilot, powered flying controls of the type to be fitted to the Comet and sweep back increased to 45 degrees.

Above: TG306, the second DH.108, showing the modified canopy. Below: By comparasion, VW120, the third machine, with a modified nose and better cockpit streamlining. *(Both DH via BAe Hatfield)*

WV120 shows off its undersides.
(author's collection)

The mainplane was again attached to a standard Vampire fuselage but during construction the airframe was fitted with all the necessary cables and pipe lines for the installation of full automatic recording instrumentation. A boosted engine known as the Goblin 3 was installed and the aircraft flew for the first time at Hatfield on 23 August 1946 and quickly attained true level speeds above the 616 m.p.h. of the World's absolute speed record. Geoffrey de Havilland gave a polished display of aerobatics in this aircraft at the Radlett SBAC Show on 12/13 September after which the machine was prepared for an attempt on the record over the official course near Tangmere.

Geoffrey Jnr left Hatfield on 27 September with the intention of making a high speed practice flight low down over the Thames Estuary after a dive from 10,000 feet. Twenty minutes later eye witnesses saw the aircraft break into several large pieces and fall into Egypt Bay, northeast of Gravesend, Kent. Nearly all the wreckage was recovered, including the engine, which examination showed not to have been at fault. The subsequent enquiry established that the structure had failed under the very great loads experienced at air speeds in the region of Mach 0.9.

Previous trials with TG306 had shown that a much improved performance could be obtained if the pilot's seat was lowered, the canopy redesigned and an elongated and more pointed nose fitted. After trials with a revised nose on Vampire TG281, a third and DH.108 was similarly equipped and fitted with an even more powerful Goblin 4.

Serialled VW120, it first flew at Hatfield on 24 July 1947 in the hands of John Cunningham, who succeeded Geoffrey de Havilland Jnr as chief test pilot and continued the research flying until, a year later, enough data had been compiled for the aircraft to be spared for an attempt on the 100 km. International Closed-circuit speed record.

Entered jointly by the manufacturers and the owners, the Ministry of Supply, and piloted by John Derry, VW120 lapped the pentagonal course near Hatfield on the evening of 12 April 1948 to set up a new record speed of 605.23 m.p.h. The same aircraft and pilot exceeded the speed of sound in the UK for the first time on 9 September during a 41 minutes flight when Derry climbed on oxygen to 40,000 feet and exceeded Mach 1 in a dive to 30,000 feet. Two days later he gave a demonstration of aerobatics at the SBAC Show at Farnborough and on 1 August 1949 took VW120 to Elmdon for the SBAC Challenge Trophy Race in which it had been entered by Sir Geoffrey de Havilland. In poor weather conditions he lapped the short course at 488 m.p.h. but was unable to overtake either John Cunningham's Vampire 3 VV190 or T. S. Wade's Hawker P. 1040 VP401.

Not long after this, the aircraft was handed over to the Ministry of Supply and went to RAE Farnborough where it joined the original slow speed prototype. Its career ended on 15 February 1950 in a crash that killed the pilot, Squadron Leader John Stewart Rowland Muller-Rowland DSO, DFC.

The test flight was supposed to examine the effects of change from sub-sonic to transonic flight, but the aircraft is thought to have broken up whilst in a dive. The inquest into Muller-Rowland's death was opened two days later by North Bucks Coroner, Mr E T Ray, at Bletchley. Witnesses told of hearing an explosion. Some wreckage came down at Little Brickhill, while the cockpit came down near Bow Brickhill church. Other pieces were found as far away as Husborne Crawley. Muller-Rowland's body was found near Sandy Lane, between Bow Brickhill and Woburn Lane. Because of the secrecy of the aircraft the local police sealed the area to keep the public away, and after the crash police officers visited local schools to appeal for any 'souvenirs' to be returned. It was thought that the accident was due to a failure of the pilot's oxygen supply.

DH.109

This type number was not used, but was intended to apply to a Naval strike aircraft built to Specification N.8/49

DH.110 Sea Vixen

The DH.110 design was first proposed in 1946 as a later generation naval all-weather fighter and was the final and largest development of the Vampire-Venom theme. It was also amended to meet an advanced RAF night fighter requirement but detail design and construction did not start until 1948 when the Air Ministry issued a Specification for an transonic, two seat, all-weather fighter similar to the DH.110 design and ordered two prototypes. These were built at Hatfield under the direction of J. P. Smith.

It was to be a stressed skin, twin boom monoplane with the swept wing that had been aerodynamically proven on the DH.108. The machine was equipped with powered controls incorporating 'a feel' an artificially created 'force feedback' to produce an opposition to the pilot's movement of the controls that was proportional to ther aerodynamic loads acting on the control surfaces. The aircraft was armed with four 30 mm. Aden guns and powered by two Rolls-Royce Avon engines side by side in the rear of the fuselage nacelle. The pilot's cockpit was offset to port to provide sufficient working space for a radar operator below and behind on the starboard side. Radar equipment included a hydraulically driven scanner in a fibre-glass radome in the nose.

The first prototype, WG236, flew for forty-six minutes at Hatfield on 26 September 1951 piloted by John Cunningham and first exceeded the speed of sound in a shallow dive on 9 April 1952.

WG240, the second prototype, flew on 25 July of that year but on 6 September John Derry and his flight test observer Tony Richards were killed when WG236 broke up during demonstrations at the Farnborough SBAC Show. WG240 did not fly again until 11 June 1954 after modifications which included an all moving tailplane, cambered leading edge extensions outboard of the wing fences and reduced ventral fin area.

WG236, the first prototype DH.110, is seen at Hatfield. *(DH via BAe Hatfield)*

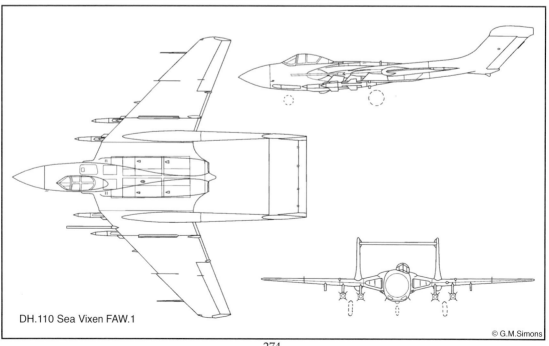

DH.110 Sea Vixen FAW.1

© G.M.Simons

XF828, the semi-navalised prototype, in flight, now fitted with a nose-mounted instrument probe. *(DH via BAe*

The RAF passed the DH.110 over in favour of the Gloster Javelin but the Royal Navy decided to abandon Sea Venom modernisation in favour of the larger twin engined DH.110, re-worked to naval standards. This involved an 80 % redesign at Christchurch under the direction of William A. Tamblin AFRAeS AMINA. and included the provision of arrester hooks, hydraulic nosewheel steering, power folding wings and long stroke undercarriage. The Aden guns were removed.

An order was placed by the Ministry of Supply in February 1955 for three pre-production development aircraft and a contract signed for an initial, but substantial, Admiralty production batch. A further contract was awarded in June 1959 followed by a repeat order on 25 August 1960. The first Ministry of Supply aircraft, the intermediate, fixed wing, semi-navalised prototype XF828, designated Sea Vixen Mk. 20X, flew at Christchurch piloted by Lt. Cdr. J. Elliot on 20 June 1955. He had already made touch-and-go landings on HMS *Albion* in the second prototype, WG240, fitted with long travel oleos on 23 September 1954 and the first arrested deck landing by XF828 was made on HMS *Ark Royal* on 5 April 1956.

Production Sea Vixen F.A.W.ls were assembled at Christchurch using undercarriage units built by De Havilland Propellers Ltd., radomes made at Hatfield and stub and extension wings sub-contracted by Folland Aircraft Ltd., Hamble and De Havilland's Portsmouth factory. At the time they were the heaviest aircraft ever to enter British naval service and had performance and armament equal to any contemporary land based fighter. They were also the first British interceptors to dispense with guns and in the all-weather fighter role were equipped with Ferranti pilot attack sight and armed with four De Havilland Firestreak infra-red homing missiles and twenty-eight two-inch air-to-air rockets stowed in two retractable fuselage containers.

For alternative strike/reconnaissance duties the Firestreaks were interchangeable with four 500 pound or two 1,000 pound pylon-mounted bombs, or alternatively clusters of six three-inch air-to-surface rockets, packs of 124 two-inch air-to-air rockets or drop tanks.

XJ474, the first production Sea Vixen F.A.W.l, flew at Christchurch on 20 March 1957 and together with XJ475 took part in trials at Boscombe Down, RAE Bedford and at sea in HMS *Ark Royal*. They also made 166 deck landings on HMS *Centaur*.

In November 1957 700 Squadron, 'Y' Flight, of the Service Trials Unit began a working up programme with early production Sea Vixens which included three weeks in HMS *Victorious* during which three Sea Vixens made 172 deck arrested landings, 23 at night.

On 2 July 1959, 892 Squadron, the first Sea Vixen unit, was formed at Yeovilton around the crews and

XF828, the semi-navalised prototype, is seen at on the runway at Farnborough in 1955. *(DH via BAe Hatfield)*

XP924 was originally an FAW.2 and served with 899 NAS before being retired from frontline service and converted to a D.3 standard as a drone aircraft.

1963 at XP918, the 119th aircraft. It was superseded by the F.A.W. Mk. 2 which, in addition to the retractable rocket packs, carried four Red Top infra-red homing missiles on pylons under the wings or, alternatively, four Bullpup air-to-surface missiles for ground strafing. They were recognised by the deepened tail booms which extended forward of the wing to house additional fuel.

Twenty-nine Sea Vixen F.A.W. Mk. 2s were built and the first entered service in July 1964 with 899 Squadron, the Initial Training Unit for the type. The squadron sailed for the Far East in HMS *Eagle* in December that year and during the Aden withdrawal in 1967 one of its Sea Vixens, carrying the British flag, was the last aircraft to leave. It re-embarked with 14 Sea Vixen F.A.W. Mk. 2s in October 1970 but was disbanded in February 1972.

Main training was provided by the Naval Air Fighter School, Yeovilton, formerly 766 Squadron. Its first F.A.W. Mk. 2, XS582, arrived on 7 July 1965 and two months later it received XJ580, first of a number of the earlier mark converted to F.A.W. Mk. 2 standard.

In the flying tanker role Sea Vixens F.A.W. Mk. 2s of 892 Squadron, flown off HMS *Hermes* off Cyprus in 1967, refuelled B.A.C. Lightning F. Mk. 3 fighters of 56 Squadron during local defence exercises. Six of 892's F.A.W. Mk. 2s provided the Navy's aerobatics at the

aircraft of 700 Squadron. They embarked in HMS *Ark Royal* during a voyage from Devonport to Gibraltar in February 1960, and returned the 1,000 miles nonstop to Yeovilton in 1 hour 54 minutes on 18 June to attend the Naval Air Day display with two other Sea Vixen squadrons, 766 and 890, the latter from HMS *Hermes.*

All Sea Venom squadrons, including 893 and 899 at Yeovilton, were re-equipped with Sea Vixens. A further development was the manufacture by Flight Refuelling Ltd. of the Mk. 20 underwing drogue type refuelling pack to enable a tanker Sea Vixen to refuel another by the 'Buddy System'. Trials were made at Hatfield by test pilots Chris Capper and Peter Barlow, and in May 1961 a Sea Vixen remained airborne eight hours two minutes using this system.

Australia had also shown an interest in the type and two crated examples were despatched by SS *Ballerat* in June 1960 to RAAF Edinburgh near Adelaide.

Production of the Sea Vixen F.A.W. Mk. 1 ended in

Two Sea Vixen FAW.1 (XJ571 & XN694) of 899 Sqn, one refuelling the other at a Farnborough Air Show. *(author's collection)*

	DH.110 Powerplants		
Mark number	Engine		
DH.110	two Rolls-Royce Avon		
Sea Vixen FAW1 and 2	two 10,0000 pounds static thrust Rolls-Royce Avon 208		

DH.110 Specifications

Mark:	DH.110	Sea Vixem FAW.1 Sea Vixen FAW.2
Span:	50 feet 0 inches	50 feet 0 inches
Length:	52 feet 1½ inches	55 feet 7 inches
Height:	10 feet 9 inches	10 feet 9 inches
Wing area:	648 square feet	648 square feet
AUW:	-	35,000 pounds FAW.1
		37,000 pounds FAW.2
Max Speed:	-	645 mph FAW.1
		640 mph FAW.2
Ceiling:	-	48,000 feet

Farnborough Show in September 1968.

Twelve Sea Vixen F.A.W. Mk. 2s of 893 Squadron, detached from RNAS Yeovilton for ten days to take part in the 1968 Cyprus defence exercises, flew nonstop to RAF Akrotiri with refuelling from RAF Victor tankers en route. The distance, 2,200 miles, was the longest range achieved by the Sea Vixen or by a whole squadron of naval aircraft.

By 1970 some of 890 Squadron's aircraft were in use by Airwork Ltd., operators of the Fleet Requirements at Yeovilton.

A small number of Sea Vixens subsequently saw service in the less glamorous role of drones, being redesignated Sea Vixen D.3. Only four were converted to the D.3 standard, though three more were sent to Farnborough but not converted.

DH.111

The DH.111 was a design project that is surrounded by confusion. It was most certainly a design to compete in Specification B.35/46, in response to Operational Requirement OR.229. From that point the confusion starts. Some sources say it was a four engine swept-wing jet medium bomber with a cruising speed of 500 kt and a ceiling of at least 55,000 feet. Other sources say it was a heavy bomber design based on DH.106 Comet Even more sources record that the designation was not used to avoid confusion with the Handley Page HP.111.

DH.112 Venom/Sea Venom

The DH.112 was a high performance, single seat fighter-bomber developed from the Vampire to make best use of the high thrust of the Ghost jet engine. Originally known as the Vampire F.B. Mk. 8, it was an entirely new design having a thinner aerofoil section wing with sweep back only on the leading edge which permitted speeds closer to Mach One.

The seventy-five gallon jettisonable fuel tanks on the wing tips were the first to be fitted to an RAF fighter, wind tunnel tests demonstrating that this was more efficient than pylon-mounted tanks at half span.

The first prototype Venom, VV612, first flew at Hatfield on 2 September 1949, and after trials the type went into large scale production at Chester and by the Fairey Aviation Co. Ltd. at Ringway as replacement for the Vampire FB. Mk. 5 to Air Ministry Specification 15/49. A scheme for building 160 Venom FB. Mk. Is starting with WL892, by the Bristol Aeroplane Co. Ltd. at Filton, was abandoned.

The armament consisted of four 20 mm. British Hispano Mk. 5 cannons in the nose and 2,000 pounds of bombs or eight 60 pound rocket projectiles on racks under the wing. Wing fences were fitted to eliminate tip stall on the approach and the first aircraft for the RAF flew in June 1951.

An early production aircraft, WE256, was to have been flown by John Derry in the Jubilee Trophy Race at Hatfield on 23 June but bad weather prevented it showing its paces before the type was issued to squadrons of the Second Allied Tactical Air Force in Germany. Their first experimental operation took place at Wunsdorf in September 1952, but initial teething troubles imposed a number of flight limitations. When these were removed the Venom quickly established a high reputation, not only in the ground attack role but also for its manoeuvrability and climb as a high altitude interceptor, as demonstrated by the first prototype fitted with reheat at the Farnborough Show in September 1952.

During 1954 Venom F.B. Mk. Is re-equipped the Middle East Air Force and in the following year an improved version designated Venom F.B. Mk. 4 was produced. The prototype, WE381, first flew on 29 December 1953 and was fitted with a later mark of

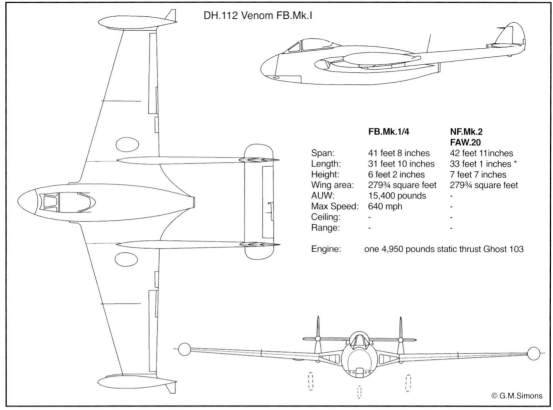

DH.112 Venom FB.Mk.I

	FB.Mk.1/4	NF.Mk.2 FAW.20
Span:	41 feet 8 inches	42 feet 11inches
Length:	31 feet 10 inches	33 feet 1 inches *
Height:	6 feet 2 inches	7 feet 7 inches
Wing area:	279¾ square feet	279¾ square feet
AUW:	15,400 pounds	-
Max Speed:	640 mph	-
Ceiling:	-	-
Range:	-	-
Engine:	one 4,950 pounds static thrust Ghost 103	

© G.M.Simons

Ghost, with hydraulically operated ailerons having artificial feel to give improved control at high Mach numbers. The aircraft also had redesigned tail surfaces with kidney shaped fins and rudders to prevent excessive yaw and possible rudder locking at low air speeds. Late production Venom F.B. Mk. 4s were also equipped with an ejector seat, and replaced the F.B. Mk. 1 in Germany. Venom F.B. Mk. Is of 14 Squadron

RNZAF and F.B. Mk. 4s of 60 Squadron, based at Tengah by the Far East Air Force, were responsible for the air defence of Singapore and made many attacks on Malayan terrorists. One out-dated Venom Mk. 1 was flown at Farnborough in 1955 with R.F.D. high speed target towing equipment in underwing containers.

The intermediate mark numbers were allocated to two seat fighter derivatives built to follow on from the Vampire N.F. Mk. 10. They originated with the private venture Venom Mk. 2 night fighter, G-5-3, first flown at Hatfield on 22 August 1950 and demonstrated by John Derry at the Farnborough Show the following month. It used standard Venom wings and tail booms fitted to a new and wider fuselage

As the *De Havilland Gazette* for February 1954 said *'Venom Fighters of the RAF somewhere in Germany'* (DH via BAe Hatfield)

The prototype Venom N.F. Mk.2 G-5-3 in flight. *(DH via BAe Hatfield)*

accommodating pilot and radar operator side by side for efficient team work, and under the direction of William A. Tamblin was developed at Christchurch into the Venom N.F. Mk. 2 with A.I. radar in an elongated nose.

The first production machines went to 23 Squadron, Coltishall, in 1953, where they made their operational debut in July the following year. Many were modified to Venom N.F. Mk. 2As with the dorsal fins of the Vampire T.Mk.11, clear view canopy and the kidney shaped fins and rudders of the Venom F.B. Mk. 4. The bullet fairings at the intersection of tailplane and fin were transferred to the trailing edge to reduce the tail buffeting at high Mach numbers.

In parallel to the F.B. Mk. 4, the N.F. Mk. 3, first flown on 22 February 1953, had power operated ailerons, a wholly inset tailplane, improved A.I. radar in a completely symmetrical radome, and clear view hinged canopy with power jettison.

Evaluation of de Havilland's Venom 2 prototype G-5-3 by the Royal Navy as WP227 led to the construction at Christchurch of all-weather fighter prototype WK376 to Specification N. 107, strengthened for catapult take off and equipped with deck arrester hook. It was designated Sea Venom N.F. Mk. 20 and made carrier trials from HMS *Illustrious* on 9 July 1951.

The Christchurch design team produced power operated folding wings for the third prototype, WK385. Production aircraft were fitted with an improved canopy which could be jettisoned under water, a fairing on top of the tail pipe to house the arrester hook and small wing tip slats. Designated Venom F.A.W. Mk. 20, the first production aircraft,

WM500, flew on 27 March 1953 and WM567, the 50th and last, on 6 June 1955. Modifications to the RAF's two seat Venoms were applied to the naval version, creating the F.A.W. Mk. 21 with power operated ailerons; a clear view clam shell jettisonable canopy; Martin-Baker Mk. 4 ejection seats; long stroke undercarriage and provision for Rocket Assisted Take-Off Gear (RATOG). The engine was an uprated Ghost 104.

Deliveries started with WM568, first flown on 22 April 1954, and ended with XG680, which flew on 6 June 1957. The next aircraft, XG681, was the first of a later version known as the Venom F.A.W. Mk. 22 with Ghost 105 engine. The final aircraft was XG737.

890 Squadron was re-formed with Sea Venom F.A.W. Mk. 20s at Yeovilton on 20 March 1954 and embarked in a carrier after converting to F.A.W. Mk. 21s, the deck landing trials with which had been made by the Boscombe Down test pilot Commander S. G. Orr on HMS *Albion* in the summer of that year. 809, an existing all-weather squadron, gave up its Sea Hornets for the new equipment and eventually carriers *Albion, Ark Royal* and *Eagle* were all equipped with Sea Venoms, which co-operated with F.B. Mk. 4s from Cyprus in the Anglo-French intervention in Egypt.

On 1 November 1956 they strafed five enemy airfields, destroying 14 aircraft including some MIG 15s and on ensuing

WX787, a production DH.112 Venom NF.Mk.3 with the inset tailplane and dorsal fin. *(DH via BAe Hatfield)*

days attacked airfields, tanks and road convoys all over the Nile Delta.

The Sea Venom was used by 831 Squadron on airborne early warning duties and as it was also one of the few night fighters which could intercept jet bombers such as the Canberra, its crews were provided with pressure breathing waistcoats and modified oxygen equipment. The experimental department at Christchurch under William A. Tamblin equipped Sea Venom Mk. 21 XG663 with blown flaps, using air bled from the compressor of the Ghost engine in 1956. In deck landing trials on *Ark Royal* in April, a reduction of 15 knots in stalling speed was achieved. Later a Venom N.F. Mk. 2 was used in the development of reverse thrust.

Another Venom used for development was F.B. Mk. 4, WL813, piloted by M. P. Kilburn who made the first air firings at Aberporth of the D.H. Firestreak guided missile, destroying a Firefly drone. Service trials of the Firestreak were conducted at Ford by 700 Naval Trials Squadron, one of whose test vehicles was XG607. Royal Navy firing trials began early in December 1958 when three Sea Venom F.A.W. Mk. 21s of 893 Squadron were catapulted off HMS *Victorious* in

the Mediterranean and recorded 80% direct hits on Malta-based Fireflies. While *Victorious* was refitting, these aircraft had been flown to Christchurch for the installation of the Firestreak power supply, control equipment and launching pylons of the type then under development for the DH.110 Sea Vixen.

Such was the Vampire's popularity overseas, export versions were offered under the designations F.B. Mk. 50, N.F. Mk. 51 and N.F. Mk. 52 for the day fighter, night fighter and naval fighter respectively.

A number of F.B. Mk. 50s equipped 6 Squadron of the Royal Iraqi Air Force at Habbaniya in 1955 while 150 F.B. Mk. Is and 100 F.B. Mk. 4s were built by a consortium of three companies in Switzerland for the Swiss Air Force. A scheme for Fiat to build the F.B. Mk. fifty in Italy as the G.81 was shelved and the Italian Air Force received only two British-built machines. In 1956 34 Squadron of the Venezuelan Air Force was equipped with twenty-two British F.B. Mk. 4 Venoms.

The Royal Swedish Air Force Venom received N.F.

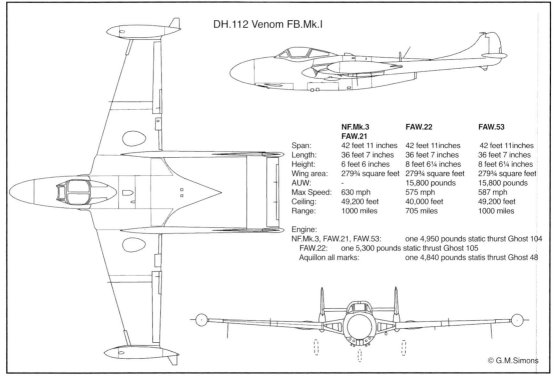

DH.112 Venom FB.Mk.I

	NF.Mk.3 FAW.21	FAW.22	FAW.53
Span:	42 feet 11 inches	42 feet 11inches	42 feet 11inches
Length:	36 feet 7 inches	36 feet 7 inches	36 feet 7 inches
Height:	6 feet 6 inches	8 feet 6¼ inches	8 feet 6¼ inches
Wing area:	279¾ square feet	279¾ square feet	279¾ square feet
AUW:	-	15,800 pounds	15,800 pounds
Max Speed:	630 mph	575 mph	587 mph
Ceiling:	49,200 feet	40,000 feet	49,200 feet
Range:	1000 miles	705 miles	1000 miles

Engine:
NF.Mk.3, FAW.21, FAW.53: one 4,950 pounds static thurst Ghost 104
FAW.22: one 5,300 pounds static thrust Ghost 105
Aquillon all marks: one 4,840 pounds statis thrust Ghost 48

© G.M.Simons

The Swedish type J33, a De Havilland DH 112 Venom Mk 51, belonging to F 1 Hässlö in the air

Mk. 51s (33001-33062) built at Chester and Ringway designated J33 and fitted with Ghost engines built at Trollhatten, Sweden by the Svenska Flygmotor Company and shipped to England for installation. At least four later flew for Svensk Flygtjanst A.B. in civil markings as SE-DCA, 'CD, 'CD and 'CE on military target towing contracts. SE-DCD was subsequently presented to the Air Force Museum at Malmslatt.

Four Sea Venom Mk. 20s were erected in France by S.N.C.A. du Sud-Est and equipped with Fiat-built Ghost 48 engines as S.E. Aquilon 20 prototypes, equivalent to the export Sea Venom Mk. 52 and first flown 20 February 1952. They were followed by the single French-built Aquilon 201, No. 05 F-WGVT, with short stroke undercarriage and ejector seats for catapult trials at the RAE Farnborough in November 1954. Sud-Est built seventy-five Aquilon 202s with long stroke undercarriages, forty single seat Aquilon 203s and the unarmed Aquilon 204 trainer with short stroke undercarriage.

The F.A.W. Mk. 53 built at Christchurch for the Royal Australian Navy differed from the F.A.W. Mk. 21 only in its radar and combat equipment. In one of these, Lt. J. Overbury R.N. accompanied by Lt. Cdr. Kable R.A.N. established a new inter-city record between Rome and Malta on 2 July 1955 at an average speed of 534 m.p.h. The Mk. 53s equipped 808 Squadron R.A.N., formed at Culdrose on 23 August 1955 starting with WZ893. After a working up period over the Channel they embarked for Australia in HMAS *Melbourne* in March 1956 but early in the following year a small defect was found in the wing structure of FAA and RAN Sea Venoms causing a temporary ban on catapulting after which the Australians were based ashore at Nowra, N.S.W.

With the introduction of the DH.110 Sea Vixen in 1960, the Sea Venoms of the Royal Navy were progressively withdrawn from service and hundreds were reduced to scrap at Lossiemouth.

DH.113 Vampire

The DH.113 design was a Vampire 5 fitted with a two-seat cockpit similar to that of a Mosquito and powered by a Goblin 3 turbojet. Such grafting, made possible by the similarity in diameters of the Vampire nacelle and the Mosquito fuselage, provided accommodation for pilot and radar operator side by side in a lengthened nose carrying A.I. Mk. 10 radar.

Two prototypes G-5-2 and G-5-5 were built, the first of which flew at Hatfield for the first time on 28 August 1949 piloted by G. H. Pike, only a few days before demonstration at the Farnborough Show. Standard armament of four 20 mm. Hispano cannon was retained and provision made for a pair of one hundred gallon underwing fuel tanks at half span. Trials led first to a deletion of the fin acorns and to a slight increase in fin area, and finally to the taller rudders and increased tailplane span of the Venom.

The DH.113 was intended for export and twelve were ordered by

Four DH.113 Vampire NF.Mk.10s from 25 Squadron are seen at West Malling on 22 February 1952. *(author's collection)*

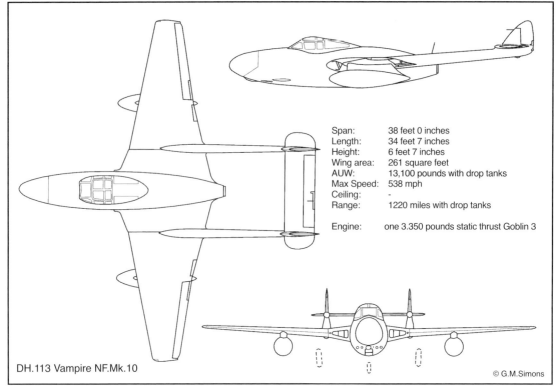

Span:	38 feet 0 inches
Length:	34 feet 7 inches
Height:	6 feet 7 inches
Wing area:	261 square feet
AUW:	13,100 pounds with drop tanks
Max Speed:	538 mph
Ceiling:	-
Range:	1220 miles with drop tanks
Engine:	one 3.350 pounds static thrust Goblin 3

DH.113 Vampire NF.Mk.10

© G.M.Simons

the Egyptian Government in October 1949 but when the export of arms to Egypt was banned, they were taken over by the RAF under the designation Vampire N.F. Mk. 10 as an interim type pending the delivery of Meteor and Venom night fighters. Allotted serials commencing WP232, they were first issued to 25 Squadron at West Malling in July 1951 to replace Mosquito N.F. Mk. 36s. 23 Squadron, Coltishall was similarly re-equipped in the following September when 151 Squadron re-formed at Leuchars as the third Vampire N.F. Mk. 10 unit.

The Vampire N.F. Mk. 10's short, 2½ year, service career was limited to the above three home defence squadrons, each of which had an establishment of sixteen fighters, and by the time the type had been completely phased out in May 1954 at least twenty-five new and unused aircraft were still at storage units. A few were retained for trial purposes such as WP249 which was evaluated at the A&AEE Boscombe Down while WP250 went to Radlett to be flown

Two views of the prototype DH.113 Vampire night fighter.

The picture above is of the aircraft before painting on 28 August 1949. Fully painted, it appeared at the Farnboroigh air show the next month.

Right: G-5-2 with experimental tail surfaces.
(both DH via BAe Hatfield)

by Handley Page for experimental work on boundary-layer suction laminar flow wing sections. From 1953 to 56 it flew with various five feet test sections outboard of the port tail boom, using air tapped from the engine compressor. A dummy section was fitted on the starboard side to avoid asymmetric drag.

WP240 which was to have been flown by John Cunningham in the abortive Jubilee Trophy Race at Hatfield on 23 June 1951, was used in 1955 to air test the Sea Vixen radome.

A total of ninety-five Vampire N.F. Mk. 10s were built, sixty-two at Chester, some being delivered to the Italian Air Force under the designation Vampire N.F. Mk. 54. One was evaluated by the Swiss Air Force as J1301. A number of surplus RAF machines were fitted with improved cockpit canopies and retained for use by 1 and 2 Air Navigation Schools at Topcliffe and Thorney Island. These remained in service until 1959, but a considerable number returned to de Havilland's Chester works to be re-worked and re-equipped internally to N.F. Mk. 54 standard as interim all weather fighters for the Indian Air Force. These were delivered by air in two main batches via Blackbushe and Bahrein between August 1957 and February 1958.

DH.114 Heron

The DH.114 was a modern counterpart to the pre-war DH.86, just as the Dove was supposed to be a modernised DH.89. It was first considered in 1945 but the market did not then exist and it was not until 1949 that detail designs began under the direction of William A. Tamblin.

Emphasis was on rugged simplicity in order to produce a truly economical vehicle for short or medium stage services in areas without proper airfields. It was devoid of complicated hydraulics, the undercarriage was fixed, and the engines, ungeared, unsupercharged Gipsy Queen 30s, were renowned for reliability and long inter-overhaul life. They drove two bladed De Havilland variable pitch airscrews and the aircraft's small field performance was consequently exceptional.

The type name of 'Heron' was chosen and the prototype, G-ALZL, first flown at Hatfield by G. H. Pike on 10 May 1950, was built largely from existing components, including Dove outer wing panels as well as Dove nose and tail units joined by lengthened keel, roof and side members. Accommodation was for two pilots and fourteen passengers, but three extra seats could be fitted if no toilet were carried.

At the end of 180 hours development flying during

Above: 7.30 pm, 10 May 1950, and the prototype DH.114 Heron G-ALZL takes to the skies for the first time.
Below: The same aircraft in company colours in flight. *(both DH via BAe Hatfield)*

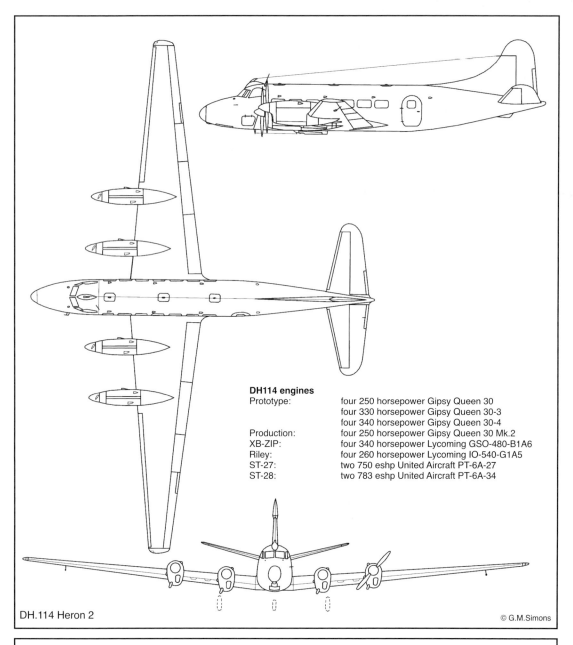

DH114 engines

Prototype:	four 250 horsepower Gipsy Queen 30
	four 330 horsepower Gipsy Queen 30-3
	four 340 horsepower Gipsy Queen 30-4
Production:	four 250 horsepower Gipsy Queen 30 Mk.2
XB-ZIP:	four 340 horsepower Lycoming GSO-480-B1A6
Riley:	four 260 horsepower Lycoming IO-540-G1A5
ST-27:	two 750 eshp United Aircraft PT-6A-27
ST-28:	two 783 eshp United Aircraft PT-6A-34

DH.114 Heron 2

© G.M.Simons

DH.114 Heron Specifications

Mark:	Heron 1 & 2	Mk.1B, 2B, 2C	Mk. 2D, 2E, 3, 4
Span:	71 feet 6 inches	71 feet 6 inches	71 feet 6 inches
Length:	48 feet 6 inches	48 feet 6 inches	48 feet 6 inches
Height:	15 feet 7 inches	15 feet 7 inches	15 feet 7 inches
Wing area:	499 square feet	499 square feet	499 square feet
Tare weight:	7,960 pounds	7,985 pounds	8,150 pounds
AUW:	13,000 pounds*	13,000 pounds**	13,500 pounds***
Cruise:	160mph	165 mph	183 mph
Ceiling:	18,500 feet	18,500 feet	18,500 feet
Max range:	805 miles	805 miles	915 miles

* prototype 12,500 pounds   **Heron 2C 13,150 pounds   ***XB-ZIP 14,450 pounds

A typical interior of a Heron in the early 1950s. The cabin height was six inches more than the Dove. *(author's collection)*

which the original tailplane gave place to one with dihedral, the prototype left for tropical trials at Khartoum and Nairobi. In May 1951 a high pressure sales drive began, during which it bore many insignia including those of Morton Air Services Ltd., BEA, Japan Air Lines, and during a fortnight's visit to Scandinavia in 1954, the Norwegian registration LN-BDH. Trial installation of the Gipsy Queen 30-3 was made in 1951, of the Gipsy Queen 30-4 in 1956 and later 'ZL was brought up to full production standard for Jersey Airways Ltd. with Gipsy Queen 30 Mk. 2s.

New Zealand National Airways Ltd. (NZNAC) obtained the first production Heron, which left Hatfield on its 13,000 mile delivery flight on 2 April 1952 and exactly a year later inaugurated services with three others across the Cook Strait between Wellington, Nelson and Blenheim. The second, third and fifth machines opened the Oslo-Stavanger service of Braathens SAFE Air Transport on 18 August 1952 but only seven Herons were built at Hatfield before the production line was transferred to Chester.

G-AMTS, the last of the seven Hatfield-built examples, was the prototype Heron 2 with retractable undercarriage, first flown on 14 December 1952. Without the drag of the undercarriage it was 20 m.p.h. faster than the Heron 1 and had an improved fuel consumption. Production continued at a slow rate and the 143rd Heron was completed at Chester during May 1961. The type saw service in thirty countries and later

operated as Heron 1B or 2B at an increased all-up weight of 13,000 pounds. As in the case of the Dove, the A suffix was reserved for Herons with special furnishings for the American market.

In February 1955 two IBs, G-ANXA and 'XB, replaced Rapides on the Scottish ambulance runs and on BEA's scheduled services between Renfrew and Benbecula and Renfrew and Barra, where their short take off ability was put to good use on the beach airstrip. In the south, Cambrian Airways Ltd. operated a Heron 1B and two Heron 2Bs between Cardiff and the Midlands, Belfast, Jersey and Paris. Heron 1B F-OANQ, formerly in the Cameroons as F-BGXU, had flown 7,000 hours since 1958 on Transpac's inter-island services in New Caledonia, while three former NZNAC Heron Is of Fiji Airways Ltd. connected Suva with Nandi, 135 miles away.

The Heron 2 soon found use as a luxury private transport, a role in which it excelled in the business world for many years. In that year, ZS-DIG was supplied to the Anglo American Corporation of South Africa Ltd.; CGG to the Governor General of the Belgian Congo to replace a Dove with the same markings; and XG603 in RAF markings to the British Joint Services Mission. This was the first Heron to go into service in the USA, having been flown out by the northern route for the personal use of the British Ambassador in Washington. It was forerunner of a similar VIP Heron, XH375, delivered to the Queen's Flight at Benson in May 1955 and later flown extensively by HRH Prince Philip, the Duke of Edinburgh. This in turn led to two VVIP series 3 aircraft delivered to the Queen's Flight in April 1958, one of which was flown to Ghana by the Duke on 22 November 1959. The Heron C. Mk. 4, commencing XR391, was introduced in May 1961.

The first production Mk. 2B was the 50th machine - Saudi Arabian SA-R5 - the personal aircraft of Prince Talal al Saud. First of that version to fly, however, was the G-ANOL *'Excalibur'* used by HRH Princess Margaret during her visit to the West Indies in 1955. In company with a later model, VP-BAN, it flew on the routes of Bahamas Airways Ltd. as VP-BAO.

Major modifications included the wide chord rudder introduced in 1955, and De Havilland fully feathering propellers, first demonstrated on the 82nd aircraft, G-ANCJ, at the 1955 SBAC Show. These props

Although it was the Duke of Edinburgh's personal Heron, XH375 was used extensively by The Queen's Flight both at home and overseas. It was in natural metal finish with an Edinburgh green cheat line. *(via AVM J de M Severne)*

The Queen's Flight DH.114 Herons were finished in overall fluoresent red by the end of 1961. This may well have been a colour that made them highly visible, but was not popular with passengers, groundcrews or aircrews. *(via AVM J de M Severne)*

were available as an optional extra, thus changing the designation to Heron 2C. Two examples, G-ANUO and 'OHB, with executive interior operating at an even higher all-up weight of 13,500 pounds were designated Heron 2D, and based at London's Heathrow Airport to maintain communications with Shell interests in Amsterdam. The Canadian Comstock Company used CF-HLI for industrial surveys and coast to coast executive flying in Canada. Others were used for similar purposes by Rolls-Royce Ltd., Vickers-Armstrongs Ltd. and English Electric Aviation Ltd. A custom built version, G-APMV, with four VIP and eight other seats and also an electric galley, was known as the Heron 2E and was based at Turnhouse by Ferranti Ltd. A number of other de luxe Herons were used overseas, PH-ILA with Phillips of Eindhoven; N4789C in Alaska; I-BKET by Signor Agnelli of the Fiat Company in Italy; CN-MAA by the Sultan of Morocco and XB-ZIP by the Banco Nacional de Mexico. The last mentioned had a considerably improved performance after being fitted in 1959 with 340 h.p. Lycoming engines

by Vest Aircraft de Mexico S.A.

The 14 seat Heron 2B served for many years with major airlines. They also served with Communications Flights in the air forces of Saudi Arabia, South Africa, Ceylon, Iraq, West Germany, Jordan and Ghana.

By 1957 airline Herons were being replaced by larger aircraft, which created a cascade down effect. In May 1961 the Royal Navy replaced five Sea Devon communications aircraft with a similar number of ex-civil Heron 2s. Delivered to Lee-on-Solent under the designation Sea Heron C. Mk. 20, they included two former Jersey Airlines machines and three surplus West African Airways aircraft specially overhauled by the manufacturer at Leavesden.

Mexico's Lycoming engined Heron was forerunner of conversions made in Australia by Connellan Airways of Alice Springs, and in Florida by Riley Aeronautics, who produced Riley Herons with even

The almost classic standard De Havilland aircraft delivery photograph. Heron 2 '120' was delivered to the South African Air Force in December 1955. It was one of the first to be fitted with the wide chord, bulged rudder. *(DH via BAe Hatfield)*

Left: Heron 2 I-BKET, supplied to the FIAT Motor Company for executive use. *(DH via BAe Hatfield)*

Below: Prinair was by far the largest single user, worldwide, of the D.H. Heron, having operated no less than thirty-five of them at one time or another. Most were converted in the airline's own workshops by a subsidiary known as Caribbean Aircraft Development Industries (CADI) by replacing the original Gipsy Queen 30 engines with four Continental IO-520s. *(author's collection)*

better payload and performance by fitting turbo-supercharged Lycomings.

An even more extensive remanufacture was undertaken by Saunders Aircraft Corp. Ltd. of Gimli, Manitoba, who replaced the four Gipsy Queens by two 715 e.s.h.p. United Aircraft PT-6A-27 propeller-turbines. The first such conversion, designated the ST-27, was made to the former British Joint Services Mission Heron 2, XG603, which first flew at Dorval as CF-YBM-X on 18 May 1969. Among a number of other surplus Herons sent to Canada for ST-27 conversion were the Queen's Flight aircraft XH375 and XM295, ferried in 1969 as CF-YAP and CF-XOK. These were delivered to Aerolineas Centrales de Colombia as ST-27s HK-1287 and to Skywest Canada as CF-XOK respectively early in 1972. The R.A.F.'s penultimate Heron, XR391, and the Kuwaiti 9K-BAA, followed as CF-CAT and 'NX, and after conversion were sold to Bayview Air Service, Slave Lake, and Otonabee Airways, Peterborough, as C-FCNT and 'NX respectively.

When supplies of used Herons dwindled,

Saunders began the basic engineering for the ST-27B (later known as the ST-28), wholly built at Gimli with 783 e.s.h.p. PT-6A-34s, partial pressurisation and operating at the increased all-up weight of 14,500 pounds. The prototype, C-FYBM-X, (actually a rebuild of Heron 14087, originally S.A.A.F. 727 and later G-ASUU) first flew at Gimli on 17 July 1974. All work terminated however after 12 ST-27s and the ST-28 prototype had been built.

The ultimate Heron conversion was the Saunders ST-27: the Saunders was lengthened by eight feet six inches to accommodate up to twenty-three passengers. It was powered by two 750-shp Pratt and Whitney Canada PT6A-34 turboprop engines. Here is CF-LOL operating for St Andrews Airways. *(author's collection)*

DH.115 Vampire Trainer

The removal of night interception equipment from the de Havilland DH.113 in 1950 and the fitting of dual controls to create a private venture jet trainer was a logical step. The prototype, marked as G-5-7, known as the DH.115 Vampire Trainer, was built in the Christchurch factory and statically exhibited at the Farnborough SBAC Show in September but was not airborne until J. W. Wilson made the first 25 minute flight at Christchurch on 15 November.

At the conclusion of company trials the prototype was handed over to the RAF as WW456 for Service evaluation, first at 204 Advanced Flying School and then at the Central Gunnery School, Leconfield. The programme was completed on 26 April 1951 and in September the aircraft performed at the Farnborough Show, then was handed over to the Christchurch Technical School as a ground instructional airframe. In February 1952, the design was adopted as the standard RAF advanced trainer and ordered to Specification T. 111 under the designation Vampire T.Mk. 11.

This marked the beginning of a new era when RAF pilots qualified for their 'wings' on jet aircraft. Student pilots graduating from the Hunting Percival Provost were converted to a jet of fighter-like performance with side by side seating in a pressurised cabin. It was equipped with two 100 gallon underwing fuel tanks and could be used for fighter navigation, the demonstration of compressibility effects, or for combat training equipped with dual inter-connected gunsights and two 20 mm Hispano cannon. For other armament training, provision was made the carrying eight twenty-five pound rockets and eight twenty five pound practice bombs; or 500 pound bombs with rockets; or two 1,000 Ib. bombs.

Deliveries began with WZ414, first flown on 19 January 1952, and the first units to receive Vampire Trainers were 202 and 208 Advanced Flying Schools at Valley and Weston Zoyland, and the Fighter Weapons School, Leconfield. They were issued to 5 FTS at Oakington in 1954 and two years later replaced the Balliol to become the first jet trainer used by the RAF College, Cranwell. They were also issued to fighter squadrons as communications and check aircraft and to most Station Flights. Operational experience showed the need for modifications that included a central blind flying panel; side by side ejector seats; a one piece, clear view canopy and long dorsal fins.

Before quantity production began, two pre-production Vampire Trainers, WW458 and WW461, were also built at Christchurch, the first of which flew on 1 December 1951. Both were delivered to RNAS Culham early in 1952 for Navy evaluation, resulting in the delivery of 73 Sea Vampire T.Mk.22 aircraft, commencing XA100 and ending XG777, for FAA training squadrons at Lossiemouth and elsewhere. The DH.115 was also used for communications duties with Sea Venom squadrons and as Admirals' Barges. Second line Fleet Air Arm units using the T.Mk.22 included 736, 738, 749, 764 and 781 Squadrons.

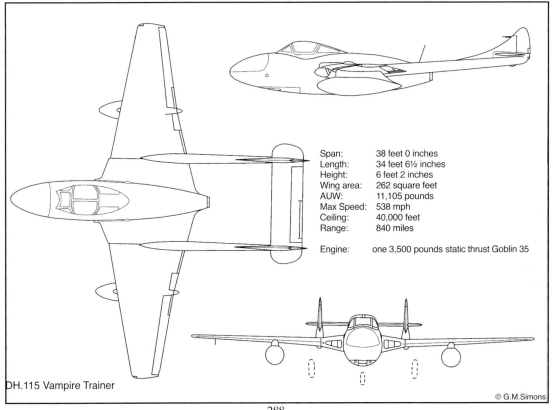

Span:	38 feet 0 inches
Length:	34 feet 6½ inches
Height:	6 feet 2 inches
Wing area:	262 square feet
AUW:	11,105 pounds
Max Speed:	538 mph
Ceiling:	40,000 feet
Range:	840 miles
Engine:	one 3,500 pounds static thrust Goblin 35

DH.115 Vampire Trainer

© G.M.Simons

Above: the prototype DH.115 Vampire Trainer G-5-7 with its original tail assembly.

Right: The Vampire Trainer development aircraft WZ419, showing the clear-view canopy , dorsal fairings, ejector seats and other modifications. *(both DH via BAe Hatfield)*

When production ended in 1958, 804 Vampire Trainers had been built, 427 at Chester, the first aircraft from which had flown in October 1951. They included large numbers of the T.Mk.55 export variant which equipped the air forces of more than twenty countries, including Sweden, where it was locally designated J28C, and India, where additional Vampire Trainers were erected by Hindustan Aircraft Ltd.

Construction of 41 examples commencing A79-801 of the T.Mk.33 with imported Goblin engines, was undertaken at Bankstown by De Havilland Aircraft Pty. Ltd., the last five of which were completed for the Royal Australian Navy as T.Mk.34s, equivalent to the Sea Vampire T.Mk.22 and later fitted with ejector seats as T.Mk.34As. Sixty-nine T.Mk.35s commencing A79-600 were delivered in September 1957, but whereas the T. Mks. 33 and 34 had the old type fins and canopy, the T.Mk.35 had the later type and was fitted with increased tankage and non-skid hydraulic brakes. All T.Mk.33s were then converted to this standard but retained their original fuel capacity and were designated T.Mk.35As. They were used for night flying, instrument approaches and armament practice and British-built T.Mk.11s served a similar purpose with 14 Squadron, RNZAF at Ohakea and with the Royal Rhodesian Air Force.

Three T.Mk.55s were allotted British civil status for overseas delivery and demonstration; construction number 15485 as G-ANVF prior to handing over to the Finnish Air Force as VT-1 in April 1955; construction number 15798 was shipped to Buenos Aires as G-AOXH in November 1956 for a demonstration tour of South America by George Errington who handed it over to the Chilean Air Force on 16 April 1957; and construction number 15802 for which the marks G-APFV were reserved but which was an exhibit at the 1957 SBAC Show and went to the Lebanese Air Force as L-160 instead.

By 1965 the RAF.'s only active Vampire Trainers were six kept at 1 FTS Linton-on-Ouse, for training

G-ANVF, the Vampire T.Mk.55 civil demonstrator aircraft, showing the clear-view canopy fitted to later production aircraft. *(DH via BAe Hatfield)*

A line up of Swiss-built Vampire T.Mk.55s at Dubendorf Airfield, Switzerland. *(author's collection)*

foreign students. In January 1966 they were transferred to 7 FTS Church Fenton, and thence to 3 FTS Leeming, where their last operational sortie took place on 29 November 1967 when a Flight of four performed formation aerobatics, with a final flypast, led by one of the replacing Jet Provosts.

A few remained in service with the Central Air Traffic Control School, Shawbury, until November 1970 and with 3 Civilian Army Co-operation Unit at Exeter until the end of 1971.

DH.116

This was a design project intended to modernise the Sea Venom alll-weather fighter for the Fleet Air Arm. To speed up delivery, the basic Venom fuselage was to have been slightly modified to house a more modern radar set and mated to a new thin-section, swept wing.

Although a development contract was signed, for a pair of prototypes, Royal Navy policy changed in favour of a larger twin-engined aircraft and the DH.116 was shelved in favour of the DH.110, eventually to be adopted as the Sea Vixen.

DH.117

Submission to Operational Requirement F.155T, a specification issued by the Ministry of Supply for an interceptor aircraft to defend the United Kingdom from high-flying supersonic bombers. The DH.117 was designed with a straight wing and was to be powered by two Gyron Junior turbojets and one Spectre rocket in the tail, with a crew of two seated in tandem. Provision was not made for Red Hebe as per the specification request, the De Havilland team preferring the company's own line of missiles that would culminate in Red Top. The design was not built.

DH.118

A specification issued by British Overseas Airways Corporation in October 1956 for a long haul turbojet transport for service in 1962 gave rise to design studies by several major aircraft manufacturers.

The De Havilland proposals were given the type number DH.118 and envisaged a 120-147 seater powered by four 17,000 pound static thrust Rolls-Royce Conway engines pod-mounted beneath the wings. It was to have a fuselage 137 feet 6 inches long, and a span of 137 feet. The aircraft was to be capable of nonstop transatlantic flights at an all-up weight of 240,000 pounds and have a superior performance to the Boeing 707.

This was a replacement design for the abortive Comet 5 and an important feature of the design was its ability to operate from existing runways. According to data given in Parliamentary debate in November 1956, BOAC was thinking in terms of 25 to 30 DH.118s at a cost of some £56 million, but in February 1957 an official announcement stated that the project had been dropped.

DH.119

The DH.119 was a design proposal that emerged at the end of 1956 in response to a requirement from British European Airways.

The 119 had a swept wing, mid-mounted tailplane and four Rolls-Royce RA29 Avon engines of 12,000 pounds thrust mounted behind the rear wing spars, with air intakes below the wings. With an all-up weight of 160,000 pounds, accommodation was provided for up to ninety-five passengers.

For political reasons, the 119 was evolved into the joint BEA / BOAC airline requirement: the DH120.

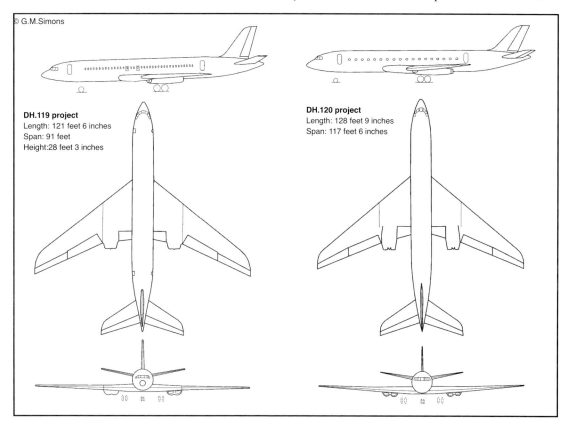

© G.M.Simons

DH.119 project
Length: 121 feet 6 inches
Span: 91 feet
Height:28 feet 3 inches

DH.120 project
Length: 128 feet 9 inches
Span: 117 feet 6 inches

DH.120

Shortly after submitting the DH.119, De Havillands proposed a joint project in order to meet the requirements of both BOAC and BEA. Similar to the DH.119, the project featured the same wing/engine layout but was powered by either four Rolls-Royce RB140s or RA29 Avons, with an all-up-weight of 190,000 pounds. Neither BEA or BOAC favoured the design, given that it was a compromise to meet both specifications and, in BEA's case the aircraft was much larger than they required. The project was quickly superseded in the project office by a dedicated project, once again for BEA.

(Airco) DH.121 Trident

In 1955 a series of short-term studies was undertaken for a short-range high density airliner to replace BEA's Viscounts. The highly aerodynamic design, with blown flaps and laminar flow wings, was originally put forward powered by Rolls-Royce RB109 Tyne engines, and later possibly with twin Conway engines.

Three projects became serious contenders for the BEA order, the Avro 740, Bristol 200 and De Havilland DH.121. During 1957, the Conservative Government decided to use one of the few new major commercial contracts as a carrot to encourage the British aviation industries to reorganise themselves into larger groupings.

As a consequence of the government's conditions for tendering for the order, a delay was incurred as the manufacturers began discussing prospective partnerships. De Havillands proposed a consortium under the old name of Airco (Aircraft Manufacturing Company) with Hunting, Fairey and Bristol. It was also intended to include Saunders Roe (in which de Havilland was a shareholder) in a subcontract capacity, with Handley Page offering assistance.

Not surprisingly, Bristol did not want to play

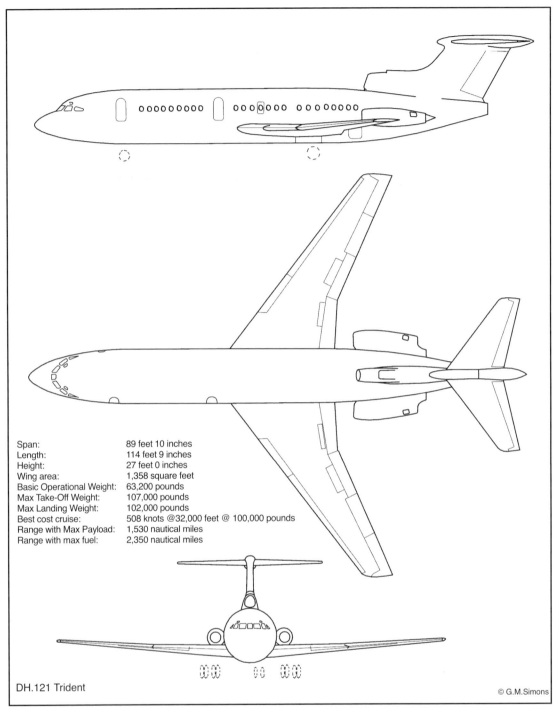

Span:	89 feet 10 inches
Length:	114 feet 9 inches
Height:	27 feet 0 inches
Wing area:	1,358 square feet
Basic Operational Weight:	63,200 pounds
Max Take-Off Weight:	107,000 pounds
Max Landing Weight:	102,000 pounds
Best cost cruise:	508 knots @32,000 feet @ 100,000 pounds
Range with Max Payload:	1,530 nautical miles
Range with max fuel:	2,350 nautical miles

DH.121 Trident

© G.M.Simons

second fiddle to De Havilland and decided to link up with the Hawker Siddeley Group.

It appears that there was a strong prejudice within BEA for using any product of the Bristol Aircraft company and that they were also not confident in Avro as a civil aircraft builder. On the other hand, De Havilland was the only British manufacturer with previous jet transport experience. It was also armed with all the valuable data from the Comet crashes, had

major experience in structural fatigue and a good after-sales service. A further factor was that De Havilland was used to working with Rolls-Royce, and Bristol (with their own engine company) was not, and of course the 121 was the natural follow-on to the Comet.

BEA decided in 1958 that the 121 best met its requirements, even though Bristol continued to press their case for some time with the Model 200, which the government appeared to prefer, due to the stronger financial resources of the Bristol-Hawker Siddeley joint venture.

BEA was adamant that the 121 was to be the selected aircraft, so on 1 August 1958 approval was given for BEA to place an order with De Havilland for twenty-four 121 aircraft with an option for an additional twelve. BEA and De Havilland worked closely on the new project, tailoring it specifically for the airline's requirement. It could now accommodate up to 117 passengers and was powered by Rolls-Royce Medway engines. That it would certainly have been a world beater was clear, and it could have been developed further as there was much potential in the Medway engine for growth variants.

This was not to be, however, for when in early 1959 there was a sudden dip in traffic growth BEA panicked, fearing it would now be operating a huge fleet of new aircraft but would be unable to fill all the seats. Despite reistance from De Havilland, the DH.121 was cut down in size to accommodate only eighty passengers, and the Medways were replaced by the less powerful Rolls-Royce Spey.

Right: Work proceeds on the first batch of DH.121 fuselages at Hatfield.

Below: Nearing its final form the mock-up of the Trident flight deck shows the cockpit arrangements as derived by Airco to suit the requirements of British European Airways. *(both DH via BAe Hatfield)*

The DH.121 design team was led by C. T. Wilkins. Following the inclusion of De Havillands into the Hawker Siddeley Group the DH.121 became entirely a De Havilland project and Airco was disbanded. With its distinctive plan form and 35 degrees of wing sweepback, the DH.121 obviously owed much to the celebrated Comet 4 but was far more efficient aerodynamically because the mainplane had a cleanness only possible with rear mounted engines. Also the main undercarriage legs carrying four wheels

The DH.121 production line at Hatfield. Closest airframe to the camera is the prototype, later to be registered G-ARPA. *(DH via BAe Hatfield)*

each pivoted about the rear spar and turned through 90 degrees before folding inwards so that the wheels were housed in the fuselage and not inside the wing. The nose wheel was offset to port to retract sideways. For lateral control split ailerons were fitted, only the inner portions of which were used at high Mach numbers, and double slotted flaps worked in conjunction with leading edge slats. To ensure complete safety the powered controls were operated by three completely separate hydraulic circuits, a distinctive feature which, combined with the three engined layout, led to the adoption of Trident as an appropriate type name in September 1960.

In typical mixed class configuration, 75 passengers sat 4-6 abreast while for coach class working the 66 feet 10 inches long pressurised cabin accommodated 97 passengers six abreast. All fuel was carried in the wing and to ensure rapid turn round a high landing weight in relation to maximum take off weight enabled more than one stage to be flown without refuelling. The Trident could land within 40 minutes of a full load take off, having covered 180 miles with still enough fuel for 700 miles in its tanks. The aircraft was also unique in satisfying the Corporation's demand for automatic landing and the entire fleet was equipped with 'autoflare' with full automatic landing capability added

In full BEA colours, G-ARPE is rolled out. *(DH via BAe Hatfield)*

The prototype DH.121 Trident gets airborne from Hatfield in the hands of John Cunningham and Peter Bugge and three other crew members on 9 January 1962. *(DH via BAe Hatfield)*

later through Smith's Flight Control System.

By the end of 1959 preliminary structural testing had begun and a fuselage nose section had been subjected to water tank pressure testing. The first DH.121 was rolled out at Hatfield on 4 August 1961 and by September taxying trials had been completed with two ground running engines installed and the airframe systems had been checked. The Spey turbojet was airborne for the first time on 12 October in Avro Vulcan XA902, a test bed in which Speys were tested under Trident flight conditions prior to the first flight of the prototype early in 1962. The next six aircraft joined the flight test programme later in 1962 to ensure

the issue of a full Certificate of Airworthiness in time for first deliveries to be made to British European Airways by mid 1963.

At one stage De Havilland had invited representatives from Boeing to Hatfield to view the Trident line, in the hope of a joint production deal. However, a reciprocal trip to Boeings in Seattle saw nothing of that company's future plans being revealed to the team from De Havilland.

As has been well documented, Boeing produced an aircraft similar to the original DH.121 specification. called the Boeing 727-100. Whereas the Trident went on to achieve a production of some 117 aircraft, well

High above a cloudscape, Trident G-ARPB poses for the company photographer. *(DH via BAe Hatfield)*

over 1,800 727s were manufactured, and led to future developments such as the Boeing 737 and 757.

Only 23 of the initial order for 24 Tridents actually entered service because the penultimate aircraft, G-ARPY, crashed at Felthorpe, Norfolk during its maiden flight on 3 June 1966 as the result of a deep stall, with the loss of test pilots Peter Barlow, George Errington and two other crew. The early production fleet remained in B.E.A./British Airways service until the survivors were withdrawn in 1975 and flown to Prestwick to be cocooned and, eventually, scrapped.

Development of this very successful transport as the Hawker Siddeley HS.121 Trident 1C, the stretched Trident IE, the long span 2E and high capacity 3B is outside the scope of a book devoted to De Havilland history.

DH.122

The DH.122 was a proposed DH.121 Trident variant for the British Overseas Airways Corporation to compete with the Vickers VC.10. It was not proceeded with.

DH.123

A series of design studies were made under the designation of DH.123 in 1959 for a Heron/Dakota replacement seating up to 36 passengers. One study which reached the active project stage envisaged the installation of two de Havilland Gnome P.1000 propeller-turbines and although brochures were available at the Farnborough SBAC Show in September 1959 it was decided not to manufacture until the results of a market survey were known.

In January 1961 an announcement was made which stated that the project had been dropped in favour of the DH.l26.

DH.124

This designation was not used to avoid any confusion with the Handley Page HP.124.

DH.125 Jet Dragon

The DH.125 was the jet successor to the Dove executive transport, fitted in the modern manner with two rear mounted Bristol Siddeley Viper 20 turbojets and 'T' tail.

At the time of its initial announcement in February 1961 a wooden mock up was already complete and on 6 April it was stated that an initial batch of thirty was being laid down for delivery in 1963. The DH.125 was fully pressurised and air conditioned for the carriage of two crew, six passengers in large executive armchairs, and generous baggage, at a cruising speed of 450-500 m.p.h. over stages up to 1,500 miles. The fuselage and cabin was cylindrical but a foot wider than that of the Dove in order to give the same headroom as the Heron and the one piece mainplane had large double slotted flaps and air brakes. The DH.125 was designed to operate from short runways, employ

Early examples of the 125 breed! From left to right: G-ASEC, G-ARYC, G-ARYB and G-ARYA. *(DH via BAe Hatfield)*

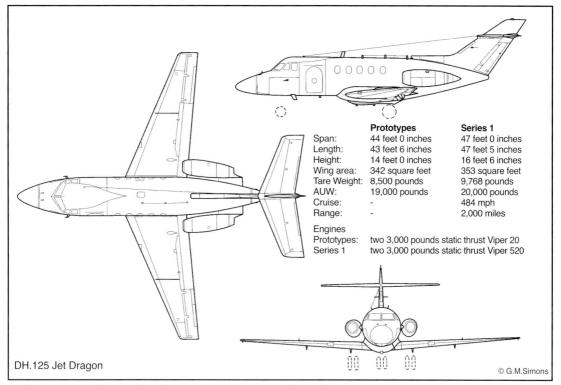

	Prototypes	Series 1
Span:	44 feet 0 inches	47 feet 0 inches
Length:	43 feet 6 inches	47 feet 5 inches
Height:	14 feet 0 inches	16 feet 6 inches
Wing area:	342 square feet	353 square feet
Tare Weight:	8,500 pounds	9,768 pounds
AUW:	19,000 pounds	20,000 pounds
Cruise:	-	484 mph
Range:	-	2,000 miles

Engines
Prototypes:	two 3,000 pounds static thrust Viper 20
Series 1	two 3,000 pounds static thrust Viper 520

DH.125 Jet Dragon

© G.M.Simons

moderate approach speeds and operate at a cost per mile closely approximating that of the Dove.

It was designed by a De Havilland team led by J. Goodwin and for a short time was known as the Jet Dragon. An initial batch of 30 Series 1 aircraft was laid down in the Chester factory but two prototypes, slightly shorter in span and length, were built in the experimental shop at Hatfield. The first, G-ARYA, made its first flight of 56 minutes on 13 August 1962 piloted by Chris. A. Capper and the second, 'YB, followed on 12 December. These were used for the certification programme and in the autumn of 1964 the 8th production aircraft, G-ASSI, made an extensive sales tour of the USA and Canada, which ensured a steady market in North America for more than a decade. So great was the impact made by the De Havilland label in North America that it was deemed good sales practice to describe the American model as the DH.125 rather than the H.S. 125.

The subsequent development and commercial history of De Havilland's world-beating 'mini jetliner' took place after the firm was absorbed into the Hawker Siddeley Group and is therefore outside the scope of this book.

G-ASSI, the DH.125 North American demonstrator airborne near Hatfield in 1964. (*DH via BAe Hatfield*)

DH.126

This project was similar to the DH.125 with two rear mounted turbofan engines, but enlarged to supersede the projected DH.123 as an ultra-short-haul Dakota replacement. Designed to carry 35-50 passengers over distances up to 600 miles, it was studied by Airlines of New South Wales for routes in New Guinea, Papua and Queensland, and by UnitedArab Airlines for Middle East services in 1964.

DH.127

Proposed delta-winged strike fighter for Royal Navy as Blackburn Buccaneer replacement, early 1960s. The design featured two Rolls-Royce Spey engines with vectored thrust and two RB.108 lift jets in the nose to lower approach speed. It was not proceeded with.

DH.128

Use of this design number has not been located.

DH.129

Use of this design number has not been located.

DH.130

Some sources suggest that this was a supersonic airliner design that was incorporated into the Hawker Siddeley HS APG 1011 project. Very little else is known.

OTHER 'DE HAVILLAND AIRCRAFT'

The De Havilland Aeronautical Technical School

This was founded at Stag Lane in 1928. The 'Tech School' as it was known came about when company expansion made it advisable to develop the existing apprentice scheme to include a wide variety of practical and theoretical engineering subjects. The first 'workshop' was just a corner of a maintenance shop, but later a complete building was allocated with little in it apart from benches. An evening technical institute was established at Stag Lane with A. T. Eadon as Principal and staffed by De Havilland designers, aerodynamicists and stressmen who trained students up to AFRAeS. standard and beyond.

The School was extended at this time to include design and drawing departments which allowed students to design their first original full sized aeroplane and subsequently to build it. This was the Gipsy powered TK.1 two seat biplane, in which Geoffrey de Havilland Jnr. came 5th in the 1934 Kings Cup Race.

The School grew into a significant training college which produced a number of significant designers and engineers over the years.

At the outbreak of war, part of the School was occupying the former Moth Minor erecting shop at Hatfield, but this was completely destroyed when a Ju.88 bombed it on 3 October 1940. R. W. Reeve returned from White Waltham to take over as Principal in 1941 and after the de Havilland Experimental Department moved out of Salisbury Hall, London Colney, and vacated the two hangars on the estate in which the two prototype Mosquitoes had been built, the School moved in and remained for eight years.

During this time the original Wright Flyer Biplane became due for return to the United States after many years on exhibition at the Science Museum, London, and the School's expertise was honoured when it was invited to build an accurate replica to replace it. Work started in March 1946 and the completed aircraft was handed over to the Museum two years later by Sqn. Ldr. Reeve in the presence of Sir Geoffrey de Havilland, Frank T. Hearle and those who had made it, on 29 October 1948. A working replica of the Wright brothers' twelve horsepower water-cooled engine was a later project which ran quite successfully on the test bench before it was also presented to the Museum by Sir Geoffrey on 25 April 1951.

The progress of the College continued with the move first to De Havilland's factory at Hatfield and much later, when the School transferred to purpose-built accommodation at Astwick Manor, Hatfield. Opened by Lord Salisbury on 18 June 1949, the curriculum expanded considerably into design, production and maintenance courses backed up by practical experience in the adjacent factory but no more full scale construction was undertaken by students.

The College undertook the construction of aircraft as part of its engineering instructional syllabus. Several Moths were hand-built and flown by the students. The last of these was a Moth Major, G-ADIO, built at the College in 1935.

However, long before this time, a growing emphasis on design and development had spawned a fully-fledged College aircraft design section and in 1934 it was agreed that the students should design and build their own aeroplane. A Dutch student named Juste van Hattum unintentionally began the distinctive, if brief, TK series of designs by inscribing upon the drawings in his native tongue 'Tekniese Kollege No. 1' and so the 'TK' appelation stuck!

When the Second World War brought the series to an end, four aircraft of widely differing types had been built, the last of which was numbered T.K. 5.

TK.1

The TK.1 was designed and built in the Stag Lane days of De Havilland. Supervising the project was the responsibility of Marcus Langley, who was described as lecturer in aircraft design at the College.

Conventional in design and appearance, it was not surprising that the students' first effort should have resembled the Moths upon which they had worked already. The TK.1 was an all-wood tandem two-seater biplane with open cockpits and an experimental 80 hp DH engine. This was rapidly replaced by a 120 hp Gipsy III inverted engine, and the machine closely resembled a regular de Havilland machine. Fuel capacity was 12 gallons in a top-wing centre-section tank with gravity-feed to the engine.

With differential ailerons mounted to the lower wings only, the straight wings put the front cockpit directly under the top wing. The tail assembly was conventional but, departing from parent-company style, the rudder was statically mass-balanced rather than aerodynamically balanced.

Registered somewhat aptly as G-ACTK, the first flight was undertaken by Hubert Broad in June of 1934 under 'B' conditions as E-3. The following month the TK.1 went to Martlesham Heath for its certificate of airworthiness trials and, in response to an urgent plea from Geoffrey de Havilland (who wanted to race it in the King's Cup Air Race), it was completed in a single day just before the event. It was decreed 'a workmanlike job' and had no difficulty in passing its trials. In the race on 13/14 July, it came fifth at 124.24 mph.

The TK.1 was destined to have but a short life. Sold in February 1936 to Flt Lt Edward Fielden and converted by its new owner into a single-seater, it was scrapped later the same year.

Its span was 27 feet 0 inches, length 24 feet 0 inches. The wing area 183½ square feet. The tare weight was 944 pounds. all up weight 1,450 pounds. The aircraft had a maximum speed 118 m.p.h and crusied at 100 m.p.h. The initial climb 900 feet per minute.

The Moth-like lines of the first of the College's own-design aircraft is clearly visible in this picture of G-ACTK.

TK.2

The series of aircraft designed and built by the students of the de Havilland Technical College progressed to the TK.2 in 1935 and was aimed expressly at speed and performance with the goal of winning races, in particular the King's Cup Air Race.

One example of this two-seat low-wing monoplane was built, but it appeared in three distinct guises and was by far the most successful of all the TK machines.

The design of the all-wood TK.2 was conventional, with a large and well-rounded top rear decking comprising of fabric-covered stringers on lightweight formers. Pilot and passenger sat side-by-side in an enclosed cockpit. It turned out that it was only ever flown as a single-seater, a long-range

The TK.2 in its 1936 configuration with revised cabin and rear decking. *(author's collection)*

fuel tank being fitted in the passenger seat.

A single box spar absorbed all the loads in the RAF 34 section wing that tapered straight from root to tip. The wing was plywood covered with split trailing-edge flaps fitted.

The undercarriage comprised two rubber-in-compression shock struts enclosed in aerofoil-section fairings and terminating in fork-mounted wheels contained in spats. Power was provided by a 140 hp Gipsy Major IC with a fixed-pitch metal propeller.

The first flight was carried out at Hatfield on 16 August 1935 by Hubert Broad under the Class B markings E-3. The machine then went to Martlesham Heath for its official trials for Certificate of Airworthiness, which were completed by 29 August. The registration G-ADNO was allocated and the machine was prepared for the King's Cup Air Race that September. It came fourth in the Race at 165.88 mph.

In 1936, race preparations included the re-design of the cabin transparencies to produce a more refined aerodynamic effect, and the permanent conversion of the machine to a single-seater with a large fuel tank of 36 gallon capacity fitted behind the pilot. The machine came sixth in the King's Cup Race at 172.5 mph and later won the Heston-Cardiff race at 190 mph.

For the 1938 season, changes to the TK.2 were more dramatic. The engine was replaced by a 140 hp Gipsy Major II, the cabin glazing improved still further and, most significantly, the wing-span reduced by four feet. At the same time, the fuselage rear decking was revised to reduce wetted area. In this form it won the Heston-Cardiff race at 187.5 mph, and the Heston-Isle of Man race at 168.4 mph.

The TK.2 spent the war years on company communications duty as E-0235 and was resurrected after the war to break the 100 km closed circuit class record in August 1947 at 178.33 mph. For this the machine had acquired its third engine – a Gipsy Major 10 Mk.1. However, the aircraft's days were numbered as disaster of an insidious nature put an end to the machine later that year. The Air Registration Board discovered structural deterioration when the aircraft came up for its Certificate of Airworthiness renewal and ordered that it would require expensive reconstruction. At this stage it was decided to scrap the machine.

William Patrick Ingram 'Pat' Fillingham was De Havilland's chief production test-pilot from 1939 onwards. Prior to that he was trained at the DH Technical School. It was he who flew the TK.2 during the war and raced the aircraft in 1947. He said that it was a good performer although it was extremely difficult to slow down for landing and the flaps had little effect in this direction. The result was that the aircraft tended to float extensively on flare-out which gave it poor short-field performance.

Experience gained in this design was applied to the DH.88 Comet and therefore the contribution of this machine was both relative and related. It was sleek, fast and did its intended tasks remarkably well.

G-ADNO, c/n 1998, was completed at Hatfield 1935 and powered by one 147 horsepower De Havilland Gipsy Major. It was first flown on 16 August 1935 as E-3, and was modified and test flown as E-5 in 1938 with span reduced to 28 feet 0 inches and 140 horsepower De Havilland Gipsy Major II. The original span was 32 feet 0 inches, length 22 feet 5 inches. Wing area 125 square feet, tare weight 1,049

The TK.2 in its later configuration. Even though the span was reduced, the paint scheme makes it look even smaller! *(author's collection)*

pounds. all-up-weight was 1,600 pounds. The maximum speed was 182 m.p.h, initial climb l,150 feet per minute with the short span wings that had

a wing area of 119 square feet. In this form the tare weight was 1,140 pounds and the all-up-weight was 1,650 pounds.

TK.3

The T.K. 3 remained only a design project but it may have had some influence on the design of the

D.W.I low-wing, single seat ultra light monoplane built at Hungerford, Berks, by De Havilland Aeronautical Technical School students the Hon. Andrew Dalrymple and A. R. Ward in 1937.

TK.4

'The most intriguing light racing machine seen in this country since the days of the original DH. 71 Tiger Moth monoplane' is how *Flight* described the TK.4.

Besides a number of then-unique features in design and construction, it was also the smallest aeroplane ever built in Great Britain. Under the supervision of Squadron Leader O W Clapp and E W Dodds of the College, the students prepared the whole effort themselves. Some 400 pages of stress analysis, representing six months' work, went into its development.

The wing featured a fully-symmetrical wing-section which was extremely shallow in chord-depth ratio, so much so that the loads were equally divided amongst four spars. Retractable Handley Page slots, each thirty-six inches long, were arranged to lie flush with the leading edge when closed, and there were split trailing-edge flaps. Five degrees of dihedral and two of incidence were incorporated.

The moulded cockpit cover was made of a new material called Perspex. Extensive use was made of balsa wood for fairings and tailplane and rudder ribs while the rudder and elevators were formed entirely of this material. The rear fuselage decking was formed in Elektron, a magnesium alloy.

What was then considered a novel technical feature was a fully-retractable undercarriage. This retracted inwards so that the wheels were stowed just behind the engine inside the forward fuselage. The hydraulic retracting mechanism used Dowty-type struts designed by the students with the help of the patentees. The students made all the component parts and sent them to Dowty for assembly. No brakes were fitted as it was considered

that the drag of the sprung tailskid combined with the small-diameter wheels would be enough to slow the aircraft on landing.

The College design team selected the 140 hp Gipsy Major II fitted with a variable-pitch airscrew to power the aircraft. Engine cooling and carburettor intake were combined into one centrally-mounted air scoop under the propeller hub. The air outlet was through a slot under the nose in the undercarriage wheel bay. Cowlings were flush-mounted and secured using the then-new Dzus fasteners while all controls were operated by Teleflex conduit-and-cable instead of the usual cable and pulley system.

Only one machine, G-AETK, was built and this was first flown on 30 July 1937 by de Havilland test pilot Robert John Waight under the Class B registration of E-4. The machine was taken almost immediately to Martlesham Heath for Certificate of Airworthiness testing. It was described as handling well up to its maximum speed of 235 mph but the stalling speed, flaps up, was very high at 95 mph.

The certificate of airworthiness was granted on 1 September, whereupon it was entered for the King's Cup Air Race on 11 September. Penalised by the handicappers, it a was scratch machine and finished 9th at 230.5 mph. The initial rate of climb was 1,350 feet per minute.

On 1 October, while practising for an attempt on the 100 km class record for the benefit of *Flight's* photographer, Waight pulled a steep turn and entered a high-speed stall from which recovery was impossible. He was killed instantly and the TK.4 totally destroyed.

This was a brave effort to create a racing aircraft and its demise was due to the as-yet not fully understood phenomenon of the high-speed stall.

Short-lived but very fast: the ill-fated TK.4 with test-pilot R J Waight. The remarkably small size of the machine is clearly evident in this picture. *(author's collection)*

Although it had been proved in laboratory and demonstrated in wind-tunnels, it was not fully appreciated that the TK.4 in a steep turn had a stalling speed as high it not higher than a Spitfire.

The span was 19 feet 8 inches, the length 15 feet 6 inches, tare weight 931 pounds / All-Up-Weight 1,357 pounds. The aircraft's designed maximum speed was supposed to be 215 m.p.h.

TK.5

Before the demise of the TK.4, there was encouragement to design and build a new machine and so, in the summer of 1937, the students sought to experiment with an unusual shape. A circular aerofoil with the pilot in the middle was strongly favoured but then, after intervention by Captain Geoffrey de Havilland, it was decided to look once more at the canard form. So it was that, in 1938, work began on what was to become the TK.5. This was a single-seat machine but, unlike all other projects, it was to be a pusher machine with a canard tailplane and elevator at the nose and a swept-back wing with vertical stabilisers near the tips at the tail. The engine was mounted at the rear of the fuselage behind the wing trailing edge.

The main fuselage forward of the wing was built around a spruce framework with plywood covering to the sides and lightweight metal panels for the top and part of the underside. The rear portion of the fuselage incorporated the engine mount of welded metal tube, the major part of it being covered by the aluminium engine cowlings.

Two wooden spars with plywood diaphragms and solid balsa-wood tips formed the structure of the plywood-covered front stabiliser which was provided with a light alloy leading edge. Similar construction was used in the main wings with wood-framed vertical fins and rudders outboard of the aileron centre-span position. Initially, these fins were to be entirely above the wing but as built they were to extend beneath the wings as well. The mainplane was swept back so that the centre of gravity was in front of the wing, thus demanding a 'lifting tailplane' effect from the canard.

Power came from a 145 hp Gipsy Major 1C high-compression engine. The undercarriage was of tricycle arrangement with a castoring front wheel. Oleo springing was employed and Bendix brakes were fitted to the main wheels.

Registered G-AFTK, the completion of the aircraft was overtaken by the declaration of war, but late in 1939 Geoffrey de Havilland Jnr attempted the first

Above: A three-quarter rear view of the TK.5 - if time had been spent in a wind tunnel with a model, the reasons for the design refusing to get airborne might have been discovered!

The size of the TK.5 can be gauged by the student standing by the nose! *(both author's collection)*

flight at Hatfield. The machine would not leave the ground and after several attempts, the project was abandoned due to the pressure of other activities in time of war.

So why did the aircraft refuse to become airborne? Firstly it appears that the centre of gravity was too far forward. The front stabiliser had a total area of 19.8 square feet of which less than 38 percent was given to the movable elevator surfaces. It is thus most likely that there was insufficient front stabiliser elevator power to pitch the nose up for take-off. Clearly either the front elevators should have been very much larger in area or the entire front stabiliser should have been combined as an all-flying surface to lift the aircraft's nose.

As it was, the machine possessed insufficient elevator area to regulate pitch, particularly at low speed. Without propeller slipstream, it is estimated that the TK.5 would have needed a ground speed in excess of 80 mph before the nose could be lifted. The difficulty is that by this time the main wing would have been producing so much lift as to press the nose down on the ground. It was a novel design at a time when the aerodynamics had yet to be established fully. A wind-tunnel model would have helped.

The machine's span was 25 feet 8 inches, length 18 feet 3 inches. The wing area was 117 square feet. The all-up-weight was estimated as 1,366 pounds with a projected maximum speed 177m.p.h. The design team estimated an initial climb of 1,165 feet per minute with a ceiling of 22,100 feet..

TK.6

While the TK.5 was on test, the Technical School had already planned the TK.6. This was a less-radical design to a proven layout and resembled the TK.2. A span of 34 feet and a length of 22 feet was combined in this fixed undercarriage design with a Gipsy Major II. The design sadly coincided with the TK.5's problems and the onset of the war.

Cierva C.24 Autogyro

One machine that has always been a distinct 'oddity' in the DH production sequence is the Cierva C.24 Autogyro. The De Havilland Aircraft Co. Ltd. was responsible for the design and construction of this rotary wing aircraft, the Cierva Autogiro Company's sole contribution being the rotor assemblies. It thus found a place in the standard de Havilland constructor's number sequence.

It was a two seat cabin autogiro of similar construction to the De Havilland DH.80A Puss Moth, fitted with tricycle undercarriage and the three bladed rotor of the Cierva C.19 Mk. IV autogiro. One aircraft only, G-ABLM, c/n 710, powered by a 120 horsepower Gipsy III, was built at Stag Lane and first flown by Senor Juan de la Cierva in September 1931.

After trials at both Stag Lane and Hanworth, a Certificate of Airworthiness was issued on 23 April 1932. Flown by Cierva, the aircraft toured Europe in the following May and June and flew in the Brooklands-Newcastle Race at 103 and 5 m.p.h. piloted by R. A. C. Brie on 6 August 1932. Shown at the Fifty Years of Flying Exhibition at Hendon in July 1951. It was then stored by the London Science Museum without its engine, latterly at Hayes, Middlesex. Restored for static exhibition by Hawker Siddeley apprentices at Hatfield 1973/74, complete with engine but with parts of the rotor drive missing, it was eventually transferred to the De Havilland Mosquito Museum, Salisbury Hall.

Rotor diameter 34 feet 0 inches. Length 20 feet 0 inches. Tare weight 1,280 pounds. All-up weight 1,800 pounds. Maximum speed 115 mph. Cruising speed 100 mph. Range 350 miles. Rotor speed 200

The De Havilland designed and built Cierva C.24 autogyro *(author's collection)*

De Havilland Aircraft Pty Ltd.

The De Havilland company started up in Australia early in 1927 when Major Hereward de Havilland took a DH.60 Moth, G-EBPP, by sea to Perth and flew it to Melbourne, where he rented a shed at the back of the town to assemble imported Moths.

On 7 March, less than seven years after the move to Stag Lane, an Australian subsidiary, De Havilland Aircraft Pty Ltd., was incorporated and became the first of a world-wide chain of overseas holdings.

Initially DH.60 Moth, DH.60G Gipsy Moth and DH.60M Moth airframes were imported for erection and sale but even before the arrival of G-EBPP, kits of parts for three Cirrus engined DH.60s had been supplied to QANTAS and completed as G-A UFJ for its own flying school at Longreach, and as G-AUFI and 'FK for the West Australian Airways school at Perth W.A.

Later the De Havilland Aircraft Pty. Ltd. undertook manufacture of DH.60G and DH.60M Moths at Bankstown, Sydney and in 1941 some 41 DH.94 Moth Minors were completed from components and materials shipped from Hatfield. Australian production thereafter amounted to-

DH.82A Tiger Moth	1,085
DH.98 Mosquito	212
DH.83 Fox Moth	2
DH.100 Vampire	80
DH.84 Dragon	87
DH.115 Vampire Trainer	73

In addition the company was also responsible for the design and construction at Bankstown Aerodrome, Sydney of the G.2 wartime troop carrying glider and the three-engined Drover postwar transport aeroplane.

DHA.G.1/2

The G1 glider was designed to meet a Royal Australian Air Force requirement for a transport glider to specification 5/42.

Two prototype gliders, sometimes known as Experimental Glider 1, were ordered from De Havilland Australia, but as DHA were already committed to build DH.82 Tiger Moth basic trainers and DH.84 Dragon navigation trainers, most of the work was carried out by subcontractors, with much of the build work on the two prototypes being carried out on the fifth floor of a Mill in Camperdown, Sydney.

It was a high-wing cantilever monoplane of all wooden construction, making extensive use of plywood. It used the cockpit canopy of the DH.84 Dragon, but was otherwise an original design. The aircraft's undercarriage used a single mainwheel behind a long nose skid, and a wooden tailskid. The crew consisted of a single pilot with seats for six passengers.

The first prototype made its maiden flight on 14 June 1942, and was accepted by the RAAF on 11 October 1942, with the second prototype following on 17 November.

A production order was placed with DHA for a modified version, but with the threat of invasion less likely, as well as the availability of Douglas Dakota transports and Waco Hadrian gliders from the United States, only six were ordered. The G2 was of similar layout to the G1, but had a slightly larger fuselage and a shorter span wing which could be broken into three parts to aid transportation. The first production G2 flew on 20 March 1943 and was delivered to the RAAF on 6 May 1943, with the remaining five following in July that year. They saw little use, most of them being stored, with the first G2 being used for glider conversion training.

The first G2, serial number A57-1, was modified in 1948 by the Government Aircraft Factory for trials of a suction airfoil, the modifications included the fitting of a 96 hp Ford Mercury 95A engine. Trials continued until 1951.

The first production G.2 glider, A57-1, is seen at Laverton, Victoria in 1942. *(author's collection)*

DHA.3 Drover

Design work on the DHA.3 began in 1946 after DHA identified a need to replace the DH.84 Dragon then in widespread use in Australia. Although the British parent company's Dove was being produced at the same time, DHA saw that the Dove was not entirely suitable for Australian conditions. Using the Dove as a starting point, DHA designed an aircraft with three four-cylinder Gipsy Major engines instead of the Dove's two Gipsy Queen six-cylinder engines and a fixed tailwheel undercarriage instead of the Dove's retractable tricycle undercarriage. Like the Dove, the DHA-3 was sized to carry eight or nine passengers with a single pilot.

The result was an aircraft with the same wingspan as the Dove and a slightly shorter fuselage. The name 'Drover' was selected by Sir Geoffrey de Havilland after suggestions were invited from DHA employees, the winner being Thomas King from the Drawing Office.

The first DHA-3 Mk.1 Drover took to the air at Bankstown Airport on 23 January 1948 piloted by Brian 'Black Jack' Walker, DHA's chief test pilot. The aircraft was subsequently flown by Walker to Melbourne for trials by the Australian Department of Civil Aviation, a flight of 460 miles, achieving 140 mph and a fuel consumption of approximately 22 gallons per-hour. During trials a single-engine rate-of-climb of 240 feet per-minute at sea level was obtained.

The type entered service with the Australian Department of Civil Aviation (DCA, now the Civil Aviation Safety Authority) in 1949, the DCA operating the first two aircraft. QANTAS and the Royal Flying Doctor Service took delivery of their first aircraft in 1950, eventually receiving five and six new aircraft respectively. QANTAS placed the Drover into service on its routes in what was then known as the Territory of Papua and New Guinea.

After entering service, by 1952 the design's shortcomings were became apparent. These included the aircraft's lack of power, especially in hot weather, and an unfortunate tendency for propellers to fail in-flight, resulting in the loss of two aircraft.

On 16 July 1951 VH-EBQ, the third Drover built, crashed in the Huon Gulf near the mouth of the Markham River off the coast of New Guinea after the centre engine's propeller failed. The pilot and the six passengers on board were killed.

The prototype Drover, VH-DHA, operated by the Australian Department of Civil Aviation, ditched in the Bismarck Sea between Wewak and Manus Island on 16 April 1952. The port propeller failed, a propeller blade penetrated the fuselage and the pilot was rendered unconscious; the ditching was performed by a passenger. On this occasion the three occupants survived the ordeal to be rescued.

A third aircraft, VH-EBS, suffered a propeller failure while still on the ground in September the same year.

The propeller problem was overcome by replacing the De Havilland variable-pitch propellers with Fairey Reed fixed-pitch ones, modified aircraft being re-designated the DHA-3 Mk. 1F. All but the

The prototype Drover, VH-DHA, over the De Havilland Aircraft Pty Ltd factory at Bankstown Airport, Sydney, in 1948. *(author's collection)*

The prototype VH-DHA after roll-out.

Left: Drover VH-EBQ, the third aircraft built, on roll-out from the Bankstown factory in 1950 prior to delivery to QANTAS for New Guinea internal services.

The role in which the Drover is best remembered was with the Royal Flying Doctor Service in outback Australia. Drover Mk.3A VH-FDC delivers a stretcher patient to a waiting ambulance at Broken Hill NSW. The Mk.3A had Lycoming engines and other improvements including dihedral tailplane. *(all author's collection)*

three aircraft that had crashed by that time were brought to this standard. The propeller change, however, did nothing to improve the type's performance. In a bid to improve lift all Mk. 1F aircraft were further modified with double slotted flaps in place of plain flaps, and were once again re-designated, this time as the DHA-3 Mk. 2.

Sixteen aircraft had been delivered by the end of 1952, but the problems suffered by the type stalled further sales for several years. The last four of the twenty Drovers built were produced in 1953 but were not sold until 1955 and 1956. In another bid to rectify the type's poor performance DHA re-engined seven Mk. 2 aircraft with Lycoming O-360 engines driving Hartzell feathering constant-speed propellers. Changes were also made to the flap control system and the tail wheel assembly.

The first modified aircraft, re-designated as a DHA-3 Mk. 3, was returned to its owner, the Royal Flying Doctor Service of Australia on 4 June 1960.

Three Mk. 3s were later further modified; two aircraft operated by the New South Wales section of the RFDS were modified in 1962 as the Mk. 3a with the tailplane altered to have a much greater dihedral and the span increased by two feet. The third was modified as a Mk. 3b with an increase in maximum take-off weight of 300 pounds to 6,800 pounds.

The RFDS had its Drovers modified to Mk. 3 standard in the early 1960s and operated the type until late in the decade, when more modern aircraft such as the Beechcraft Queen Air were acquired. The seventh Mk. 3 was acquired second-hand from the Department of Health by the RFDS as a Mk. 2 and then modified. The RFDS Mk. 3s were configured to carry the pilot, two medical staff and two stretcher patients and were operated in the Northern Territory and outback New South Wales and Queensland.

The Drover became fairly well-travelled for an Australian design; apart from their initial use in Australia, New Guinea and Fiji, second-hand Drovers were registered in the Western Pacific Islands (Solomon Islands) and operated by New Hebrides Airways Ltd. and Air Melanesiae in the New Hebrides, and others were registered in New Zealand and the United Kingdom in addition to further examples making their way to Fiji.

By the end of the 1950s only nine Drovers were still in airline service worldwide. The last Drover to operate scheduled services in New Zealand was with Great Barrier Airlines was withdrawn from service in 1985 and replaced by a BN.2A Islander.

De Havilland Aircraft of Canada Ltd.

Founded in 1928 as a subsidiary, De Havilland Canada was first located at De Lesseps Field in Toronto, before moving to Downsview in 1929.

As detailed elsewhere in this book, De Havilland Aircraft of Canada Ltd. erected forty DH.60M Moths, one DH.61 Giant Moth and at least twenty-five DH.80A Puss Moths from small components made at Stag Lane.

Immediately prior to and during the Second World War, large scale production of wholly Canadian-built Hatfield designs took place at Downsview, Toronto:

DH.82A Tiger Moth	25
DH82C Tiger Moth	1528*
DH.83C Fox Moth	54
DH.98 Mosquito	1134

* Plus 200 fuselages shipped to Britain.

After the war, de Havilland Canada began to build designs uniquely suited to the harsh Canadian operating environment, starting with the DHC.1 Chipmunk, and continuing through the remarkable Beaver - Otter - Caribou family of short take-off and landing aircraft.

The company also continued production of several British De Havilland aircraft and later produced a licence-built version of the American-designed Grumman S2F Tracker. In 1962 the Avro Canada aircraft production facility was transferred to de Havilland Canada by their then-merged parent company, UK-based Hawker Siddeley.

Details of the later DH.5 Buffalo, DHC.6 Twin Otter, and DHC.7 are outside the scope of this book, since all went into production after the parent company became part of HSA Ltd.

The original DH Canada factory - a wooden shed on a railway siding at Mount Dennis, Ontario adjacent to De Lesseps Field. The factory later moved to Downsview. *(author's collection)*

The pre-war Downsview site, showing assorted Moths and DH.89 Rapides under construction and modification. (*author's collection*)

DHC-1 Chipmunk

The Chipmunk was designed to succeed the de Havilland Tiger Moth biplane trainer that was widely used during the Second World War.

Wsiewołod Jakimiuk, a Polish prewar engineer, created the first indigenous design at De Havilland Aircraft of Canada Ltd. It was an all-metal, low wing, tandem two-place, single-engined aircraft with a conventional tailwheel undercarriage and fabric-covered control surfaces. The wing was also fabric-covered aft of the spar.

CF-DIO-X, the Chipmunk prototype, flew for the first time at Downsview, Toronto, on 22 May 1946 with Pat

Fillingham, test pilot from the parent de Havilland company, at the controls. The production version of the Chipmunk was powered by a 145 horsepower De Havilland Gipsy Major 8 engine while the prototype was powered by a 145 horsepower De Havilland Gipsy Major 1C.

158 DHC-1B-1 (145 horsepower Gipsy Major 1C) and 60 DHC-1B-2 (known in RCAF service as the

G-AKDN was first registered in the UK on 14 August 1947 as a DHC.1A-1. (*author's collection*)

A trio of Chipmunks - WB566, WB556 and WB555 - line up for the camera before entering into service with the RAFVR. *(author's collection)*

Mk. 30) with 145 horsepower Gipsy Major 10-3 and one-piece canopy were built in Canada, 111 were built at Hatfield and 889 at Chester. The British-built aircraft were mainly T.Mk.10s for the R.A.F. (145 horsepower Gipsy Major 8) to Specification 8/48 commencing WB549, and export T.Mk.20s for the air forces of the Arab Legion, Burma, Ceylon, Colombia, Denmark, Egypt, Iraq, Ireland, Lebanon, Portugal, Saudi Arabia, Syria, Thailand and Uruguay.

A small number of civil Mk.21s were built for Air Service Training Ltd. at Hamble; the Ministry of Civil Aviation, at Stansted; and for Australia, Indonesia, Japan and Tanganyika. Sixty others were built under licence by Indústria Aeronáutica de Portugal S.A. (OGMA) in Portugal.

When declared surplus, large numbers of Service aircraft were civilianised in Canada, Britain and Australia as Mk.22 or Mk. 22A (with increased fuel) for worldwide sales. Five single seat Mk. 23 agricultural conversions were made in Britain between 1958 and 1966, and another, G-ATTS. was modified by Hants and Sussex Aviation Ltd., Portsmouth in 1966 as test bed for the 118 shaft horsepower Rover TP-90 gas turbine.

Australian conversions included the Sasin SA-29

Spraymaster and the Aerostructures Sundowner sport single seater.

Chipmunk G-AOSU was re-engined with a 180 horsepower Lycoming 0-360-A1A flat four air-cooled engine and first flown at Lands End (St. Just) airport Cornwall, went into service at Bicester as a glider tug for the RAF Gliding and Soaring Association in September 1975. G-ARWB was exhibited at the 1976 Farnborough SBAC Show as test bed for the 200 horsepower Bonner engine.

One Canadian-built Chipmunk, CF-CYT-X, was powered by a 210 horsepower Continental IO-260-C for acrobatic purposes and first flew with this engine piloted by J. P. Huneault at Quebec on 16 July 1969. Others, known as Super Chipmunks, were reworked in the USA by Art Scholl and others for international competition aerobatics with 260 horsepower Continental G0-435s.

Large numbers of Chipmunks of various marks still survive.

Data for T.Mk.10: Span 34 feet 4 inches. Length 25 feet 5 inches. Wing area 172½ square feet. Tare weight 1,425 pounds. All-up-weight 2,100 pounds. Max. speed 138 mph. Cruise 119 mph. Initial climb 840 feet per minute. Range 280 miles.

DHC.2 Beaver

After World War Two De Havilland Canada management turned to the civilian market for work, aware that military contracts were unlikely to guarantee business. The company hired Punch Dickins, a famous bush pilot, as Director of Sales and he began an extensive programme of collecting requests from other pilots, to understand what they needed in a new aircraft. Almost without variation, the pilots asked for tremendous extra power and STOL performance, in a design that could be easily fitted with wheels, skis or floats. When de Havilland engineers noted that this would result in poor cruise performance, one pilot allegedly replied *'You only have to be faster than a dog sled'*. Other suggestions included full-sized doors on both sides of the aircraft so it could be easily loaded no matter which side of a dock it tied up on. The doors had to be wide enough to allow for a 45 Imperial gallon drum to be rolled up into the aircraft.

On 17 September 1946, de Havilland put together a design team consisting of Fred Buller, Dick Hiscocks, Jim Houston and Wsiewołod Jakimiuk, led by Phil Garratt. The new aircraft was to be all-metal using *'...steel from the engine to the firewall, heavy aluminum truss frames with panels and doors throughout the front seat area, lighter trusses toward the rear and all monocoque construction aft'*. There were plans to fit the evolving design with a British engine, but this limited power, so the wing area was greatly increased in order to maintain STOL performance. When Pratt & Whitney Canada offered to supply war-surplus 450 hp Wasp Jr engines at a low price, the aircraft ended up with extra power as well as the original long wing. The result was unbeatable STOL performance for an aircraft of its size.

After much testing and with adjustments and improvements, the innovative machine, eventually offered on wheels, skis, floats or as amphibian, was ready for the sales circuit. The first flight of the DHC-2 Beaver was in Downsview, Ontario when the prototype CF-FHB-X was taken into the air by Russell Bannock on 16 August 1947. The first production aircraft was delivered to the Ontario Department of Lands and Forests in April 1948.

Initial sales were slow, perhaps two or three a month, but as the machine was demonstrated sales started to improve. A key event in the Beaver's history occurred the following year, when the US Army started looking for a new utility aircraft to replace their Cessnas. The competition quickly boiled down to the Beaver and the Cessna 195 but the Beaver outperformed the 195 and with the outbreak of the Korean War, led to orders for hundreds of aircraft.

Above: De Havilland Canada DHC-2 Beaver AL.1 G-CICP/XP820 of the Army Air Corps Historic Aircraft Flight Trust. This machine had been operated by the Army Historic Aircraft Flight until funding from the MoD was withdrawn and the the aircraft were gifted to the new company and entered operated on the civil register.

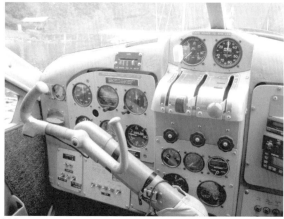

Right: The cockpit of a Beaver. The control yoke could be swung over so the aircraft could be flown from either seat. *(both author's collection)*

C-FYRR is a Beaver Mk.1 and first flew in 1957. It is seen here fitted with amphibious undercarriage. *(author's collection)*

Soon orders increased from around the world. When production finally ceased in 1967, 1,657 DHC-2 Beavers had been built.

The Beaver was designed for flight in rugged and remote areas of the world. Its short takeoff and landing capability made it ideal for areas normally only accessible by canoe or foot. Because it often flew to remote locations, often in cold climates, its oil reservoir filler was located in the cockpit and oil could be filled in flight. A series of upgrades to the basic design were incorporated. One major customer introduced the use of flat steps replacing the earlier tubes, a feature that is now almost universal. In 1987, the Canadian Engineering Centennial Board named the DHC-2 one of the top ten Canadian engineering achievements of the 20th century.

Forty went to the British Army Air Corps as Beaver A.L.Mk.1 and one, G-ANAR, to the De Havilland Aircraft Co. Ltd., Hatfield 1953 as Beaver 2 with 550 h.p. Alvis Leonides 502/4, increased span and fin area.

The 1,535th airframe was converted on the production line with lengthened fuselage, larger vertical tail surfaces and 578 e.s.h.p. Pratt and Whitney PT6A-6 propeller turbine as the Turbo Beaver, or Beaver 3, CF-PSM-X, first flown December 30,1963. Although the Beaver 2 was not proceeded with, a total of 60 Beaver 3s was built.

Specification:
Beaver 1: Span: 48 feet 0 inches. Length: 30 feet 3 inches. Tare weight: 2,810 pounds. All-Up-Weight: 4,820 pounds. Cruise: 137 m.p.h.

Beaver 2: Span: 48 feet 8 inches. Length: 31 feet 9 inches. Tare weight: 3,255 pounds. All-Up-Weight 5,100 pounds. Cruise 156 m.p.h.

Beaver 3: Span 48 feet 0 inches. Length 35 feet 2 inches. Tare weight: 2,590 pounds. All-Up-Weight: 5,100 pounds. Cruise 140 m.p.h.

DHC.3 Otter

When De Havilland Canada began design work on the 'King Beaver' - the Otter's original name - in January 1951, it was trying to extend the company's line of rugged STOL utility transports. The single-engined, high-wing, propeller-driven DHC-3 Otter was conceived to be capable of performing the same roles as the Beaver, but was considerably larger, in company parlance a veritable 'one-ton truck' as compared to the Beaver which was regarded as the 'half-ton truck'.

Using the same overall configuration as the earlier and highly successful DHC.2 Beaver, the new design incorporated a longer fuselage, greater-span wings, a cruciform tail, and was much heavier. Seating in the main cabin was for 10 or 11, whereas the Beaver could seat six. Power was supplied by a 600 hp Pratt & Whitney R-1340 geared radial. The version used in the Otter was geared for lower propeller revolutions and consequently lower airspeed. The electrical system was 28 volts D.C. Like the Beaver, the Otter could be fitted with skis or floats.

The prototype, CF-DYK-X, was first flown by George Neal on 12 December 1951. The Otter received Canadian certification in November 1952 and entered production shortly thereafter. A total of 466 was built before the type went out of production.

The Otter served as the basis for the very successful Twin Otter, which features two wing-mounted Pratt & Whitney Canada PT6 turboprops, but that design is outside the scope of this book.

The DHC-3/CC-123/CSR-123 Otter was used until 1980 by the Royal Canadian Air Force and its successor, the Air Command of the Canadian Forces. It was used in Search and Rescue, as the 'CSR' denoting Canadian Search (and) Rescue (type 123) and as a light utility transport, 'CC' denoting

Left: A production DHC.3
Otter for Phillipine Air Lines.

Below: A US Army U-1A
starts up in July 1967 at the
Hue Citadel Airfield,
Republic of Vietnam
(both author's collection)

Canadian Cargo. During the Suez Crisis, the Canadian government provided assistance to the United Nations Emergency Force and the Royal Canadian Navy carrier HMCS *Magnificent* carried four Otters from Halifax to Port Said in Egypt early in 1957, all four flying off unassisted while the ship was at anchor. This was the only occasion when RCAF fixed wing aircraft operated from a Canadian warship. It was also operated on EDO floats on water and skis for winter operations on snow. The EDO floats also had wheels for use on runways (amphibious). It was used as army support dropping supplies by parachute, and also non-parachute low-speed, low-altitude air drops, to support the Canadian Army on manoeuvres. In the end it was operated by the Primary Air Reserve in Montreal, Toronto, Edmonton and Winnipeg, with approximately 10 aircraft at each base, as well as by the RSU (Regular (Forces) Support Units) at those bases. It was usually flown with a single pilot (Commissioned Officer) in the left seat and a Technical Air Crewman (NCO) in the right seat. The Kiowa helicopter replaced it in Air Reserve squadrons.

The Otter was also sold to the air forces of Burma, Chile, Colombia, Ghana, India, Indonesia and Norway. About 100 were used by the world's civil airlines, bringing the number of countries which bought the Otter new to 36.

Two Otters, G-ANCM and G-AOYX, were delivered as civil demonstrators to the De Havilland Aircraft Co. Ltd., Hatfield and were eventually disposed of in India and Portugal respectively.

Span: 58 feet 0 inches. Length: 41 feet 10 inches. Tare weight: 4,165 pounds. All-Up-Weight: 7,600 pounds. Maximum speed: 160 m.p.h. Cruise: 139 m.p.h. Initial climb: 850 feet per minute. Range: 960 miles.

DHC.4 Carribou

The De Havilland Canada company's third STOL design was a big step up in size compared to its earlier DHC Beaver and DHC Otter, and was the first DHC design powered by two engines. The Caribou, however, was similar in concept in that it was designed as a rugged STOL utility aircraft.

Prototype CF-KTK-X was first flown by test pilots George Neal and David Fairbanks at Downview on 30 July 1958.

On 22 October 1959 the company's civil demonstrator, CF-LAN, made a globe-circling four month tour of 47 countries. It crossed the South Atlantic to the Azores, visited the UK and continued through four continents to Australia. Sales were made to the RAAF and to the air forces of Ghana, Kuwait, India and Kenya.

The Caribou was primarily a military tactical transport that in commercial service found itself a small niche in cargo hauling. Impressed with the DHC4's STOL capabilities and potential, the U.S. Army ordered five for evaluation as YAC-1s and went on to become the largest Caribou operator, ordering 173 in 1959 for delivery in 1961. The AC-1 designation was changed in 1962 to CV-2, and then C-7 when the U.S. Army's CV-2s were transferred to the United States Air Force in 1967. U.S. and Australian Caribous saw extensive service during the Vietnam War.

The majority of Caribou production was destined for military operators, but the type's ruggedness and excellent STOL capabilities requiring runway lengths of only 1200 feet also appealed to some commercial users. US certification was awarded on

DH Canada's original DHC.4 Carribou demonstrator CF-LVA in flight. *(DH via BAe Hatfield)*

23 December 1960. Ansett-MAL, which operated a single example in the New Guinea highlands, and AMOCO Ecuador were early customers, as was Air America, (a CIA front in South East Asia during the Vietnam War era for covert operations).

Some U.S. Caribou were captured by North Vietnamese forces and remained in service with that country through to the late 1970s. Following the war in Vietnam, all USAF Caribous were transferred to Air Force Reserve and Air National Guard airlift units pending their replacement by the C-130 Hercules in the 1980s.

All C-7s have now been phased out of U.S. military service, the last example serving again under U.S. Army control through 1985 in support of the U.S. Army's Golden Knights parachute demonstration team. Other notable military operators included Australia, Brazil, Canada, India, Malaysia and Spain.

Other civil Caribou aircraft entered commercial service after being retired from their military users.

Span: 95 feet 7½ inches. Length: 72 feet 7 inches. Height: 31 feet 9 inches. Wing area: 912 suare feet. Tare weight: 16,920 pounds. All-Up-Weight: 28,500 pounds. Economical cruise: 181 m.p.h. at 7,500 feet. Initial climb: 1,575 feet per minute. Maximum range: 1,280 miles.

RAAF DHC-4 Caribou A4-299 from 38 Squadron celebrating 45 years of service. *(author's collection)*

And Finally...

It is common practice for author's to list other books that they have used in their research - this title is unusual in that it is based entirely on contemporary material from De Havilland - Aircraft Manuals, Sales Literature technical documentation and the two internal publications *De Havilland Enterprise* and *De Havilland Gazette*, combined with official civil service and military test reports as archived in the Technical Library of the Aeroplane and Armament Experimental Establishment (A&AEE) at Martlesham Heath, and later Boscombe Down supplied to me by Terry Heffernan, their Librarian, from 1976 onwards.

Throughout this entire project there has been one detail of historical fact that I have not been able to solve - that

of why the signwriters at De Havillands varied the ways of painting the five-digit military serials on the side of fuselages. It cannot be a simple one-off mistake, for it would have been soon corrected. But from as early as World War One, right through to the early 1950s, there appears to have been some form of 'consistency' of using a separator-marker of either a dot or a dash between the letter(s) and numbers, much to the annoyance of the serial-collector / recorders who claim it is totally wrong and claim '... it could not have happened' despite the photographic evidence to the contrary!

No doubt as with previous works of mine assorted 'professors' - usually American - will accuse me of

These pairs of sample pages from two De Havilland type manuals show how the company recorded and distributed information about their products.

Even in the mid-1930, the company was using both Imperial and Metric measurements, for the simple reason that they were trading internationally.

They also show one other important detail, even the company was aware that any figures quoted were, at best, nothing but an estimate.

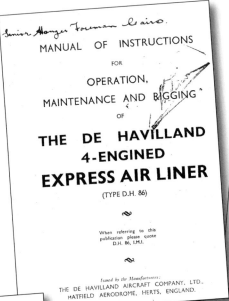

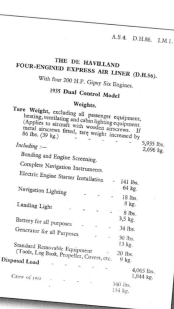

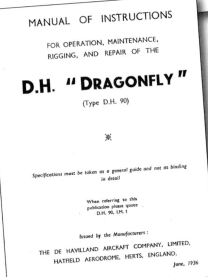

Page 11 of the Dragonfly manual explains it succinctly: *'It must be borne in mind that local conditions of temperature, humidity and barometric pressure have an important influence on aircraft performance'*

It continues *' The figures quoted in this publication should be regarded, therefore, as the most accurate estimate it is possible to make, and used as a guide only.*

What was good enough for De Havillands, is good enough for me!

plagiurism or, of an even more henious crime, that of making use of the online encyclopedia Wikipedia!

For the record, I have been gathering primary source documents since the early 1970s, and of course some of it appears online now - Indeed, I have supplied Wiki with data since it's inception, so it is not surprising at all that there are similarities between my written work and assorted online entries! If I use material I have provided to Wiki, then am I plagiurising myself? It seems that many of these academics completely miss the point that if any two people record history to any degree of accuracy, then the details are likely to broadly be the same and this becomes even more apparent the more condensed the item is. There are only so many ways to say 'the sun rose in the east', and of course, a fact cannot be copyrighted!

Given my use of primary source documentation, I thought it may be of interest to share judst a few fragments of the original source material, despite many items being photo-copies of the original carbon copies, that in some cases have also been microfilmed!

Page 1 of an 6 page report on the special handling trials performed on DH.86A aircraft by A&AEE at Martlesham Heath in 1936.

`C.A.`

Report No. M/636,c/C.A.

December 1936.

$\to$ `TO`

`TL.`

TECHNICAL REFERENCE LIBRARY.
A. & A. E. E., R. A. F.

AEROPLANE AND ARMAMENT EXPERIMENTAL ESTABLISHMENT,

MARTLESHAM HEATH.

Special Handling Trials on
D.H.86a Aeroplanes.

A.M. Ref:- 564022/36/R.D.A.6.

A. & A.E.E. Ref:- M/4478/15 - C.A.104.

In accordance with arrangements made at a meeting at the Air Ministry on 23rd October 1936, two pilots from this Establishment visited Croydon on 27th October, to fly a D.H.86a. and a D.H.86 aeroplane belonging to Imperial Airways. It was found that the D.H.86 aeroplane offered for trial (ACVY) had been flown at this Establishment a few days earlier, and its handling qualities were well known. No flight was, therefore, made on it on this occasion; a flight was made on D.H.86a. AEAP.

D.H. 86a AEAP

The unpleasant directional characteristics previously reported on ADYH (see A. & A.E.E. Report M/636,b/C.A.) are also present on this aeroplane but are less marked. When making a turn with ailerons only, there was not the same tendency for the nose to turn in the opposite direction. The controls were somewhat more in harmony than on ADYH and the ailerons were definitely better. The aeroplane, nevertheless, requires hard flying the whole time. The weight on the flight was 10,250 lb. with the centre

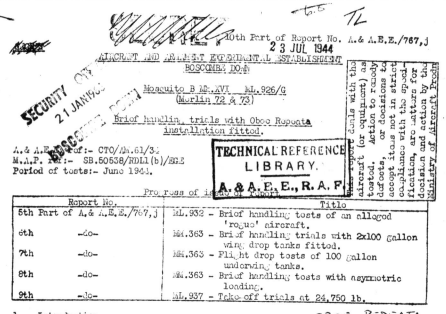

2 3 JUL 1944

AIRCRAFT AND ARMAMENT EXPERIMENTAL ESTABLISHMENT
BOSCOMBE DOWN

Mosquito B Mk.XVI   ML.926/G
(Merlin 72 & 73)

Brief handling trials with Oboe Repeata
installation fitted.

A.& A.E.E. Ref:- CTO/AM.61/32
M.A.P. Ref:- SB.50538/RDL1(b)/EGE
Period of tests:- June 1944.

TECHNICAL REFERENCE
LIBRARY.
A.& A.E.E., R.A.F.

Progress of issue of report

Report No.		Title
5th Part of A.& A.E.E./767,j		ML.932 – Brief handling tests of an alleged 'rogue' aircraft.
6th	–do–	MM.363 – Brief handling trials with 2x100 gallon wing drop tanks fitted.
7th	–do–	MM.363 – Flight drop tests of 100 gallon underwing tanks.
8th	–do–	MM.363 – Brief handling tests with asymmetric loading.
9th	–do–	ML.937 – Take-off trials at 24,750 lb.

1.   Introduction.   OBOE REPEATA

      Mosquito ML.926/G is a Bomber Mk.XVI version modified to carry an Oboe Repeata installation beneath the fuselage.   This equipment is surrounded by a blister made of transparent plastic material painted externally, and attached to modified bomb doors, this is shown in the photograph attached.   As this blister was of considerable size (the overall dimensions were approximately 8½ ft. long, 2½ ft. wide, and 3½ ft. deep) tests have been made to determine its effect on the handling characteristics of the aircraft.

      The tests have not been completed as the blister was damaged during diving trials, but sufficient experience has been gained to enable an assessment of the general handling characteristics to be made.

2.   Condition of aircraft relevant to tests.

      2.1.   General. The aircraft was basically a standard B. Mk.XVI powered by Merlin 72 and 73 engines driving 3-blade D.H. Hydromatic propellers (Type A5/147).   The enlarged bomb doors were replaced by modified doors to which the blister, described in para. 1, was fixed.   The following standard items of external equipment were also fitted:

          Bulged side panels to the cabin enclosure in place of the original panels with observation blisters.
          Attachments for 50 gallon wing drop tanks, (the tanks were not however carried).
          Recess for the F-type transmitter at the rear end of the fuselage, with a wooden blanking disc.
          Whip aerial on the top of the rear of the cabin enclosure.
          Ice guards on the carburetter air intakes.
          Multi-stub engine exhausts.
          Fuel cooler under starboard wing, sealed off.
          Pitot head mounted on the leading edge of the fin.
          Twin RAE-type static vent plates, one on either side of the bomb aimer's compartment.

      2.2.   Controls. The aircraft control surfaces were standard.   In particular, the tailplane was of the "medium" size, the elevators were metal covered and had standard horn balances, and a standard "inertia weight"

                                                      /giving

1944, and A&AEE were conducting tests on many different Mosquitoes - the stack of original reports on this type were at least four feet high!

Opposite: just a sample page from one of the pre-war *DH Gazettes*.

Reserve.

SOUTH AFRICA
Baragwanath, home of D.H.
South Africa.

AUSTRALIA
D.H. Factory at Mascot,
Sydney.

INDIA
D.H. Servicing Shops at
Karachi.

Airscrew Division:
Machine Shop.

CANADA
D.H. Factory at Toronto.

Airscrew Division:
Multiple Blade Forming.

Aircraft Division:
Paint Spraying.

ENGLAND
Hornet Moth.

CHINA
Express Air Liner of

Acknowledgements

A book of this nature would not have been possible without the help of many people and organisations.

For many years Darryl Cott, the Staff Photographer at BAe Hatfield, and Stuart Howe of the De Havilland Aircraft Museum at Salisbury Hall were the very greatest of help and assistance, the former making freely available to me the tremendous archive from the 'DH Days' that were then in his care. I also wish to record my thanks to Gary Bishop of BAe Product Support for allowing me access to the techical details and specifications of so many aircraft.

It goes without saying that my deepest possible thanks go to the late Group Captain John Cunningham CBE, DSO and Two Bars, DFC and Bar, De Havilland test pilot and an all-round gentleman!

Thanks are also offered to the usual 'guilty suspects' for their endless, unfailing support over the years: John Stride, David Lee, John Hamlin, Vince Hemmings, Brian Cocks, Martin Bowman, Mick Oakey, Ian Frimston, Warrant Officer Paddy Porter BEM and many others too numerous to mention, but not forgotten! Finally, thanks also go to Laura Hirst, Matt Jones, Charles Hewitt and everyone else at Pen & Sword!

I am indebted to many people and organisations for providing photographs for this story, but in some cases it has not been possible to identify the original photographer and so credits are given in the appropriate places to the immediate supplier. If any of the pictures have not been correctly credited, please accept my apologies.

Whilst mentioning photographs, it may seem strange to see something that was applied to the reverse of photographs used in this book, a simple publication clearance stamp. Unfortunately this has become especially important to show due to the growth of a plethora of websites who seem to think that it is perfectly acceptable to take any image and apply their own watermark to it and then demand exorbitant 'fees' from authors. Well guys, I have news for you, this book was compiled with images scanned from prints obtained before the internet and you opportunists were around, and to prove it, here is the rubber stamp stating that *'Photograph Courtesy of British Aerospace Hatfield. This photograph may be published without payment of any fee'*, and is just a representative of the many hundreds so marked I have in my collection and have used. It was applied by Darryl and thus ensured that so many rarely seen images could appear here in print. We discussed and eventually decided that rather than just crediting BAe Hatfield we would also add the letters 'DH', for after all, they were the source of the original photographs!